The Blackwell Reader in Pastoral and Practical Theology

The Blackwell Reader in Pastoral and Practical Theology

Edited by
JAMES WOODWARD AND STEPHEN PATTISON

Consultant Editor
JOHN PATTON

Blackwell
Publishing

© 2000 by Blackwell Publishing Ltd
except for editorial material and organization © 2000 by James Woodward and
Stephen Pattison

BLACKWELL PUBLISHING
350 Main Street, Malden, MA 02148-5020, USA
9600 Garsington Road, Oxford OX4 2DQ, UK
550 Swanston Street, Carlton, Victoria 3053, Australia

The right of James Woodward and Stephen Pattison to be identified as the Authors
of the Editorial Material in this Work has been asserted in accordance with the UK
Copyright, Designs, and Patents Act 1988.

First published 2000

10   2009

Library of Congress Cataloging-in-Publication Data

   The Blackwell reader in pastoral and practical theology / edited by
James Woodward and Stephen Pattison : consultant editor, John Patton.
     p. cm. – (Blackwell readings in modern theology)
   Includes bibliographical references and index.
   ISBN 978-0-6312-0744-3 (hardback) – ISBN 978-0-6312-0745-0 (paperback)
   1. Pastoral theology.   2. Theology, Practical.   I. Woodward, James, 1961-
II. Pattison, Stephen.   III. Patton, John, 1930-   IV. Series.
   BV4011.B54   1999
   253 – dc21   99-36072
                                                      CIP

A catalogue record for this title is available from the British Library.

Set in 10.5 on 12 pt Plantin
by Graphicraft Ltd, Hong Kong
Printed and bound in Malaysia
by KHL Printing Co Sdn Bhd

For further information on
Blackwell Publishing, visit our website:
www.blackwellpublishing.com

Contents

List of Contributors   viii

Acknowledgments   x

Preface   xiii

An Introduction to Pastoral and Practical Theology
STEPHEN PATTISON AND JAMES WOODWARD   1

**Part One   Modern Pastoral and Practical Theology
in Historical Perspective**
Introduction to Part One   23

1   The Meaning and Importance of Pastoral Theology   27
        SEWARD HILTNER

2   Introduction to Modern Pastoral Theology in the
    United States   49
        JOHN PATTON

3   The Emergence of Pastoral and Practical Theology
    in Britain   59
        PAUL BALLARD

**Part Two   Approaches and Methods in Pastoral
and Practical Theology**
Introduction to Part Two   73

 4 The Nature of Practical Theology   77
     ALASTAIR CAMPBELL

 5 Pastoral Theology in a Pluralistic Age   89
     DON BROWNING

 6 Practical Theology as Transforming Practice   104
     ELAINE GRAHAM

 7 Interpreting Situations: An Inquiry into the Nature of
     Practical Theology   118
     EDWARD FARLEY

 8 Practical Theology as a Theological Form   128
     EMMANUEL LARTEY

 9 Some Straw for the Bricks: A Basic Introduction to
     Theological Reflection   135
     STEPHEN PATTISON

**Part Three   Relating Theory and Practice to Perspectives
and Issues in Pastoral and Practical Theology**
Introduction to Part Three   149

10 Pastoral Theology and Sociology   151
     MICHAEL NORTHCOTT

11 Liberation Theology and Political Theory   164
     PETER SEDGWICK

12 Ecclesiology and Pastoral Theology   173
     NICHOLAS BRADBURY

13 Christian Morality and Pastoral Theology   182
     NICHOLAS PETER HARVEY

14 Spirituality in a Postmodern Era   192
     MARIE MCCARTHY

15 Sketching the Contours of a Pastoral Theological
Perspective: Suffering, Healing, and Reconstructing
Experiencing 207
CHRIS SCHLAUCH

16 The Relationship between Pastoral Counseling and
Pastoral Theology 223
GORDON LYNCH

17 How Sexuality and Relationships have Revolutionized
Pastoral Theology 233
BONNIE J. MILLER-MCLEMORE

18 Culture, Religious Faiths, and Race 248
MARTIN FORWARD

19 What is the Relevance of Congregational Studies for
Pastoral Theology? 257
BRYNOLF LYON

20 Towards Dialogue: An Exploration of the Relations
between Psychiatry and Religion in Contemporary
Mental Health 272
MARK SUTHERLAND

21 Management and Pastoral Theology 283
STEPHEN PATTISON

Part Four   Evaluating Pastoral and Practical Theology
Introduction to Part Four 297

22 An Introduction to Evaluation in Pastoral Theology
and Pastoral Care 300
STEPHEN PATTISON AND JAMES WOODWARD

23 Pastoral Care as Performance 311
DAVID LYALL

Bibliography 320

Index 335

Contributors

Paul Ballard is Head of the Department of Theology and Religious Studies at Cardiff University.

Nicholas Bradbury is an Anglican parish priest working in the Diocese of Bristol.

Don Browning is Professor of Religious and Psychological Studies at the University of Chicago.

Alastair Campbell is Professor of Ethics in Medicine at the University of Bristol.

Edward Farley is Professor of Theology at Vanderbilt Divinity School.

Martin Forward is Lecturer in Pastoral and Systematic Theology at Wesley House, Cambridge, UK.

Elaine Graham is Samuel Ferguson Professor of Social and Pastoral Theology at the University of Manchester.

Nicholas Peter Harvey is a freelance English Roman Catholic writer and theologian.

Seward Hiltner (1909–84) was Professor of Pastoral Theology at Princeton University.

Emmanuel Lartey is Senior Lecturer in Pastoral Studies at the University of Birmingham.

David Lyall is a Senior Lecturer in Christian Ethics and Practical Theology at the University of Edinburgh.

Gordon Lynch is a practicing counselor and teacher of counseling at University College, Chester.

Brynoff Lyon is Associate Professor of Practical Theology and Pastoral Care at the Christian Theological Seminary in Indianapolis, Indiana.

Marie McCarthy is a member of the clinical and training staff of the Center for Religion and Psychotherapy of Chicago.

Michael Northcott is a Senior Lecturer in Christian Ethics and Practical Theology at Edinburgh University.

Bonnie J. Miller-McLemore is Associate Professor of Pastoral Theology at Vanderbilt Divinity School.

Stephen Pattison is Senior Research Fellow in Practical Theology at Cardiff University.

John Patton is Senior Professor of Pastoral Theology at Columbia Theological Seminary, Decatur, Georgia.

Chris Schlauch is Associate Professor of Pastoral Psychology and Psychology of Religion in the School of Theology, Boston University.

Peter Sedgwick is Assistant Secretary of the Church of England's Board for Social Responsibility.

Mark Sutherland is an Anglican mental-health chaplain working at the Maudsley Hospital, London.

James Woodward is an Anglican priest working as the Master of the Foundation of Lady Katherine Leveson, Temple Balsall, in the Diocese of Birmingham, and Honorary Research Fellow at Cardiff University.

Acknowledgments

This Reader is, in part, the product of a long process of consultation with students, teachers, and researchers of pastoral and practical theology. A number of individuals helped inform and shape early drafts of our framework. They have extensive teaching and research experience which was used to inform the choice of readings and articles that would best act as a resource. We record our thanks to Elaine Graham (University of Manchester); David Lyall, Duncan Forrester and Michael Northcott (University of Edinburgh); Mark Pryce (University of Cambridge); Heather Walton (University of Glasgow); Frances Ward (University of Manchester); Frank Turner (University of London); Emmanuel Lartey (University ot Birmingham); Robin Gill (University of Kent), and Gordon Oliver (Diocese of Rochester). The process of refining the framework and choice of readings and articles was a slow and careful one and the final responsibility for this present framework remains with the editors.

John Patton of Columbia Theological Seminary has been a constant source of support and formative advice on this work. He has commented on a wide variety of material and ensured that we had access to influential American writers and researchers to balance the material in the Reader. A particular thanks to Paul Ballard and Cardiff University for supporting Stephen Pattison in his appointment to a Senior Research Fellowship and enabling him to have time to complete the project. James Woodward wishes to thank the Diocese of Birmingham and the Governors of the Foundation of Lady Katherine Leveson for their support.

The staff of Blackwell Publishers had the confidence and vision to take the project on and have encouraged the editors at all stages of its production. Our thanks to Alex Wright, Martin Davies, Clare Woodford, Joanna Pyke, and Lisa Eaton.

Finally the editors would be grateful for any feedback about this book. Please feel free to comment on all aspects of this volume. Please write to the editors c/o James Woodward, The Master, The Foundation of Lady Katherine Leveson, Temple Balsall, Knowle, Solihull, West Midlands, B93 0AL.

The editors and publishers gratefully acknowledge the following for permission to reprint copyright material:

Don S. Browning: "Pastoral Theology in a Pluralistic Age," in *Practical Theology*, edited and with an Introduction by Don S. Browning (Harper & Row, 1983), © 1983 by Don S. Browning. Reprinted by permission of HarperCollins Publishers Inc.

Alastair V. Campbell: "The Nature of Practical Theology," in *Theology and Practice*, by Duncan B. Forrester (Epworth Press, 1990), © 1990 Epworth Press. Used by permission of Methodist Publishing House.

Edward Farley: "Interpreting Situations: An Inquiry into the Nature of Practical Theology," in *Formation and Reflection: The Promise of Practical Theology*, edited by Lewis S. Mudge and James N. Poling (Fortress Press, 1987), © 1987 Fortress Press. Used by permission of Augsburg Fortress.

Nicholas Peter Harvey: "Christian Morality and Pastoral Theology," from *The Scottish Journal of Pastoral Theology*, 52 (1999) pp. 106–15. Used by permission of the editor and the author.

Seward Hiltner: from *Preface to Pastoral Theology* (Abingdon Press, 1958). Used by permission of the publisher.

Emmanuel Lartey: "Practical Theology as a Theological Form," from *Contact*, 119 (1996), pp. 21–5. Used by permission of the author and the *Contact* editorial board.

Brynoff Lyon: "What is the Relevance of Congregational Studies for Pastoral Theology?," from *Journal of Pastoral Theology*, edited by Nancy J. Ramsay and John Patton (1991). Used by permission.

Stephen Pattison: "Some Straw for the Bricks: A Basic Introduction to Theological Reflection," from *Contact*, 99 (1989), pp. 2–9. Used by permission of the author and the *Contact* editorial board.

Preface

Welcome to *The Blackwell Reader in Pastoral and Practical Theology*. This short preface describes the nature of the book and how to use it.

THE AIM OF THE BOOK

This book aims to give students of pastoral and practical theology, together with those involved in ministry and pastoral care, some basic written resources for understanding and expanding their knowledge of this burgeoning subject.

SOME BACKGROUND

Pastoral or practical theology is becoming an increasingly important part of theological study and education on both sides of the Atlantic. A century ago, pastoral theology was mainly a matter of instructing those training for ministry in the skills and aptitudes that they needed for practical tasks such as visiting people in their homes or baptizing babies. Nowadays, particularly within the Protestant tradition upon which this Reader largely draws, it has become more sophisticated and complex. More, and different kinds of, people, some of whom are not committed to a particular religious belief, take courses in this subject at universities, colleges, and seminaries.

For preliminary purposes, pastoral or practical theology can be defined as a prime place where contemporary experience and the resources of the religious tradition meet in a critical dialogue that is mutually and practically transforming (Pattison with Woodward 1994).[1]

An important theological method lies at the heart of this Reader. This method holds together experience and tradition, practice and theory as interdependent realities. These elements need to engage and connect with each other within the Christian faith tradition. This dynamic and holistic approach should involve the whole person and his or her community.

A number of dimensions of the theoretical traditions around pastoral and practical theology are reflected in the Reader. Furthermore, a number of examples of how these traditions relate to a diverse number of areas are also considered. One important aspect of practical and pastoral theology is that it is a subject area which is always moving, changing, and adapting.

These preliminary remarks about pastoral and practical theology are expanded upon as the Reader progresses.

WHAT IS IN THIS BOOK?

This is a Reader, not a textbook. Taken as a whole, this book presents an overview of the whole field of pastoral and practical theology. However, this is presented in the form of selected, free-standing articles and extracts on key topics. There is no continuous narrative that works readers through a syllabus from one particular perspective. This is partly because there is no syllabus or approach that is universally accepted. Pastoral and practical theology is a diffuse and fragmented subject area in terms of basic understandings, concepts, and methods.

We have tried to provide items that relate to most major topics that are currently of significance in pastoral and practical theology. We have also attempted to extend the scope and nature of the field by including topics that we believe will, or should be, of increasing importance in the future.

Many of the items and extracts included have been published before. They are included because they have proved to be of lasting use to students and teachers in pastoral theology. They address important issues; often they are out of print or difficult to get hold of because they are in journals. Thus, the Reader acts as a source of classic texts that are of proven value.

However, it also contains much new material. Seventeen of the articles have been specially written or revised by authoritative writers

in the field of practical theology. They have been commissioned because there appeared to be an important gap in teaching and learning resources that needed to be filled. This makes the Reader an
original resource for new thinking and learning in pastoral theology.

Each article has been carefully selected or commissioned after
extensive consultation with teachers and students about what they
would find most useful in a book like this. We have tried, as far as
possible, to select articles that are very readable – we would like the
book to be enjoyable and accessible, as well as useful! Inevitably,
however, some items are more demanding than others.

At the beginning of each article or extract, the editors explain why
it has been chosen, and the significance of the particular piece within
the fields of practical and pastoral theology. Following on from each
article, there are a number of critical points and questions that can
be used by individuals or groups to extend thought and discussion
on the topic concerned. We also provide suggestions for further
reading on topics which readers can follow up in the comprehensive
bibliography at the end of the book.

How to Use this Book

Most Readers are not designed to be read from cover to cover. This
one is no exception. Topics, styles, and approaches in the different
articles are all very different. The editors have made no attempt to
homogenize the articles on the grounds that there are many voices
representing different perspectives in pastoral theology, and these
should be allowed to speak for themselves. We envisage three main
types of readership and use for the book.

Students on pastoral, practical, and applied theology courses will probably find it most useful to get a sense of the entire contents of the
book by quickly skimming through it. This will give a good overview
of topics that are currently regarded as important in the whole area
of pastoral and practical theology. Thereafter, it will probably be
helpful to read articles on particular topics as they emerge in lectures
and seminars. The questions, suggestions for further reading, and
concluding bibliography should prove useful when it comes to preparing for seminars, assignments, and examinations.

Teachers on pastoral, practical, and applied theology courses who already
have a good sense of the field will be able to select particular articles

for seminar discussion, follow-up reading to lectures, assignments, and perhaps as the basis of examination questions. Here again the questions, suggestions for further reading, and concluding bibliography should be useful.

General readers and those who have acquired this book from a sense of curiosity about the field will find that it gives a good overview of pastoral and practical theology if they read most of the articles herein. However, they may well find it more rewarding to pick on topics that are of particular relevance to their own interests or work. Any of the items selected should make sense in its own terms and it will offer significant and accessible insight into topics that are of particular but not exclusive relevance to pastoral practitioners of all beliefs and persuasions. For those who are more interested in issues and topics than general approaches, the best place to start might be in Part Three.

THE SHAPE OF THE BOOK

Although each extract and article is free-standing, the book is structured into five main sections, each of which has a short editorial introduction of its own.

1 A historical perspective

This section of the book contains three items that place the modern discipline and field of pastoral and practical theology in a historical perspective. The scope, methods, norms, and nature of pastoral theology have changed enormously over the last century. This section aims to give a sense of the evolution that has taken place, particularly since the Second World War, on both sides of the Atlantic. It gives background about where we have come from and why we presently think of, and study pastoral theology in the way that we do.

2 Methods in pastoral and practical theology

One of the main ways in which pastoral and practical theology has changed over the last half century is in terms of acquiring a concern for the right kinds of methods for relating theology, action, and practice. There has been an explosion of concern about methods in, for example, theological reflection on practice and implementing the insights of faith. This second section provides six extracts and papers giving examples of what methods are used in pastoral theology and how they work.

3   Relating theory and practice to issues in pastoral and practical theology

It is all very well to understand how pastoral and practical theology has developed historically and to know something of its methods, but for many people the point of undertaking study in this area is to have a better sense of how to think about what they do in relation to particular events, issues, or topics. This third part of the Reader provides material that does exactly that. Twelve topics or issues are considered that raise interesting issues and problems in both theory and practice. This is the largest section of the book, and probably the one that will provide most immediate and concrete interest in terms of seeing the value of pastoral and practical theology.

4   Evaluating pastoral and practical theology

Pastoral theology attempts to relate theory and practice together in such a way that both are changed and enriched. Does it succeed in doing this? What is the value of adopting the approaches and methods of pastoral theology? Often questions like these are ignored in subjects that are academically confined. One of the original aspects of this book is that we believe that they are important questions to ask not only of religious professionals, but also of approaches and courses. In this section, therefore, two items are included that try to begin to raise critical questions about the significance and value of all aspects of pastoral theological activity.

Bibliography and index

The book concludes with an extensive bibliography of up-to-date and authoritative sources in pastoral and practical theology, followed by a thematic index. These provide tools both for further exploration and for revision on the particular topics that form the exciting and pluriform world of pastoral theology.

J.W.
S.P.

Note

1 Do not be put off by this slightly abstract definition. There is a full discussion of the actual nature, meaning and definitions of pastoral and practical theology in the first paper in this volume.

An Introduction to Pastoral and Practical Theology

STEPHEN PATTISON AND JAMES WOODWARD

This introductory essay provides some basic orientation to the broad field of pastoral and practical theology. It considers some key questions that newcomers to this area might ask in trying to understand something of its nature. The essay leans heavily upon the authors' own experience of being involved in pastoral theology. It is, therefore, phenomenological and descriptive in approach, not normative or comprehensive. Many of the ideas and themes touched on in the essay are developed in later papers throughout the Reader, so referencing here is minimal.

ARE PASTORAL AND PRACTICAL THEOLOGY THE SAME THING?

Pastoral theology and practical theology are sometimes talked about as if they are completely different things; at other times, as if they were exactly the same. The question therefore arises: what are the differences and similarities between these two terms and what they appear to denote?

Pastoral theology is an older term than practical theology. It goes back far into the history of the Christian community and is related to the need to guide, heal, reconcile, and sustain that community (Clebsch and Jaekle 1975). A pastor is literally a shepherd who looks after a flock. Drawing on imagery from the Old Testament, Jesus described himself as "the good shepherd" of his "sheep," i.e. his followers (John 10.11). This usage was developed by early Christian leaders who were therefore described as pastors.

Pastoral theology might be seen in broad terms as the theological reflection and underpinning that guided pastoral care directed towards ensuring the individual and corporate wellbeing and flourishing of the Christian "flock." It was the theological activity and tradition associated with "shepherding" or pastoring. Many people, particularly within the Catholic tradition, still use the term "pastoral theology" to describe the theological activity that guides and informs practical pastoral action such as distributing sacraments, marriage preparation, burying the dead, etc. (Duffy 1983; Hunter 1990: 873ff).

Practical theology is a term that emerged in the German Protestant tradition as part of the academic theological curriculum in the late eighteenth century. Although pastoral care was seen as one important area of concern in practical theology, its concerns extended beyond this to specialist interest in worship, preaching, Christian education, and church government. The purpose of practical theology was to apply theological principles to these activities. Practical theology has tended to be preferred as a term that includes pastoral theology within the mainstream Reformed tradition. Anglicanism, however, has tended to use the concept "pastoral theology" when talking about theology relating to practical action.

Pastoral theology and practical theology have different historical backgrounds and uses. Some people prefer the term pastoral theology to describe the theological activity that undergirds and accompanies pastoral care. Others prefer to see themselves as practical theologians because this may permit a wider vision of practical action that is not simply confined to looking after the narrow Christian community and its narrowly pastoral concerns. It also allows an escape from the rural and agricultural meanings that underlie the word "pastoral," together with unfortunate connotations that contemporary Christian people are like sheep.

Nowadays, there is a lot of common ground between pastoral theology and practical theology. Ultimately, both are concerned with how theological activity can inform and be informed by practical action in the interests of making an appropriate, effective Christian response in the modern world.

In contemporary North America, theologians have often been keen to identify themselves distinctively as either pastoral or practical theologians. The former have tended to focus upon issues concerned with and arising from the practical Christian pastoral care of individuals and groups (Gerkin 1997; Patton 1990). The latter have perhaps been more traditionally "academic" and scholarly, concerned with establishing broad theoretical theological and ethical frameworks for understanding issues and situations that extend beyond the immediate pastoral task and church community (Browning 1991). In some ways, practical theologians who are interested in examining and establishing theologically informed norms and values for action might be designated moral theologians, especially within the Catholic tradition. However, it is clear that the concerns of practical and pastoral theologians overlap in many areas. The difference between them seems, in the present context, to be more one of emphasis than substance.

In contemporary Britain, the traditions of pastoral and practical theology are far less well-developed and defined than they have been in the USA. This means that any putative differences between pastoral and practical theology are mostly disregarded (Ballard 1986). For the pragmatic British, either name will do as a broad designation of the subject area that deals with the relationship between the faith and theological traditions, and practical issues and actions that are concerned with human wellbeing. In this sense, pastoral and practical theology may be regarded as the same thing for contemporary purposes. It is acknowledged, however, that meaningful historical and other distinctions might be made between these two concepts by those who have a mind to do so.

WHAT ARE APPLIED THEOLOGY AND PASTORAL STUDIES?

The trend in Britain at the moment is towards calling all theological activity that tries to relate theory and action in practical ways "practical theology." However, two other terms are also in common usage.

"Applied theology" is usually basically the same kind of activity as pastoral or practical theology, acting particularly as a synonym for the latter in some contexts. Some people object to the use of applied theology instead of practical theology because they believe this implies that theology is not affected by an interaction with practical issues. In this sense, "theoretical" theology is given immunity from having to change in the light of experience. Practical theology might be taken to imply a more mutual, dialogical process than the simple application of theological truths and conclusions in practice.

"Pastoral studies" is a term used in Britain from the 1960s onwards to describe the kind of courses undertaken by students that were oriented towards helping them to understand and improve their professio al pastoral work (Ballard 1986). Although there was often a good de i of theological work and reflection in these courses they were not well integrated into the wider theological enterprise in the way that practical theology is coming to be. The aim of pastoral studies courses was broadly "to develop critical reflection on, and knowledge of, environment, society, the person, and theology, in relation to the pastoral task" (Pattison 1983: 23). While this aim remains legitimate, it can easily be subsumed under the designation of pastoral theology or practical theology. In the early 1990s, the British pastoral studies teachers' conference decided to change its name to the British and Irish Association for Practical Theology. This was intended to signify a broadening of scope for pastoral studies.

CAN PASTORAL THEOLOGY AND PRACTICAL THEOLOGY BE CLEARLY DEFINED?

It is certainly possible to define pastoral theology and practical theology clearly. However, it is probably not very useful to do so. The trouble is that definitions differ. The contents and scope that they imply also differ. There is no one universally accepted definition of either term. Some definitions exclude important elements that are included in others. Others are so brief, compressed, or general as to be almost meaningless. Pastoral and practical theology is a diffuse and changing field that involves many diverse participants, methods, and concerns, as will be seen throughout this book. In the absence of any orthodoxy, there is no need for anyone to subscribe to any particular definition as authoritative. Here, however, are a few definitions that may help in trying to gain a sense of some of the relevant elements of pastoral and practical theology.

In the North American *Dictionary of Pastoral Care and Counseling*, an authoritative reference book, Protestant pastoral theology is given a threefold definition as

1   Traditionally, the branch of theology which formulates the practical principles, theories, and procedures for ordained ministry in all its functions. . . .

2 The practical theological discipline concerned with the theory and practice of pastoral care and counseling. . . .

3 A form of theological reflection in which pastoral experience serves as a context for the critical development of basic theological understanding. . . . Here pastoral theology is not a theology *of* or *about* pastoral care but a type of contextual theology, a way of doing theology *pastorally*.   (Hunter 1990: 867)

A British dictionary of pastoral care (Campbell 1987: 201) defines pastoral theology as, "The theological study of the Church's action in its own life and towards society, in response to the activity of God." More recently, another dictionary suggests that "Pastoral theology (what Browning calls 'strategic practical theology') primarily concerns the church disciplines of religious education, pastoral care, preaching, liturgy, mission, evangelism and social ministries" (Atkinson and Field 1995: 42). This particular dictionary argues that pastoral theology is "a wide term admitting of many different definitions." Finally, a theologian who does not regard himself as a "pastoral theologian" defines pastoral theology rather cynically as "the gentle art of running a church that makes a healthy profit" (Cupitt 1994: 20).

Practical theology has also been variously defined. The *Dictionary of Pastoral Care and Counseling* provides another threefold definition of practical theology. It may be

1 A field of study in clergy education covering the responsibilities and activities of the minister and usually including preaching, liturgics, pastoral care, Christian (church) education, and church polity and administration.

2 An area or discipline in clergy education whose subject matter is the life and activity of the church as it exists in the present.

3 An area or discipline of theology whose subject matter is Christian practice and which brings to bear theological criteria on contemporary situations and realms of individual and social action. (Hunter 1990: 934)

Whyte defines practical theology much more simply as "The theology of practice" (Campbell 1987: 212), while Forrester suggests that it is "The theological discipline which is primarily concerned with the interaction of belief and behaviour" (Richardson and Bowden 1983:

455). Meanwhile, the *New Dictionary of Christian Ethics and Pastoral Theology* asserts, following Browning, that

> all theological thinking . . . is essentially practical. The social and intellectual context in which theology is brought into conversation with the vision implicit in pastoral practice itself, and with the normative interpretations of the faith handed down in the traditions of the church. Theology thus arises from practice, moves into theory, and is then put into practice again.   (Atkinson and Field 1995: 42)

A great deal of time could be spent on analyzing where these definitions agree and differ. It is worth noting a few points in the present context.

First, often definitions of pastoral and practical theology overlap. This suggests that it is probably futile to try and separate these areas either definitionally or in practice. Furthermore, it allows students of this area to define the subject as broadly as they like.

Second, there are some significant commonalities that can be summarized:

- Pastoral and practical theology are concerned with practice.
- They are also concerned with relating practice to the Christian theological tradition.
- The Christian community, the church, and its work is a very important focus for pastoral and practical theology.
- Practical and pastoral theology have traditionally been closely, associated with the ministry of the church.
- An important focus for pastoral or practical theology is contemporary practices, issues, and experiences that bear upon or form a concern for the Christian community.

The articles in this *Reader* aim to explore the nature, concerns, methods, and scope of practical theology, showing its diffuse and diverse nature. They will substantiate and question the kinds of definitions outlined here. Readers may care to return to these definitions later on to identify which of them best describe the field of pastoral and practical theology.

Here is the editors' own provisional working definition of pastoral and practical theology:

> Pastoral/practical theology is a place where religious belief, tradition and practice meets contemporary experiences, questions and actions and conducts a dialogue that is mutually enriching, intellectually critical, and practically transforming.   (Pattison with Woodward 1994: 9)

This definition is based on our experience of engaging in practical theology. It is a phenomenological definition rather than a normative one. That is to say that it describes what in our view practical theological activity does now. It is rather general and very broad. So, for example, it does not confine itself to the pastoral work of the church or the tasks of Christian ministers, though it certainly does not exclude them either. This definition is just one way of thinking about pastoral theology. It suffers from all the problems that any definition does in trying to cope with a wide, open and developing sphere of activity.

How is Practical/Pastoral Theology Practical?

Practical theology justifies the first part of its name by the fact that it is concerned with actions, issues, and events that are of human significance in the contemporary world. While it is possible to study issues like the family, marriage, or poverty in a theoretical way, for their own sake or out of a sense of curiosity, practical theologians take note of such issues because they wish to have an impact upon them. Whether it is a question of deciding what kinds of counseling are most appropriate for use within the church and its ministry, or helping to determine what an appropriate response might be to world poverty, the work of practical theology is to help generate concepts, norms, and actions that will be of practical utility and make a difference. In this sense, practical theology helps to direct and shape the concrete service of the Christian community in the world.

If practical theological activity fails to take into account the realities of the contemporary human condition, or if it produces high-flown theory that cannot be understood or applied in practice, it is arguable that it forsakes an important part of its identity and value. This does not mean, however, that practical theology has to adopt a dogmatic, instructive, minute, or monolithic approach to things.

HOW IS PRACTICAL THEOLOGY THEOLOGICAL?

Practical theology is theological in two main ways. In the first place, it takes the insights and resources of the Christian religious tradition of belief and practice, such as the Bible, theology and liturgy, as primary resources for its understanding and activity. Second, it aims to make a contribution to Christian theology and understanding. Thus, practical theologians may be able to help alter, deepen, or even correct theological understandings.

For example, a study of the contemporary human emotion of shame might reveal that the Christian theological tradition of atonement has overemphasized guilt at the expense of shame so that shamed people find little to help them within that tradition (Patton 1985). This might suggest that the theological tradition has to be revised or reconceptualized in some way more adequately to address the human condition and also to reflect the reality of divine salvation. A similar revision of Christian views of God occurred in the aftermath of the Holocaust when it became apparent that understandings of the nature of God needed to be changed in the face of the reality of experience of unimaginable mass suffering. While the theologians who have produced new ideas about the "crucified God" (Moltmann 1974) in the face of the Holocaust may not have seen themselves as practical theologians, it is precisely this taking experience seriously and then reflecting on its implications for theological understanding that characterizes the theological aspect of practical theology.

WHAT IS THE SCOPE OF PRACTICAL THEOLOGY?

In principle, the scope of practical theology is almost infinite. Any issue that is of practical contemporary human and religious concern may become the focus for practical theological consideration. Often, the kinds of issues that most concern practical theologians are those that relate to or become problematic in the life of the church and the church's ministry. These will change over time. At one time, a good deal of effort was devoted to exploring the implications of counseling and psychotherapy for the church community, relating this to ideas of salvation. More recently, practical theologians have become concerned about the nature of religious communities, family groups, spouse and child abuse, etc. (Glaz and Moessner 1991).

There is no reason at all why practical theology should not extend its interest beyond the confines of the Christian religious community to consider and influence issues of wider human interest such as the situation of people with mental health problems or world poverty. The only limit to the scope of pastoral theology is the amount of time and resources that people have to devote to it.

WHAT ARE THE METHODS OF PRACTICAL THEOLOGY?

The methods employed in pastoral or practical theology are as varied as is demanded by the issues that are being considered. Different issues or phenomena require different approaches and methods. Thus a consideration of financial debt and its implications for people's lives and worldviews (Selby 1996) will require a different approach and methods from, say, a study of shame and guilt in the individual (Patton 1985). In the first case, some knowledge of economics will be vital. In the second, it will be important to gain a good knowledge of individual psychology. Similarly, different theological themes and methods will need to be employed in varying circumstances.

All of which means that practical theologians need to be flexible in the methods they use. They must be prepared to engage in inter-disciplinary learning, because the theological tradition does not in itself provide all the information about the modern world that is needed to have a good understanding of many issues. Furthermore, an important skill that is needed is that of selecting and interpreting appropriate evidence from many sources, including theological ones. Only thus can reasonably clear and well-informed judgments be reached.

In practice, practical theologians use a wide variety of sources and methods in their work. Historical and textual methods may be used to understand and interpret theological insights and sources. Empirical methods such as surveys and questionnaires may be used to establish the nature of contemporary beliefs and behavior, or the nature of a particular human need in a locality. The capacity to be able to reflect upon and articulate something of the theological significance of human experience is highly valued in practical theology, as is the capacity to interpret meanings, myths, and symbols that shape people's views of themselves and their world. At all points, however, methods are only deployed if they are relevant to the task of arriving at an appropriate pastoral theological response to a situation.

One important methodological concept that should be noted is that of induction. Often thinking uses a deductive method whereby conclusions are deduced from authoritative principles or texts. Thus some people would deduce from the biblical example of Jesus caring for the poor and the meek that Christians in the contemporary world should also care for these groups or individuals. An inductive method proceeds the opposite way by looking at the reality of things as they seem to be and then formulating principles or general truths from this.[1] While both induction and deduction can form part of the practical theological process, induction has a particularly important place. Practical theologians often assume that it is necessary to take the "text" of contemporary reality as seriously as tradition and historically derived principles so that theology is addressed by and addresses contemporary concerns in all their multiplicity and confusion (Gerkin 1997).

WHAT ARE THE OUTCOMES OF PRACTICAL THEOLOGICAL ACTIVITY?

Practical theological activity is in itself transformative as a process for those who undertake it. The attempt to understand and respond to contemporary human issues from a theological perspective is likely to affect people's views of themselves and the world, however infinitesimally. This represents a kind of transformation or change.

Another outcome that may come from the practical theological process are different ways of thinking about and understanding phenomena or situations. These may be expressed in the form of written or spoken words such as books, articles, or speeches. It may also be hoped and expected that the practical theological process will lead to people changing their attitudes and beliefs in practice so that they actually begin to behave differently. So, for example, an effective practical theology of poverty might result in people thinking differently and in a more sophisticated way about this topic because new concepts have been developed at the theoretical end. At the same time, new ways of behaving and acting in response to poverty may be identified and implemented by, say, a church community (Green 1987).

Practical theology is often deeply committed to the notion of understanding leading to and from action, or praxis (Pattison 1997a). This means that it aspires to be transformative in both theory and practice. Practical theology cannot change the world on its own. Indeed, its contributions may indeed be modest and limited. However, it can make a real difference to its practitioners and the context that surrounds them.

WHO ARE THE PRACTICAL THEOLOGIANS AND WHERE DO THEY WORK?

Practical theology as a discipline has one of its main roots within the academic setting of universities, seminaries, and colleges. Here practical theologians undertake writing, research, education, and training that equip people with the basic outlook and methods of this subject.

It would be a mistake, however, to see practical theology as exclusively or narrowly an academic, or academically confined activity that is only undertaken by people who have gained qualifications in practical theology and self-consciously adopt the label "practical theologian." Many different kinds of people in different settings, with a variety of qualifications and interests, are interested in relating religious ideas and beliefs to practical situations and issues. Some of these people may not regard themselves as Christians.

Over time, practical theology has become far less clerical, male, and ecclesiastically-concerned and -dominated. However, the church community remains an important setting for people, especially pastoral workers, to conduct practical theological activity. Settings where religious people have a ministry, or confront practical issues and problems such as mental health problems, unemployment, or the future of work are also important places for this activity. It will often be the case that theologically trained clergy or pastoral workers may take a lead in trying to initiate practical theologizing. However, groups and communities may well be the place where this is done so that the final result in terms of concepts or actions are the product of a corporate process in which all learn, contribute, and grow, including, sometimes, people from outside the identifiable religious community.

Academics and non-academics, church employees and lay people, can all contribute something to the field of pastoral theology from their different settings and knowledge bases if there is a basic willingness to learn from one another. Thus, practical theological activity at its best may straddle the gaps between academy and church, church and wider community, education and experience, tradition and contemporary context, lay and ordained, individual and group. No group or individual has the monopoly on how, where, or when practical theology should be done, or on who should be "allowed" to undertake it. It could even be argued that those who are outside the Christian religious community could profit from becoming critical practical theologians of their own activities in so far as these are informed by action-guiding ideologies and faith systems (Pattison 1997b).

WHAT IS THE STARTING POINT FOR PRACTICAL THEOLOGICAL ACTIVITY?

Usually, the starting point for practical theological activity is some kind of theoretical or practical concern that seems to demand attention. So, for example, someone might be concerned about how a particular theological concept or idea might be related to the lives and practices of people in everyday life. An instance of this is the idea that God desires to save and heal people physically, mentally, and spiritually. A practical theological approach might then be to try and assess how, and in what ways, God's healing work is made real and might be made more real in the contemporary world. Within the same realm of illness and healing, it might be asked how contemporary experiences of illness and healing, e.g. of cancer, mental distress, or Aids can be better understood in the light of the Christian tradition of salvation and healing (Pattison 1989; Woodward 1990, 1995).

Wherever the practical theological consideration of illness and healing starts, whether with theological principles or contemporary experiences, the aim is to understand better what is going on, with a view to knowing how best to respond to the issue or situation. As we have already noted, engaging with issues like illness, health, unemployment, debt, poverty, etc. may also lead to some changes in theological insights and concepts, and in how these are understood and interpreted. Thus, a process of dialogue in which both theory and practice might be seen differently lies at the heart of practical theological activity.

Sometimes practical theology starts with ideas and examines their implications for practice. Sometimes it starts with practice and looks at how this might affect ideas and concepts. This kind of process might be thought of as a kind of conversation between theory, theology, and practice. In this conversation, all the conversation partners are changed by the interaction which occurs.[2]

WHAT ARE THE ESSENTIAL CHARACTERISTICS OF PRACTICAL THEOLOGY?

Because practical theology is a very diverse field in which many people are involved, employing a large variety of different approaches and methods, it is difficult to give a comprehensive and universally applicable list of the characteristics and ingredients that go into this activity. Here are some of the elements that may, or perhaps should, be typical of much contemporary practical theology:

(1) Practical theology is a *transformational activity*. That is to say, that both in terms of process and outcome it aims to make a difference to people, understandings, and situations in the contemporary world.

(2) Practical theology is not just concerned with the propositional, the rational, and the logical in life and theology. It needs to find an important place for parts of human experience and data like the emotions, the symbolic, and the irrational if it is fully to address the human condition. Artistic and imaginative ways of thinking about and expressing pastoral theological insights are also important (Campbell 1986; Capps 1993; Deeks 1987; Wilson 1988).

(3) Practical theology is *confessional and honest*. This means that it is committed to looking at the world through the "lenses" of a particular committed faith perspective or inhabited worldview. It attempts to bear witness to the truth and relevance of religious experience in dialogue with the contemporary world. In trying to be truthful about the world and religious experience, practical theology must be prepared to admit to and live with huge black holes in understanding and experience. So, for example, the problem of

suffering when it appears in the form of young children dying of cancers must not be ideologically glossed by platitudes about the goodness of God. Instead, practical theologians must seek better ways of thinking about and responding to situations. Above all, they must not deny the real experience of people who find themselves or their loved ones suffering for no explicable reason.

(4) Practical theology is *unsystematic*. Because it continuously has to re-engage with the fragmented realities and changes of the contemporary world and the issues it presents, much practical theology is not systematic or complete. It provides shafts of light into situations and issues rather than final answers or durable solutions. It is, in a way, "throwaway" theology that always has to reinvent its tasks and methods. As such, it must always be flexible and provisional. This contrasts with some traditional kinds of theology that have claimed to be universally valid, complete, essentially unchangeable and unchallengeable, because of their historical role and authority in the life of the church.

(5) Practical theology is *truthful and committed*. It is part of the role of practical theology as an intellectually sophisticated and honest activity to try and discern the reality of situations in all their complexity and then to keep faith with that reality, resisting temptations to gloss over awkward aspects. At the same time, there is often a commitment not just to seeing the world in a different way, but also to doing something to change it. Practical theology does not just try to stand above practice in a detached way to analyze it, it is also committed to helping people and situations change.

(6) Practical theology is *contextual and situationally related*. This means that practical theology is committed to being a kind of "local theology" (Schreiter 1985). It gives priority to the contemporary context or situation in which it is involved rather than to other situations, other times, and other places. While historical data, classic texts such as the Bible, and experiences from elsewhere may help practical theology in its task, its main concern is to explore and contribute to immediate contexts, situations, and practices.

(7) Practical theology is *sociopolitically aware and committed*. Having learned much from the example of praxis-based liberationist theologies that apply the tools of suspicion to theology as well as to the social and political order, much contemporary practical theology is very aware of the challenges presented to both theory and practice by social and political movements and trends. It is, in turn, often

committed to understanding and promoting the view from "below," i.e. that of those groups and individuals who experience institutionalized injustice and oppression in such a way that their voices are not heard and their interests are ignored. Women, gay people, and people of color are just some of the groups whose perceptions challenge pastoral theology to become more sociopolitically aware and committed.

(8)   Practical theology is *experiential*. It takes contemporary people's experiences seriously as data for theological reflection, analysis, and thought. It also gives them high status alongside traditional authoritative texts like the Bible, that contain the deposit of people's religious witness and experience in the past.

(9)   Practical theology is often *reflectively based*. Theological reflection on lived contemporary experience is an important starting point for engaging in practical theology. It is by people thinking through and analyzing their own experiences and the issues and situations that they face that the process of practical theology actually gets going. An important outcome of practical theology is to deepen and enrich this kind of theological reflection.

(10)   Practical theology is *interrogative*. Often theology has been thought of as monolithic and instructional, telling people what the nature of reality and the divine is. Practical theology, however, is more interested in asking good questions about the nature of reality and practice than in trying to confine them within the restraints of traditional theological orthodoxy.

(11)   Practical theology is *interdisciplinary*. That is to say, it uses the methods and insights of academic and other disciplines that are not overtly theological as part of its theological method. Theology in itself, it is maintained, cannot reveal all that one needs to know adequately to respond to contemporary situations and issues. Thus economics, sociology, psychology, and other disciplinary findings and perspectives must be utilized (Pattison 1986).

(12)   Practical theology is both *analytical and constructive*. It helps people more fully to understand what kind of situation they are in, and the theological themes that may be relevant to it in its analytical phase. However, it may also help people to construct ideas about how they might change and where they might like to move in its positive, constructive, normative, or prescriptive role.

(13)   Practical theology is *dialectical and disciplined*. Proceeding by way of a kind of critical conversation, many contemporary

practical theologies hold in creative tension a number of polarities such as

- theory and practice
- the religious tradition emanating from the past and contemporary religious experience
- particular situational realities and general theoretical principles
- what is (reality) and what might be (ideal)
- description (what is) and prescription (what ought to be)
- written texts and the "texts" of present experience
- theology and other disciplines
- the religious community and society outside the religious community

Disciplined conversation in the midst of these polarities allows practical theology to be both discerning and creative.

(14) Practical theology is *skillful and demanding*. Although all manner of people with or without qualifications in "practical theology" can become involved in the practical theological process, there is much to learn about how to work with different methods, types of material, situations, etc. There is thus much scope for individual and group development if people wish to become involved in this kind of activity at a deep level.[3]

CONCLUSION

Pastoral or practical theology is a diverse and developing field that can be both exciting and confusing in equal measure for the newcomer. In this introductory essay, we have tried to give a basic outline of some of the main features of contemporary practical theology as we have seen and experienced it as practitioners in this field.

The terminology of "pastoral" versus "practical" theology was discussed and we suggested that there is no one view about which of these terms should predominate over the other. Some of the cognate terms and synonyms for pastoral and practical theology such as applied theology and pastoral studies have also been touched upon. Here again, confusion and diversity of usage reign, allowing students, practitioners, and scholars in the field much scope for shaping their own definition and usage. Definitions of pastoral and practical theology were examined and shown to be diverse, but with some significant commonalities of focus and concern.

We then discussed the ways in which practical theology can be seen as both genuinely practical and authentically theological. The wide scope of practical theology was considered, before we moved on to a discussion of some of the methods that can be used in this activity. The possible outcomes of practical theological activity in terms of both theological understanding and practice were outlined before looking at the practical theologians and where they might undertake their work. After examining possible starting points for practical theological activity, some of the characteristics that might be typical of contemporary theologies were briefly listed.

We hope that this very condensed overview of the whole subject area will help readers to orientate themselves in pastoral and practical theology. The remaining papers in this volume should help to fill out the very abstract picture that has been presented here. It may be helpful to return to this essay after reading some or all of these contributions that help to demonstrate the breadth and diversity of pastoral and practical theology.

In the meanwhile, here are some questions for further consideration that may help in the critical assimilation of the material in this essay:

• Are there any significant differences between pastoral theology and practical theology?
• Is it useful to try to define practical theology? How might it be defined?
• What are the main characteristics of contemporary pastoral and practical theology? Are there any that are missing from the account in the essay?
• Which aspects of pastoral and practical theology seem interesting and attractive? Which are off-putting?
• Who should engage in pastoral and practical theology and to what ends?

Notes

1 See further extract from Hiltner later in this Reader (chapter 1).
2 See Pattison below (chapter 9) for more on the conversational model in practical theology (pp. 135–43).

3   For more detail of these characteristics of practical theology, see Pattison
    with Woodward (1994).

References

Atkinson, D., and Field, D. (eds.) (1995), *A New Dictionary of Christian
Ethics and Pastoral Theology*, Leicester: Inter-Varsity Press.
Ballard, P. (ed.) (1986), *The Foundations of Pastoral Studies and Practical
Theology*, Cardiff: HOLI.
Browning, D. S. (1991), *A Fundamental Practical Theology*, Minneapolis:
Fortress Press.
Campbell, A. (1986), *Rediscovering Pastoral Care* (rev. edn.), London: Darton,
Longman & Todd.
Campbell, A. (ed.) (1987), *A Dictionary of Pastoral Care*, London: SPCK.
Capps, D. (1993), *The Poet's Gift*, Louisville: Westminster/John Knox Press.
Clebsch, W., and Jaekle, C. (1975), *Pastoral Care in Historical Perspective*,
New York: Jason Aronson.
Cupitt, D. (1994), *After All*, London: SCM Press.
Deeks, D. (1987), *Pastoral Theology: An Enquiry*, London: Epworth Press.
Duffy, R. (1983), *A Roman Catholic Theology of Pastoral Care*, Philadelphia:
Fortress Press.
Gerkin, C. (1997), *An Introduction to Pastoral Care*, Nashville: Abingdon Press.
Glaz, M., and Moessner, J. S. (eds.) (1991), *Women in Travail and Transi-
tion*, Minneapolis: Fortress Press.
Green, L. (1987), *Power to the Powerless*, Basingstoke: Marshall, Morgan,
and Scott.
Hunter, R. (ed.) (1990), *Dictionary of Pastoral Care and Counseling*, Nashville:
Abingdon Press.
Moltmann, J. (1974), *The Crucified God*, London: SCM Press.
Pattison, S. (1983), "Pastoral Studies: Dustbin or Discipline?," *Contact*,
80: 22–6.
Pattison, S. (1986), "The Use of the Behavioural Sciences in Pastoral
Studies," in Ballard (1986): 79–85.
Pattison, S. (1989), *Alive and Kicking: Towards a Practical Theology of Illness
and Healing*, London: SCM Press.
Pattison, S. (1997a), *Pastoral Care and Liberation Theology*, London: SPCK.
Pattison, S. (1997b), *The Faith of the Managers*, London: Cassell.
Pattison, S., with Woodward, J. (1994), *A Vision of Pastoral Theology*, Edin-
burgh: Contact Pastoral.
Patton, J. (1985), *Is Human Forgiveness Possible?*, Nashville: Abingdon Press.
Patton, J. (1990), *From Ministry to Theology*, Nashville: Abingdon Press.
Richardson, A., and Bowden, J. (eds.) (1983), *A New Dictionary of Theology*,
London: SCM Press.

Schreiter, R. (1985), *Constructing Local Theologies*, London: SCM Press.

Selby, P. (1996), *Grace and Mortgage*, London: Darton, Longman, & Todd.

Wilson, M. (1988), *A Coat of Many Colours*, London: Epworth Press.

Woodward, J. (ed.) (1990), *Embracing the Chaos: Theological Responses to AIDS*, London: SPCK.

Woodward, J. (1995), *Encountering Illness*, London: SCM Press.

Part One

Modern Pastoral and Practical Theology in Historical Perspective

INTRODUCTION TO PART ONE

1 The Meaning and Importance of Pastoral Theology
Seward Hiltner

2 Introduction to Modern Pastoral Theology in the United States
John Patton

3 The Emergence of Pastoral and Practical Theology in Britain
Paul Ballard

Introduction to Part One

Pastoral care, together with the pastoral theology that has accompanied and supported it, has been an important part of the life of the Christian church since its earliest origins. The history and evolution of pastoral theology and pastoral care, or the cure of souls (*cura animarum*) is a long and fascinating one. Early pastoral theological reflection was mostly firmly earthed in experience and practice. Ideas and concepts arose from experience, while the point of ideas, doctrines, and concepts was to illuminate and guide practice and experience. So, for example, the insistence in the early church upon the doctrine of the bodily incarnation of God in Jesus so that he really suffered in the flesh upon the cross may be seen as a theological response to the reality of martyrs being bodily tortured, dying for their faith, and needing to find a theological rationale or value for this (Pagels 1982). Many of the figures who laid down the roots of Christian theology such as Saint Paul, Saint Augustine, and Pope Gregory the Great devised their theologies directly in the light of their experience of practical, pastoral situations. Theology was not what we would now call an academic activity whereby full-time individual thinkers and writers could practice their craft in an educational setting more or less independently of the religious community, its liturgical activity, and its practical concerns (Farley 1983b).

It is not possible here to explore the early historical roots and practices associated with pre-Reformation pastoral care and pastoral theology. Readers who would like to do this are advised to consult, for example, McNeill (1977), Oden (1983, 1984), and especially relevant articles in Hunter (1990). It is perhaps useful, however, to mention in this context that the essential ingredients of pastoral activity have been described by two church historians looking at the *cura animarum* from its earliest inception as those of healing, guiding, sustaining, and guiding (Clebsch and Jaekle 1975). Clebsch and Jaekle suggest in their historical survey that in any particular era one or other of these elements is uppermost. More recently, Howard

Clinebell, a contemporary North American pastoral theologian, has argued (1984) that these elements should be supplemented by that of nurturing.

The historical focus of this Reader is mainly liberal Protestant pastoral and practical theology in the twentieth century. Perhaps the most important single figure before 1900 in the modern evolution of this kind of theology was the German Reformed theologian, Friedrich Schleiermacher (1768–1834). It was he who fundamentally defined the basic modern understanding of the term "practical theology" within the academy. Practical theology, which he saw as a set of techniques for governing and perfecting the church, is the "crown" of a theological "tree" whose roots were in philosophical exploration. Between the roots and the crown lay the trunk which consisted of historical, exegetical, and dogmatic studies of the Christian tradition. The idea was that student clergy would study philosophical and historical theology and then apply this to the work of church leadership and governance in practical theology. In this context, practical theology was divided into two parts. The first, church government, consisted of activity directed toward the wellbeing of the church community as a whole, e.g. polity, legislation, discipline. The second, church leadership, is where the more individually-oriented pastoral tasks of healing, sustaining, guiding, teaching, conducting liturgy, preaching, and shepherding fit in (Schleiermacher 1988).

While Schleiermacher may have created a theoretically prominent place for practical theology within the theological curriculum it has, perhaps, never had the intellectual attention that it deserves. Furthermore, the context and character of practical and pastoral theology has changed radically since the early nineteenth century. Since the Second World War, pastoral theology and practical theology have experienced a renaissance in the English-speaking theological world, striking out in new and very varied directions. The papers in this part of the Reader are designed to fill in the background to this development which has radical discontinuities with traditional practical and pastoral theology, as well as retaining some similarities.

The first paper is an extract from Seward Hiltner's important book, *Preface to Pastoral Theology* (1958). Published in the USA soon after the Second World War, this volume asserted the significance and importance of pastoral theology as an integral part of theological study, not just as a set of techniques. Drawing upon considerable interdisciplinary experience of dialogue with psychology and psychoanalysis, Hiltner argues that pastoral theology is more than the application in practice of theories derived from academic study of theological ideas. It is a place where theological ideas and contemporary experiences meet in such a way that both are changed. The implication is that pastoral practice and experience might contribute directly to the corpus of theological knowledge. This assertion of the intellectual relevance of practice and contemporary human experience has been an important guiding idea in the evolution of contemporary pastoral and practical theology.

From a younger generation than that of Seward Hiltner, John Patton, a contemporary American pastoral theologian, brings the story of developments in Protestant pastoral theology in the USA up to date. Patton describes the evolution of, and main trends in contemporary US pastoral theology. The papers by Hiltner and Patton should both be of interest to students outside North America. As in so many other areas of life, the USA has provided many of the key ideas and concepts that have helped to shape pastoral and practical theology in other countries.

Finally in this section, Paul Ballard, a long-standing British practical theologian, describes the evolution and character of British pastoral and practical theology over the last half century. Trends in the USA have had an enormous influence in Britain. However, there are some significant differences and strengths on the British scene derived from different intellectual and organizational factors and arrangements such as the teaching of theology in publicly-funded universities and colleges rather than just in church seminaries.

The papers in this section will provide useful historical background and context for students in pastoral and practical theology on both sides of the Atlantic. Having a sense of where this set of disciplines and practices has come from should help understanding of the shape and nature of pastoral and practical theology today. This will be useful in evaluating the papers in succeeding sections that may assume some background historical knowledge.

References

Clebsch, W., and Jaekle, C. (1975), *Pastoral Care in Historical Perspective*, New York: Jason Aronson.

Clinebell, H. (1984), *Basic Types of Pastoral Care and Couselling*, London: SCM Press. (American edn published by Abingdon Press in 1984.)

Farley, E. (1983b), *Theologia: Fragmentation and Unity in Theological Education*, Philadelphia: Fortress Press.

Hunter, R. (ed.) (1990), *Dictionary of Pastoral Care and Counseling*, Nashville: Abingdon Press.

McNeill, J. (1977), *A History of the Cure of Souls*, New York: Harper and Row.

Oden, T. (1983), *Pastoral Theology*, San Francisco: Harper and Row.

Oden, T. (1984) *Care of Souls in the Classic Tradition*, Philadelphia: Fortress Press.

Pagels, E. (1982), *The Gnostic Gospels*, London: Penguin Books. (American edn published by Random House in 1979.)

Schleiermacher, F. (1988), *Christian Caring: Selections from Practical Theology*, Philadelphia: Fortress Press.

1

The Meaning and Importance of Pastoral Theology

Seward Hiltner

Introduction

Seward Hiltner (1909–84) was an American Presbyterian minister who eventually became Professor of Pastoral Theology at Princeton University. A clinical student of Anton Boisen, the founder of Clinical Pastoral Education (CPE), Hiltner did perhaps more than anyone else to establish and foster pastoral theology as an area of serious, distinctive academic and practical concern. His thinking both reflected and helped to stimulate the contemporary renaissance in pastoral and practical theology as serious, critical academic as well as pragmatic concerns.

In his pioneering book *Preface to Pastoral Theology* (1958), Hiltner argues that pastoral theology is not just the application of principles taken from other theological disciplines to practice, nor is it simply about improving skills and technique or giving practical hints and tips. Instead, pastoral theology should be seen as a legitimate and central theological discipline in its own right. Unlike other theological disciplines, it is an operation- or experience-focused theological discipline that contributes directly to the understanding of revelation and theology from the "shepherding perspective." The "shepherding perspective" basically means regarding experience and theology from the vantage point of the practice of pastoral care, broadly understood.

Hiltner was heavily influenced by the correlational method of Paul Tillich who was engaging in theological dialogue with the insights and practice of psychodynamic psychology at this time. This dialogue permitted theology and psychology to learn from and be mutually illuminative of each other. While this particular dialogue may now be in abeyance, the importance of establishing a dialogue between theology and contemporary experience and taking experience seriously as a datum of theological significance has become a major part of the contemporary identity of pastoral theology.

FROM *PREFACE TO PASTORAL THEOLOGY*

Task

What is pastoral theology? How important is it? To whom?

It is the thesis of this book that pastoral theology is a formal branch of theology resulting from study of Christian shepherding, that it is just as important as biblical or doctrinal or historical theology, and that it is no less the concern of the minister of the local church than of the specialist.

[. . .]

The meaning of pastoral theology

Pastoral theology is defined here as that branch or field of theological knowledge and inquiry that brings the shepherding perspective to bear upon all the operations and functions of the church and the minister, and then draws conclusions of a theological order from reflection on these observations.

This means, first, that pastoral theology comes out of inquiry from the shepherding perspective. I hold that there are two other perspectives cognate with shepherding, which I call "communicating" and "organizing," which should also lead to branches of theology. . . .

Second, the definition asserts that pastoral theology is a branch of theology in the strict sense of the term.[1] It has the same kind of autonomy as any other branch of theology – biblical, doctrinal, historical, ethical, and so on – although all branches are of course interrelated. But pastoral theology is not derivative from the other branches except in the same sense in which all branches derive in part from one another.[2]

Third, the definition implies that pastoral theology is an operation-centered or function-centered branch of theology rather than what we shall call for lack of a better name a logic-centered branch of theology.[3] Within the whole body of divinity what is distinctive about the operation-centered inquiries such as pastoral theology is that their theological conclusions, or theory or basic principles, emerge from reflection primarily on acts or events or functions from a particular perspective. There are other branches of theology, such as biblical theology or doctrinal theology, whose organizing principle is of a different nature. The study of the Bible, or biblical theology, is centered logically around anything that contributes to understanding the meaning, devolopment, and significance of that book and the people and events and experiences lying behind the book. The study of doctrine is organized systematically and logically around the relation of doctrines to one another and their mutually reinforcing capacity to give testimony to the total faith. From these focal concerns each of the logic-centered fields of theology pursues its special investigations, which of course include the questions of practical significance and implication.

The logic-centered fields of theology are so obviously indispensable that they have led unwittingly to a misconception, namely, that any branch of theology must proceed as they do. They find their focuses in something that is overridingly logical and necessary, such as the Bible, the interrelation of doctrines, the development of history, or the meaning of morals. The contention here is that there is another kind of branches of theology, whose focuses are a particular perspective upon operations.[4] We distinguish three such branches, of which pastoral theology is one. A picture of the "body of divinity" is indicated schematically in [figure 1, see p. 30].[5]

Fourth, our definition suggests that pastoral theology is systematic, as any branch of theology must be, but that the principles around which the system is organized are those given by the nature of the shepherding perspective.[6] For instance, doctrinal theology is organized systematically around doctrines and their interrelationship. It uses the common currencies of the faith – such as God, sin, salvation – primarily in terms of the relation of their meaning to one another. Pastoral theology, like any branch of theology, also uses these common currencies of the faith. But it organizes its material according to the data secured from inquiry according to the shepherding perspective. Thus pastoral theology is not a different kind of theology in terms of ultimate content. It is not a competitor of any other branch of theology, but its principle of self-organization is uniquely its own, just as theirs are.[7] As we shall see in this brief historical inquiry about pastoral theology, confusion about these apparently abstract points led sometimes to odd conclusions about pastoral and practical theology.

Fifth, our definition of pastoral theology enables us to use a method in relation to it that is consistent with the standards for any critical theological method.[8] How do we approach critical and discriminating inquiry in any branch of theology? We first acknowledge that we do not bring a blank mind, that our whole previous experience with the faith and with the world affects the questions and presuppositions we bring. In so acknowledging, we are in a better position to see what is in the material we are studying. So it is with pastoral theology. We do not come at this with minds wiped blank of experience with the faith. We acknowledge our views and convictions, and thus become more open to what study of this particular kind, namely, reflection on acts viewed from the perspective of shepherding, has to teach us.

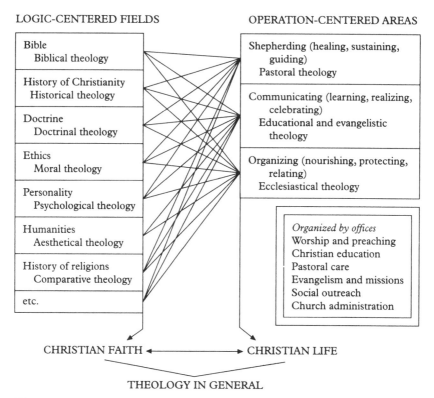

LOGIC-CENTERED FIELDS   OPERATION-CENTERED AREAS

Bible
   Biblical theology

History of Christianity
   Historical theology

Doctrine
   Doctrinal theology

Ethics
   Moral theology

Personality
   Psychological theology

Humanities
   Aesthetical theology

History of religions
   Comparative theology

etc.

Shepherding (healing, sustaining,
   guiding)
   Pastoral theology

Communicating (learning, realizing,
   celebrating)
   Educational and evangelistic
   theology

Organizing (nourishing, protecting,
   relating)
   Ecclesiastical theology

Organized by offices
Worship and preaching
Christian education
Pastoral care
Evangelism and missions
Social outreach
Church administration

CHRISTIAN FAITH ⟷ CHRISTIAN LIFE

THEOLOGY IN GENERAL

Figure 1 The body of divinity: the organization of theological knowledge and study

Our method proceeds from and through revelation as in any branch of theology, in the sense in which William Temple defined revelation as the "coincidence of event and appreciation."[9] We seek to cultivate the appreciation, the reception, the assimilation, the understanding – recognizing that only so can we know the event. The event may indeed exist independently of our appreciation, but we never know it so. So revelation calls not for the stifling of inquiry but for the most discriminating inquiry that can be made.

All realms of theological inquiry involve relationship between faith and culture. Sometimes the questions raised in culture – for example, What kind of stability can man have in a world of instability? – can be answered by faith.[10] And at times questions asked within the faith – for example, How can a man avoid simple repetition of actions he deplores? – can have at least partial answers given by the world of culture – perhaps to this question the insights of psychology into our inner ambiguous motivations. Material of tremendous potential significance for the questions of theology is now available in the personality sciences. When pastoral theology studies this material, as it pertains to the perspective of shepherding, it is following not a nontheological or an extratheological method but something that is part of method in every branch of theology. Faith can remain faithful and relevant only when it is in constant and discriminating dialogue with culture.

In concluding this initial discussion of the meaning of pastoral theology, it will be well to note briefly the definitions that are excluded. First, pastoral theology is not merely the *practice* of anything.[11] The practice or functions or events are examined reflectively and thus lead to theory. Any merely practical study of practice, if it failed to lead to fundamental theory, could not be pastoral theology.

Second, pastoral theology is not merely applied theology. Such a notion implies that principles are acquired through, for example, study of the Bible or of Christian doctrine and that these are applied in one-way fashion to acts and functions. We acknowledge fully that study of Bible and doctrine results in principles that may and must be applied. We assert further, however, that the process moves the other way also, that adequate critical study of events from some significant perspective makes creative contributions to theological understanding. Pastoral theology, like any branch of theology, applies some things learned elsewhere. But it is more than that as well.

Third, pastoral theology is not just pastoral psychology or pastoral sociology under a new name. The data considered may frequently be the same. What pastoral theology insists on is that the knowledge gained from observation and reflection be placed in a theological context. The principal criteria and methods employed are themselves theological. Pastoral psychology deals with insights emerging out of psychological inquiry for any and all aspects of the pastor's work and thought. Pastoral theology deals with the theological theory of the shepherding perspective upon the pastor's acts and functions. There is much overlap; but the two studies are not identical in scope, method, or aim.

Fourth, pastoral theology is not, as it has sometimes been held to be in the past, the theory of all the functions and operations of pastor and church. Such a view has seldom been held to completely, for the theory of preaching was usually excluded from the rubric of pastoral theology. We hold equally that pastoral theology cannot be the theory of all pastoral operations save preaching, for that gives it a kind of "Whatever is left over" definition. We believe attempts to define pastoral theology in this way will lead to either imperialism or amorphousness, as in the past, and we reject both.

Finally, we reject the possible conception of pastoral theology is the link between the organized fields of theological study and the acts and functions of minister and church. We reject this for two reasons. On the one hand, it implies that study of operations and functions cannot lead through reflection and systematization to a branch of theology, and we believe it can and must do so. We reject it, on the other hand, because it implicitly defines any branch of theology in terms of what we have called a "logic-centered" point of reference. We must acknowledge the great importance of bringing together the findings from the logic-centered fields with those from the function-focused fields. But we believe this task is the job of all the branches and is not a function that can be performed by any alleged "master discipline."

As we shall see in the historical chapter, some astute theologians in the nineteenth century proposed a branch of theology known as "practical theology," which would in turn have subbranches, of which pastoral theology might be one. There are two senses in which our conception of pastoral theology agrees with the intention behind the formation of practical theology. The first is the implication that the study of operations can and must be theological in character, must somehow lead to theological understanding. The second is that pastoral theology is not the sole branch of theology that can emerge from proper study of the functions of pastor and church.

With other aspects of this nineteenth-century idea of practical theology, we must take issue. We do not believe there is or can be a discipline of "practical theology" or "operational theology" that can be regarded as coordinate with biblical theology, doctrinal theology, and historical theology, and seen in the same series. The branches of theology whose focus is operations are *collectively* coordinate to the branches of theology whose focus is some logical reference point, such as the Bible. Further, we do not believe there can be a master perspective on acts and operations that would swallow all the others, any more than there can be a master perspective in the logic-centered fields, such that Bible would swallow up doctrine or history or ethics or that doctrine would consume the others.

Pastoral theology, to present the definition in slightly different language, is an operation-focused branch of theology, which begins with theological questions and concludes with theological answers, in the interim examining all acts and operations of pastor and church to the degree that they involve the perspective of Christian shepherding.

Importance of pastoral theology

There are five reasons why the study of pastoral theology is important today. The first is the peculiar nature and extent of the need for shepherding in our time. In our country more people belong to churches, both absolutely and proportionately, than at any previous time. Joining the church and professing faith in Jesus Christ do not automatically eliminate personal needs and problems. The churches and ministers now have an opportunity to help many persons to whom previously they would have been denied access.

Whatever one's diagnosis of our present cultural climate – age of anxiety, trend toward conformity, confusion in moral standards, or cult of success – the deepest need is to come somehow to a valid sense of meaningfulness. At least the start toward this must often be made through shepherding. But the details of the shepherding process must be up to date or they will not make contact. In the culture in which the shepherding metaphor was first developed, the single shepherd, with his crook to guide and redirect the strays, took his sheep into green pastures by day and at night brought them to the safety of home. Today a sheep grower has to help the pasture by fertilizer, by alternate plantings, or by irrigation. He adds vitamins and antibiotics to the sheep diet. He does these things, not because sheep are inherently more complicated now than they used to be, but because modern knowledge enables him to do more about helping more sheep in more dimensions of their life. The spiritual shepherd of today has as much obligation as the literal shepherd to bring his methods up to date, in order to meet the peculiar needs and dangers of our time.

A second reason why the study of pastoral theology is important lies in the development of new knowledge, new tools, and new professions that bear upon helping and healing. The new knowledge that is coming from psychology, from psychiatry, from anthropology, and from other sources is not easy to assimilate; but its riches are such that no thoughtful person can set them aside.[12] This knowledge is about more than methods and techniques. It may teach the spiritual shepherd the equivalent of how to prevent the grass from disappearing from a green pasture through knowledge of irrigation, crop rotation, and tree planting.

There are new problems and opportunities through the rise of new helping professions or through extension of functions among older helping professions such as the medical. Some modern shepherds, it is true, may be quacks, consciously or otherwise. In either event they need to be so recognized. But what is the shepherding function of the ordained minister in relation to the shepherding actually being carried out by the social worker, the psychiatrist, the student personnel worker, the clinical psychologist, the leader of group therapy, and all the others?[13] It is not the minister's Christian faith that distinguishes him from them. They too may well be Christians. How does he cooperate with them? Where do their skills extend beyond his and his beyond theirs? These questions and relationships demand continued study and discussion at a basic theoretical level as well as in terms of daily practice. Without a pastoral theology the minister has no theoretical structure to use in trying to answer them but must resort to a kind of practical opportunism. And we must speak not only to the question of the ordained minister as shepherd but also to that of the universal pastorhood of believers when some of those unordained Christian shepherds have skills and knowledge to which the ordained do not profess.

Third, pastoral theological study is important because without it the acts of shepherding, though they be many and mighty, will not illumine our understanding of the faith. In the United States it is clear that there is much shepherding activity within the churches. But it is not always clear that this is based on understood Christian presuppositions, and that reflection upon the activities is regarded as something more than the application of psychology or sociology in a purely practical sense.[14] Unless pastoral *theology* is studied, we lose many of the best opportunities with which God has provided us for deepening and correcting our understanding of the faith and that of those we try to help.

Fourth, the study of pastoral theology is important because of the peculiarly psychological intellectual climate of our time. Harry A. Overstreet has suggested that the language of our century is psychological in a way not true of any previous age.[15] Whether the psychology is good or bad, true or false, it is a mode of thinking in some respects unique to our time. Unless this modern man learns that this psychological language may also be a theological language, he is disposed to relegate theology as irrelevant to his thought and his concerns. There seems to be a growing amount of popular psychological thought that really deals with theological questions but that, by failing to acknowledge accurately the theological context, distorts theology and drives a deeper wedge between a misunderstood theology and an apparently more "comfortable" psychology. These trends should be arrested. Pastoral theology, studying shepherding in the light of theological questions and returning with theological answers, can take full account of psychology but can help prevent the false bifurcation that many now believe to represent the relation of theology and psychology. Of course there are difficult problems in this relationship. But the real problems are quite different from those posed in the popular mind.

Finally, the study of pastoral theology is important in the context of our general theological revival today. The renewed and widespread concern among laymen as well as clergy for a deepened understanding of biblical and doctrinal theology, and sometimes of historical and moral theology, is incomplete unless there is a new depth to pastoral theology. And at this point . . . there is no clear *structural* norm in our Protestant tradition. From this tradition we can learn much about attitude, about concern, about diligence, and even about content. But on how to think about and study pastoral theology, and organize our insights into basic principles, we hear no uniform voice of tradition. This makes it all the more important that the best constructive study be brought into this area.

The general point in this section, the importance of a pastoral theology – and not alone of a pastoral psychology, an applied theology, a pastoral practice, or even a right spirit – is deserving of brief illustration. Let us suppose a psychiatrist or clinical psychologist to be studying "acceptance" as he finds this in his therapeutic work. In many instances he may discover that, precisely at the point where the patient or client comes to feel most deeply that the psychiatrist accepts him, there is where he feels also at the same time most threatened. Prior to this time the patient has always held the secret reservation that, if the psychiatrist really knew what he was like, the proffered acceptance would be withdrawn. Now he must accept the fact that he is accepted as he is. But the immediate result, while not without its liberating aspects, makes him feel threatened in a new way. Previously many of his energies had been devoted to defending something unacceptable in himself. Now that he knows this part has been accepted, these energies must henceforth be used for some purpose other than concealing or fighting the unacceptable. This places before him a whole new range of possibility. It means change, and it threatens. Previously, automatic reactions decided what he would feel and do. Now he must bear responsibility as a human being, aware of his fallibility and sin, but inescapably aware also that his responsibility cannot be avoided by denial of its existence. Later on he will feel released. For the moment he may well feel torn between release and the new sense of threat at the loss of old defenses and the plain obligation of new responsibility.

From experiences like this the psychiatrist may properly generalize that there are occasions when a new step in development is, while ultimately liberating, temporarily threatening. He may properly conclude that one should be careful about pushing people in even the best directions in view of the threatening potentiality of recoil.

It is clear that processes are revealed here by the psychiatrist that are of interest to any brand of theologian. The acceptance that has been transformative has been in spite of the inner conviction of unacceptability. But this acceptance, while ultimately a blessing if the person lives through the threat, is temporarily ambiguous. From such studies the pastoral theologian may conclude, tentatively, that he should guard against any temptations to see movement toward freedom or toward acceptance as unalloyed and unambiguous goods.

The pastoral theologian, dealing with such data, will carry his questions further. He may well say in this type of situation it would appear that just when love that has long been offered is finally recognized and received as love, at precisely that moment does judgment seem to be felt most terribly. The depth of one's unacceptability is recognized only as this has been accepted by something not of one's own creation.

At this point the pastoral theologian may find his thoughts turning to Paul with special reference to Romans.[16] Paul drives home the point that the law judges and condemns us, and that only by accepting the reality of God's love and his grace through Jesus Christ can we find new life. Presumably a pastoral theologian will see a genuine relationship between Paul's statements and the process the psychiatrist is reporting on. But the pastoral theologian cannot conclude that, having found it in Paul, his work is done, that all he need do thereafter is go about finding other instances of how right Paul was. Perhaps Paul did experience all the complexities and ambiguities that may exist in the relation between love and judgment. But we cannot assume this in advance, even of Paul. Study of the processes of such relationships may augment Paul's understanding, indeed may even help in our understanding of Paul's experience. In certain basic principles Paul may indeed remain normative. But it is still our task, as in every age, to rediscover the relevance of these. And we have also the job of exploring the relevance and truth of associated or related principles. Perhaps new tools are available for the study of processes that were previously unexaminable. Paul may be right without being adequate. We can never forget Paul and by implication all traditional theological wisdom. But this can never be a substitute for observing our pastoral experience, generalizing on it theologically, and checking it against the wisdom of the Christian ages. Where the study is of the shepherding perspective on functions and operations, it is pastoral theology.

NOTES

1   This means that theology, or any of its branches, is to be understood as an attempt to articulate the faith more or less systematically, in one or more of its aspects, from one or more perspectives. So viewed, theology is human and fallible; but its intent and concern are always to move toward articulation and clarification of the faith in all its dimensions. Theology has inescapably an intellectual dimension. We have to think about it by using the same tools with which we think about anything else. But the intellectual activity is never to be seen as divorced from faith and experience, as if it were only a passive ordering of things after their occurrence. It bears creatively upon our assimilation of the faith itself and therefore of anything that may be called experience. Any branch of theology, in order to qualify, must, therefore, emerge from the faith, examine with all possible intellectual tools some basic aspect or dimension of the faith, and return to the faith with a creative and systematic account of its fallible but illuminating findings.

2   The word "autonomy" runs some risks of being misunderstood, even when we qualify it at every point by indicating the interrelationship of the several branches of theology. By analogy what I want to say is what Paul Tillich says in using the terms autonomy, heteronomy, and theonomy in a different connection. If the branches of theology were heteronomous, they would be related but in the pattern of a power structure such that some would engulf others. If they were merely

autonomous without genuine relationship, they would be anarchic. In the other context Tillich uses the term "theonomy" to indicate the fulfillment of man, man's law, through God, God's law. Autonomy not seen in this context is not true autonomy but anarchy. See Paul Tillich, *Systematic Theology* (Chicago, Ill.: University of Chicago Press, 1951) I, p. 147ff.

Any branch of theology that regarded itself as the whole of theology would be either anarchic or imperialistic. While it cultivates rightly the subject matter peculiar to its nature, it also pays attention to the subject matter that is common currency for every branch. It aims at precision in what is unique about it, but it also brings its offerings to the common table. If pastoral theology exists and is important, as this volume contends, then it is necessary for its autonomy to be recognized in order that it may not prematurely be the victim of an intellectual or theological heteronomy that would, for example, regard it as merely practical without the ability to make genuinely theological contributions.

3   What I am calling the "logic-centered" fields of theological inquiry are sometimes referred to as the "theological sciences." This term is unsatisfactory, not only because of the specialized way in which the term "sciences" is now used, but also because it implies that no real knowledge is involved unless it is organized in a certain way. We call these fields "logic-centered" to suggest that the key to their distinctive nature lies in a "logical" organization of subject matter. The logical organization of the subject matter in each field leads, then, to certain consequences which, potentially, enrich the whole.

For instance, biblical scholars now use linguistic analysis, archaeology, paleography, oriental history, and other special methods and disciplines in the pursuit of their inquiry that has the Bible as its logical center. A good deal of their work on these special methods has little immediate transmissive value to the ordinary church member. But the pursuit of the special investigations that follow from the logical focus is in the long run important even for that church member.

The point here is not of course to argue the case for the biblical scholar's need to pursue archaeology or oriental history, for he can do that far better himself. It is, rather, by clarifying the nature of the distinctive way in which he organizes his inquiry, to indicate that another way of organizing a branch of theological study may also be both possible and necessary. This point must be made in order to lay claim to the right of pastoral theology to be a theological discipline, even though its principle of organization is function-centered rather than logic-centered. Proper study of functions with resulting systematization of knowledge leads to a body of knowledge and not merely to skill or technique.

4   From the latter part of the nineteenth century until today the principal
    scheme of organizing theological knowledge that was used in the the-
    ological seminaries was fourfold, involving biblical, systematic, his-
    torical, and practical, theology. The overall error in this plan was the
    attempt to deal with practical theology, so-called, as if it were co-
    ordinate with each of the other items. If by practical theology we mean
    those branches of theology whose organizing center is functional rather
    than logical, then they are to be seen as structurally co-ordinate with
    all the logic-centered branches of theology viewed collectively, not as
    co-ordinate with each of them viewed separately. Whatever is felt to be
    the appropriate number of fields, logic-centered or functioncentered,
    the whole number in each group is structurally co-ordinate with the
    whole number in the other group. To regard practical theology or any
    branch of operationfocused theology as one of a list of branches that
    are otherwise logic-centered is to force on a branch like pastoral the-
    ology organizational and structural criteria that prevent its making its
    inherent contribution to the whole body of divinity.

5   Figure 1 (on p. 30) attempts to represent the shape of the body of
    divinity according to the principles already indicated. On one side
    are the logic-centered fields and on the other the operation-centered
    areas. Each is shown connected with the other, as interpenetrating, as
    engaging in two-way communication. The primary point is not to
    argue for a specific number of fields and areas, but to demonstrate
    the proper mode of relationship among the fields and areas. If it is
    objected that this outline lacks unity because it insists on two different
    ways of organizing theological inquiry, two answers can be given. The
    first is that all attempts to deal with theological inquiry without making
    this distinction result either in an antipractical bias or in detheologizing
    the operational studies. In other words, I did not make the distinction
    but only discovered it. Second, the kind of unity that is needed for
    the richest theological inquiry is that which emerges from two-way
    communication at all points. No single field or area has the respons-
    ibility for integration in such a way that any other field can dispense with
    its integrative obligation. It is simply a fact that this linkage function
    must be shared or it cannot be performed at all. But that cannot be
    done by the equivalent of back-slapping, acting as if there were no
    distinction in the organizing principles of the two types of theological
    inquiry. And it certainly cannot be done if the fields treat the areas like
    illegitimate theological children fit only to apply what has been learned
    elsewhere and incapable of creative theological contribution.

6   Against a common misconception, we need to protest that system does
    not refer to something imposed or superadded as a kind of intellectual
    Procrustean bed in which data are made to lie whether they fit or not.
    The best system is that which demonstrates the reality of relationship

among the items so far as real knowledge goes, and then declares honestly its ignorance where the relationships are unclear or unknown. The fact that systems can and sometimes do become chains and walls is not the fault of system as such as I have defined it, but comes from an uncurbed desire to round things off whether the rounding stage has been reached or not.

It is my contention that pastoral theology, like any branch of theology, must become systematic in the sense defined above. In theology the question of system has been complicated because doctrinal theology has often used the term "systematic theology" for itself. Indeed, it is necessary for doctrinal theology to be systematic in order to be intelligible and coherent. But this use, although unintentionally, has sometimes obscured the fact that every theological discipline must be systematic, that is, must bring together into a statement the representation of the relationships actually seen among items of the data, including statement of that about which there is ignorance or unclarity. In other words, any good system is open, even though struggling to represent adequately all the relationships it sees among its data.

If every branch of theology has the obligation to be systematic, the question then arises: systematic about what or around what? The principal answer is that it systematizes its data around the content of its unique organizing center. The biblical scholar is systematic about the Bible, not only in the sense that he overlooks none of its books, but also in the sense that all his data – whether they come from textual, historical, exegetical, archaeological, or other forms of inquiry – are systematically organized around the Bible. The historical theologian organizes his data systematically around a historical center, which he usually interprets as chronological sequence but which may assume other developmental forms. The system of the doctrinal theologian is focused around his logical organizing center of doctrinal relationship and coherence.

What has been said so far is adequate as a statement of what the system is centered about so long as we are considering that which is distinctive or unique within each branch of theology. But this is not all that needs to be said about the center of the system. Every branch of theology uses the common currencies of the faith – God, man, sin, and so on – without which it would not be a part of theology at all. In so far as each branch of theology has the obligation not only to pursue its unique task, but also to bring its contribution to the village green of theological integration, it has also, as a secondary focus for systematizing its knowledge, the common currency.

While dealing with its sister branches, any theological discipline rightly systematizes its knowledge around that organizing center that is different from that of other branches. This is the system of what might be called its domestic policy. In its foreign policy, however, each branch of theology must take more care to systematize both around the common currency and around the special focus.

Our special concern is of course the system that is proper to pastoral theology. Around what shall its data be systematized? The answer is that the primary center for its system is its organizing principle, which I have defined as shepherding when shepherding is understood as a perspective present in all pastoral events and dominantly important in some. Like any other branch, pastoral theology must use the common theological currency for a basic part of its content. But in domestic policy, while using the common currency in communication with its sister disciplines, it nevertheless organizes and systematizes itself around that which is distinctive, namely, shepherding. The organizing principle is also the focus of system.

This volume divides the shepherding perspective into three aspects: healing, sustaining, and guiding. As an inquiry what pastoral theology is systematic about is the actual process by which shepherding – healing, sustaining, or guiding – is brought about. When this knowledge is put together into a system, although an open one, clarifying the common currency of the faith, we have a systematic pastoral theology. Any demand to pastoral theology that its primary focus of system be something else, such as systematic doctrine or Bible or morals, would be denying its claim to be a branch of theology. While this book itself is only an introduction to such a statement of systematic pastoral theology, it does later on attempt to illustrate the meaning of system in pastoral theology in the sense described.

But pastoral theology has a foreign as well as a domestic policy. It is not the sole discipline that studies shepherding in the generic sense. So, each in its own way, do psychiatry, clinical psychology, social work, and other disciplines. In relation to these disciplines around what does pastoral theology organize itself? The answer is, around the common currency of the faith, although with special reference still to its shepherding perspective on that faith.

It is so obvious that the pastoral theologian can learn from contact with these other shepherding disciplines that the case need not be argued here. But the question may then be asked: How does his system center differ from theirs? The answer is not that he is a Christian and they are not, for many of them are. It is, rather, that the activity of beginning with theological questions, bringing them to the shepherding material, and returning either with theological answers or with new theological questions is the focal thing about his pastoral theological discipline. These workers, as persons or as Christians, may indeed do the same thing, as many of them now do so helpfully for all concerned. But doing this is not necessarily inherent in their discipline as such.

Pastoral theology, then, in summary, needs to be as systematic as any other branch of theology. That which distinguishes the center of its system within the body of divinity is its inquiry after and drawing conclusions from the exercise of the shepherding perspective. In relation to the shepherding disciplines which as disciplines are not theologically oriented, its system is focused around the common currency of the Christian faith. Thus the system of pastoral theology may be called bifocal, depending on whether it is speaking within the body of divinity or in relation to human knowledge in general.

Pastoral theology must have full commerce with every discipline that is studying shepherding. And every bit of relevant insight it discovers about shepherding, regardless of source, must be considered in the light of its theological significance. If the commerce is not open and free, the system finally becomes rigid and irrelevant. But if the inquiry is not theological, then new truth has no apparent theological root or implication; and vitality comes to be associated with nontheological orientations. If both tasks are carried out, then pastoral theology becomes an open and inquiring and theologically focused system, enriching the whole body of divinity and having an impact on nontheological disciplines as well as learning from them.

7   The principle around which data are organized, data in which one has some emotional investment, is often closer to one's personal center than he realizes. There tend to be resistances to the other fellow who appears to be using one's data but is organizing them in a different, and of course inferior, way. When the data involve the many similar elements that botany and pharmacology have in common, although organized in different ways, the resistance may not be strong. But when we deal with the kind of material found in the social and psychological sciences and in the humanities, resistances are greater.

The disciplines such as psychiatry or social work that are most closely co-ordinate with the function-centered theological disciplines tend to be in their present form of relatively recent development. They do not have the masses of data in their short history that other disciplines with longer study and self-conscious inquiry lay claim to. To the older disciplines these parvenus never appear to be quite autonomous or respectable. Social work, for instance, has been particularly beset on these grounds. Not only is it accused by sociology, psychiatry, and clinical psychology of borrowing most of its data; it is often alleged to be destroying their meaning by the way it organizes them and the uses to which they are put. Needless to say, this is not a good picture of the facts. It is the parvenus who, whatever their claim to autonomy, are generally more sinned against than sinning. But when a newcomer becomes big enough, he may act exactly as does the sophomore conscious only that he is no longer a freshman. For illustration see some aspects of education in our century.

For pastoral theology the implications of this discussion are obvious. To be sure, it deals with something as old as the church itself. But the study of it in the form we advocate, leading to a branch of theology in the full sense, is recent. It is, therefore, a parvenu. So long as it kept its place as practical, deluding itself that it merely applied what had been found out elsewhere, its existence was safe but dull, uncreative, and intellectually dishonest. Now that, at least in the person of this author, it alleges its theological character and an autonomy similar to that of other disciplines, something other than a passive parallelism will have to take place. Perhaps other theologians are so uniformly enlightened that they will rejoice unambiguously at the emergence of this talking sibling. It is more likely that the pastoral theologian will meet some new resistances from within and without the theological fold. This is good; for it means, at last, genuine encounter. An adult may spank a baby, but he does not fight it. Pastoral theology wants to be encountered – accepted as a sibling if possible – but better fight and even lose than to be mentally clothed with diapers.

8   The relative lack of attention to theological method by any except professional theologians suggests that this matter should be discussed, however briefly, if we are to demonstrate that pastoral theology conforms to the essential canons of any critical theological method. This may be done most briefly and sharply by speaking to three basic questions. First, how can theology be open and inquiring when it spends so much time looking backward, even asserting that in Jesus Christ there is already a final revelation? Second, how can theology be relevant to man's needs when it seems concerned only with *Heilsgeschichte* rather than with history or culture in general? Third, if theology articulates faith, how can it possibly do justice to doubt and despair?

As to the question about the backward look, we may note first that every science or discipline has some touchstone or basic principle on which it proceeds until or unless this is qualified or corrected. The history of any science is partly about the disentangling of what is truly basic from the particular and limited forms in which that has been seen. In physics such a principle would be that energy can be neither created nor destroyed. When atomic energy was discovered, this principle seemed to be threatened because it contradicted the form in which the general principle had previously been seen. What then occurred was a restatement of the principle on the basis of a wider understanding of the forms it could assume.

What Christian thought has been agreed on is that the nature and character of God have been revealed in the character and acts and existence of Jesus Christ, that this revelation has involved actual events and is therefore historical and not merely symbolical, and that the nature of God as revealed is about his dealings with men and about their response to him for good or for ill in some kind of personal rather than Olympian or "first-cause" sense. When a statement is made about God apart from God's dealings with man, an abstraction is being made from the total revelation. It may be necessary to do this, but the mischief comes if one forgets he is abstracting. The revelation in Jesus Christ is final in that no further basic clue needs to be given or new type of work needs to be done by God for the salvation of man. But the assimilation and understanding of the revelation by man is never final, nor is that work of God ever done that attempts to help man receive the revelation.

In terms of methodological principle the relation of the backward look (or the consolidation of principles) to inquiry (future-oriented instability) is now more similar in the sciences and in theology than for many centuries. As the sciences emerged in Western history, their movement has been from a study of the remote toward that of the near. They began with astronomy, moved to physics, and on to chemistry and biology. Only in recent years have psychology, sociology, and scientific anthropology been explored. The serious efforts of the "near sciences" have compelled a wrestling with the observer in a way that was not necessary for many years in the "remote sciences." The latter too are now examining the observer. In the sciences the backward look is both a resting upon a hard-won touchstone and a questioning of every possible premise. It includes examination not only of what is out there but also of what is in here.

Christian thought sees a vital and organic connection between its belief in the final revelation of God in Jesus Christ and the need for future-oriented theological inquiry. At best man's understanding and reception of the revelation is incomplete; most theologians regard it as distorted. Inquiry is necessary to correct our understanding of the revelation, which is not merely about God out there but about his relation to us. And inquiry is relevant about the vital details of life, for these are not made explicit in the revelation itself. Without the touchstone inquiry could not proceed. But every belief and presupposition about our understanding of the revelation is open to future-oriented inquiry.

The second question asked how theology could be relevant to man's needs when it seemed concerned only with the knowledge of salvation rather then with knowledge and culture in general. Of course it is true that theology is focused on the knowledge of salvation, but any authoritarianism or pietism that defines this in purely compartmenatalized terms does injustice to the witness of the Bible that man is saved either as a whole or not at all. The theologians have of course taken different stands about the relation of theology to culture. Methodologically speaking, however, all great theologians have taken culture, or human knowledge in general, quite seriously. In his day Thomas Aquinas was a daring innovationist by insisting on relating Aristotelian thought to theology. Even those theologians of past and present, such as Karl Barth, who believe that theology is kerygmatic exposition and who are wary that any culture-related apologetic is letting the camel's nose in the tent, make use of and take for granted many of the results of culture-related inquiry such as historical criticism of the Bible. The biblical theologian does not wait cringing lest some new scrolls be discovered that force him to rethink something. Instead he regards the archaeological search as a positive instrument of his own methodology. To be sure, it may raise new questions, and there is always potential tension. But this is sought, not evaded, as a part of the task of theological inquiry itself.

The third question asked how it is that, if the task of theology is to articulate faith, it can possibly do justice to doubt and despair. If it claims to have the answers, how can it possibly take seriously the questions? The basic reply to this is that, while Christianity or theology may have the answer, no theologian or other man ever has the answer untinctured by the doubt, struggle, and despair to which the question refers. Theological method must be rigorous in avoiding the equation of our understanding of the faith from the faith itself as it must be in God's eyes. The more usual way to state this is in terms of the Protestant principle of God's judgment upon us lest we think we are God, on our ways, our thoughts, and even our church.

This point has unusual importance for method in pastoral theology. The would-be shepherd who believes that he possesses faith unmixed with doubt cannot help the doubting and deceives himself. If he knows anything basic about himself, he recognizes that doubt in some form has been a part of his past and is within his present. He is, therefore, able to accept both the doubt and the implicit faith in those he would help, not simply identifying himself with the one and rejecting the other. In the process of helping and the never-ending self-reflection that is a vital part of the helping and the inquiry the shepherd is aware that the theology – as the reception and assimilation of faith – is always in the making and never finished.

9   William Temple, *Nature, Man and God* (New York: Macmillan, 1934), p. 315.

10 This is the way Paul Tillich puts it in discussing his theological method as one of "correlation." He writes, "The method of correlation explains

the contents of the Christian faith through existential questions and theological answers in mutual interdependence" (*op. cit.*, p. 60). Not everything is yet clear about Tillich's use of the key term "correlation" to describe his theological method. Plainly he intends by it to establish theological relevance; theology does not talk in a corner by itself but speaks to the vital questions men ask. Thus he says to the theologian that culture and life cannot be neglected, and to the ordinary man that faith has a message for him. But to what extent is correlation a two-way method? Tillich apparently solves this problem by indicating that theology deals with matters of ultimate concern and other disciplines with preliminary concerns. But this does not solve the problem. No one can say in advance when the emerging knowledge or insight is going to be ultimate or only preliminary. Nor does it seem sufficient to say that the sacred may erupt from the profane.

Knowledge or insight of the utmost importance to theology may emerge at any time from a discipline that seems far removed from theology, and it hardly seems fair to say that that discipline has no claim to what it has discovered.

We believe that a full two-way street is necessary in order to describe theological method. If we hold that theology is always assimilation of the faith, not just the abstract idea of the faith apart from its reception, then it becomes necessary to say that culture may find answers to questions raised by faith as well as to assert that faith has answers to questions raised by culture. Tillich apparently hesitates to put the matter this way, and there is obvious risk to the ultimate meaning of faith in so putting it. But if psychiatry, for example, enables us to help someone to turn a corner and thence move on into the faith, how can we avoid saying that culture has given the answer to a problem posed by faith – provided we believe that our understanding of faith is never known apart from such actual concrete processes?

In the hands of Tillich there are great virtues in the word "correlation" as a key to theological method. In lesser hands we may wonder about the term, perhaps especially concerning methodology in the function-oriented branches such as pastoral theology. Much of the history of these disciplines shows them either remaining linked in purely reproductive and uncreative fashion with practice while failing to move on to articulated theory, or else devising some systematic theory without explicit recognition of how theory is evolved from practice. It would be desirable if a key methodological concept could be found that would guard against these prevalent distortions.

"Dialectic," especially if used along with "correlation," has something to be said for it. For it can suggest the recognition of tension or opposition within what nevertheless remains a real relationship. But its tension connotation may exaggerate differences that are only verbal or perspectival in character, even if it avoids a Hegelianism. A word has been sought, so far in vain, that would connote movement back and forth, acknowledging agreement or contribution when real, retaining tension when real. Explorations thus far may be briefly reported.

"Interconnect" in mechanics means that movement of any one part that moves each and every part. An interconnected theological method could mean that movement, inquiry, or discovery would imply and necessitate study of the way in which all theological disciplines are thereby affected, as well as the search for that movement in all other disciplines that interconnectedly moves one's own.

"Interpenetrating" implies that anything moving toward depth in one discipline may do so for others also. "Interrelated" is like "correlated" but connotes, rather, one that finds its unity than two discovering what they have in common. "Intervolve," meaning to involve one with another, would be more promising if it did not look like a misprint. "Nexus" means precisely "interconnection" but in practice tends to suggest merely a point of juncture. We even toyed with "amphidetic," which means to be bound all around. Certainly that has been the conclusion of this verbal search.

11 We use the term "method" to mean more than "practice," however skilled, and more than "technical means." Every discipline, including theology, uses technical means. But technical means govern inquiry only after assumptions have been made, history and context have been reviewed, and a specific subject of inquiry set. After technical means have been employed, much yet remains to be done. Data must be organized, their significance and relationships must be assessed, and implications need to be drawn from them. Method in any discipline is that which engages critically in all these procedures and not solely in those which use the technical means peculiar to the discipline.

12 See my "Bibliography and Reading Guide in Pastoral Psychology," *Pastoral Psychology*, vol. V, no. 50 (January 1955).

13 See my "Psychotherapy and Counseling in Professions Other than the Ministry," *Pastoral Psychology*, vol. VII, no. 62 (March 1956).

14 Although I must reject certain aspects of the book's content, Albert C. Outler's *Psychotherapy and the Christian Message* (New York: Harper, 1954) is nevertheless an important call to a consideration of these presuppositions. So is an earlier but in some respects a more deep-reaching book, *Psychotherapy and a Christian View of Man* by David E. Roberts (New York: Charles Scribner's Sons, 1950). William E. Hulme in *Counseling and Theology* (Philadelphia: Muhlenberg Press, 1956) also attacks this question but with a tendency to find an answer too quickly in parallelism of psychology and theology.

15 Harry A. Overstreet, *The Mature Mind* (New York: W. W. Norton, 1949), p. 1.

16 See especially Rom. 3:19–25, 27–8; 4:16–17; 5:1–5; 7:1–6; 8:1–11; 10:5–13.

SOME POINTS FOR FURTHER CONSIDERATION

- Is Hiltner right to argue that pastoral theology should be seen as a distinctive theological discipline that has its own contribution to make to theological understanding?
- In what other ways might pastoral theology be understood apart from those which Hiltner advocates?
- Is Hiltner's vision of pastoral theology an attractive or an unattractive one? What are its strengths and weaknesses?
- Hiltner is very interested in establishing dialogue with psychological insights into the human condition. What other disciplines and methods should be taken seriously by contemporary pastoral theology, and why?
- What other contemporary theologies are primarily operation- or experience-centered? How do they compare with Hiltner's in terms of scope and method?

FOR FURTHER READING AND EXPLORATION

Hiltner expands the arguments summarized here in Hiltner (1958). For more about Hiltner himself, along with Tillich, Boisen, and Clinical Pastoral Education, see relevant articles in Hunter (1990). For the application of CPE see e.g. Foskett and Lyall (1988). Tillich's critical correlational method is outlined in his own *Systematic Theology* (1951–63), especially in volume 1 of that work. It can be seen in action in dialogue with existentialism and psychology in *The Courage to Be* (1952). It has been refined and developed in practical theology by, for example, Browning (1983, 1991) and Graham (1996) whose work is summarized in papers later in the present volume.

References

Browning, D. (1983), *Religious Ethics and Pastoral Care*, Philadelphia: Fortress Press.
Browning, D. (1991), *A Fundamental Practical Theology*, Minneapolis: Fortress Press.

Foskett, J., and Lyall, D. (1988), *Helping the Helpers*, London: SPCK.
Graham, E. (1996), *Transforming Practice*, London: Mowbray.
Hiltner, S. (1958), *Preface to Pastoral Theology*, Nashville: Abingdon Press.
Hunter, R. (ed.) (1990), *Dictionary of Pastoral Care and Counseling*, Nashville: Abingdon Press.
Tillich, P. (1951–63), *Systematic Theology*, vols 1–3, London: Nisbet.
Tillich, P. (1952), *The Courage to Be*, London: Nisbet.

2

Introduction to Modern Pastoral Theology in the United States

JOHN PATTON

INTRODUCTION

John Patton is a Senior Professor of Pastoral Theology at Columbia Theological Seminary, Decatur, Georgia. He has made a number of seminal contributions to the development of modern pastoral and practical theology in his books (Patton 1985, 1990, 1993). While his influence has been mainly felt in the USA, Patton's work is widely respected and influential throughout the English-speaking world of pastoral theology.

In the present, specially commissioned article Patton traces the main influences that have shaped contemporary (mainly Protestant) pastoral theology in the USA. Broadly, the tradition represented by psychologist William James, pastoral educationalist and mental health survivor Anton Boisen, and by Seward Hiltner has been the chief influence upon the method and content of late-twentieth-century academically-based pastoral theology. However, as Patton notes, the somewhat individualistic and psychological bias of that tradition is coming under challenge as concerns about ethics, hermeneutics, and contextual issues such as race, gender, class, and power come to the fore in a more pluralistic world. Patton concludes that US pastoral theology now faces the challenges of developing better pastoral anthropologies, exploring the boundaries between pastoral care and ethics, understanding the implications of change, learning how better to learn theologically from experience, how to deal with the implications of factors such as gender, culture, and faith tradition for pastoral care, and exploring major problem issues in pastoral care.

Many of the methods, issues, and concerns that Patton describes have resonances within the British context. This is not surprising, as North American and European cultures have much in common. Furthermore, the American pastoral theology "industry" is much larger and more coherent than its counterpart in Britain. This means that many ideas and techniques are inevitably imported, often with enormous advantage and profit to all concerned. So, for example, experiential theological learning through Clinical Pastoral Education, with its accompanying emphasis on the importance of pastoral supervision to enhance learning, has been imported to a greater or lesser extent into many British pastoral training opportunities.

INTRODUCTION TO MODERN PASTORAL THEOLOGY IN THE UNITED STATES

Although there are a number of ways in which one might interpret the modern history of pastoral theology in the United States, it is reasonable to argue that its origins can be most clearly seen in the thought of philosopher William James, hospital chaplain Anton Boisen, and theological school professor Seward Hiltner. This pastoral theology of the James, Boisen, Hiltner tradition was developed in the graduate programs which explicitly brought psychology into theological education, in clinical pastoral education and in the specialized ministries of pastoral care and counseling.

The James, Boisen, Hiltner Tradition

William James was not a theologian and, although he was deeply concerned with religion, he was very explicit in his avoidance of theological judgments and affirmations. Nevertheless, his philosophy contributed to American pastoral theology in a number of ways.

James believed that religious experience constituted important data for human knowledge. His study of such experience in the Gifford Lectures of 1901 and 1902, published as *The Varieties of Religious Experience*, argued that in the intense and the extreme examples of a type of experience, one could see more clearly the true nature of a phenomenon.

Second, as a philosopher and psychologist James concerned himself more with function than with truth. Most important was whether or not a particular belief or practice produced a worthwhile result. The study of the action and effectiveness of a phenomenon were judged to be as important as its ultimate truth.

Third, James was concerned with studying phenomena themselves more than thought or categories ordering or classifying those phenomena. He argued against the narrow empirical philosophers and scientists and sought a broader and more inclusive empirical thought. James's philosophy was concerned with what Clifford Geertz later called "thick description." James's interest in extremes, the concern for function and with richness of description all contributed to modern pastoral theology's focus upon experience.

Congregational minister Anton Boisen, recognized as the founder of clinical pastoral education in the United States, was a follower of James in several important ways. Like James, Boisen was concerned with the function of theological belief. The positive relationship of a belief to experience was more important than its relationship to religious tradition. Following James in his concern for function, Boisen viewed the achievement of a moral life as more important for the believer than what he believed. This was a major interpretive key for him in understanding human goals and needs.

This latter concern was not arrived at simply through participating in the experience of others but grew out of Boisen's own experience as a patient with a psychiatric illness. He interpreted his illness and the illness of others as an attempt to achieve a moral resolution of a problem. Extreme behavior was not just crazy or irrational. It had a purpose which could be achieved or fail to be achieved. Thus, the time of crisis in such an illness was one in which a caring person who was knowledgeable in both theology and psychology could be extremely valuable.

For Boisen, the real evil in mental disorder is not to be found in the conflict but in the sense of isolation or estrangement experienced by the patient, and his statement that "loneliness is more terrible than anxiety" expresses the primary dynamic for the development of mental hospital chaplaincy. Moreover, he demonstrated that the chaplain was not just in a position to be helpful to patients in supporting them in crisis, he was in position to learn theology "empirically" – from the kind of extreme experiences that James had presented in his Gifford Lectures. Boisen understood both patient and chaplain to be learners from the crisis experience, not just learners about crisis but learners about themselves. Thus he contributed to the breaking down of the rigid barriers between patient and pastor and between illness and health that have become an important part of the clinical pastoral education movement.

Seward Hiltner, who was a professor of pastoral theology at the University of Chicago Divinity School and later at Princeton Theological Seminary, carried out his work as a pastoral theologian in the tradition of both James and Boisen. Like James he was concerned with experience and with function and, thus, with developing an empirical theology. As a minister and theologian, he was concerned like Boisen, not with just studying crisis and moral dilemmas, but with ministering to persons experiencing them.

Growing out of this pastoral concern, Hiltner left his graduate study of theology to become a student in clinical pastoral education and, later, the executive director of the Council for Clinical Training. After some years in this position and in another administrative position in religion and mental health, he completed his PhD in theology and for the rest of his career was an influential writer and professor of pastoral theology.

About the same time that Hiltner established the program in Religion and Personality at the University of Chicago, around 1950, similar graduate programs were established at other schools of theology, e.g. at Boston and Northwestern universities, and at the Southern Baptist Seminary in Louisville. The establishment of these graduate programs as new fields of study in theological education was one of the three most important features in the development of modern pastoral theology in America. The other two features were the recognition of clinical pastoral education as a recognized part of the theological education and the development of specialization in pastoral care and counseling as a dimension of ministry.

In America in the 1960s, 1970s, and 1980s chaplains, pastoral counselors, and clinical pastoral education supervisors became a significant part of religious ministry, although they were not always accepted as fully legitimate by the church. In developing the clinical pastoral method, Anton Boisen followed James's view of experience and some of James's methods of examining it. He believed that we learn about human life and God's relation to it by examining concrete human experiencing and the narrative descriptions of it as presented in case records and personal histories. As Boisen's method developed in situations other than mental hospitals and among pastoral supervisors who had not had the kind of struggle which Boisen had, the examination of experience moved toward the "verbatim" or written report of pastoral conversations and away from extensive case histories of individual patients.

In a wide variety of clinical settings students have been asked to recall in as much detail as possible what was said and done in, for example, a visit with a patient in a hospital room. At the beginning this is not easy for the student to do, but with the suggestion that some notes on the visit be written as soon as possible after it, and with practice, verbatims become easier to write. When the verbatim is written in its final form, the student takes the notes that he or she has written and develops them into a narrative with dialogue between student and patient.

Obviously, what is written is not exactly what happened in the event. Seward Hiltner used to tell his students to write in detail in the verbatim what had happened – "by hook or crook, but not by sheer fabrication." His comment recognized that there would inevitably be the use of imagination in the writing of the narrative, but the assumption was that the event as written could be as useful in the student's learning as the event as it had actually happened. The writer of an event reveals important things about himself or herself in the way that the narrative is constructed. The important thing to note is the value given to the recovery of pastoral care events and the student's experiencing of them.

Two other features of American clinical pastoral education are particularly important in understanding it. First, theoretical knowledge is developed out of practice as well as contributing to it. On a study leave in America an European pastoral theologian noted that the most distinctive thing about clinical pastoral education was that students enter it "without thorough training beforehand." Students are allowed, even invited, to make mistakes in their pastoral work, to learn from them, and even to question pastoral theory on the basis of their experience.

The second feature is the focus on the person of the student participating in the educational process. This is based on three assumptions: (1) the way one cares for others is inescapably related to the way one cares for oneself; (2) pastoral caring always involves *being* someone as well as *doing* something; and (3) one can best learn about oneself and how to care for others through experiential and reflective participation in caring relationships.

The Development of Specialized Ministries of Care

The development of specialized ministries in pastoral care and counseling has also been an important part of American pastoral theology. Students have been educated in theological schools and clinical centers according to the standards of the Association for Clinical Pastoral Education and the American Association of Pastoral Counselors. The primarily theological questions raised by the specialized pastoral care ministries have been: (1) In what way are they related to the traditional functions of ministry? and (2) How do they make use of theology in their theory and their practice? A significant amount of American pastoral theology has been written in response to these questions.

In recent years, the James, Boisen, Hiltner tradition in American pastoral theology has been most affected by three particular concerns: ethics, hermeneutics, and context.

Pastoral theology and ethics

One of Hiltner's students, Don Browning, has been most influential in expressing the first of these concerns. Browning has questioned the heritage of Boisen and Hiltner as the primary basis for modern pastoral theology and has developed his theory out of the ethical rather than the phenomenological side of William James's philosophy. Under the pressures of pluralism, Browning argues, the very goals of our care often come under question; therefore, our care should be guided by a more explicitly normative discipline. Pastoral theological method needs to be reconstituted under the guidance of a critical, practical moral theology (as Catholics would call it), or theological ethics (as Protestants would call it) or religious ethics (as philosophers would call it).

Although assenting to the importance of "case material" or actual experience in ministry, Browning's primary means of relating theology to practice has been through the application of ethical principles to pastoral situations. His method has involved identifying the type of moral reasoning operative in pastor and parishioner or counselor and client, encouraging an intentional application of moral guidance, and thus offering a more priestly model of ministry. The theology in pastoral care and counseling may most effectively be seen in the practical theological application of moral reasoning to particular life situations.

Hermeneutics and pastoral theology

Charles Gerkin and others have based their pastoral theology not on ethics, but on principles of hermeneutics. The pastor and parishioner are seen as interpreters of their worlds. In the light of the faith tradition which they represent, pastors offer to their parishioners and counselees wider horizons of interpretation and more nearly adequate frames of meaning for their lives. The moral guide in Browning, in Gerkin becomes a hermeneut or interpreter, one who is more akin to the biblical prophet than the priest.

Probably the most important contribution the hermeneutical perspective has made to the clinical method of pastoral theological education has been challenging the assumption that it is simple to move from experience to theology. There is, in fact, a rather sophisticated process which goes on when one takes pastoral experience with theological seriousness. Experience is shaped by the language we use to describe it; therefore we inevitably must deal not just with the experience itself but with the language and the hermeneutical or interpretive process used to communicate it. The interpreter of experience can never get completely beyond her interpretation of it. On the other hand, there is something in experience which is beyond words and which reminds us of the limits of our words, something that warns us not to take our words too seriously. There is no such thing as uninterpreted experience. Observation and interpretation are complex realities in our processing of event and experience. Language and interpretation are not all there is.

Moreover, pastoral theology is not just concerned with human experience, but human experience in relationship to God and to other persons. Although *one* cannot move from experience to theology without becoming involved in the circle of event and interpretation, *persons in relation and in ministry* can escape or at least limit the problem. The life of the community of faith and the actions of ministry involve dimensions that are beyond words even though they are dependent upon words and interpretation for increased effectiveness and understanding. Relationship and action are related to interpretation in a way similar to the relationship of Word and Sacrament. Each is inadequate without the other, and each is dependent upon the other for the development of its full meaning and purpose.

Context in pastoral theology

Concern with context has been the most important recent feature of pastoral theology in the United States. In fact, a central part of the ministry of pastoral care today is discerning the contexts most relevant for understanding a pastoral situation. There are multiple contexts to be taken into account.

Context may be defined as the whole situation, background, or environment relevant to a particular circumstance or event. Contextuality means that the social situation in all of its uniqueness informs the thought and action of one's reflection. Recognition of specific contexts for care involves hearing and remembering that, first, tries to discern what is specific and perhaps unique to a particular person or situation and, second, remains open to the discovery of what appears to be common to many persons and situations. This dual perspective assumes that knowledge of what is specific and particular contributes to what is more general, and that what appears to be common contributes to the understanding of what is specific and particular.

The contexts that have been most influential for pastoral theology have been race, culture, gender, and power. African American pastoral theologians have begun to influence how care is offered and interpreted. Persons from many different cultures are seeking specialized pastoral care and practicing it. Feminist and womanist pastoral care specialists and theologians are calling attention to issues that male practitioners and theorists have long ignored, such as gender bias in diagnosis and treatment or pastoral anthropologies where culture-based characteristics of males are assumed to be normative. Increased attention has been given to power and political influence as issues in the giving and receiving of care.

Continuing Issues for American Pastoral Theology

Growing out of this history, a number of issues continue to be important for pastoral theology in the United States. The ones that follow are some of the most important.

1 Developing a "pastoral" anthropology, informed by how the process of responsible caring affects one's understanding of what is normatively human and which deals with both the "is" and "ought" of human being.
2 Exploring the borderline between pastoral care and ethics which includes interdisciplinary discussions of the allocation of health care resources as well as the development of case material which demonstrates both ethical and pastoral dimensions of care.

3   Developing a more useful and profound view of the process of change
    in human beings through the exploration of clinical, theological, psy-
    chological, and cultural interpretations of the change process and the
    relationship of developmental and crisis views of change.
4   Developing a more sophisticated pastoral theological method that
    examines now theology may be learned from experience, including
    how one can learn, clinically, to be a better theologian.
5   Critically examining the issues of contextualization in ministry, pastoral
    care, and theology, including how issues such as gender, culture, and
    faith tradition affect the care process.
6   Exploring the major problem issues in pastoral care, e.g. illness and
    health, addiction, the family, etc., in relation to a relevant anthropology
    and ecclesiology.

BIBLIOGRAPHY

Aden, L., and Ellens, H. J. (eds.) (1990), *Turning Points in Pastoral Care*,
    Grand Rapids: Baker Book House.
Browning, D. S. (1983), *Religious Ethics and Pastoral Care*, Philadelphia:
    Fortress Press.
Hiltner, S. (1958), *Preface to Pastoral Theology*, Nashville: Abingdon Press.
Holifield, B. (1983), *The History of Pastoral Care in America*, Nashville:
    Abingdon Press.
Hunter, R. J. (ed.) (1990), *Dictionary of Pastoral Care and Counseling*, Nashville:
    Abingdon Press.
James, W. (1982), *The Varieties of Religious Experience: A Study in Human
    Nature*, New York: Penguin.
Lapsley, J. N. (1972), *Salvation and Health: The Interlocking Processes of Life*,
    Philadelphia: Westminster Press.
Neuger, C. C. (ed.) (1996), *The Arts of Ministry: Feminist-Womanist Ap-
    proaches*, Louisville: Westminster/John Knox.
Patton, J. (1993), *Pastoral Care in Context*, Louisville: Westminster/John
    Knox Press.
Smith, A. (1997), *Navigating the Deep River: Spirituality in African American
    Families*, Cleveland: United Church Press.
Stokes, A. (1985), *Ministry After Freud*, New York: Pilgrim Press.

SOME POINTS FOR FURTHER CONSIDERATION

• To what extent do you recognize the description that Patton
   gives of Protestant pastoral theology in North America? What
   seems familiar? What seems unfamiliar to you?

- Do you think Patton's description of pastoral theology is an attractive and/or interesting one? Which elements do you value? Which do you think are of limited value?
- From your own understanding, do you think that Patton has correctly identified the main elements that shape, influence, and form the methods and subject matter of pastoral theology?
- What do you think should lie at the center of pastoral theology in terms of methods, contents, and concerns?
- From your own understanding of pastoral theology and the pastoral task, do you think that the US tradition that Patton describes omits any elements and features that you would think important, e.g. ecumenical perspectives, attention to scripture, the importance of lay perspectives, doctrine, etc.? Why are those elements important?
- If you are not a North American Protestant, how far do you think Patton's kind of pastoral theology would fit your own needs and context? If you are a North American Protestant, what do you think would be the problems that people who are not from your tradition might have with this kind of approach?

For Further Reading and Exploration

For more material on Boisen and Clinical Pastoral Education see the relevant articles in Hunter (1990), also Foskett and Lyall (1988) and Foskett (1984) who discuss CPE in the British context. A useful history of pastoral care and theology in the USA may be found in Holifield (1983) as well as in the relevant articles in Hunter (1990). For the process of reportage and interpretation involved in theological reflection used in CPE, see, e.g., Patton (1990, 1993). The relationship of ethics to pastoral care and theology has been explored by Browning (1976, 1983) and summarized by Pattison (1993) and Graham (1996). The challenge of wider contextual factors to pastoral theology from the perspectives of race, culture, gender, and power may be approached through, for example, articles in Hunter (1990), and the contributions of Lartey (1997), Glaz and Stevenson-Moessner (1991), Graham and Halsey (1993), and Couture and Hunter (1995), as well as in many of the remaining articles in this Reader.

References

Browning, D. S. (1976), *The Moral Context of Pastoral Care*, Nashville: Abingdon Press.

Couture, P., and Hunter, R. (eds.) (1995), *Pastoral Care and Social Conflict*, Nashville: Abingdon Press.

Gerkin, C. (1991), *Prophetic Pastoral Practice*, Nashville: Abingdon Press.

Gerkin, C. (1997), *An Introduction to Pastoral Care*, Nashville: Abingdon Press.

Glaz, M., and Moessner, J. S. (eds.) (1991), *Women in Travail and Transition*, Minneapolis: Fortress Press.

Graham, E., and Halsey, M. (eds.) (1993), *Life Cycles: Women and Pastoral Care*, London: SPCK.

Lartey, E. (1997), *In Living Colour*, London: Cassell.

Pattison, S. (1993), *A Critique of Pastoral Care*, 2nd edn., London: SCM Press.

Patton, J. (1985), *Is Human Forgiveness Possible?*, Nashville: Abingdon Press.

Patton, J. (1990), *From Ministry to Theology*, Nashville: Abingdon Press.

___ 3 ___

The Emergence of Pastoral and Practical Theology in Britain

PAUL BALLARD

INTRODUCTION

Paul Ballard is one of the pioneering figures in the rise of postwar British pastoral studies and practical theology, having taught the subject at Cardiff University since the late 1960s. Through his own writings and initiatives, he has had a considerable personal influence on this area (Ballard 1986; Ballard and Pritchard 1996). From this vantage point, he is in a good position to chart the rise, changes, and nature of British practical theology in this specially commissioned article that to some extent complements the article by John Patton (chapter 2 above).

The article surveys and accounts for the interesting, but uneven rise of practical theology in Britain over the last fifty years. From very small beginnings, this is a disciplinary area that has become increasingly significant in British academic theology and church life. It is now being taught and studied in a variety of institutions, including state-funded universities and colleges. The sheer variety and plurality of participants, opportunities, methods, and contexts for practical theology in Britain means that the discipline has emerged in a rather uneven way. In particular, pastoral or practical theology has been less shaped by the needs of students for ministry and by clerical concerns than its American counterpart, from which it has taken much. Many students and researchers in pastoral theology in Britain are not, and do not intend to become clergy, although there are many who do hold ecclesiastical offices. Indeed, some of the most influential theorists in British pastoral theology came from other disciplines such as psychiatry and medicine. This introduces an interesting, creative, diffuse, occasionally confusing and frustrating dimension to pastoral theology in terms of its participants, contents, methods, and areas of interest. While pastoral and practical theology continue to grow in size and influence in Britain, it is important to realize that this is an area of concern which is still relatively small, particularly compared to other theological and non-theological academic disciplines. Perhaps this helps to account for a historic lack of contributions from women and members of ethnic minorities to the discipline, a deficit which is only now beginning to be remedied.

THE EMERGENCE OF PASTORAL AND PRACTICAL THEOLOGY IN BRITAIN

Since the end of the Second World War, what is known as pastoral, practical, or applied theology in Britain has undergone a number of important changes and developments. Indeed, it could be said that this field had undergone a transformative renaissance. From a time when it looked as if this kind of theology might disappear altogether as a field of interest, practical theology has ceased to be the Cinderella of the theological world. It has become one of the fastest-growing and most popular areas within the contemporary theological curriculum.

Pastoral theology is now taught with increasing seriousness and sophistication to aspiring clergy in most, if not all, traditional denominational theological colleges and courses (i.e. seminaries). It is also taught in some of the theological departments in publicly-funded universities. Increasingly, it is studied by lay people, non-Christians, and those in emergent churches such as those of the Black communities in Britain. Furthermore, people can study it by a variety of different methods and in different institutions such as Bible colleges, distance learning courses and 'new' universities and university colleges which did not offer courses in practical theology before around 1990. There are large numbers of qualifications at undergraduate and postgraduate level now available exclusively in pastoral theology. More and more people are undertaking postgraduate qualifications in it up to the level of PhD.

In this brief article I will try to outline some of the factors that account for the current renaissance in pastoral and practical theology in Britain since the last war. Inevitably, this has to be a partial, thumbnail sketch, for the story is complex, uneven and diverse. First, it is important to understand the broad context of church organization in Britain.

The British Context

The British Isles are divided into five different countries: England, Scotland, Wales, Northern Ireland, and Eire or Southern Ireland. The first four of these form the United Kingdom and are loosely Protestant historically. The last named is an independent nation that was traditionally dominated by Catholicism, a religious affiliation that is influential throughout Britain.

In England, the traditionally dominant Christian denomination was the (Anglican) Church of England, a state-established episcopal church. Its counterpart in Scotland is the Church of Scotland, a state-established, Calvinist-influenced presbyterian church. Neither Northern Ireland nor Wales have established churches. All these countries have a wide range of well-known denominations, e.g. Methodists, Baptists, Congregationalists, including most recently, the growing Black churches and independent evangelical churches. Clearly, the established churches have had more historic resources and influence than other denominations in their countries.

It is probably true to say that ecumenical cooperation and some theological homogenization is increasing between churches of all kinds, including the Catholic church. This growing cooperation was symbolized by the establishment of the Council of Churches for Britain and Ireland in 1990. This new body supplanted the British Council of Churches and included the Catholic church as a full member for the first time. It is against this confusing ecclesiastical background that the renaissance of pastoral or practical theology has to be discussed.

What Was There Before?

Some kind of pastoral or practical theology has long been part of British life. Britain has had its own pastoral theorists, stretching back over the centuries. For example, the famous English poet-priest, George Herbert, wrote a treatise about parish ministry in the seventeenth century. The saintly nineteenth-century bishop of Lincoln, Edward King, published a set of pastoral lectures that he gave to ordinands as professor of pastoral theology at Oxford University.

In Scotland, training for pastoral ministry in the Church of Scotland was integrated into the nineteenth-century university system as 'practical theology', following the paradigm of Friedrich Schleiermacher (Schleiermacher 1988). Ordinands educated in Scotland studied liturgy, poiemenics ('shepherding' or pastoral care), and homiletics ('preaching' – a very important skill for Calvinist ministers of the word). Meanwhile, Catholic seminarians were tutored in sacramental theology and administration, including the use of the Confessional, in their preparation for ministry.

A number of features characterized this British pastoral theological tradition up till around the 1960s.

1 Pastoral theology was taught only by clergy only to aspiring clergy.
2 The focus of this theology was upon the practical work of clergy.
3 This kind of articulated theology was largely devoted to giving practical 'hints and tips', for example, about how to conduct a successful household visit to parishioners, or how to baptize a baby without dropping it. There was a lack of undergirding theory as well as a certain amateurism about how people could actually be helped.
4 The clergy who were the objects of this pastoral education were being trained for work in parishes or congregations. In these parishes most people could be assumed to be Christians.
5 Finally, pastoral or practical theology was not intellectually demanding. It was not thought to have an important part to play in theological theorizing. This was the domain of scholars who studied the Bible, Church History, Dogmatics and Philosophical Theology. Practical or pastoral theology was simply a way of transferring theological truth into some kind of practice.

So What Happened?

The clerical, pragmatic paradigm of pastoral theology was revolutionized in Britain in the second half of the twentieth century. Now many different kinds of people are studying or contributing to some kind of practical or applied theology in a variety of different settings in lots of different ways. What, then, are the factors that have brought this about?

Here are just some of the strands of influence that have combined in various ways to move pastoral theology away from a theoretical, clericalized amateurism towards being the significant, lively, pluralistic and increasingly sophisticated area of study and practice that it is today.

The rise of professional ministry

Before the early nineteenth century, there was little if any specific training for ministry. Clergy in the Church of England, for example, read the New Testament in Greek after taking a non-theological degree at Oxford or Cambridge as a preparation for taking holy orders. The main qualification for being a minister was to be a literate gentleman of good character. Clergy lived much as other gentlemen, taking services where necessary and playing a part in the parishes to which they were appointed much like other members of their class. So, for example, they acted as magistrates, givers of charity, teachers, and even physicians if no doctor was available (Russell 1980). The pages of novels such as those of Jane Austen and George Eliot are full of clergy such as these.

The nineteenth century saw the rise of distinctive 'professions' such as medicine, with their own common and specific training for aspirants to membership. Seeing the rise of trained and licensed practitioners, clergy began to aspire to be professionals with their own distinctive dress, training and standards. It was in the nineteenth century that theological colleges or seminaries were founded for all ordinands to attend before ordination. It was then, too, that chairs in pastoral theology such as the one that King occupied were founded for Anglicans at, for example, the universities of Oxford and Dublin.

The clerical profession has often developed in different ways from other professions. However, the impetus to become more professional and to be recognized as such by other professions has been a powerful foundational factor in the desire to ensure that clergy have a proper knowledge and skill base. The late-twentieth-century advocates of pastoral theology have been able to appeal to the latent benefits of professionalism to legitimate the development of their discipline. It is this that has opened the doors to more practical, professional development in theological seminaries and courses for ministry. Thus pastoral studies became an examinable subject in Anglican theological courses for ordination in the early 1980s. Similar developments took place in other denominations at around the same time.

The crisis and diversification of ministerial role and identity

Since the days of George Herbert and Edward King, British society has become more secularized. Church communities have lost much of their formal influence and power, and the clergy have largely lost their unquestioned place in their local communities. At the same time, there are fewer people going to church, there is less money to spend from historical resources (e.g. land, investments) and fewer people are willing to become clergy. All this has helped to provoke a crisis in ministerial role and identity. What are clergy for, and what role should they perform in church and community?

It was this kind of question that helped to provoke new thinking about pastoral work in the early 1960s – the decade of 'secular' theology and 'the death of God' in theological circles.

On the one hand, some people thought that the secular world of Dietrich Bonhoeffer's 'man come of age' presented opportunities for clergy to embrace the world and to come to understand it on its own terms. They advocated the knocking down of mental and sometimes physical barriers between church and world and so saw pastoral work as a kind of general community work (Davies 1973). Industrial Mission, i.e. sending representative Christian persons into the secular world of work in factories and commerce to learn from and contribute to it, was one response to this kind of thinking.

On the other hand, some clergy and thinkers felt that what was needed was a reassertion of religious identity. They believed in concentrating on what religious ministers distinctively had to offer by way of religious insight, spirituality, sacraments and prayer (Martin Thornton 1961).

Whichever response was adopted, the clerical role had become problematic both in theory and practice. It could no longer be uncritically assumed. This provided a powerful impetus to pastoral theological reflection and for the acquisition of new skills and knowledge of whatever kind was thought to be appropriate.

New fields and paradigms

The postwar years saw an acceleration in the pace of secularization and the decline of confidence in traditional clerical skills and roles. They also witnessed the rise of new skills and professional paradigms that could be applied by clergy to their work.

Social work, community work, psychotherapy and counselling all began to seem like credible ways of working usefully to facilitate human wellbeing beyond traditional religious communities and paradigms. It became important for clergy seeking to establish their relevance in a secular society to explore these ways of working.

Thus, the early 1960s saw the rise of Frank Lake's Clinical Theology Association which explored the relationship between pastoral care, psychodynamic thought and counselling and theology. Slightly later, the Westminster Pastoral Foundation started to offer training and counselling under Christian auspices. Organizations like the Institute of Religion and Medicine offered opportunities for clergy to begin to enter into mutual dialogue with doctors.

All this was symptomatic of the need for clergy to explore new ways of doing and being relevant in the highly professionalized world of state-provided welfare-for-all that was then reaching its zenith.

It is no accident that the first modern British university course in Pastoral Studies, a postgraduate Diploma, was inaugurated in Birmingham in 1963 to explore the relationship between theories of wellbeing, theology and practice at this very time. Much of the course was devoted to acquiring and evaluating the counselling, groupwork, and community work skills and perspectives that were then coming into vogue. All the students on the course at that time were clergy, especially hospital chaplains who felt the pressure for a meaningful role in a technologically-oriented, professional environment perhaps more acutely than most. The Birmingham Diploma's interdisciplinary, interprofessional, experience-based paradigm was to become very influential in shaping courses in pastoral studies and pastoral theology in Britain subsequently.

Theological underpinnings

The twentieth century has seen a decisive turn to the human in theology. If traditional theology was tempted to focus on the nature of God and a world and life beyond this one, twentieth-century theology has located itself as a firmly human activity situated within human-created language and so focusing on the human condition. Early influential pioneers of the dialogue between theological and non-theological discourses and practices included Paul Tillich and the 'secular' theologians of the 1960s. Perhaps the most famous symbolic expression of this trend in Britain was the publication of Bishop John Robinson's *Honest to God* in 1963.

Since then, the turn to the human, and the presence of God in this world, has received important impetus from the various liberation theologies (e.g. feminist theology, black theology, gay theology) that have emerged around the world. Gustavo Gutierrez remarks on the task of contemporary theology, 'the question is not how . . . to speak of God in an adult world, but how to proclaim him as Father in a world that is not human' (Gutiérrez 1974: 69).

Many modern theologies focus on the importance of lived experience, practice, action and the primacy of human need. This adds impetus to the need to study practical theology with its emphasis on the human condition and needs, rather than on traditional kinds of more abstract theology. Within a perspective informed by human concern and liberationist praxis, pastoral theology has moved towards the centre of the theological enterprise. It is no longer a subject that is only to be considered only after thorough study of more traditional theological disciplines.

The turn to the practical in education

It is not just liberation theologians who believe that a theory-practice paradigm of thought and education is important. Over the last few years of the twentieth century, the British government began to stress the need for education to be related to work and employment (Barnett 1994).

It is no longer thought to be a virtue to study an abstract subject such as history or theology for its own sake. The increasingly inclusive, expanding mass higher education system aims to equip all students with skills and competences that are specifically relevant to work. Thus, many theologians are increasingly keen to relate their subjects to students' practical needs and interests. Students themselves are anxious to study courses that will equip them with practically-oriented knowledge and skills.

Both students and teachers are faced with increasing expense and diminishing state support for higher education. This provides a powerful incentive for experience-based and -relevant education such as that which is provided by pastoral theology.

Once students become employed, they are increasingly expected to undertake relevant continuing professional development. In the case of clergy and pastoral workers, practical theology is an obvious place to seek this. This partly explains the mushrooming of postgraduate, post-work-experience pastoral theology qualifications.

Beyond the clerical paradigm: the turn to the laity

One of the most remarkable and distinctive developments in British pastoral theology is the way in which it has gradually moved beyond the clerical paradigm. Many people who study or research in pastoral theology in Britain today are not clergy and do not intend to be clergy. Indeed, they may not necessarily be Christians or members of any religious group.

The rise of lay people and non-clerical concerns in the arena of pastoral theology is probably due to a number of factors. First, much pastoral work in churches and other institutions is now done by lay people. This is due partly to the absence of sufficient clerical personpower. It is informed by very positive theologies that emphasize the ministry and gifts of all people, not just clergy.

Second, and related, it has become clear that promoting human well-being within a religious understanding or context is in no way something that is just of interest to clergy.

Third, the British tradition of educational opportunities in universities being open to all who are suitably qualified provides a welcome ethos of openness and inclusiveness. Pastoral theology is thus usefully forced to be in principle a public discourse, not the province of particular ecclesiastical interest groups.

Finally, the liberal ethos that is implicit in the turn to the secular and the human means that pastoral theology cannot easily exclude any human being who wishes to learn from it, or to contribute to it.

North American influences

The influence of North American trends and methods upon the development of British pastoral and practical theology has been an important one. The dominance of counselling as a paradigm for pastoral practice set an important agenda for pastoral theology in the 1970s and 1980s. The methods of Clinical Pastoral Education with its emphasis on systematic reflection on practice have had a continuing influence on the shape of pastoral education. The theologies of Tillich, Hiltner and the 'secular' theologians of the 1960s all helped to shape British pastoral theology.

British pastoral theology has perhaps been able to preserve a greater sense of the importance of the community, the secular, the public, pluralism, and the non-professional than its North American counterpart (Wilson 1983). However, there are still very few full-time pastoral theologians teaching or researching in this field. Thus many of the most important ideas and techniques used in this area are imported from the work of colleagues in North America.

Conclusion

British pastoral theology has been transformed in the second half of the twentieth century. Before the last war it was, broadly speaking, a severely practical, atheoretical discipline that was marginal to mainstream theological endeavours and uninformed by the human sciences and professional skills. It was exclusively focused upon the work of clergy.

Now it is becoming a growing and diverse field which is gradually developing a theoretical literature as well as skills of reflection upon practice of many different kinds. It is gradually moving towards the centre of contemporary theological endeavour, as well as outwards to embrace many practical contemporary issues and concerns such as poverty, the future of work, and the nature of community.

In many ways, it is not possible to define or circumscribe British pastoral and practical theology at the present time. The discipline is developing in many different directions and places.

In this article, I have emphasized the evolution of pastoral theology as an academically-based discipline. However, even an organization like the British and Irish Association for Practical Theology which was founded in 1994 to give voice and shape to this disciplinary interest does not contain all the people who teach and research in this area. There are many important pastoral theological partners outwith the university and the seminary. So, for example, the Association of Pastoral Care and Counselling, the Clinical Theology Association, and the Industrial Mission Association are all important contributors to pastoral theology in so far as they try to relate theology, insights from human sciences, and practice together.

Generally, British pastoral theologians welcome and enjoy the breadth, width and inclusiveness of practical theological endeavour today. We are in no hurry, and indeed in no position, to start shutting out interesting contributions just because they do not come from people who call themselves pastoral or practical theologians or because they come from outside the academy. The sheer diversity and fragmentation of this burgeoning field at the moment can be confusing. On the whole, however, the confusion is interesting and creative.

The distinctive and shared concerns of British pastoral theology are reflected in the articles that make up the remainder of this Reader. They are, of course, in many ways similar to those of American colleagues.

SOME POINTS FOR FURTHER CONSIDERATION

- Which aspects of British pastoral theology do you find interesting and attractive?
- Are there any significant emphases, approaches, or areas of concern that you think British pastoral theology does not take seriously enough?
- What are the main strengths and weaknesses of British practical theology?
- If you are British, to what extent is the kind of pastoral theology that Ballard describes relevant to your interests and needs? If you are not British, what are the problems that arise in trying to understand and appropriate this kind of approach?
- If you have read the previous articles by Hiltner and Patton, what are the main similarities and differences between what you know of British and North American pastoral theology?

FOR FURTHER READING AND EXPLORATION

Paul Ballard's thought can be further explored in Ballard (1986) and Ballard and Pritchard (1996). Ballard (1986) contains more material on the history of pastoral theology in Britain, as does Pattison (1993) and Graham (1996). Perhaps the best history of the pastoral role and ideology amongst Anglicans is still Russell (1980). For definition and discussion of terms like pastoral theology, practical theology and pastoral studies in the British context see Campbell's *Dictionary of Pastoral Care* (1987) which contains a representative, though somewhat dated, collection of topics and authors writing in pastoral theology in Britain. For more on the uniquely British concept of 'pastoral studies' see Pattison (1983) which also discusses the interdisciplinary nature of this activity, for which see also Ballard (1986). Some of the most important written contributions to the evolution of British pastoral theology have been made by R. A. Lambourne (first director of the Birmingham Diploma in Pastoral Studies), Michael Wilson (Lambourne's successor), Alastair Campbell (an American trained Scottish pastoral theologian), Anthony Dyson (Anglican professor of social and pastoral theology at Manchester University), David Deeks (an English Methodist),

Emmanuel Lartey (a Ghanaian Methodist who is presently director
of the Birmingham course) and by Elaine Graham (Dyson's successor
in Manchester). See further, e.g. Lambourne (1963), Wilson (1983,
1988), Campbell (1981, 1985), Deeks (1987), Lartey (1997) and
Graham (1996). This selection is invidious as there are many others
writing in, and helping to shape the discipline in Britain. This can
be seen from other contributions to this Reader and by consulting
the main British journal of pastoral studies and pastoral theology,
Contact. An important addition to the width of British pastoral theology from a basically evangelical perspective is Atkinson and Field's
New Dictionary of Christian Ethics and Pastoral Theology (1995).

References

Atkinson, D., and Field, D. (eds.) (1995), *A New Dictionary of Christian
Ethics and Pastoral Theology*, Leicester: Inter-Varsity Press.
Ballard, P. (ed.) (1986), *The Foundations of Pastoral Studies and Practical
Theology*, Cardiff University: HOLI.
Ballard, P., and Pritchard, J. (1996), *Practical Theology in Action*, London:
SPCK.
Barnett, R. (1994), *The Limits of Competence*, Buckingham: Open Univer-
sity Press.
Campbell, A. (1985), *Paid to Care?*, London: SPCK.
Campbell, A. (1986), *Rediscovering Pastoral Care*, London: Darton, Longman
& Todd (2nd edn. 1987).
Campbell, A. (ed.) (1987), *A Dictionary of Pastoral Care*, London: SPCK.
Carr, W. (1997), *Handbook of Pastoral Studies*, London: SPCK.
Davies, J. (1973), *Every Day God*, London: SCM Press.
Deeks, D. (1987), *Pastoral Theology*, London: Epworth Press.
Dyson, A. (1977), "Pastoral theology – towards a new discipline," *Contact*
78: 2–8.
Graham, E. (1996), *Transforming Practice*, London: Mowbray.
Gutiérvez, G. (1974), "Liberation, theology and proclamation," *Concilium*,
6: 69.
Hurding, R. (1998), *Pathways to Wholeness: Pastoral Care in a Postmodern
Age*, London: Hodder & Stoughton.
Lambourne, R. A. (1963), *Community, Church and Healing*, London: Darton,
Longman & Todd.
Lartey, E. (1997), *In Living Colour: An Intercultural Approach to Pastoral
Care and Counselling*, London: Cassell.
Pattison, S. (1983), "Pastoral studies – dustbin or discipline?" *Contact* 80:
22–6.

Robinson, J. (1963), *Honest to God*, London: SCM Press.
Russell, A. (1980), *The Clerical Profession*, London: SPCK.
Schleiermacher, F. (1988), *Christian Caring*, Philadelphia: Fortress.
Thornton, M. (1961), *Pastoral Theology: A Reorientation*, London: SPCK.
Wilson, M. (ed.) (1983), *Explorations in Health and Salvation*, Birmingham: University of Birmingham Department of Theology.
Wilson, M. (1988), *A Coat of Many Colours*, London: Epworth Press.

Part Two

Approaches and Methods in Pastoral and Practical Theology

INTRODUCTION TO PART TWO

4 The Nature of Practical Theology
Alastair Campbell

5 Pastoral Theology in a Pluralistic Age
Don Browning

6 Practical Theology as Transforming Practice
Elaine Graham

7 Interpreting Situations: An Inquiry into the Nature of
Practical Theology
Edward Farley

8 Practical Theology as a Theological Form
Emmanuel Lartey

9 Some Straw for the Bricks: A Basic Introduction to
Theological Reflection
Stephen Pattison

Introduction to Part Two

The papers and extracts in this Part of the Reader pick up, develop, and move on from the background papers contained in Part One. Having gained a preliminary sense of the nature and history of contemporary practical and pastoral theology it is now possible to begin to look more closely at some of the main ideas, approaches and methods that can inform it. Practical and pastoral theology are developing, dynamic activities that attempt actively to relate to contemporary experience and situations. There is a sense, then, in which the heart of pastoral theology is to be found not so much in clear, monolithic theoretical definitions but more in the various methods and approaches that are used to engage theology and practice in fruitful interaction.

In general terms, the papers in this Part move from broad approaches to pastoral and practical theology to looking at particular methods for doing it. In his paper "The nature of practical theology" (chapter 4), Scottish theologian Alastair Campbell discusses the nature of contemporary practical theology. He suggests that it must be redefined as a distinctive branch of theology. It has the task of selecting "contemporary situations from the life of the church and the world and setting them alongside the current theories and research conclusions of biblical scholars, church historians and systematic theologians." This process will generate proposals for action that will in turn create fresh situations for study.

Campbell's approach, like those of many others in this Part, is implicitly a dialogical one between theory and practice, theological tradition and contemporary life. It is complemented and amplified in the extract that follows, "Pastoral theology in a pluralistic age" (chapter 5) by US theologian Don Browning. Coming from a background of passionate commitment to developing relevant, proactically-related theological ethics, Browning argues that practical theologians must employ what he calls a "revised correlational method" to their work. This method takes both the theological tradition and the contemporary situation very seriously and attempts to engage them in critical dialogue together. The aim is to arrive at normative ways of seeing the human situation which can then be related to contemporary ideas and practices in pastoral work. Browning's influence here has been profound and seminal in the development of contemporary pastoral and practical theology.

It is at this point that the first woman writer, Elaine Graham, enters this volume. As in many other areas of life, the formal discipline of pastoral and practical theology has hitherto unfortunately often been dominated by men. Gradually, however, women are making themselves visible in this area. Elaine Graham is an English theologian who has adapted and further developed Don Browning's "revised correlational method" in the light of feminist and postmodern thought and experience. Graham proposes a role for practical theology that focuses on understanding and articulating the experiences of faith communities in her specially commissioned paper, "Practical theology as transforming practice" (chapter 6). It should enable faith communities to practice what they preach, as well as to preach, i.e. articulate, what they practice.

The first three chapters in this Part of the Reader all show a concern for critically and dynamically relating contemporary experiences, situations, and practices to theological and other ideas and traditions. This expresses something of the essence of contemporary practical theology. The concern for specific aspects of this relationship is spelt out more fully and concretely in the last three papers included here.

In an extract from his influential paper "Interpreting situations: an inquiry into the nature of practical theology" (chapter 7), US theologian Edward Farley dwells upon the importance of analyzing different kinds of situations theologically as a discipline of faith. He not only demonstrates the complexity of understanding particular kinds of situation, he also proposes that such activity should be seen as a hermeneutical act, an act of interpretation. This notion of active interpretation is a very significant one in contemporary practical theology.

Further light is thrown upon interpretation, theological analysis of situations, and the process of doing practical theology generally by Emmanuel Lartey. A Ghanaian theologian, Lartey draws on his experience of teaching pastoral theology at an English public university to outline a number of different models of practical theological process in "Practical theology as a theological form" (chapter 8). Lartey helps to locate some of the theological approaches outlined in the previous papers. It may, therefore, be helpful to read his paper before the others or in the case of having difficulty understanding them. He also outlines his own "pastoral cycle" model of practical theology.

The last paper in this part, "Some straw for the bricks: a basic introduction to theological reflection" (chapter 9) by English theologian Stephen Pattison, is designed to help people to start to become effectively involved in theological reflection. Drawing on the work of many other theologians like Browning and Lapsley, together with the notion of interpretation, Pattison suggests that practical theological reflection that relates theory, theology, and practice effectively can best be conceived as a kind of conversation. Those who are interested in starting to do practical theology rather than reflecting upon its assumptions and methods might find this paper the best one to start with in this Part of the Reader.

Several general points can be made at this juncture by way of critical comment on all the papers in this Part. First, it should be noted that notions of pastoral theology and practical theology are often confused, used differently, or used synonymously. This reflects a genuine confusion and plurality in the field with which students and practitioners have to live.

Second, it is worth pointing out that implicit in all of these papers are two undergirding questions that are distinctive to practical theology and which constantly exercise its exponents. First, in what way is practical theology *practical*, i.e. how does it affect, and in what ways is it affected by, contemporary concerns, situations and realities? Second, in what way is practical theology *theological*, i.e. how does it relate to theological ideas, traditions, and faith communities?

Finally, there are a number of persistent tensions and questions that flow through most of the papers to a greater or lesser extent, either implicitly or explicitly. First, there is considerable diversity and disagreement about the nature of pastoral and/or practical theology and the methods that it should employ, though there is much consensus also. Second, there is a lack of consensus about the purpose of practical theology. Several purposes are proposed for it. Third, and related, there is an issue about who pastoral or practical theology is for, and who should undertake it, e.g. lay people, clergy, congregations, academics. Similarly, fourth, there is considerable disagreement about the methods that might be employed in pastoral and practical theology, though there is some consensus around the importance of the general activity of interpretation of situations and traditions. Fifth, there is a tension between the relative importance that should be accorded to theology and the religious tradition originating in the past over against contemporary experience and non-theological disciplines and understandings. Finally, it is not clear whether the focus of pastoral and practical theology should be upon the overt religious community or whether it should engage wider issues and communities.

None of these questions or tensions is resolved in the papers below. This open-endedness and unresolvedness may be a distinctive identifying feature of critical pastoral and practical theology at the present time. It is one of the things that makes this discipline interesting. Perhaps it may be taken to reflect the theological tradition of openness to God's inexhaustibility, incomprehensibility, and continuing revelation in the contemporary world.

4

The Nature of Practical Theology

ALASTAIR CAMPBELL

INTRODUCTION

Alastair Campbell is a Scottish Presbyterian theologian who, after studying in California, taught practical theology at the University of Edinburgh for many years. Now an ethicist with an international reputation, Campbell is Professor of Health Care Ethics at the University of Bristol in England. He was perhaps the most influential British pastoral theologian in the 1980s, editing the definitive *Dictionary of Pastoral Care and Counseling* (1987). His work has had a decisive, lasting, and seminal influence, particularly in the theory and practice of pastoral care.

In this paper on the nature of practical theology in the modern world, Campbell poses the question, "Is practical theology possible?" He then tries to define the basic nature and approach that practical theology should take as a discipline. This is done by critically comparing the approaches of two pastoral theologians, Eduard Thurneysen and Seward Hiltner. Both these approaches have severe limitations. Thurneysen's is dogmatic, ecclesio-centric, and deductive in nature. Hiltner's tends toward pragmatism, induction, and theological conservatism. From recognizing these limitations and considering the changing situation of the world, Campbell then goes on to redefine the nature and scope of contemporary practical theology. It must, amongst other things, be "politically aware and theologically courageous."

He suggests that practical theology must study specific social structures and individual institutions, whether ecclesial or secular. It should not be limited, in scope or subject matter, to the ordained ministry of the church. Practical theology must have a lateral, dialogical, relationship with other theological disciplines rather than being inductive. It must expect to be fragmentary and poorly systematized. Its "findings" will be mostly in terms of concrete proposals that are transformative for restructuring individuals, communities, and society, whether within the church or outside. This set of features, Campbell suggests, will give redefined practical theology a distinctive, coherent, and complementary role alongside other theological disciplines.

THE NATURE OF PRACTICAL THEOLOGY

Some academic subject matters have a quaintly old fashioned ring; 'moral sciences' for example or 'natural philosophy'. 'Practical theology' has a similar odd sound today. To the theological outsider it must sound remarkably like a contradiction in terms, whilst to the professional theologian it may carry undertones of an unscholarly pragmatism or a tendency towards liberal theology. Yet perhaps the juxtaposition of these two terms is an important one. It may, by its oddity, encourage us to ask the question, 'Is practical theology possible?' This would be a question similar to the familiar one about the possibility of metaphysics. It is asking for a formal definition of the subject matter which will meet adequate criteria of meaning, consistency and relationship to other disciplines whose status is not in doubt. In this chapter I shall attempt some answers to this question of possibility, by focusing specifically on writings in the theology of pastoral care.

Although it may sound antiquarian, the term 'practical theology' appears to be of relatively recent usage. It first makes its appearance in German nineteenth-century theological treatises, the most celebrated of which was F. D. E. Schleiermacher's posthumous work, *Die Praktische Theologie nach den Grundsätzen der Evangelischen Kirche*.[1] Schleiermacher described it as the 'crown of theological studies', its tasks being the setting out of 'the method of the maintaining (*Erhaltung*) and perfecting (*Vervollkommnung*) of the church'.[2] This emphasis on the church-based nature of the discipline is an important one for the subsequent development of practical theology, particularly when we remember that is Schleiermacher's terms the church is the fellowship of those who share in God-consciousness.

In other nineteenth-century text books, the subject was subdivided into various branches related to the different functions of the ministry: homiletics, liturgics, catechetics, poimenics and occasionally halieutics ('man fishing') and works of charity. J. J. Van Oosterzee's large volume[3] provides a good illustration of this approach. It contains a wealth of common-sense advice to trainee ministers concerning preaching, conduct of services, catechetical instruction, and both 'general' and 'individual' pastoral care. Significantly, a very short concluding section mentions 'labours beyond the sphere of one's own congregation'. The author feels uncertain whether such non-congregational matters are strictly within the domain of practical theology.

As the text books multiplied in the late nineteenth century the concern with the teaching of techniques became paramount. Thus, as Seward Hiltner remarks in a brief historical sketch of the recent history of the subject:

> The notion of 'hints and helps', implying the right to dispense with structural and theoretical considerations, to set aside scholarship in this area, and to appeal to the more degraded forms of practicalism, helped to drive most systematic books out of this field by the turn of the century.[4]

Such a development meant that the discipline became divorced from the important new movements in systematic theology and biblical studies. Far from being the 'crown' of divinity it became its poor relation. We may note certain difficulties inherent in the basic approach to the subject which led to this collapse:

1. The relationship between practical theology and historical and dogmatic theology was seen largely as a deductive one, practical theology being understood as *applied* theology, just as, say, civil engineering is applied physics. Thus Oosterzee, arguing in the same terms as Schleiermacher that the other theological sciences exist to serve practical theology, declares that 'It teaches the minister of the Gospel to apply . . . the knowledge which he has already acquired in the theoretic domain.'[5] Such a relationship, however, is not satisfactory for either side. On the one hand it removes the independent status of practical theology, making it into a subsection of dogmatics, whilst on the other hand it opens systematic theologians to charges of irrelevance and inapplicability from practical theologians. The result of this uneasy relationship was the drifting apart of the two disciplines.

2. The question of whether practical theology was an 'art' or a 'science' remained unresolved. Where the subject became the teaching of techniques by 'craftsmen pastors' to 'apprentice pastors' it tended to degenerate into 'a pastoral medicine chest for all conceivable and inconceivable ailments',[6] and its status within an academic environment became questionable.

3. Most unfortunate of all was the total identification of the discipline with church-directed functions of ministry. Since the church was seen in Schleiermacher's terms as the fellowship of the pious, this meant the imprisoning of practical theology in the world of the religiously minded. One sees this most clearly in the dubious position which 'missions' and 'works of charity' had in the nineteenth-century view of the principal functions of ministry. Since the clergyman had become a kind of chaplain to the godly-minded, his relationship (and the relationship of the church he served)

to the world outside became of secondary concern. Spiritual maintenance was the keynote and practical theology provided the manuals which well ensured the perfection of the church. This type of definition of the scope of the subject meant that it was quite ill-equipped to cope with the radical questioning of the place of the church in the world evident in post-liberal theology.

Can an approach to the subject be found which avoids these pitfalls? There appears to have been little interest in recent theological writing in the construction of a comprehensive definition of practical theology.[7] However, the area of the *theology of pastoral care* has received considerable attention and we may look to this field for the main lines of the contemporary debate.

From postwar writing in the theology of pastoral care two works may be singled out for special attention: Eduard Thurneysen's *A Theology of Pastoral Care*, and Seward Hiltner's *Preface to Pastoral Theology*. Each book in its own way has attempted to set the theology of pastoral care within the general context of the subject matter of theology and each has implicitly a view of practical theology as a whole.

Thurneysen's definition is reminiscent in some respects of Schleiermacher's view. He states that '. . . pastoral care occurs within the realm of the church . . . it presupposes membership in the body of Christ, or has this membership as its purpose'.[8] However, although Thurneysen's view of pastoral care is clearly church-centred, its ultimate definition derives from a theology of the Word of God. Pastoral care is concerned with the 'specific communication to the individual of the message proclaimed in general in the sermon to the congregation'.[9] The message to be proclaimed is that of the forgiveness which is at the heart of the Gospel.

One may see in this formulation of Thurneysen's one way of establishing coherence in the discipline of practical theology. The normative concept is that of the Word of God, which may take several forms in its communication to the believer. That aspect known as 'pastoral care' has as its *differentia* the uniqueness of the one-to-one encounter, but in the last analysis all is dependent on the Word as witnessed to in scripture and tradition. One could summarize Thurneysen's view by saying that practical theology is best understood on the homiletical model, the model of proclamation.

A very different view is put forward by Seward Hiltner in his *Preface to Pastoral Theology*. Hiltner proposes a division of the subject matter of divinity into two types of field: the 'logic-centred' field and the 'operation-centred' field. The first category includes within it biblical theology, historical theology and doctrinal theology. The second category is Hiltner's redefinition of practical theology. He subdivides the operation-centred field into three 'perspectives': Shepherding, Communicating and Organizing. These three perspectives replace the traditional division of practical theology into the offices of the ministry.

By using the term 'perspective' Hiltner is trying to convey the notion that there are several different ways of regarding the offices and functions of the church, each in itself a valid way. Anything that is done within the life of the church may be viewed from a shepherding (or pastoral) perspective, or from the perspective of communicating (compare Thurneysen's proclamation category) or that of organizing (that area traditionally described as church discipline). Against the background of this restructuring of the subject matter Hiltner is now in a position to offer his own definition of pastoral theology:

> Pastoral theology is defined as that branch or field of theological knowledge and enquiry that brings the shepherding perspective to bear upon all the operations and functions of the church and the minister, and then draws conclusions of a theological order from reflection on these observations.[10]

We may note that Hiltner is arguing for an *inductive* rather than a *deductive* approach to practical theology. Instead of the other theological disciplines laying down the norms for understanding the practical functions, Hiltner is suggesting that the study of the practical functions will produce some theological insights.[11]

These brief summaries of Hiltner's and Thurneysen's theories may have served to draw attention to some of the contrasts between them. It is very clear that they approach the definition of practical theology from opposite ends of the theological spectrum. Consequently each approach provokes its peculiar set of problems. Thurneysen's definition locates practical theology firmly within the framework of scripture, tradition and the ongoing preaching of the Gospel. In such an analysis practical theology is bound to be subservient to biblical and historical theology, the ground on which it stands being identical with that of these two disciplines. Yet we might question whether the very coherence of Thurneysen's position has not meant an undesirable narrowing down of the understanding of the mission of the church. Preaching, understood primarily as verbal communication, has been given such a normative position that the call of the church to heal and serve the needy, the poor and the outcast[12] finds no clear place; moreover it must be asked whether the *koinonia* of those gathered in Christ's name can be adequately understood in a purely kerygmatic context. Again, Thurneysen's insistence on membership of the church as a precondition or an indispensable goal of pastoral care rules out the possibility that God may be at work outside the church as well as within it. In short, Thurneysen buys coherence and consistency at too high a price. The categories of verbal communication and adherence to church membership confine too narrowly the potential scope of practical theology.

Quite another set of problems arises from Hiltner's approach to the subject. He is very concerned to earth theology in the human sciences and to allow the insights of contemporary experience in general, and of the counselling situation in particular, to revitalize the church's understanding of its task. Thus practical theology accepts concepts from depth psychology, sociological theory and group dynamics, since they all contribute to the fresh theological understanding that can come from the operation-centred fields. It is strange how unaware Hiltner seems to be of the fundamental methodological problems which his definitions create. His division of the body of divinity into logical and operational fields hardly solves the basic problem of how the present experience of the church is related to its historical basis as attested to in scripture. Indeed the division he proposed severely deepens the cleavage between the two.[13] Again his theology seems to have no place for the category of revelation – even in the negative sense of deliberately espousing 'natural theology'. It simply ignores all the questions to do with historicity and uniqueness. A fellow American theologian has acutely characterized the theological inadequacy of Hiltner and many of his followers:

> If revelation at least remains a live issue for Tillich and Thurneysen, it hardly seems to be a vital problem in the American tradition of pastoral care, which in the footsteps of Ritschl, Troeltsch and Harnack has thought it could proceed quite as well without the excess baggage of Nicaea, Chalcedon, etc. It has been content to derive its 'theological' bearings essentially from psychological case studies and clinical pastoral relationships, the results of which is a *derivative* or functional theology, in which theology *functions* now and then to help out in the solution of some practical problem.[14]

More surprising still is Hiltner's implicit assumption that the 'operations' of the church are a kind of given from which practical theology may begin. By bringing different perspectives to bear (the shepherding, the communicating, etc.) on these operations new theological truth is to be gained. Yet surely what the churches and their ministers are, or do, at any given time or place is bound to be sociologically and culturally conditioned to a very large extent. It is hardly a place from which to *begin* theologizing from whatever perspective. The very *existence* of the churches needs a theological justification and what their ministers *do* is open to more radical questioning than simply whether they are effective communicators, organizers and pastors. There is no place in Hiltner's definition of the practical disciplines for a radical theological critique of the churches in the light of a question like Bonhoeffer's celebrated self-interrogation in prison: 'What is bothering me incessantly is the question what Christianity really is, or indeed who Christ really is, for us today.'[15] We can find in Hiltner an ecclesiastical conservatism more profound (because less open to theological correction) than that of Thurneysen.

Our investigation to this point has led to a negative answer to the question about the possibility of an independent and viable practical theology. The type of definition proposed by Thurneysen effectively subsumes the subject under dogmatic theology whilst the formulations of Hiltner, despite his admirable intentions, leave the subject in the limbo of pragmatism. It would be audacious to suppose that some new and original solution could now be offered which will avoid the criticisms made of previous viewpoints. Yet a hint of a solution may be gained from the persistent re-appearance of the problem of church-centredness which has been evident in one form or another since the first definition by Schleiermacher. It seems that the articulation of the nature of practical theology is intimately related to one's understanding of the relationship between the life of the church and the life of the world 'outside the church'. Practical theology's concern for operations and its relatedness to specific situations needs to be grounded in some systematic conceptualization of the church–world relationship.[16]

One begins the quest for re-definition, then, by asking why the things that are done by Christians are done, and what their relationship is to the things done by non-Christians. (Put in another way, one does *not* accept the functions of church and ministry as given.) An answer to this can be given in the following terms: the actions of Christians are celebrations of and attestations to God's reconciling work in the world which begins and ends in Jesus Christ. The relationship of these actions to those of non-Christians is one of both similarity and difference. The similarity is that *all* human actions both participate in and fall short of the purposes of God. The difference is that those who profess belief and adhere to membership of the church have been called to *make explicit* the celebration of God's work.

This understanding of the nature of the church was elaborated in a World Council of Churches report on evangelism published in 1967:

> Since God is constantly active in the world and since it is his purpose to establish *shalom*, it is the Church's task to recognize and point to the signs of this taking place. The Church is always tempted to believe that the activity and presence of God are confined within the boundaries it draws round itself and to think that *shalom* is only to be found within them. But the whole world was implicated in the death and resurrection of Christ. Hence everything in the world may have a double aspect. Each time a man is imprisoned, tortured or destroyed, death is at work. But each time a man is a true neighbour, each time men live for others, the life giving action of God is to be discerned. . . . So God, as he moved towards his final goal, is using men and women, both inside and outside churches, to bring signs of *shalom*. . . . What else can the churches do than recognize and proclaim what God is doing in the world?[17]

The emphasis in this report on 'what God is doing in the world' was a familiar one in the new explorations in theology of the 1960s. It reflected reactions to the 'death of God' and the 'secular theology' debates, and it found a particularly strong expression in the writings of Joseph Fletcher, J. A. T. Robinson and Paul Lehmann.[18] Since that era things have moved on in the theological debate. There is now more awareness of the radical political implications of the theology which takes the notion of a historically active God seriously. The 'option for the poor' of political theology generally and of liberation theology in particular has presented a challenge to the whole ideological foundation of Western theology and biblical scholarship. We are now so far removed from the seemingly secure ecclesiastical world of Thurneysen and Hiltner that there is surely no way back to an uncritical 'churchiness' in practical theology. At the same time the liberal optimism of the 1960s with its confidence in secular institutions is also radically under question. The new agenda for practical theology must therefore be both politically aware and theologically courageous. Religious language is not to be swept aside by simplistic translations into secular alternatives, but when religious imagery is used, it must be subjected to the acid test of a relevance, beyond a personalist salvation, to a social and political renewal. This is the inescapable atmosphere within which one must attempt a practical theology today.

Against the background of these challenges facing practical theology, we may now sketch out a re-definition of its nature and scope.

(1)   Practical theology is concerned with the study of specific social structures and individual initiatives within which God's continuing work of renewal and restitution becomes manifest. These may be found either inside or outside the life of the church.

(2)   Practical theology can no longer take the functions of the ordained ministry as normative for its divisions of subject matter and delineation of scope. The ordering of the fellowship of believers is of concern to the practical theologian, but only as part of the wider question of the place of the witnessing, serving and loving community within the whole economy of salvation. A consequence of this is that instead of 'missions' and 'acts of charity' being seen as peripheral to the scope of the discipline, they move into the centre of its concern. If a division of subject matter is necessary at all, it may perhaps be found in the threefold nature of the church's life – *kerygma*, *koinonia*, *diakonia* – provided always that these are understood in ways that open the church to the world.[19]

(3)   The relationship between practical theology and the other theological disciplines is *neither inductive* (cf. Hiltner), *nor deductive* (cf. Thurneysen). The relationship is to be seen as a 'lateral' rather than a 'linear' one.

Practical theology juxtaposes concrete situations of witness, celebration and service with the findings and formulations of the biblical, historical and philosophical subjects in the theological corpus. It does this not in order to correct according to some canon of relevance, nor in order to be corrected according to some canon of orthodoxy. It is more an exercise in creative imagination, the interplay of idea and action, with all the ambiguity and inconclusiveness which this implies.[20]

(4)   Because of the 'situation-based' method it employs, practical theology can be expected to be fragmentary and poorly systematized. If it is constantly seeking out and presenting newly emerging situations, it cannot at the same time present a comprehensive and coherent account of itself. (Yet in this respect it perhaps differs only in *degree* not in *kind* from the other theological disciplines where the constantly increasing volume of research and proliferation of alternative theories militate against a statement of a 'position' which will not subsequently be questioned.)

(5)   The 'findings' of practical theology can be expected to be mostly in the form of *concrete proposals* for the restructuring of the church's life of witness, fellowship and service, for the style of life of individual Christians within the 'secular' structures of society, and for the renewal and reforming of the secular structures themselves.[21] At the same time such proposals must then become the subject of fresh theological reflection if practical theology is not to return to a new form of 'hints and tips', but one with a fashionable political emphasis. The discipline must remain a critical one, and this it can achieve by retaining its relationships with the other disciplines in the theological corpus. There can be no excuse for a practical theology based on an outmoded biblical theology, or on a poorly reasoned set of theological categories. Practical relevance must never be equated with an unreflective pragmatism lacking in self-criticism and historical perspective.

This brief survey of the recent history of practical theology has suggested that the subject must be redefined if it is to be reinstated as a viable branch of theological study. The redefinition proposed sets it the task of selecting contemporary situations from the life of the church and the world and setting them alongside the current theories and research conclusions of biblical scholars, church historians and systematic theologians. This in turn generates proposals for action which create fresh situations for study. Such a definition is designed to give practical theology a method and momentum of its own which sets it apart from the other branches of theology, whilst articulating its relationship to them. It is an attempt to create a discipline which is both practical and critical.

But it would be naive to suppose that the case for the possibility of practical theology now rests proven. An obvious weak spot in the definition may at once be identified: On what criteria is one to select the 'concrete situations' for study and experiment especially when these are to come from outside as well as inside the life of the church? Do practical theologians have the temerity to suggest that they can discern where God is at work, say in international politics, or in the works of writers and artists, or in the dilemmas of modern technological society?

Perhaps one must answer that such boldness *is* indeed required. In an age when destruction seems ever closer at hand – whether from environmental degradation, world political unrest, the crippling social problems of 'developed' societies, the debilitation of world hunger and increasing poverty, or the ending of it all in nuclear holocaust – it seems that *some* branch of theology must be concerned with matters which directly affect human well-being in whatever future awaits us. This appears to be a task especially suited to a recreated 'practical theology', one which treads a difficult path between practical relevance and theological integrity.

Nevertheless, the possibility of such a practical theology is only minimally established. It is only in the implementation of the kind of objectives that this essay has proposed that the discipline can either establish its viability, or join its nineteenth-century predecessor on the scrap heap of old confusions.

NOTES

1 Berlin 1850.
2 Ibid., pp. 27f.
3 J. J. Van Oosterzee, *Practical Theology: A Manual for Theological Students*, tr. M. J. Evans, London 1878.
4 Seward Hiltner, *Preface to Pastoral Theology*, Abingdon 1958, p. 48.
5 Oosterzee, p. 3.
6 Ibid., p. 2.
7 This observation is based solely on a study of works published in English until recently. There is now some revival of interest marked by the publication of the following: T. C. Oden, *Pastoral Theology: Essentials of Ministry* (Harper and Row 1983) and Don S. Browning (ed.) *Practical Theology: The Emerging Field in Theology, Church and World* (Harper and Row 1983).
8 Eduard Thurneysen, *A Theology of Pastoral Care*, John Knox Press 1962, p. 53.
9 Ibid., p. 15.
10 Seward Hiltner, *Preface to Pastoral Theology*, p. 20.
11 This is most clearly seen in an extended footnote (*Preface*, p. 222) in which Hiltner distinguishes his position from that of Tillich's method of correlation. Hiltner argues that Tillich is mistaken in supposing that the answers must always come from the side of theology. In his view a 'two way street' is possible: '. . . it becomes necessary to say that culture

may find answers to questions raised by faith as well as to assert that faith has answers to questions raised by culture.'

12 Matt. 25.31ff; Luke 10.25–37; Luke 4.18.

13 It is significant that Hiltner's division of theological subjects has never been seriously discussed since he proposed it in 1958. Indeed even his close associates, contributing to a *festschrift* (*The New Shape of Pastoral Theology*, ed. W. B. Oglesby Jr.) make merely passing reference to it.

14 Thomas C. Oden, *Contemporary Theology and Psychotherapy*, Westminster Press 1967, p. 57.

15 Dietrich Bonhoeffer, *Letters and Papers from Prison*, The Enlarged Edition, SCM Press 1971, p. 279.

16 We must dintinguish this question of *practical theology* from the questions more appropriate to *philosophical theology* of the relationship between 'Christian knowledge' and 'worldly knowledge' (faith and culture). The practical theological question is related specifically to action and interaction.

17 *The Church for Others*, Final Report of the Western European Working Group, Department on Studies in Evangelism, WCC, Geneva 1967, p. 15.

18 See especially Paul Lehmann, *Ethics in a Christian Context*, SCM Press 1963.

19 See J. C. Hoekendijk, *The Church Inside Out*, SCM Press 1964: H. Küng, *On Being a Christian*, Collins 1978; J. Moltmann, *The Church in the Power of the Spirit*, SCM Press 1977.

20 The conceptual models for the type of relationship proposed are to be found in Liam Hudson's converger/diverger categories (*vide Contrary Imaginations*, Methuen 1966 and *Frames of Mind*, Methuen 1968), in M. L. Johnson Abercrombie's description of the influence of schemata on the perception of new situations (*The Anatomy of Judgement*, Hutchinson 1960) and in the distinctions between 'lineal' and 'non-lineal' communication drawn by Marshall McLuhan and others (E. Carpenter and M. McLuhan, *Explorations in Communication*, Beacon Press, Boston 1960). There is now an increasing interest in the place of such imaginative associations in theology, see for example, S. McFague, *Metaphorical Theology*, SCM Press 1983.

21 Examples of such proposals can be found in church reports on nuclear war, legislation for abortion, changing attitudes to marriage, etc. The task of practical theology, however, is to subject the presuppositions and arguments of all such reports to critical scrutiny. Within the specific field of pastoral theology there is an interesting trend towards the sociopolitical dimension. See especially P. Selby, *Liberating God: Private Care and Public Struggle*, SPCK 1983. This, again, requires ongoing critical assessment from theological scholars as part of the general debate about the status of political theology.

Some Points for Further Consideration

- In what specific ways does Campbell expand understandings of the scope and methods that should define practical theology.
- Do you think Campbell provides an adequate description of the scope and function of practical theology?
- In the light of your own situation and the fact that Campbell's paper is now quite old, are there any features of his notion of practical theology that you would want to add, subtract, or change?
- What do you think are the strengths and attractions of Campbell's description of practical theology? What do you like about it? What are its weaknesses? What do you dislike about it?
- To what extent does Campbell succeed in overcoming all the problems that have arisen with the other kinds of practical theology by, e.g., Schleiermacher, Thurneysen, and Hiltner?
- How practical do you think Campbell's practical theology is? Would you be able to engage in practical theology on the basis of what Campbell says here?

For Further Reading and Exploration

For further discussion of the history and distinctive features of practical and pastoral theology see editorial material and chapters 1 to 8 of this Reader as well as Ballard (1986), Forrester (1990), Browning (1991). For more of Campbell's own writings on pastoral care and pastoral theology, see Campbell (1985, 1986, 1987). For more on Hiltner, see Hiltner (1958), and chapter 1 above. The social and political nature of pastoral theology is further explored in, e.g., Couture and Hunter (1995), Selby (1983), Pattison (1993, 1997a).

5

Pastoral Theology in a Pluralistic Age

DON BROWNING

INTRODUCTION

Don Browning can be seen as the key international figure in the renaissance of practical theology in the second half of the twentieth century. Professor of Religion and Psychological studies at the University of Chicago, Browning has given new meaning and method to the concept of practical theology as well as bringing to birth an International Academy of Practical Theology where practitioners of the discipline can meet and educate one another. In his many written works Browning has argued that Christian practice must not be merely pragmatic or therapeutic. Morals, meanings, and ideals should shape a vision of humanity and the kinds of activity that help to work towards this vision. Christian practice should be based on and contribute to theologically-based ethics. This view has formed an important corrective to postwar pastoral care in the USA that uncritically took counseling and psychotherapy as its practical and ethical template.

In "Pastoral Theology in a Pluralistic Age," one of his early contributions to a new theory of practical theology, Browning argues the case for pastoral theology being understood as a "practical theology of care." This practical theology should create norms of human wellbeing and action that are publicly explicable. They should be based on reflection upon the Judeo-Christian tradition. This is brought into dialogue with contemporary situations and insights via the use of a revised correlational method – a methodological device that Browning adopts and adapts from previous thinkers like Paul Tillich and David Tracy. This will allow pastoral theology to regard itself as "an expression of theological ethics" concerned with religio-ethical norms. It can then make specific recommendations for action and practice in the lives of individuals who are being cared for.

Browning's writing is often complex and theoretical, so it is not necessarily straightforwardly practical in the sense that one can go out and start to apply it instantly and simply. It is not easy to see how the method of critical correlation can be carried out in practice. Which bits of the religious tradition, or of the situation under consideration are to be taken into account, for example? While many people would sympathize with the need to draw upon religious and philosophical norms, some would question whether pastoral or practical theology is mainly to be defined in such ways. Not everyone would be happy with seeing pastoral theology mainly as ethics. Campbell (1987) and Pattison with Woodward (1994), for example, see pastoral theology as a critical, exploratory, and dialogical process which explores and creates meanings and is also in some ways aesthetic. For them, practical theology is much looser, softer-edged, and more diverse than it is for Browning. Perhaps pastoral theology should be seen as an exploratory, transformational game, not a matter of setting out prescriptions and rules. Perhaps, too, Browning's method does not take contemporary practice seriously enough. Whatever the weight of these criticisms, Browning's thought and critical correlational methods have had an enormous influence on the shape of contemporary practical theology, upon which others have built (see, e.g., Graham in chapter 6 below).

PASTORAL THEOLOGY IN A PLURALISTIC AGE

What is the future of pastoral theology? In this [article] I advance a primarily theological and normative answer to this question. I do not speculate about the sociological fortunes of pastoral theology. Rather, I risk some vision of what pastoral theology *should* become if it were true to itself and true to that religious tradition which has evolved out of our Jewish and Christian heritage.

My present hopes for the future of pastoral theology are continuous with the view put forth in my *Moral Context of Pastoral Care.*[1] Pastoral theology should rediscover itself as a dimension of theological or religious ethics. It is the primary task of pastoral theology to bring together theological ethics and the social sciences to articulate a normative vision of the human life cycle. Pastoral theology involves stating the appropriate relation between a moral theology of the human life cycle and psychodynamic, developmental, and other social science perspectives that describe or explain how human development comes about.[2] In addition, pastoral theology should express a theology of those pastoral acts through which this normative vision of the human life cycle is appropriately mediated to individuals and groups in all of their situational, existential, and developmental particularity. Furthermore, pastoral theology in the future increasingly must express itself within a pluralistic society of diverse religio-cultural assumptions, differing cultural disciplines, and conflicting ethical patterns of life. . . .

Although this vision of pastoral theology can be stated rather simply, the overall project is exceedingly complex. There are, however, unique features to this proposal that may have productive consequences for the long-term health of both pastoral theology and the allied practices of pastoral care, pastoral counseling, and pastoral psychotherapy.

Interest in pastoral theology has languished behind interest and development in pastoral care, pastoral counseling, and pastoral psychotherapy. We have made advances in our technologies of intervention into such life-cycle issues as adolescence, sexuality, marriage, adulthood, aging, and death. But our normative theological visions of these milestones of the life cycle have received less and less of our attention. More and more, I fear, we have tried to intervene into these life-cycle issues with increasingly diffuse and confused normative theological images – images that should serve, when properly stated, as meaning contexts for our pastoral work. We borrow from the psychotherapeutic and developmental psychologies. But we are sometimes oblivious to the fact that we appropriate from them not only scientific information and therapeutic techniques but various normative visions of human fulfillment that are often neither philosophically sound nor theologically defensible.[3]

In the remainder of this chapter, I want to present an outline for a discipline of pastoral theology, or what could just as appropriately be called a practical theology of care. . . . I will do this by pointing to the range of questions with which pastoral theology as a discipline should concern itself. To facilitate this, it will help to present the main facts of a pastoral case. It is a problem that calls for a pastoral response informed by both theological ethical and psychodynamic perspectives.

Mary Jones is a twenty-seven-year-old public school nurse. She has just made an appointment with a Protestant chaplain in a major metropolitan hospital. Although she is Roman Catholic, she has sought out a Protestant clergyman to get advice about the possibility of having an abortion. Mary has been married but has been divorced for slightly over one year. She has been employed for five years. When she got her divorce she returned to the city where she grew up and where her father and siblings reside. Her entire family is Roman Catholic. She has no plans to marry the father of her child. She was referred to the chaplain by her psychotherapist, who felt he was unable to help her make the decision about the abortion.

She believes that divorce, extramarital sex, and abortion all are sins. Yet she is somewhat attracted by the possibility of actually having the child. On the other hand, she wonders whether her traditional Catholic values will serve her well at this time.

The chaplain reported that a kind of cost–benefit analysis characterized her thought about the possibility of having an abortion. On the cost side, if she had the abortion she would (a) probably feel guilty, (b) lose a child which, in fact, she had always wanted, and (c) incur some health risks. On the benefit side, she would (a) not jeopardize her relationship with her family, (b) be free of the burden of raising a child, (c) not lose her nursing job, and (d) not incur other embarrassments.

The chaplain took note of this attempt to sort out her options, but he also made some inquiry into her developmental history. He learned that she was the oldest child of a lower-middle-class Irish Catholic family of three children. She remembers having strained relations with her mother as a young child. This appeared to be due to the jealousy that existed between herself and her younger sister for which her mother always held her responsible. Her mother died, however, when she was eleven years old. At that time a remarkable transformation came over her. She assumed the position of the head of the house. She did all of the cooking, cleaning, and other household work. Her father praised her for this profusely and she called her father the most "wonderful man in the world." She talked this way about her father in spite of the fact that he had a persistent problem with alcohol. After graduation, she went to nursing school and later married a medical student. Mary helped put her husband through medical school. The divorce came after her husband became established as a doctor and "seemed not to need or really appreciate her anymore." Having the baby would at least mean "having someone to take care of," and "someone who would appreciate her."

In contrast to the typical case discussed in the pastoral care literature where ethical issues are generally overlooked, the presenting problem is here clearly ethical. In addition, because Mary is already in therapy it is inappropriate for the chaplain to redefine the situation totally in the direction of the psychodynamic and motivational issues. Yet, I would contend that even to handle the ethical issues responsibly (consistent with the religio-ethical commitments of the Christian ministry), this chaplain should keep psychodynamic perspective in mind as horizon and background in his ethical considerations. The very essence of pastoral care is found in addressing the religio-ethical dimensions of human problems with an equal consideration for the dynamic-motivational issues as well.

I want to reflect on this case from a religious perspective, an ethical perspective, and a psychodynamic perspective – in that order. In doing this, I hope to outline the discipline of pastoral theology. It will be a hierarchical ordering of the issues of pastoral theology. By this I mean that the religious issues are fundamental (although not in all respects determinative) of the ethical and the psychodynamic issues. Even though this is true logically and methodologically, this does not necessarily mean that in all pastoral care cases the pastor must always place religious or ethical issues before psychodynamic ones. Care always entails a focus-ground structure. In some cases, psychodynamic issues should be in the foreground, but if the religious and ethical dimensions are in the background and the pastor knows how to articulate the way they are operative, the care and counseling being offered is none the less pastoral in the proper and full sense of the word.

The following propositions will, I hope, advance my point of view:

(1) *Pastoral theology should be understood as philosophical reflection on the major themes of the Judeo-Christian tradition with special regard for the implication of these themes for a normative vision of the human life cycle.* It may be surprising to hear me refer to pastoral theology as a type of philosophical reflection. But to understand it in this way will have great clarifying consequences for a variety of pastoral care ministries, especially those ministries such as institutional chaplains or pastoral psychotherapists who must articulate their role before various professions and constituencies within the public world. It is difficult for chaplains to explain intelligibly to a doctor or social worker their role identity in narrowly confessional terms. It is better to articulate one's faith assumptions in a more public and philosophical language. And it is certainly better to do this rather than lapsing, due to discomfort with narrowly confessional language, into the jargon of the social sciences as is the case with so many of our pastoral specialists today.

I am proposing here a revised correlational method of doing pastoral theology (practical theology of care) analogous to the revised correlational method proposed by David Tracy in the arena of fundamental theology.[4] This method is different from the Tillichian model which correlates questions from an analysis of existence with answers from Christian revelation.[5] The revised model critically correlates both questions and answers found in the Christian faith with questions and implied answers in various secular perspectives (the human sciences, the arts) on common human experience.[6] It is interesting to speculate on the similarities between the revised correlational model and the Hiltner-Williams model of "correlation of perspectives."[7] The Hiltner-Williams correlational method is closer to Tracy than it is to Tillich. The Hiltner-Williams model was basically a philosophical approach to pastoral theology. It certainly started with faith, but it brought the intuitions of faith into the public arena, fostered public discussion, reflected critically on the facts of faith, and attempted to advance publicly defensible reasons for the relevance of faith within the context of the public hospital, the public healing disciplines, and other public communities that are the context for our common lives.

The chaplain in this case should understand his task in a publicly and philosophically articulated way. If this chaplain chooses to guide this woman toward a particular attitude toward abortion, it will be better if he can defend his stand publicly, that is philosophically, even though the beginning point of his position may be grounded in faith. Here, as always, it should be faith seeking understanding. A purely confessional view of pastoral theology will no longer serve either the pastoral minister functioning increasingly within the context of a pluralistic and secular culture or the chaplain and pastoral psychotherapist who must function within various pluralistic (and therefore public) interdisciplinary contexts. This first point will become more clear as we complete our discussion of the following propositions.

(2) *Pastoral theology must attempt to discern and articulate the relevance to care of both the religious dimension of common experience as well as the explicit faith themes of the historic Judeo-Christian tradition.* This proposition follows directly from the first. If pastoral theology is to have a public character, it must concern itself with both the explicit themes of our historic faith as well as the tacit religious dimensions of everyday experience.

The desire to care for another person, whether it comes from a minister or a secular therapist, presupposes certain attitudes of a religious kind. Deciding to care for another person assumes certain convictions that that person is worth valuing and caring for, not just for certain instrumental purposes, but intrinsically and with regard to some wider, if not ultimate, standard of value and worth. A variety of contemporary philosophers and theologians (Stephen Toulmin, David Tracy, Schubert Ogden, Bernard Lonergan, Paul Tillich) have argued that all of our finite judgments about both truth and value presupposed limit-experiences and a "limit-language" about wider measures of the true and the valuable.[8] David Tracy, following Lonergan, illustrates the function of limit-language in the area of scientific judgments. For the scientist to be rigorous and constantly open to the truth, he or she must ask such questions as "Can these answers work if the world is not intelligible? Can the world be intelligible if it does not have an intelligent ground?"[9] Tracy is suggesting that at the outer limits of the scientist's enterprise, there exist certain assumptions about the intelligibility of the world that are finally of a religious kind.

I believe that something similar exists in all acts of care. This, I feel, is what both Thomas Oden and I were getting at some fourteen years ago in our respective books entitled *Kerygma and Counseling* and *Atonement and Psychotherapy*.[10] Both of us believed we discerned a kind of limit-experience behind the attitude of acceptance that is fundamental to all good psycho-therapies, even secular ones, regardless of their other differences.[11] We both argued that every specific attitude of therapeutic acceptance presupposed a deeper judgment about the ultimate acceptability of the person, not just to the therapist, but to some ultimate ground that bestows all value and assigns all acceptability.[12] We both believed that this limit-experience requires a "limit-language" to give expression to it (although we did not use this Tracy-Toulmin terminology in those days) and that religious language is precisely the language that serves that function. We differed, however, in that Oden insisted that only the symbols formed by the revelation of God in Jesus Christ (*Deus Pro Nobis*) provided this language,[13] whereas I insisted on a correlational method (maybe even a revised correlational method) that correlated our secular intuitions of this ground with the language of revelation.[14]

If pastoral theology can be philosophical enough to discern and articulate the limit-assumptions behind every act of care, pastoral practitioners can take their place more comfortably in the various pluralistic contexts that characterize contemporary ministry in both its specialized and generalized forms. Even this chaplain can profit from this bifocal perspective on his relation by Mary Jones. This chaplain may want to ground his care for her under the rubric of the love of God in Jesus Christ. But he also should be aware that this faith assumption is not altogether different from the limit-assumptions that secular therapists (even the therapist in this case) also make. Even the secular therapist must answer the question, why do I care for this person? Why is this person worth helping? Why am I obligated to help? These questions point to limit-assumptions that taper off into religious faith. The chaplain is fed by both sources of faith – those of common experience *and* explicit religious traditions. The difference between the minister and the secular therapist is not that one has faith and the other doesn't; it is rather that the minister has the additional resources of a specific religious tradition. Recognizing this fact makes it possible for the minister to take his or her place more gracefully in the contemporary pluralistic situation characterizing the helping disciplines today.

But the fuller task of pastoral theology is to give philosophical expression to the norms for the human life cycle explicitly found in the major themes of the Judeo-Christian tradition. Once again, it should be a matter of faith seeking understanding. Our task is to state the norms not just for the faithful (although certainly for them), but also to determine whether these norms have general public meaning, that is, whether they have general significance even for those who are not explicitly Christian. Is there some-thing about Christian attitudes and norms of behavior that is valid for our mental health system, for our educational system, for our public policies with the aged and ill? Obviously, we cannot address these issues in the public arena from a narrowly confessional stance. This is why pastoral theology in the contemporary pluralistic situation should have an increasingly public and philosophical character.

(3) *Pastoral theology should understand itself as an expression of theological ethics, primarily concerned with the religio-ethical norms governing the human life cycle.* This proposition is the most novel of the four that I am advancing and the one that signals most clearly the facet of pastoral theology being neglected today. Pastoral care is frequently seen as a religious enterprise, but we overlook the ways it is also an ethical enterprise. In this case, the situation is clear: this woman is asking for ethical guidance. Would most of our ministers, chaplains, and pastoral counselors know how to give it? Would they attempt to avoid the ethical issue and retreat to a psychodynamic reduction of her concerns? In this case, that would be doubly inappropriate since she already has her psychotherapist. Would one simply try to help her make a decision that she could live with and feel comfortable with? Once again, her therapist can also do this!

But how do we proceed? What are our ethical methodologies? Once again, a philosophical or moral-philosophical perspective may help us sort out our theological-ethical options and do so in such a way as to communicate our stance in a reasoned way to our pluralistic moral situation. First, what kind of ethical thinking is Mary herself doing? In spite of Mary's rather traditional religious convictions, her style of ethical thinking is anything but classically Catholic in character. Her cost-benefit analysis is clearly, in the terms of moral philosophy, a kind of teleological thinking. Teleological moral thinking, moral philosophers tell us, always tries to answer the question of what we should do by trying to determine which act will bring about the greatest amount of good over evil. The teleologist is always interested in consequences; the moral thing to do is that which will bring into reality the greatest amount of good consequences when good is given a nonmoral (although not immoral) meaning, such as when we use it to refer to good health, good music, good food, and good times.

At first glance, one might think that she is a teleologist of a specifically utilitarian kind. Mary in her cost-benefit analysis is trying to calculate the good over evil that will come about as a consequence of different courses of action. Utilitarians invariably get into just this kind of calculations. But Mary is not a utilitarian, as we will soon see. She is much closer to another kind of teleological thinking – an ethical egoist perspective, typical of so much of the ethical thinking in the contemporary cultural situation.[15]

Mary is not a utilitarian because she is not doing her calculations – her cost-benefit analysis – with the good of the larger community in mind. A utilitarian always does his or her calculations with the larger community in view, trying to determine which act or rule, if followed, will produce the greatest amount of good over evil for the largest number of people.[16] Mary is not doing this. Mary is doing her cost-benefit analysis in terms of the amount of good over evil that will accrue solely to herself. This is the kind of ethical thinking that a teleologist of the ethical egoist kind invariably ends up doing. We should be reminded that some ethical egoists do things that indirectly create good for others, but they always do them primarily because of the good that will come to them. Mary is an ethical egoist in that sense. Each of the values she is weighing has significance first of all for herself; as of yet, she has asked no questions about the welfare of her family, the larger society, or the child she may someday have. In terms of Lawrence Kohlberg's stages of moral development, Mary may be somewhere between stage two (the instrumental-hedonistic stage) and stage three (the conventional good-girl bad-girl orientation).[17]

The chaplain has enough ethical sophistication to know that his own point of view is considerably different from that of Mary Jones. Although a Protestant, he agrees with the classical Catholic position about the sanctity of life, even the life of the fetus in its earliest stages. He agrees on this issue with a group of contemporary ethicists, both Protestant and Catholic, such as Paul Ramsey, Germain Grisez, and John Noonan.[18] But he also believes that the Catholic position puts too much emphasis upon physical life. It overlooks the possibility that God may cherish other values such as the quality of life for both the child and the mother, social integrity, and the emotional and spiritual health of all concerned. In the formal terms of moral philosophy, the counselor's position, in so far as he was aware of having one, tended toward a mixed deontological and teleological position. Deontological approaches to ethics do not first of all try to determine the morally right by calculating consequences and estimating the amount of nonmoral good an act or rule will realize. Deontological approaches to ethics try to establish the right on some first principle or intuition that is deemed to be intrinsically and self-evidently moral independent of consequences. The divine command of God, Kant's categorical imperative, and existentialist appeals to authenticity are all examples, in their different ways, of deontological approaches. The chaplain's mixed position was deontological in that the sanctity of life was for him both a revelational and intuitive given; it was teleological, however, in that he felt that this value, although always central, must sometimes be balanced with other values as well.[19] The chaplain's position is close in some respects to the theological utilitarianism of the liberal Catholic thinker Daniel Callahan, since for the chaplain, ethical thinking involves balancing a variety of social and individual values. But it also is close to James Gustafson's position when he wrote the following words in response to Paul Ramsey's strong antiabortion stand: "Paul Ramsey rests his case ultimately on a theological basis; life is sacred because it is valued by God. Good theological point. But one can ask, what other things does God value in addition to physical life? e.g., qualitative aspects of life, etc."[20] Hence, the chaplain's position would allow for the possibility of abortion, but not on narrowly egoistic grounds.

This pastoral care situation, where abortion counseling is the primary focus, is used here only to illustrate a range of ethical issues that pastoral counselors have been ignoring. Many other situations and many other issues could have been used to make my point. But this illustration alone is sufficient to raise a host of important issues. How does the counselor now proceed? Does he take a thoroughly eductive approach and let her solve this problem within her own mixed ethical-egoist and conformist values? Does he try to move her closer to his own way of thinking? Is her developmental history important? Does he need to attend to her feelings, her motivations, and her psychological makeup? What kind of helping relation should he offer her? How do the religious perspectives discussed above affect this relationship? How does the ethical perspective just mentioned affect the relation? These questions carry us into the last sections of this chapter and the heart of pastoral care – the practical judgment involved in bringing these religious and ethical perspectives together with the particularities of her situation, the strengths and weaknesses of her personality, and the initiatives and responsibilities she is likely to sustain.

(4) *Pastoral theology should be concerned with specifying the logic, timing, and practical strategies for relating theological-ethical and psychodynamic perspectives on human behavior.* The chaplain's ethical outlook led him to believe that either an abortion or having the child and putting it up for adoption were the most responsible courses of action open to her. At the same time, he ended his one-half hour interview believing that, for psychodynamic reasons, Mary Jones was strongly attracted to the idea of having the baby. But time was of the essence. A decision had to be made soon. He concluded the interview by offering to have two additional conversations. In these conversations he hoped to widen the range of her moral thinking so that she would begin to consider, in addition to her own needs, the needs of her unborn child, the needs of her family, and finally the needs of the larger society. In addition, he hoped to broaden her ethical thinking while at the same time attending to the complexities of her own developmental history.

On the moral level, the chaplain believed that there were strong arguments against having and keeping the child. Her status as a single parent, the unlikely possibility of getting assistance from her family, her lack of financial resources, the possible deleterious effects on the child of being raised without both a mother and father, and finally the growth-inhibiting consequences that having the baby would have on Mary's life, led the chaplain to take a dim view of this option. On the other hand he could morally justify both abortion or placing the child for adoption. Although he affirmed the sanctity of the unborn fetus, he saw great risks connected with the future well-being of the child is she were to have and keep the child. In addition, he held the conviction that modern society already had spawned too many alienated and emotionally deficient individuals and that the welfare of the social whole argues for either abortion or placing the child for adoption with a loving and stable family.

But there were indications, he thought, that Mary was deeply attracted to keeping the child. The chaplain's rapid scanning of her developmental history led him to hypothesize that Mary was a mildly narcissistic individual whose problems, although not grave, were prestructural in nature (located developmentally earlier than the oedipal conflict and the differentiation of the personality into ego, superego, and id). The chaplain felt that what seemed to be an oedipal relation between Mary and her father was probably superficial. Using the thought of Heinz Kohut,[21] he hypothesized that the real developmental issue was the prestructural narcissistic blows dealt to her self-esteem by her mother who constantly criticized her for mistreating her younger siblings. The father's later appreciation (accentuated by his own alcoholic and dependent needs) helped compensate somewhat for earlier narcissistic deficits. But having little understanding of what was really happening, Mary developed the strategy of enhancing her self-regard through taking care of others who needed her. This led, the chaplain thought, to an early marriage and her investment in the financial support of her husband's education. This same need might also, he believed, be behind her wish "to have a child."

All of this the chaplain held only tentatively. He did want to speak with her further. He hoped that in getting to know her better, he might gain a clearer idea about how to bring her moral discernment and her dynamic self-understanding into a closer relation. He did not aspire to take over the role now being occupied by her therapist, but he did want to promote both moral and psychological growth. At his next session, he planned to guide her into discussing her deeper feelings about the possibility of having the baby. If it emerges that having and keeping the baby does feed into her overdetermined needs to be wanted and depended upon, the chaplain then hoped to raise some carefully phrased questions designed to suggest additional moral possibilities. He would ask if she had thought about the welfare of the child, the strain it would place on her, and the possible long-term strains it might place upon society. At a later time, the chaplain was prepared to share simply and without airs of moral superiority his own moral views and the reasons he used to support them. In this way, he hoped to launch a process of moral inquiry that would at once be undogmatic in tone and dynamically sensitive to both the complexities of her developmental history as well as her level of moral thinking.

In the process of this inquiry, the chaplain hoped to offer Mary Jones a relation that was both accepting and morally serious. Both the acceptance and the moral seriousness had, for the chaplain, religious foundations.

These religious foundations can be found both in certain limit-experiences in ordinary experience (Tracy, Toulmin, Browning, Lonergan) and the major themes of the Judeo-Christian tradition. The acceptance that the chaplain will offer, if authentic, will help meet some of the needs for narcissistic support that Mary Jones will require if she is to undergo the struggle to enlarge her moral horizons. This acceptance and the value for life that it will communicate is of a piece with the religious presuppositions about the sanctity of life fundamental to the chaplain's ethical perspective on abortion. But here, as is always the case, religious convictions do not in themselves determine the final outcome of ethical deliberation. Religious convictions provide a framework and limit-language for ethical deliberation. But ethical deliberation itself requires more specific calculations about the determinate goods and values at stake in the situation at hand.

It is not the purpose of this chapter to suggest that what the chaplain did, what he believed at the moral or ethical level, and how he rationalized his choices are either right or wrong. Nor am I saying that the chaplain should be conducting this moral inquiry alone. Ideally, this chaplain would have strong relations with the larger church. The larger church, as I indicated in the *Moral Context of Pastoral Care*, would function as a community of moral discourse and moral inquiry. The chaplain's ethical deliberations would be a part of and reinforced by the ethical deliberations of the larger Christian community. Ideally, Mary Jones herself also would be a part of this community and its moral discourse. None the less, what I am saying is that the issues that the chaplain faced, the philosophical attitude that he brought to his deliberations, and his willingness to think about both ethical and psychodynamic concerns – all of this at least makes visible the agenda for pastoral theology in the future. If pastoral theology accepts this agenda, it will serve more fully and holistically human beings who live in a world that is increasingly more complex and pluralistic.

NOTES

1   Don Browning, *The Moral Context of Pastoral Care* (Philadelphia: Westminster, 1976).
2   This definition of pastoral theology is broader than that advanced in *The Moral Context of Pastoral Care*. In this book I defined pastoral theology as the theology of pastoral acts of care and associated practical theology with the task of developing a moral theology of the human life cycle. I am now willing to define pastoral theology as dealing with both (a) a moral theology of the human life cycle and (b) a theology of pastoral acts of care. Practical theology I now associate with the larger task of writing theology from the perspective of action in contrast to belief, the latter being the major task of systematic

theology. In this perspective theological ethics is a division of practical theology.

3 To give an analysis of the tacit theories of moral obligation implicit in various psychotherapeutic psychologies, I have found it helpful to apply William Frankena's categorization of different styles of ethical thinking. See his *Ethics* (Englewood Cliffs, NJ: Prentice-Hall, 1973), pp. 12–65. On the basis of his theory of virtue, one could argue that orthodox psychoanalysis contains an implicit "trait ethical egoist" theory of human fulfillment of a hedonic kind, that most of the humanistic theories (Maslow, Rogers, Perls) are "trait ethical egoist" of a non-hedonic kind, that Erikson is a "trait rule utilitarian," that most of the existentialists are "trait act deontologists," and that Kohlberg is a "trait rule deontologist."

4 David Tracy, *Blessed Rage for Order* (New York: Seabury, 1975), pp. 32–63.

5 Paul Tillich, *Systematic Theology*, vol. 1 (Chicago: University of Chicago Press, 1951), pp. 3–68.

6 Tracy, *Blessed Rage for Order*, pp. 45–7.

7 See Seward Hiltner, *Preface to Pastoral Theology* (Nashville, TN: Abingdon, 1957); Daniel Day Williams, *The Minister and the Care of Souls* (New York: Harper & Brothers, 1961).

8 Stephen Toulmin, *An Examination of the Place of Reason in Ethics* (Cambridge: Cambridge University Press, 1970), pp. 217–21; Tracy, *Blessed Rage for Order*, pp. 94–119; Schubert Ogden, *The Reality of God* (New York: Harper and Row, 1963), p. 30; Bernard Lonergan, *Method in Theology* (New York: Herder and Herder, 1972), pp. 235–45; Paul Tillich, *Systematic Theology*, vol. 32, pp. 204–10.

9 Tracy, *Blessed Rage for Order*, p. 98.

10 Thomas Oden, *Kerygma and Counseling* (Philadelphia: Westminster, 1966); Don Browning, *Atonement and Psychotherapy* (Philadelphia: Westminster, 1966).

11 Browning, *Atonement and Psychotherapy*, pp. 94–127.

12 Oden, *Kerygma and Counseling*, p. 21; Browning, *Atonement and Psychotherapy*, pp. 149–61.

13 Oden, *Kerygma and Counseling*, p. 63.

14 Browning, *Atonement and Psychotherapy*, pp. 149–73.

15 Frankena, *Ethics*, pp. 17–19.

16 Ibid., p. 34.

17 Lawrence Kohlberg, "From Is to Ought," *Cognitive Development and Epistemology*, ed. Theodore Mischel (New York: Academic, 1971), p. 168.

18 Paul Ramsey, "References Points in Deciding about Abortion," *The Morality of Abortion*, ed. John T. Noonan (Cambridge, MA: Harvard

102   *Don Browning*

University Press, 1970), pp. 60–100; German Grisez, *Abortion: The Myths, The Realities, and the Arguments* (New York: Corpus Books, 1970); John T. Noonan, Jr., "An Almost Absolute Value in History," *The Morality of Abortion*, ed. John T. Noonan, Jr., pp. 1–59.

19 The possibility of a mixed deontological and teleological ethics is explained by William Frankena in his *Ethics*, p. 52.
20 As quoted in Daniel Callahan, *Abortion: Law, Choice, and Morality* (New York: Macmillan, 1970), p. 311.
21 Heinz Kohut, *The Analysis of the Self* (New York: International Universities Press, 1971).

SOME POINTS FOR FURTHER CONSIDERATION

- What are the advantages and disadvantages of seeing practical theology as mainly a matter of religio-ethical formulation and discernment?
- How valuable and useful is it to define pastoral theology as a "practical theology of care"?
- What are the limits of Browning's vision of practical theology? Are there any important exclusions in the way he formulates this subject, e.g. in comparison with Campbell or Graham (see chapters 4 and 6)?
- What are the alternatives to seeing practical theology as a matter of critically correlating reflection on the Judeo-Christian tradition and contemporary human experience and insights from non-theological disciplines?
- What problems might arise in trying to undertake the critical correlation that might lead to a normative practical theology of care?

FOR FURTHER READING AND EXPLORATION

Browning's first foray into developing a theologico-ethical base for pastoral care is to be found in *The Moral Context of Pastoral Care* (1976). In *Religious Ethics and Pastoral Care* (1983), Browning develops and systematizes his revised critical correlational method into five stages of practical moral reasoning that should help to arrive at norms for action. In this volume, he also introduces the important corrective that it is *interpretations* of some aspects of Christian tradition that are brought into correlation with *interpretations* of contemporary human experience and secular disciplines. This move acknowledges the impossibility of engaging all aspects of everything simultaneously in critical dialogue. Browning's fullest exposition of the revised critical correlative methods is in *A Fundamental Practical Theology* (1991), a complex, systematic statement about the nature of practical theology, how it should be done, and how it relates to other theological disciplines. The seminal collection edited by Browning, *Practical Theology* (1983), from which the present paper is extracted, gives a good sense of the scope and range of the new practical theology in the USA. For explication and critique of Browning see, e.g., Pattison (1993), Graham (1996).

6

Practical Theology as Transforming Practice

Elaine Graham

INTRODUCTION

Elaine Graham was the first woman to be appointed to a senior chair in practical theology in Britain, in 1998. Professor of Social and Pastoral Theology at the University of Manchester, Graham was also the founding chair of the British and Irish Association for Practical Theology. Her published work has been much concerned with fundamentally reforming the theoretical approach of practical theology in the light of contemporary intellectual movements. Don Browning's work in creating a theological-ethical base and method for practical theology forms a foundation for Graham. However, she expands on and develops his approach to incorporate important insights from movements such as feminism and postmodernism. This is reflected in the specially commissioned paper printed here.

In "Practical Theology as Transforming Practice" Graham argues that the discipline of pastoral or practical theology should be reconceived as "the articulation and excavation of sources and norms of Christian practice." This is basically an inductive process that works from looking carefully at the practice of faith communities to theorization. Rejecting the obsession of pastoral theology with individuals, therapeutic approaches, and clerical concerns, Graham sees the work of practical theology as being primarily undertaken with and by intentional communities of faith. The quest is for practical knowledge like Aristotle's *phronêsis*. Graham situates this kind of practical theology within the uncertainties and ambiguities provided by the present postmodern context. She also draws on thinkers who have been influential in that context, such as Habermas, to illuminate the work and methods of practical theology. The ultimate end of pastoral theology is to act as an interpretative discipline that enables faith communities to give a public, critical account of the truth claims that they enact in practice. In this sense, practical theology helps communities of faith both to articulate and practice what they preach or believe and also to better articulate or preach what they practice.

This paper is complex, compressed, and highly theoretical, leaning heavily upon contemporary philosophy. It is, therefore, a demanding read. The effort expended will be worth while because Graham grapples seriously with theoretical and practical issues facing practical theology in the contemporary world. This simultaneously makes the task of practical theology more complex but also more intellectually interesting, comprehensive, and important. Graham might be criticized on a number of grounds. Her work is very abstract. It is not very clearly related to the classic Christian theological tradition (where does the Bible fit into her vision of practical theology, for example?). Her theory is not very specific about how actually to go about discerning communal performative truth claims in practice. Some would argue that she embraces too fully postmodern cultural relativism and non-realist views of God and ethics in her work. Her innovative perspective is, however, a significant development in the evolution of practical theological method.

PRACTICAL THEOLOGY AS TRANSFORMING PRACTICE[1]

Introduction

We live in an age of uncertainty: an age in which many of the foundations of contemporary Western culture seem to be dissolving. At the close of the twentieth century, it is said that we live in 'postmodern'[2] times, in which the 'grand narratives' of humanism, science and progress have been discredited (Lyotard 1984). In the face of the erosion of what Edward Farley calls 'deep symbols' – questions of identity, of the common good, of truth, hope, liberation and justice – the prospects of articulating responsible Christian witness in such a world seem daunting (Farley 1996).

Transforming Practice (Mowbray 1996) argues that the discipline of pastoral theology,[3] reorientated for a postmodern age of uncertainty, provides a method for connecting theory and practice in a reconception of faithful identity. The pastoral disciplines of personal care, social action, worship and initiation are not the 'applied' offshoots of a body of propositional theory that transcends the contingency of human activity. Rather, the ways in which Christians choose to organize their ways of being in the world, of relating to one another in community, and of enacting ritual, care and spirituality, constitute the language of authentic identity. Practical theology therefore functions in order to enable communities of faith to 'practise what they preach.'

In this commentary on *Transforming Practice*, I provide a summary of the main arguments and further discussion of some of the implications of my model of pastoral theology for a postmodern age. The chief implications of *Transforming Practice* for the discipline of pastoral theology are these: its critique of the nature of an 'age of uncertainty'; its use of feminist and gender analysis to expose the fragility and inadequacy of the categories by which modernity – and the therapeutic and clerical paradigms of Christian pastoral care – constructed its core values; and its reconception of the discipline of pastoral theology as the articulation and excavation of the sources and norms of Christian *practice*.

In keeping with the postmodern spirit of *bricolage* – enquiry which proceeds by piecing together fragments, eschewing elevated theoretical schemes, aware of the provisionality and fragility of knowledge – I suggest that the key hermeneutical criterion for a reconstructed Christian practice is the 'disclosure' of *alterity*. In practical terms, such a perspective would favour strategies which encourage empathy and solidarity with others, open up enlarged horizons of understanding and commitment and foster pastoral encounters which engender new perspectives on human experience and Divine reality. 'Disclosive practice' is, however, more than merely a procedural norm: it speaks not simply of an ecclesial communicative ethic, but serves as a metaphor for an encounter with the very nature of God.

Age of Uncertainty

> Postmodern thought . . . is a series of attitudes struck in face of questions bequeathed by modernity about the nature of rationality, the nature of subjectivity, issues of rights and responsibility, and the constitution of the political community.
>
> (Lakeland 1997: 12)

The historical and sociological epoch known as modernity is displaced by the signs of the times of 'postmodernity' and with it comes a host of voices to destabilize Enlightenment concepts of truth, human nature, knowledge, power, selfhood and language that have informed Western thought for two hundred years (Gay 1973; Kearney 1994; Reader 1997).

However, my anatomy of postmodernity does not merely conceive of intellectual debate independent of social, political and economic factors. The 'crisis' of postmodernity is not simply one of believing, but of revolutions in patterns of work and leisure, use of technology, the exercise of civic power, participation and citizenship, access to resources, relationships to the environment, and the use and abuse of scientific innovations (Hall et al. 1992). We might also include in our analysis the growth of religious pluralism and the decline of organized religion, especially in Western Europe, as signs that patterns of believing and belonging are changing. The pre-eminence of the Christian way of life can no longer be taken for granted (Davie 1994).

A frequent topic of debate concerns whether postmodernity is a successor epoch of modernity, or a critical corrective to it. My preference is for the latter analysis: as Richard Bernstein has it, the mood of postmodernity is a 'rage against humanism and the Enlightenment legacy' (Bernstein 1985: x) Postmodernity exposes the *hubris* of Enlightenment optimism, tempers the excesses of literalism, objectivism and humanism, and retrieves from the margins the repressed and hidden 'Others' of Western modernity. The postmodern is where modernity is called to account, where its confident assertions are put to the test:

> Postmodernism reminds us that we are already too determined ourselves; we can never exhaustively account for the conditions which make the world, time, knowledge, the human animal, language, possible . . . Postmodernism reminds modernity of its own constructed nature; the arbitrariness and instability of its own constructions. (Ward 1997: xxvi)

Feminist thought, whilst in many respects a child of the Enlightenment, also exhibits a postmodern scepticism towards many of the precepts of modernity. Feminists have argued that dominant views of human nature, self, knowledge, action and value are constructed *androcentrically*: that is, they assume that maleness and masculinity are the norm for adequate accounts of what it means to be human, how I achieve a sense of self, what counts as verifiable and reliable knowledge, the relationship between thought, will and action, and the sources and norms of ultimate value, truth and beauty. Once we introduce the notion of these concepts as 'gendered', however, we gain a clearer sense of some of the ways in which Enlightenment views must necessarily be revised. The challenge of feminism thus illustrates the crisis of conventional values and the necessity of accommodating diverse and heterogeneous experiences (Flax 1990).

Transforming Pastoral Theology

Christian thought and practice has, inevitably, been touched by the intellectual and social currents of postmodernity. Despite lively debate within philosophical theology, however (Ward 1997), much of this has ignited little interest on the part of pastoral, or practical, theology. Yet the practical question of the sources and norms that might inform Christian faithful witness in the Church and the world is as fundamental and problematic an issue as the purely philosophical implications of postmodernity. In the face of the collapse of the 'grand narrative' of modernity, what values of hope and obligation may now inform purposeful Christian action and vision?

One of the symptoms of postmodernity, it is said, is a resurgence of the sacred; and this opens up possibilities that go beyond either a reversion to premodern fideism or a drift into New Age eclecticism. My paramount concern is thus to remain true to the continuity of Christian witness whilst responding anew to the challenges of the present age. A necessary part of the critical reclamation of the 'boundaries' and 'horizons' (Oliver 1991) of Christian identity will therefore be a robust engagement with the ambiguities of a post-secular age:

> Set free from the compulsion to talk about God, there is a new and deeper freedom to talk about God and *not* to talk about God . . . In its engagement with the secular psychotherapies, neither does pastoral counselling need to lose its Christian identity as care offered in the community of faith. Set free from the compulsion to be 'religious', it has a genuine freedom to point beyond the secular to the One who is the source of all healing. (Lyall 1995: 107)

For most of the twentieth century, the predominant model of pastoral theology has been that of the theory and practice of individual care, prominently informed by the therapeutic models of the modern psychologies. The tasks of pastoral ministry – worship, preaching, social action, personal care, Christian formation and community-building – have traditionally been regarded as the exclusive province of the ordained clergy. However, as sociological changes have precipitated a greater demand for active participation in church life by the laity, and feminist critiques have questioned the invisibility of women's pastoral role as agents and clients of care, intensive scrutiny has been generated into the identity and aims of the pastoral task and the self-understanding of the Christian community (Graham and Halsey 1993; Lyall 1995).

Schleiermacher's original vision for Practical Theology designated the discipline as the 'crown' of theological enquiry, derivative of the higher forms of philosophical and historical theology (Schleiermacher 1966; Burkhart 1983). The burden of theological understanding and formulation was therefore directed towards the entirety of Christian practice, albeit within the service of ecclesial ministry, although it did effectively reduce practical theology to a deductive, or 'applied' theology. However, we may see a timely corrective to this within contemporary theologies of liberation which effectively turn Schleiermacher's system on its head. In their emphasis on *praxis* and context as hermeneutically primary, experience is thus envisaged as the origin, not the application, of theological formulation:

> [T]he permanent self-identity of the Christian faith cannot be presupposed . . . There is no purely theoretical centre of reference which can serve in an abstract, speculative way as a norm of identity. Truth does not yet exist; it cannot be reached by interpretation, but it has to be produced by change. (Davis 1994: 90–1)

According to this view, therefore, pastoral theology breaks out of the 'clerical paradigm' (Farley 1983a) and locates itself as the 'critical inquiry into the validity of Christian witness' (Wheeler and Farley 1991: 15). The proper object of the discipline is not the moral reasoning of the congregation (Browning 1991) or the activities of the pastor (Hiltner 1958) or 'applied theology', but the practice of intentional communities. Pastoral theology studies the whole mission of the faith-community, as expressed in its diverse practices of ordering the faithful, engaging in social justice, communicating the faith, and administering Word and Sacrament. Pastoral theology is reconceived, therefore, as the critical discipline interrogating the norms that guide all corporate activity by which the community enacts its identity.

Practical Wisdom

Looked at from other perspectives, my proposal to reconstitute pastoral theology as the theorization of Christian practice looks promising. Contemporary feminist theories regard gender identity, relations and representations as generated by performative practices of 'gendering' (Flax 1993), rather than derived from an ontological or biological dualism. Gender is a self-reflexive phenomenon: we experience ourselves as simultaneously the creators and creations of gendered culture. There are no transhistorical essences of gender, but only *practices* that realize or reinforce difference (Connell 1987; Butler 1990; Graham 1995).

Such a model presents identity and culture as 'performative'. Pierre Bourdieu's concept of *habitus* – a kind of practical knowledge within which human social action enacts and constructs culture – is a synthesis of structure and agency: a 'system of structured, structuring dispositions . . . constituted in practice and . . . always oriented towards practical functions' (Bourdieu 1992: 52). Such a *habitus* is also, I contend, necessarily embodied. Social structures are inscribed on bodily activity; embodied action creates tangible institutions.

As a working definition, we might therefore characterize practice as 'purposeful activity performed by embodied persons in space and time as the subjects of agency and objects of history' (Graham 1996: 110). Purposeful practices are the bearers of value: cultural norms are reproduced and handed down but there is also scope for creative re-rendering. Pastoral practice constitutes the *habitus* of faith; it is both inherited and indwelt but also infinitely creative: a performative practical wisdom (*phronêsis*) which we inhabit and re-enact.

Thus, the core values of communities or cultures are not to be conceived as transcendent eternal realities, but as provisional – yet binding – strategies of normative action and community within which shared commitments might be negotiated and put to work. Ethics and politics therefore become processes and practices, rather than applications of metaphysical ideals.

Community and Alterity

> There is no path to utopia . . . but the responsibility to
> seek the world 'better' or 'less cruel' persists. There
> may be no common human nature or human reality,
> but the demands of sociality continue.
>
> (Lakeland 1997: 27)

The task of articulating binding principles out of the contingency and self-reflexivity of human practice has occupied many contemporary social theorists, and their work provides some clues for pastoral theology. Here, I turn to Jürgen Habermas's idea of 'ideal speech communities' as holding out the possibility of a 'communicative ethic' that is inclusive and pluralist yet which commands sufficient respect for rational agreement (Habermas 1984, 1989; Bernstein 1985). Habermas argues that the communicative ethic which informs liberative public policy has its basis in the exercise of conversational practice. Values of truth, beauty and emancipation emerge from the transactions between groupings engaged in common tasks of transformation and action.

Habermas holds out the possibility of shared rational discourse as facilitating visions of political and moral responsibility; but his feminist critic Seyla Benhabib argues that in order for such a model to be responsive to the dynamics of gender, there must be a recognition of the radical *alterity* (otherness) at the heart of the communicative encounter. Whereas the 'generalized' other stands for a universal moral claim to human integrity, the 'concrete' other reminds us that a truly ideal speech community respects heterogeneity and difference (Benhabib 1992).

This is not a postmodern nihilism or radical relativism – which argues that truth is 'neither here nor there' (Graham 1996: 157). Rather, drawing on Donna Haraway's notion of 'situated knowledge' as a form of practical wisdom, I would argue that the virtues of hope and obligation are practised – inhabited and enacted – but always already from specific vantage-points. Thus, after Benhabib and Haraway, and in keeping with psychoanalytic, hermeneutic and feminist projects of recovering the unnamed, repressed and 'Other', I would argue that an adequate model of practical knowledge will exhibit a bias towards *alterity*, diversity and inclusivity. This is at the heart of an understanding of 'disclosive' practice which must take account of our situatedness (especially in terms of our embodiment), will be appropriately open to *alterity* (otherness) and is evinced by the provisional nature of both practice and the knowledge it embodies, rather than 'foreclosive' practices, exercising premature or authoritarian appeals to absolute truth.

> How do we present our views in the fullness of our embodied and perspectival commitment, without falling back into a . . . universalism that has rightly been criticized as expressing the will to power of those who have been able to express their views? I suggest it is not by pretending to intellectual neutrality . . . but rather by acknowledging and affirming the conditions of time and space, which limit our perspectives as well as giving them their distinctive perspectival power. . . . We should not hold our views so tightly that we cannot appreciate the perspectival truths embodied in the lives and works of others. We should think of our 'truth claims' as the products of embodied *thinking* not as eternally or universally valid *thought*. (Christ 1988: 13)

Transforming Practice

Nancy Eisland's recent work *The Disabled God* (1994) claims to advance a 'liberation theology of disability' that models many of the criteria for pastoral theology outlined above. Eisland draws upon conventional resources of personal experience, cultural factors and Christian tradition (Tracy 1981), although the parameters of each of these categories are subtly revised within a hermeneutic in which *alterity*, difference and the retrieval of 'stories seldom heard' (Milhaven 1991) are privileged as having theologically disclosive authority. The validity of theological truth-claims are 'acted out' (Eisland 1994: 95) and will be tested by their ability to animate a renewed practical wisdom for the Church: 'The struggle for wholeness and justice begins with the practices and habits of the church itself' (1994: 111).

Speaking of difference

In drawing on the *narrative experience* of two women with disabilities, Eisland refuses to render disability as if it were an ontological category. Rather, the stories bear witness to a plurality of definitions of mobility, impairment and body image. These accounts do not pathologize or victimize their narrators, but nor do they suppress the distinctive experiences of those with disabilities: 'It encompasses the recognition that disability does not mean incomplete and that difference is not dangerous' (Eisland 1994: 47).

Hermeneutics of suspicion

Christian teaching on disability, healing and illness is critically examined, and elements of *tradition* that portray disability as the result of sin, or suffering as a visitation from God to test the afflicted, or an opportunity for the 'able-bodied' to exercise charity, are found wanting. Instead, Eisland's criterion for theological authenticity within the tradition is one which empowers those with disabilities as theological subjects. They are affirmed as the authors of their own narratives of Divine disclosure:

> A liberatory theology sustains our difficult but ordinary lives, empowers and collaborates with individuals and groups of people with disabilities who struggle for justice in concrete situations, creates new ways of resisting the theological symbols that exclude and devalue us, and reclaims our hidden history in the presence of God on earth.   (1994: 86)

The symbols of faith around disability therefore have a performative power to 'create normative standards for human interaction' (1994: 91); Eisland advances a contextualized Christology of the 'disabled God . . . in a sip-puff wheelchair' (1994: 89).

Transforming communities

The truth-claims of the Gospel are thus incarnated in the worshipping community that seeks to embody the suffering but transfigured presence of the 'disabled God'. Eisland focuses on the significance for such communities of the Eucharist, a sacrament, not of exclusion, but a sign of the 'body broken for a people broken' (1994: 114). In the figure of the transfigured Christ – who retains his wounds even in a risen state – God's solidarity with suffering is realized. A vision of God embedded in human encounter and renewal animates genuinely disclosive practical wisdom: words made flesh in a community which fosters a generosity to others. Such transformative practice facilitates and encourages the exercise of the qualities of solidarity, wholeness and reconciliation, practices by which divine disclosure can be effected.

New Horizons

The process of going *beyond* the situated and concrete towards the encounter with the Other may also serve as a metaphor for the human experience of God. It speaks of authentic faith occurring at the very point of loss of certainty and self-possession: divine activity and presence are offered in the mystery of *alterity*. Thus, Eisland's thoroughly Christian incarnational theology understands the human and immediate as a 'sacrament' of the transcendent and divine: 'Our bodies participate in the imago Dei, not in spite of our impairments and contingencies, but through them' (Eisland 1994: 101).

Just as identity in the postmodern condition is contingent, performative and provisional, so theological truth-claims are to be seen as forms of *phronêsis*, or practical knowledge: faith and truth cannot be separated from practical action, which is the very vehicle and embodiment of the Word made flesh:

> Where is God? we ask. Look to the underside of history and the emancipatory struggles of oppressed peoples everywhere. Or look to the ecological quest for the wholeness and integrity of life. Or to the dialogical creation of common though shaky ground in the midst of cultural and religious differences. . . . My thesis is that the answer to the challenge of postmodernity – how to speak meaningfully of God's presence and action in the world – is already implicit in these practices. (Hodgson 1994: 65–6)

Can we regard authentic pastoral practice, therefore, as that which draws us into encounter with the 'Other', towards a deeper understanding of our own identity-in-relation? Pastoral theology is an interpretative discipline enabling faith-communities to give a public and critical account of their performative truth-claims. It attempts to capture glimpses of Divine activity amidst human practice. Pastoral theology aims to put to the test the conviction that the imperatives of hope and obligation are enshrined in transformative practice that seeks to realize a larger vision yet to come.

NOTES

1 Since *Transforming Practice* was first published, a number of other titles have appeared which attempt to debate the nature of theological and pastoral responses to postmodernity: see Farley (1996), Lakeland (1997), Reader (1997), Ward (1997) and Goodliff (1998). I have included some insights from these works in this updated commentary.

2 The terms 'postmodernism' and 'postmodernity' are related but distinct phenomena. 'Postmodernism' denotes the cultural, intellectual and aesthetic dimensions of the postmodern age, whereas 'postmodernity' indicates the sociological, economic and political contours of late capitalism. As the ensuing discussion indicates, I believe that 'the postmodern condition' is more than a crisis of ideas, although the philosophical movements of poststructuralism and deconstruction are significant elements of my analysis.

3 In *Transforming Practice* I distinguish between the two terms 'practical' and 'pastoral' theology (Graham 1996: 11–12). There is still considerable disagreement about appropriate terminology, 'practical' denoting the generic activities of Christian ministry and 'pastoral' the more interpersonal levels of care. I am increasingly moved to favour 'practical theology', given my emphasis on the discipline as the study of Christian *practice*, and to locate pastoral theology as one of a number of practical theologies, but distinguished by its focus on the theory and practice of the human life cycle. This emphasis retains something of the interpersonal nature of pastoral care and maintains some links with conventions of pastoral care as historically conceived. For purposes of clarity, and in keeping with the terminology of this volume, I retain the original nomenclature of *Transforming Practice*.

BIBLIOGRAPHY

Bauman, Z. (1989), *Modernity and the Holocaust*, Cambridge: Polity Press.

Benhabib, S. (1992), *Situating the Self: Gender, Community and Postmodernism in Contemporary Ethics*, Cambridge: Polity Press.

Bernstein, R. J. (1985), *Habermas and Modernity*, Cambridge: Cambridge University Press.

Bhaskar, R. (1989), *Reclaiming Reality: A Critical Introduction to Contemporary Philosophy*, London: Verso.

Bourdieu, P. (1992), *The Logic of Practice*, Cambridge: Polity Press.

Browning, D. S. (1976), *The Moral Context of Pastoral Care*, Philadelphia: Westminster.

Browning, D. S. (1991), *A Fundamental Practical Theology: Descriptive and Strategic Proposals*, Minneapolis: Fortress Press.

Burkhart, J. E. (1983), Schleiermacher's vision for theology. In D. S. Browning (ed.), *Practical Theology: The Emerging Field in Theology, Church, and World*, San Francisco: Harper and Row: 42–60.

Butler, J. (1990), *Gender Trouble: Feminism and the Subversion of Identity*, London: Routledge.

Christ, C. P. (1988), Embodied thinking: reflections on feminist theological method, *Journal of Feminist Studies in Religion* 5, 1: 7–15.

Connell, R. W. (1987), *Gender and Power*, Cambridge: Polity Press.

Davie, G. (1994), *Religion in Britain since 1945: Believing without Belonging*, Oxford: Blackwell.

Davis, C. (1994), *Religion and the Making of Society*, Cambridge: Cambridge University Press.

Eisland, N. (1994), *The Disabled God*, Nashville, Tenn.: Abingdon.

Farley, E. (1983a), Theology and practice outside the clerical paradigm. In D. S. Browning (ed.), *Practical Theology: The Emerging Field in Theology, Church, and World*, San Francisco: Harper and Row: 21–41.

Farley, E. (1983b), *Theologia: The Fragmentation and Unity of Theological Education*, Philadelphia: Fortress Press.

Farley, E. (1996), *Deep Symbols: Their Postmodern Effacement*, Minneapolis: Fortress Press.

Flax, J. (1990), *Thinking Fragments: Psychoanalysis, Feminism, and Postmodernism in the Contemporary West*, Berkeley: University of California Press.

Flax, J. (1993), *Disputed Subjects: Essays on Psychoanalysis, Politics and Philosophy*, London: Routledge.

Gay, P. (1973), *The Enlightenment: An Interpretation. Volume I: The Rise of Modern Paganism*, London: Wildwood House.

Goodliff, P. (1998), *Care in a Confused Climate: Pastoral Care and Postmodern Climate*, London: Darton, Longman & Todd.

Graham, E. L. (1995), *Making the Difference: Gender, Personhood and Theology*, London: Mowbray.

Graham, E. L. (1996), *Transforming Practice*, London: Mowbray.

Graham, E. L., and Halsey, M. (1993), *Life-Cycles: Women and Pastoral Care*, London: SPCK.

Gutiérrez, G. (1988), *A Theology of Liberation*, 2nd edn, Maryknoll, NY: Orbis.

Habermas, J. (1971), *Knowledge and Human Interests*, Boston: Beacon Press.

Habermas, J. (1984), *The Theory of Communicative Action*, vol. 1: *Rationality and Rationalization*, trans. T. McCarthy, Boston: Beacon Press.

Habermas, J. (1989), *The Theory of Communicative Action*, vol. 2: *Lifeworld and System: The Critique of Functionalist Reason*, trans. T. McCarthy, Boston: Beacon Press.

Hall, S., and Gieben, B. (eds) (1992), *Formations of Modernity*, Cambridge: Polity Press.

Hall, S., Held, D., and McGrew, T. (eds) (1992), *Modernity and its Futures*, Cambridge: Polity Press.

Haraway, D. (1991), *Cyborgs, Simians and Women: The Reinvention of Nature*, London: Polity Press.

Harding, S. (1986), *The Science Question in Feminism*, Milton Keynes: Open University Press.

Hiltner, S. (1958), *Preface to Pastoral Theology*, Nashville: Abingdon.

Hodgson, P. C. (1994), *Winds of the Spirit: A Constructive Christian Theology*, London: SCM Press.

Jameson, F. (1991), *Postmodernism: Or the Cultural Logic of Late Capitalism*, London: Verso.

Kearney, R. (1994), *Modern Movements in European Philosophy: Phenomenology, Critical Theory, Structuralism*, 2nd edn, Manchester: Manchester University Press.

Lakeland, P. (1997), *Postmodernity: Christian Identity in a Fragmented Age*, Minneapolis: Fortress.

Lyall, D. (1995), *Counselling in the Pastoral and Spiritual Context*, Buckingham: Open University Press.

Lyotard, J.-F. (1984), *The Postmodern Condition: A Report on Knowledge*, trans. G. Bennington and B. Massumi, Manchester: Manchester University Press.

MacIntyre, A. (1987), *After Virtue: A Study in Moral Theory*, 2nd edn, London: Duckworth.

Maddox, R. L. (1990), The recovery of theology as a practical discipline, *Theological Studies* 51, 4: 650–72.

Milhaven, A. L. (ed.) (1991), *Sermons Seldom Heard: Women Proclaim Their Lives*, New York: Crossroad.

Murphy, N., and McClendon, J. W. (1989), Distinguishing modern and postmodern theologies, *Modern Theology*, 5, 3: 191–214.

Oliver, G. (1991), Counselling, Anarchy and the Kingdom of God. Lingdale Papers 16, Oxford: Clinical Theology Association.

Rahner, K. (1968), *Theology of Pastoral Action*, New York: Herder and Herder.

Reader, J. (1997), *Beyond all Reason: The Limits of Post-Modern Theology*, Cardiff: Aureus.

Schleiermacher, E. F. (1966), *Brief Outline on the Study of Theology*, trans. T. N. Tice, Richmond, VA: John Knox Press.

Segundo, J. L. (1982), *The Liberation of Theology*, 3rd impression, Maryknoll, NY: Orbis.

Stokes, A. (1985), *Ministry after Freud*, New York: Pilgrim Press.

Tracy, D. (1981), *The Analogical Imagination: Christian Theology and the Culture of Pluralism*, London: SCM Press.

Ward, G. (1997), *The Postmodern God*, Oxford: Blackwell Publishers.

Welch, S. D. (1985), *Communities of Resistance and Solidarity: A Feminist Theology of Liberation*, Maryknoll, NY: Orbis.

Wheeler, B. G., and Farley, E. (eds) (1991), *Shifting Boundaries: Contextual Approaches to the Structure of Theological Education*, Louisville, KY: Westminster/John Knox Press.

SOME POINTS FOR FURTHER CONSIDERATION

- What are the challenges that are presented by postmodernity to practical theology? Does Graham's practical theology address these challenges adequately, or should a different approach be adopted?
- What are the strengths and weaknesses of Graham's vision of practical theology?
- In what ways does Graham's theory of practical theology add to, criticize, and differ from other theories, e.g. those of Campbell and Browning (see chapters 4 and 5 above)?

- Is it important that Graham's theory appears to have little interest in the classic resources of the Christian theological tradition? Why? What difference might be made if it did?
- How practical is Graham's vision of practical theology?

FOR FURTHER READING AND EXPLORATION

Further background to the challenges of postmodernity to theology and pastoral practice can be found in references in Graham's text, also in, e.g., Harvey (1989); Ward (1997); Goodliff (1998); Fowler (1996). For Elaine Graham's explorations in practical theology see, e.g., Graham (1995, 1996); also Graham and Halsey (1993). A critique of Graham's basic view of practical theology from a more conservative, realist perspective may be found in Biggar (1998).

7

Interpreting Situations:
An Inquiry into the Nature
of Practical Theology

Edward Farley

Introduction

Edward Farley at the time of writing this paper was Professor of
Theology at Vanderbilt University in the USA. He has written widely
and influentially on the nature of theology, especially as it relates to
the faith community and to practice. Farley's work and that of
pastoral theology have much in common and much to share with
each other. Farley believes that the everyday contemporary experience of ordinary people has theological meaning and significance. It
is for this reason that pastoral or practical theology must pay close
attention to this experience and the particular situations in which it
occurs. Theology should not just be involved in interpreting the past
and texts of the past.

In the extract which follows from Farley's paper "Interpreting
Situations," the author outlines some of the features of the hermeneutical or interpretative task that has to be undertaken in trying
to understand situations. Having demonstrated the complexities of
situational identification and analysis, Farley goes on to claim that
practical theology's fundamental mode is that of "the believer's reflective activity." In this context, practical theology becomes a part of the
religious vocation to interpret which is in no way confined to clergy
or to church matters. While practical theology is an integral part of
theology as a rigorous, academic activity, it is closely linked to the
everyday lives and concerns of ordinary people. It is thus participative

and democratic, requiring wide involvement from all Christians, not just the attention and concerns of an academic or clerical élite.

Farley's perspective considerably broadens the scope and significance of practical theology beyond clerical and academic activity. It also provides a rationale for paying close attention to contemporary experience as a source of theological data, thus complementing the approaches of Hiltner, Browning, and Graham. In addition, it provides some insight into the importance and difficulty of identifying and interpreting particular contemporary situations – part of the stock-in-trade of practical theology. Even so, it might be felt that Farley does not do much to concretize his approach or to provide steps for the interpretative process. These matters may become clearer in the papers by Lartey and Pattison that follow (chapters 8 and 9).

INTERPRETING SITUATIONS: AN INQUIRY INTO THE NATURE OF PRACTICAL THEOLOGY

Interpreting Situations as a Theological Hermeneutic

All human beings exist and act in situations and engage in interpretations of situations. This interpretive dimension of human existence does not cease with faith and with life in the community of faith. On the contrary, faith and the world of faith shape the perspective, the "taken-for-granted stock of knowledge," the weighting of what is important, all of which affect the interpretation of situations. In other words interpreting situations from the viewpoint and in the context of faith does create a special hermeneutic task, differentiable from other hermeneutic or interpretive dimensions of theology.[1] This is the reason why interpreting situations can and should be part of a deliberate and self-conscious educational undertaking, part of the church's lay and clergy education. It can be part of an educational undertaking only because it is an identifiable hermeneutics. There is not space here for an extensive exploration of the hermeneutic task of interpreting situations. Instead, I shall describe several features of such a task, items virtually unavoidable when faith engages in the interpretation of situations in a reflective and disciplined way.

A situation is the way various items, powers, and events in the environment gather together so as to require responses from participants. In this sense, any living, perhaps any actual, entity exists in situations. Situations like reality itself are never static. Living beings, we might say, live in their environments (contexts) in continuing responses to ever-changing, ever-forming situations. Situations can be very brief in time (such as a thunderstorm or a marital quarrel) or very protracted (such as the Western epoch, the nuclear age). They can also be very local (the situation of a specific family) or very global (the ecological situation of our planet). Hence, local and brief situations can occur within broader and more enduring situations. Participants in situations need not be simply individuals. Groups, communities, collectives, societies all exist in situations. Hence, it is equally proper to explore the situation of a congregation, a denomination, or the church universal. What would make such explorations theological interpretations? The following features constitute at best only an exemplary rather than an exhaustive description of a theological hermeneutic of situations.

The first task interpreting a situation faces is simply identifying the situation and describing its distinctive and constituent features. This task may sound neutral and relatively simple. It is not – for the reason that we human beings filter all situations not only through our world views, the taken-for-granted "knowledge" of our social worlds, but also through our idolatries. We are prone, therefore, to assume that the situation of conflict in Central America is "simply" a battle between Communist totalitarianism and the forces of freedom. Such a grid, needless to say, will remove most of the elements in the situation. In other words the components (powers, events, causalities) of a situation are not simply there on the surface. Discerning the components of a situation is not simply taking a photograph. It is an act of serious and even theological self-criticism. Discerning these components is a difficult task for a second reason. The "components" of a situation are not simply discrete items. A situation is not like a basket of fruit, so that discerning the situation is merely enumerating what fruits occupy the basket. The components of a situation are always different *kinds* of things, things of very different *genre*; human beings as individuals, world views, groups of various sorts, the pressure of the past, futurity, various strata of language (writing, imagery, metaphors, myths, etc.), events, sedimented social power. And we could go on and on. "Reading a situation" is the task of identifying these genres of things and discerning how they together constitute the situation.

A second task in the interpretation of situations has to do with the situation's past. Since situations are what occurs in the present, the importance of probing the past of that present may not be self-evident. Human, historical situations do not present to us the whole past. What does persist into situations is the result of repressions in the past of what tradition and its institutions permit to get through. Tradition does hand on the revelatory past – events and narratives that correct, illumine, inspire. At the same time it disguises the origins and even the existence of much of its own content, especially as these contents function to oppress, to establish and maintain power. In pre-Selma America the deep structures of racism operative in American Anglo-Saxon religion and in its churches were virtually invisible. The events and the deep presuppositions that formed and structured the communities of faith in a racist manner were not thematized in the traditioning of the churches. The history of the forming of these structures was "forgotten," repressed in the corporate memory. Certain rationalizations of these deep structures were on the surface and would be appealed to if change were advocated. A similar invisibility and disguise operates now in religious communities with regard to the role and status of women. To grasp the present situation of men and women in the churches calls for more than simply describing present policy. For the present is comprised of and structured by these disguised repressions of the past. And only a certain way of studying the past will uncover these repressions and in so doing will thus uncover something at work in the present.[2]

A third task is to correct the abstraction committed by the focus on a single situation, a situation in its brevity and its specific locality. Situations occur within situations. While it is proper to identify discrete and local situations – for instance, the changing neighborhood of a local congregation – this identification will be distortive if it isolates the situation from more comprehensive and more enduring situations. Larger and longer situations are at work when a neighborhood changes. Such a change may be tied in some way to global economics, to racial migrations, to suburbanization of the middle class. It poses issues of faith's universally human orientation. Hence, a hermeneutic even of a very local situation calls for consideration of intersituational issues, the impingement of other situations on the local situation. It cannot settle for mere internal situational analysis.[3]

A fourth aspect of a hermeneutics of situations may be the most complex of all. We have already seen that theological perspectives and criticism must be operative in all the tasks of discerning the situation. In this fourth task the theological element becomes central. Why is this the case? Let us recall what a situation is, a gathering together of powers and occurrences in the environment so as to evoke responses from the participants. A situation is something we have no choice but to respond to in some way. A situation is not, then, a neutral series of objects, something to be noted. It is a concentration of powers which impinge upon us as individual agents or as communities. The situation thus places certain demands on us. This is the case whether it is a situation of being captured and interrogated by a wartime enemy or shopping at the grocery store. The demand of the situation is multidimensional. One kind of demand occurs when the situation is imperiling, dangerous. Another kind occurs when promise and possibility are offered; another when obligation is required. Because of this demand-response feature of situations, the interpretation of situations includes the task of discerning the situation's demand.

A theological version of this task cannot avoid the insights of its own mythos into the corruption and redemption of human beings. Because of that corruption, human beings shape the demand of the situation according to their idolatries, their absolutized self-interests, their ethnocentrisms, their participations in structures of power. Faith then interprets situations and their demands as always containing this element of corruption and redemption. Situations pose to human beings occasions for idolatry and for redemption. The discernment of this dimension of the demand-response is at the very heart of a theological hermeneutic of situations.

Practical Theology as a Hermeneutic of Vocation

In the approach being explored here, practical theology as *theology* is one of the dimensions of the believer's reflective life and wisdom. Does this view of its primary location and reality dislocate it from education, from pedagogical undertakings, from the seminary curriculum? Such a consequence would be unfortunate since it would place the believer's (or church leader's) reflective life beyond the reach of the rigorous disciplining that ordered learning (education) at its best can effect. If this is so, then practical theology must be relocated not only in the pedagogies of clergy education but the pedagogies of church education. In other words the church is responsible to conduct an education which thematizes for the believer what it means to interpret, respond to, and live in situations.[4]

Does the notion of a practical theology for the believer as such eliminate the "practical theology" of clergy education, the pedagogies of preaching, education, and the like? The question uncovers a theme we have no time to explore, the theme of another intrinsic dimension of theological reflection. The reason this is a dimension and not an occasional response is that the life and interpretations of faith do not occur in general but in connection with special responsibilities. While this is not limited to the ordained ministry, church education in the past has so emphasized the educational prerequisites for its ordained leadership that this dimension has virtually been restricted to clergy. The specialized leadership of the church does constitute a situation in itself, a situation that calls for theological interpretation, and whose activities (pastoral care, church administration, and so forth) call for interpretation. Here we have "practical theology" in its more traditional sense. In the framework of this analysis practical theology has a special form because it addresses, thematizes vocation as a situation. Because ministry is itself a situation, it presupposes and needs practical theology in its fundamental sense of a hermeneutic of situations, but moves beyond that to the special requirements of the vocational situation.

What would a practical theology of ministry look like? First, it would teach practical theology as a moment of theological, reflective understanding, not isolated from but connected with the total structure of theological understanding. Second, it would include some attempt to teach practical theology itself, that is, the various hermeneutical components of the interpretation of situations. Third, since church leadership is itself a situation, it would attempt a practical theology of church leadership. Fourth, it would focus on designated areas of the situations of ministry, including preaching, education, pastoral care, and so forth. It would do this *as practical theology*. That is, it would place these activities in relation to other situations so that the theology of practical theology will include the correction of parochial and isolated approaches to these activities. Finally, it would acknowledge the distinctive and peculiar character of these activities as they reflect a double reference to action. First, each one itself is an area of action, thus, for instance, worship and liturgy. Second, each activity is focused beyond itself on areas of churchly and worldly action. It is because of this twofold action referent that the theology of each activity requires practical theology, a hermeneutic that uncovers typical structures in situations of action.

In most past and present literatures it is assumed that practical theology names one of the theological "sciences." If practical theology's fundamental mode is the believer's reflective activity, is it precluded from being a science? I have argued that this basic mode does not preclude but in fact calls for pedagogical modes of practical theology. Does it also call for or permit a scholarly mode, a mode of being a "science"? In this form the question is not very clear. If we are asking whether practical theological reflection can itself take on the character of a science, the answer is negative. The question of practical theology's relation to scholarship arises not in conjunction with its fundamental mode but in conjunction with the pedagogies which may shape and discipline that mode. The question is, accordingly, does the *teaching* of practical theology, including various thematizations of the components of practical theological reflection in interrelated areas of action, require scholarly discipline? I think the answer to this question is affirmative. What this means is that particular interpretive responses to situations can have the character of self-conscious and rigorous inquiry, can appropriate sciences and the product of sciences (linguistic, social-scientific, philosophical, etc.), and the result can be integrated into or related to other such rigorous undertakings.

What are we to say about the status of the specific disciplines of practical theology which still persist in the present form from the nineteenth-century consensus? Are homiletics, liturgics, pastoral care, and the like sciences? They seem to have their scientific status as the result of the impetus toward the independence characteristic of academic fields. Hence, they lay claim to literatures, nomenclatures, methods, professional organizations; in short, the social and formal marks of disciplines of higher education. The cost of this development has been high – clericalization and severation from the basic mode of theological reflection, independence of method from other moments or dimensions of theology, isolation even from other areas of action. My inclination at present is to say that homiletics, pastoral care, and the like name valid areas of clergy education. The problem consists not so much in their existence as pedagogical areas but in their self-understanding as separate sciences. These areas of pedagogy will be more true to themselves if they rediscover how they are rooted in the basic mode of theological reflection and how their own situations should be related to other areas. In other words they need to recover themselves as practical theology. Even if their character as independent theological disciplines is diminished by this recovery, they need not lose their rigor and integrity as areas of pedagogy that make use of scholarly resources. On the contrary, the exercise of practical theological corrective and contextualization may enable new levels of rigor and reality reference.

In conclusion, I have interpreted the problem of practical theology as the problem of correcting the clericalization of the traditional view without a total discreditation of all past correctives. Further, there appears to be a gulf opening up between the two major modern correctives of the traditional view, a gulf between churchly and praxis approaches. This is an unhappy choice because the one finds a way to focus theology on church and clerical life but praxis as such is not in view. The other finds a way to focus theology on praxis but a theology of church situationality and ministry seems to be absent. I have proposed that there is a dimension of theological reflection and understanding itself that is focused directly on situations and calls for a hermeneutics of situations. Situations are its context and object. This does not, however, preclude or discredit a practical theology of church and the activities of church leadership. These are situations in which the believer as (ordained) church leader takes responsible action and as such they are valid areas for the exercise of this hermeneutic. When it is so exercised, however, it should not be the traditional isolated treatment of these activities, but a placing of them in relation to other situations. The following seven theses summarize the argument.

(1) Practical theology is a dimension of theological reflection and understanding and therefore is all-pervasive in the faith community and not restricted to a field of clergy education.

(2) Practical theology is that dimension of theology in which reflection is directed at a living situation in which the believer or corporate entity is involved.

(3) When response to and interpretation of a situation is self-consciously responsible, it can be assisted by a hermeneutic of existing in a situation. Traditional and contemporary hermeneutics have focused primarily on understanding as it is related to and facilitated by texts, with the situation secondary to that. In practical theological hermeneutics the object of interpretation is the situation itself.

(4) A hermeneutic of situations will function to uncover the distinctive contents of the situation, will probe its repressed past, will explore its relation to other situations with which it is intertwined, and will also explore the "demand" of the situation through consideration of corruption and redemption.

(5) The clergy activities of the traditional version of practical theology are, as situations, valid and important candidates for practical theological interpretation as are the situations of the believer and churchly communities. A practical theology of these activities and environments will correct their traditional pedagogical isolation through a special hermeneutics of these situations.

(6) Practical theology like other dimensions of theology can and should be taught both in the church at large and in schools for clergy education.

(7) Practical theology as a dimension of theology and as an educational undertaking can have a rigorous character and should be supported when appropriate by the resources, tools, and disciplines of scholarship.

NOTES

1   For a beginning attempt to turn the concept of interpretation away from the text to action, although in this case on the model of text interpretation, see Paul Ricoeur, "The Model of Text: Meaningful Action Considered as Text," in *Hermeneutics and the Human Sciences*, ed. and trans. John B. Thompson (Cambridge: Cambridge University Press, 1981). Cf. also Charles Winquist's "practical hermeneutics." While he does not explicitly call for interpretation to address all kinds of situations, his approach could be consistent with that. The reason is that he sees ministry as something that facilitates interpretation in others, the interpretation being something which attends conversion and is sensitive to the depth dimension of occurrences (see *Practical Hermeneutics: A Revised Agenda for the Ministry* [Chico, Calif.: Scholars Press, 1980]).

2   The reader may recognize in these comments on tradition's obliviousness and forgetfulness Martin Heidegger's concept of *Destruktion* (*Being and Time* [London: SCM Press, 1962], 41ff), Metz's "dangerous memory," Nietzsche's genealogical method, and Derrida's deconstruction. While these concepts are not identical, they all refer to an "archaeological" dismantling of tradition for the purpose of exposing what that tradition hides in its very act of transmission. For a clear exposition of this dismantling see Sharon Welch, *Communities of Resistance and Solidarity: A Feminist Theology of Liberation* (Maryknoll, N.Y.: Orbis Books, 1985), chapter 3.

3   One of the problems with the criticisms and corrections of practical theology's parochialism is the generation of new parochialism. A situation is corrected by appeal to another pressing situation. Thus the corrective takes on the character of an "ism." To limit action to the self's situation is narcissism and privatism. To correct that by appeal to political action minus the self-reference becomes heteronomy and collectivism. To correct by appeal to the church acting in and on itself becomes ecclesiasticism. To correct by sole emphasis on the clergy and

its activities becomes clericalism. Perhaps "isms" are intrinsic to serious criticism, the game polemics must play. But analysis of situations in their intersections and interdependence may correct these correctives.

4 This statement assumes a conviction about church education that is anything but universal. The conviction is that church education is theological education. This view repudiates the distribution of subject matter such that theology is assigned to clergy education and something else is done by the church. If theology is in its primary mode a reflective and dialectical understanding evoked by the Christian mythos, then it is not only something which can and should attend the life of the believer as such, but its formation in the educational process should be all-pervasive in the church. This would mean that the church would offer a theological education in ways possible and appropriate to its particular environment, hence would teach all the fundamental dimensions of theological understanding: a hermeneutics of tradition, normative struggles with truth, and hermeneutics of praxis and situationality. In other words, it would teach practical theological understanding. See Edward Farley, "Can Church Education Be Theological Education?" *Theology Today* (Summer 1985).

Some Points for Further Consideration

- What are the main strengths and attractive features of Farley's approach to practical theology?
- Has Farley got the relationship between practical theology and other kinds of theology right?
- What does Farley add to the understanding of the nature of practical theology that is evident in other papers in this Part of the *Reader*?
- How practical is Farley's notion of situational interpretation? What problems might arise in trying to undertake situational hermeneutics?
- Is Farley right to put interpretation at the heart of practical theology? What might be the advantages and drawbacks of this emphasis?

For Further Reading and Exploration

For more on the interpretation of contemporary situations in practical theology and pastoral practice, see e.g. Capps (1984, 1990) and

Gerkin (1991, 1997). More on the educational work of developing practical wisdom in practical theology may be found, e.g., in Hunter (1990) and Patton (1990). Farley's thought can be explored in, e.g., Farley (1983b), which presents a vision of theology closely related to the practice of religious faith and the communities of faith.

8

Practical Theology as a Theological Form

Emmanuel Lartey

Introduction

A Ghanaian theologian who has trained and worked in England, Emmanuel Lartey teaches pastoral studies at the University of Birmingham as well as being chair of the British and Irish Association for Practical Theology. Lartey is particularly concerned in his published work with issues of worldwide intercultural relations and dialogue, Black theology in Britain and the relationship between counseling and pastoral care.

"Practical Theology as a Theological Form" sets out and criticizes some of the main models and methods for theological activity and reflection that are presently used in practical theology. These are the branch approach, which regards practical theology as a branch of theological knowledge; the process approach, which emphasizes method; the "way of being and doing" approach, that emphasizes the form of theological engagement; and his own "pastoral cycle" approach, which attempts to overcome some of the defects of the previous three.

This very clear, short paper should help to clarify and locate some of the issues and methods that have been raised in previous papers. It also provides some clear pointers as to how to proceed in practical theology. Perhaps the main limitation of Lartey's pastoral cycle method, and of many like it, is that it does not really illustrate the outcome of the reflective process. It could be asked: What difference does this complex, demanding process of theological activity make in theory and in practice? Maybe it is difficult to see and specify results, but practical theology will always be vulnerable to the criticism of impracticality or uselessness unless it can really demonstrate what it achieves and that it is not simply going around in ever-complexifying methodological circles.

PRACTICAL THEOLOGY AS A THEOLOGICAL FORM

The pluriformity and ambiguity of practical theology are at once its highest promise and its greatest pitfall. In this paper I wish to keep alive the importance of critical questioning of the methods and models we use in the varied exercises in which we engage in the practice of practical theology. I will be using broad brush strokes to map out areas of discourse and practice. The aim is to enable practical theologians to locate, or else, distance themselves from specific methods or models in practice today. It is necessary to indicate that this is being done from a particular social context, namely teaching a university course which focuses on an area of practical theology. We all 'inhabit' various social locations and engage in our praxis from specific social contexts. The influences on any person from within, as well as without, their social context, are many and varied. This needs to be recognized to minimize the risks of universalizing the particular or, equally heinously, particularizing the universal.

Four main interest groups appear to have been most taken by the possibilities and dangers of practical theology. These are those engaged in the study and practice of (1) ministry (specifically Liturgy and Homiletics); (2) pastoral care and counselling; (3) religious education; and (4) ethics. At times, one or other of these interest groups have sought to claim exclusive rights to the term. Each may legitimately be recognized as engaged in a form of practical theology.

There are a number of ways in which practical theology has been characterized, engaged in, or understood (sometimes by people other than those actually seeking to practise it). In my view these can be categorized into *three* distinctively different streams, although at times they flow into each other and exert relative influence upon each other. What is common to all three is a concern to relate faith (or doctrine) with practice (or life) and to do so in ways that are relevant and useful.

The Branch Approach

The first I would like to call the *branch* approach. Here practical theology is seen as a branch of theological science (or art). One of the clearest exponents of this view was Friedrich Schleiermacher, who used the image of a tree with philosophical theology being the roots, historical theology the trunk and practical theology being the branches.[1] The emphasis is upon *content* of a discipline and the method adopted is one of applicationism.

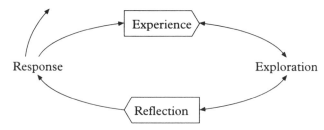

Figure 1

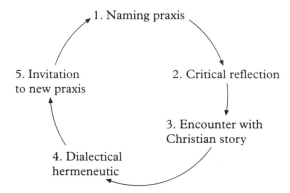

Figure 2

Practical theology has to do with 'church government', or else the 'church's action' and is derived by applying doctrinal (philosophical and/or biblical) and historical formulations to the task of church management.[2,3]

The Process Approach

The second could be termed a *process* approach. Here emphasis is laid on *method*. The main idea is to generate viable and workable methods which will enable practical theologians to deliver their goods. Tillich's method of correlation is an example of this. Here existential questions are correlated with Christian symbols which provide the answers to the existential questions. Tracy's 'revised correlational method' or 'critical correlation' seeks to refine Tillich's uni-directional question and answer method, yet offers an approach which could also be described as focusing on method.[4] Groome's 'shared Christian praxis' method of Christian formation which draws inspiration from the work of Farley, Whitehead and Browning (illustrated in figure 2), together with the various 'Pastoral Cycles' (e.g. Laurie Green's), diagrammatically represented in figures 1 and 3, would fall in the same category.[5,6]

The 'Way of Being and Doing' Approach

A third approach is one I would describe as a *form* of theological engagement. Here practical theology is understood not primarily as a branch of theological knowledge, nor simply as a method of generating theologically informed action, but rather as offering us *a way of 'doing theology' and being theologians.*[7] This approach attempts to examine the content of faith and practice. It asks questions about what the contents of our faith are, realizing that tradition, context and experience (the 'three elements in the practical theology equation') shape us in such a way that there are very many different forms of equally valid Christian faith.[8] It seeks to be reflective and thoughtful. It is concerned that faith is made manifest in practice, taking seriously the potentially transformative nature of faith and/or experience. As such it is concerned about what is being done in the name of faith. It is therefore praxis oriented. It raises methodological questions and realizes that it is important to have and use the right tools for any job. In addition, it asks questions about *who* it is that are engaged in the theological tasks, what the social location of the persons are, *who benefits from what is done*, who is *excluded* by the way things are done and who are *oppressed* by it. It asks contextual and experiential questions and challenges historical formulations in a quest for more inclusive and relevant forms. In doing so, issues of social ethics, spirituality – both personal and corporate, as well as doctrine and teaching are addressed. Moreover, it is a corporate, collaborative endeavour which listens to many different voices. It is a way of being theologians rather than a knowledge of a speciality or sub-discipline in theology. Various forms of liberation theology, such as feminist theologies and Black theologies, drawing inspiration from the Latin American experience constitute good examples of this approach. Farley has argued that this approach has historically been marginalized by the overvaluing of rationalism and the quest for scientific scholarship.[9]

Critique

Each of these approaches has inherent weaknesses. The *branch* approach undervalues the contribution which practical theology might make to the other forms of theology. It also perpetuates the 'second-class' citizenship status of practical theology by making it only and always a derived discipline dependent on knowledge and theory from the other 'more solid' fields of study. The *process* cycles may over-value method at the expense of content. They run the risk of superficiality and indeed, scavenging in various disciplines (including theological ones) in the hope of finding appropriate themes for the reflection stage. The *way of being and doing* approaches may become anti-intellectual and thus cut themselves off from an important source of critical life skills. They may over-estimate the importance of context and thus end up in a kind of corporate solipsism.

In order to address the question of how practical theology might be engaged in a University Department of Theology, I wish to present my own

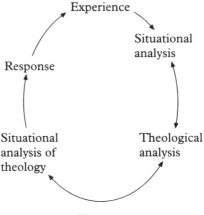

Figure 3

'pastoral cycle' suggesting some of the joys and pitfalls involved for me in my current context.

There are five phases in the process as illustrated in figure 3. I seek to point out and demonstrate that the whole process may be seen as theological and not simply the points within it labelled as such. The process normally begins with some form of concrete *experience*. This might be in the form of a placement within a hospital, hostel for homeless people, hospice, community action project, prison or counselling centre. The main point is that it involves an encounter with people in the reality of life's experiences. This phase is incarnational and suggests that practical theology must continually seek to be close to people's real experience of life. It is here that the God and 'Father' of our Lord Jesus Christ is encountered.

My preferred designation for the second phase of the activity is *'situational' analysis*. This is to indicate that it involves social and psychological analysis but also includes other perspectives on the situation encountered. It is multi-perspectival rather than inter-disciplinary, in that it realizes that it cannot completely encompass the complexity of the various necessary disciplines. What it can and must do is to bring selected perspectives from relevant disciplines to bear on the situation, in the hope of gaining a clearer understanding of what is going on. It is based on the understanding of creation which affirms that the God of all truth can be encountered in various disciplines and glimpsed through different perspectives. It also recognizes that human persons are at best limited in their perceptions but that this should not deter them from the attempt to 'see clearly'. One of the best ways, in theological terms, of gaining clear sight is *collective seeing* or *comparing visions*.

The *third* stage is the point at which faith perspectives are allowed to question the encounter as well as the situational analysis. Here the issues are: 'What questions and analyses arise from my faith concerning what I have experienced and the other analyses of it?'; 'How has Christian thought approached the issues raised?'; 'Is there a prophetic insight which may be brought to bear on the situation?' The engagement here is both personal and with the traditions of Christian faith.

In the *fourth* phase it is my faith perspectives that are the subject of questioning by the encounter and the situational analysis. The God of all creation may in reality be 'standing at the door knocking' through what has been encountered.[10] Experience and situational analysis may offer more adequate reformulations of Christian doctrine. In the *fifth* activity I, together with the group within which the whole process is set, explore what response options are available to me in the light of what has gone before and make decisions as to the preferred one. Here the person-in-community recognizes and acts responsibly in the light of the vision and the re-visioning encountered.

What is missing from the cycle, though not from the group activities on the courses each year, are the celebrations, the social and at times sporting events which are often very creative points of engagement. Especially since the groups are always international and multi-cultural.

Concerning the joys and especially the problems of maintaining a university course of study which reflects this process, in the current national climate, volumes could be written. It is perhaps sufficient to say that what is aimed at in practical theology is a relevant, meaningful, methodologically appropriate and viable form of theological activity which may be personally and socially transformative, while also being uplifting and, above all, great fun.

NOTES

1 For a clear presentation and discussion of this see J. Burkhart, 'Schleiermacher's vision for theology', in D. Browning (ed.), *Practical Theology: The emerging field in theology, church and world*. Harper and Row 1983, pp. 42–57.

2 See F. Schleiermacher, [J. O. Duke and H. Stone (eds)], *Christian Caring: Selections from 'Practical Theology'*. Fortress Press 1988; a recent critique of this is F. Woggon, 'Deliberate activity as an art for (almost) everyone: Friedrich Schleiermacher on practical theology', *Journal of Pastoral Care* 48, Spring 1994, pp. 3–13.

3 As pastoral theology is defined by A. Dyson in A. Campbell (ed.), *A Dictionary of Pastoral Care*. SPCK 1987, p. 201.

4 See D. Tracy, *Blessed Rage for Order: The new pluralism in theology*. Seabury Press 1975, esp. pp. 32–63.

5 As outlined clearly in T. Groome, 'Theology on our feet: A revisionist pedagogy for healing the gap between Academia and Ecclesia', in L. Mudge and J. Poling (eds), *Formation and Reflection: The promise of practical theology*. Fortress Press 1987, pp. 55–78.

6 L. Green, *Let's Do Theology*. Mowbray 1990.

7   Latin American liberation theology, broadly speaking, offers a particu-
    larly good example of this. See, for example, J. Segundo, *The Liberation
    of Theology*. Orbis Books 1976. Laurie Green's approach draws on this.
    See *Let's Do Theology*. Mowbray 1990, pp. 24–41.
8   Mudge and Poling, *Formation and Reflection*, p. xxxii.
9   Farley's theology as *habitus* or 'wisdom for living'. See E. Farley, *Theologia:
    The fragmentation and unity of theological education*. Fortress Press 1983.
10 See Revelation 3.20.

SOME POINTS FOR FURTHER CONSIDERATION

- Which of the forms of practical theology that Lartey describes is
  most appealing or useful from your perspective? Why?
- What are the strengths and weaknesses of Lartey's own pastoral
  cycle approach?
- Can any practical or theoretical problems with trying to undertake
  the pastoral cycle approach be identified?
- Is Lartey's claim that his is a thoroughgoing theological approach
  in terms of assumptions, method, and content justified? What
  theological criticisms might be made of his model and approach?

FOR FURTHER READING AND EXPLORATION

Many approaches to practical theological method and reflection
can be found in this Reader. See also the references in the article
and, e.g., Ballard and Pritchard (1996), Patton (1990, 1993). For
Emmanuel Lartey's own writing, see, e.g., Lartey (1987, 1997). For
a defense of practical or pastoral theology as a "useless" aesthetic
activity that informs practice but also stimulates the imagination,
see Pattison with Woodward (1994).

9

Some Straw for the Bricks: A Basic Introduction to Theological Reflection

STEPHEN PATTISON

INTRODUCTION

The author of this paper, Stephen Pattison, is a researcher in practical theology at Cardiff University. Before spending a decade conducting practical theological investigation outwith the religious and theological community in the "secular" realm of health and social welfare, Pattison taught pastoral studies at the University of Birmingham. It was here, then, that the paper reproduced here was written. Pattison found that students were keen to get started on theological reflection in practice but that the rather abstract theories of, e.g., Campbell or Browning (see chapters 4 and 5 above) did not give them much to go on to get started.

Adopting and adapting ideas of critical correlation, interpretation, dialogue, and hermeneutics, Pattison suggests the model of "critical conversation" as a fairly simple way of trying to understand and think through the complex relationship between situations and theological and other ideas and theories. Pattison argues that people who wish to engage in creative theological reflection might see themselves as being engaged in a three-way "conversation" or dialogue between their own ideas, beliefs, feelings, and perceptions; the beliefs, assumptions, and perceptions provided by the Christian tradition; and the contemporary situation which is being considered.

Pattison's approach has limitations, as he admits. It allows a good deal of subjectivity and is vague about the limits of theological reflection and its relationship to the theological tradition. This approach to theological reflection is unlikely to produce universally valid truths and doctrines, should such things be desired. Furthermore, it is mostly concerned with thinking about situations and ideas rather than with, say, feelings or actions which are also important in understanding and influencing life. None the less the paper is included here as a way in which people might start to become actual participants in and practitioners of practical theology.

SOME STRAW FOR THE BRICKS: A BASIC INTRODUCTION TO THEOLOGICAL REFLECTION

> No straw is provided for your servants and still the cry is, 'Make bricks!'
>
> (Exodus 5: 16)

Students undertaking placements on pastoral studies courses are bidden with monotonous regularity to indulge in theological reflection. This activity has a mystic flavour to it, for the teachers who demand theological reflection for the most part find it very difficult to say what it is that they are looking for. Hence the quotation from Exodus; students are being asked to make bricks without straw. The purpose of this paper is to provide one particular *entree* to theological reflection which students I have worked with seem to find helpful. I want to suggest that a good starting point for this activity is the model of a *critical conversation* which takes place between the Christian tradition, the student's own faith presuppositions and a particular contemporary situation. This model is not fundamentally original, it is drawn from the writings of many pastoral theologians whose work can be consulted if more about its background is required. Nor is the model an exhaustive one; it has drawbacks and limitations which will become apparent to some extent below. Its value, it seems to me, comes from the fact that it is simple and is a starting point for what is inevitably a very complex and demanding activity if pursued at a high level. I will come back to the model itself in a short space, but first I want to make some preliminary remarks about theology and the value of theological reflection.

Theology

The word 'theology' seems to frighten people. One suspects that the images that it brings to their minds are those of serried ranks of learned tomes written by elderly and authoritative men full of incomprehensible profundity which bear no relation to present day reality or to their own situation. Ordinary people (and most theological students are fairly ordinary) fail to see the connection between this kind of theology, which is in fact a very particular kind of theology, and the world in which they live. They most certainly feel unable to compete in the academic theological arena, and if theological reflection means doing this, they feel utterly at a loss. It is this kind of feeling which leads to people either failing to relate theology and reality at all so that belief and practice are kept in separate boxes, or to heroic and pious attempts to 'apply' the wisdom of the tomes to a reality which seems to contradict it at all points. At its worst, this can be an exercise in dull improbability. The word 'theology' must be set free from dusty academic bondage.

The first thing to be proposed, then, is that theology should be seen primarily as *contemporary enquiry*. Judging from the books in libraries, it is easy to come to believe that theology is about restating the verities of the past in ways which make them inaccessible in the present. It is very unfortunate if this impression prevails, for it is a superficial one. Most theology books, however obscure, arise from someone wanting to gain a real understanding of a question which seems to them of contemporary relevance for themselves or others. At the bottom of it all, what unites all theology is its quest for adequate and true responses to the realities of human and religious experience. Good theology is dynamic, searching and open-ended. Some of the most influential theology ever written has been a response to urgent pastoral situations (e.g. that of St Augustine) and it has been characterized by a willingness to really try and listen to and understand present realities rather than to regurgitate the answers of the past. The moral of this is that anyone who in any way tries to understand their situation in the light of faith in the contemporary world is doing theology. You do not have to start doing theological reflection on experience, if you have any questions in your mind at all relating to faith, you are doing theological reflection already! That is not to say, however, that you might not become better at it and find more adequate ways of articulating it.

Theology is active enquiry, not just historical research or intellectual gymnastics. But it is probably as well not to talk of theology, but of theo*logies* in the plural. One thing that worries people when they come to theological reflection is the thought that they might not be approaching it the right way, that they are not conforming to the norm of doing theology. The fact is that there is no formal norm. There are all sorts of ways of doing

theology which are so different that it sometimes seems that the only thing
that unites them is a common claim to be talking about God and religious
experience. Theologies work at many different levels and with very different aims, methods and concerns. In universities, for example, some theologians are mainly devoted to the history of the faith tradition or to studying
the theology of the Bible; they use historical and linguistic methods. Others
enter into dialogue with philosophy, while some see their activity as the
intellectual ordering of the faith experience of the contemporary church at
a high level of abstraction. A few study the ethical implications of the
Christian faith and others try to explore the theoretical and theological
aspects of pastoral care. Even within 'academic' theology, then, there is
considerable diversity; often scholars in one academic discipline have only a
very hazy understanding of what their colleagues are doing. Within and
outside the academic environment a thousand theological flowers blossom.
Readers may have heard of process theology, existential theology, fundamentalist theology, black theology, liberation theology, narrative theology
and others. The point is that all these theologies have very different features
and methods. The moral for the student is that if theologians are so different in their approaches and cannot agree on what theology is, there can be
no one right way of doing theology and perhaps one's own way is as good
as anyone else's. It has its own validity and usefulness within one's own
situation.

The Value of Theological Reflection

I hope I have now said enough to de-sensitize the anxious student about
the use of the word 'theology'. But I now need to demonstrate why it is
worth while to become involved in theological reflection on practical contemporary situations. The first, and perhaps best reason for theological
reflection is that it is interesting and enjoyable! To relate faith and practice
in a dialogue is a learning experience and like all good educational experience it should expand the person who does it and lead them to richer
perceptions of reality and of their own faith and thinking. This is not,
however, a kind of luxury optional extra for the leisured; developing new
perceptions and insights, or seeing old ones in a new light, actually has
practical significance. The way we perceive situations determines how we
will behave in relation to them and the sort of priorities and types of action
we might adopt. Theological reflection deepens our experience of the world
and of our own assumptions and so stops us from making unwarranted
assumptions which may be false. It also has the effect of ensuring that faith
and religious ideas do not become encapsulated and cut off from our
experience of everyday life. A constant criticism of religious people and
institutions in secular society has been that faith is kept separate from the

rest of life. Theological reflection ensures that faith remains relevant to experience and is not just kept in a separate box which is only opened on Sundays in the setting of a church community. Lastly, this activity helps to stimulate people to further theological enquiry and may make reading theological books worth the effort. Once one begins to realize that many of the questions which come out of contemporary experience have been addressed by religious thinkers in the past, there is an incentive to turn to the tools and resources of 'academic' theology for the sake of real illumination about the present day rather than simply because an essay has been set or a tutor thinks one should do so. Theological reflection on experience can make both experience and theology come alive in a new way.

The Method of Critical Conversation

As I said at the beginning, the model I want to commend as a starting point for theological reflection is that of the critical conversation. The basic idea here is that the student should imagine herself as being involved in a three way conversation between (a) her own ideas, beliefs, feelings, perceptions and assumptions, (b) the beliefs, assumptions and perceptions provided by the Christian tradition (including the Bible) and (c) the contemporary situation which is being examined. For the sake of concreteness it may be helpful to personify these elements and imagine them as people who may or may not know each other to a greater or lesser extent who come together in a room to have a verbal conversation. Each participant in the conversation will have questions to ask of the others (I shall come to the specific questions later) and each will need to get to know the others.

This model of conversation has several advantages:

1   A conversation is a concrete event which is a familiar part of everyday life even if the participants in the conversation of theological reflection are not real people.

2   The personification of participants allows the identification of starting points from different perspectives and allows heuristic clarity.

3   A real conversation is a living thing which evolves and changes.

4   The participants in a conversation are changed, both by what they learn and by the process of conversing with other participants.

5   Participation in a conversation implies a willingness to listen and be attentive to other participants.

6   Conversations allow participants to discover things about their interlocutors which they never knew before; all participants end up seeing themselves and others from new angles and in a different light.

7   The concept of conversation does not necessarily imply that participants
    end up agreeing at every point or that the identity of one overrides the
    character of the others.

8   Conversations are often difficult and demand considerable effort because
    participants start from very different assumptions and understandings.
    Considerable energy may have to be expended to try and understand
    the relevance or importance of another participant's contribution.

9   An important part of conversation may be that of silence, disagreement
    or lack of communication. This element is very important in theological
    reflection; many people suppose that if they understand the Christian
    tradition properly, they can then 'apply' its eternal truths easily to
    contemporary reality. In practice, such thinking often leads to the
    creation of dubious connections which tend to have a pious and unreal-
    istic tenor. Much more honest, perhaps, to acknowledge that there are
    enormous gaps between some situations in the contemporary world
    and the religious tradition but to maintain the belief that theological
    reflection understood as active enquiry is as much about exploring and
    living with gaps as well as with similarities.

10 Lastly, conversations can be conducted at many different levels from
    that of preliminary acquaintance to that of longterm dialogue. As par-
    ticipants get to know each other, their views of each other and of
    relevant factors in relation to each other will change and evolve to
    become more complex and sophisticated. This does not, however,
    devalue the perceptions and insights gained on the first and perhaps
    naive preliminary encounter, though later these may be radically modi-
    fied and relativized.

If what has been said so far about theological reflection as critical conversation seems to complicate that activity rather than simplifying it, it might
make more sense if it were explicated in the following more abstract way.
The notion of critical conversation between the student, Christian tradition
and the empirical situation endeavours to make students conscious of their
own presuppositions, the resources of the Christian tradition and the realities of a practical situation in such a way that each modifies and learns from
the others in a dynamic interaction. This dialogical process occurs anyway
in everyday life, the conversation model simply shapes and sharpens it.

Questions for Critical Conversation

The critical conversation which constitutes theological reflection is a structured and semi-formal one in that it proceeds via certain questions which
the participants might ask of one another. One useful set of questions for

opening up theological reflection can be derived from the creeds. Rather than taking the creeds as factual propositions, it is possible to frame questions from their basic shape. Christian creeds implicitly answer the questions, Where did we come from and why are we here? (creation), What is the purpose of human existence? (teleology), What stops us from attaining perfection and what would change that situation? (evil/salvation), In what or whom do we put our trust and what do we hope for? (eschatology). These are profoundly religious questions, but it will be noted that they can be asked of completely secular situations, thus allowing creative comparison and critique. They can also be asked of the individual student participating in reflection on practical situations. Thus they provide an opening for commencing comparison and dialogue which is in tune with the concept of theology as an interrogative and enquiring activity rather than a matter of handing down the truths of the past. Other series of questions derived from different sources might be asked. For example, the question, 'How would Jesus react to this situation or this way of perceiving?' could be posed. Again this would act as a critical starting point against which to assess and compare the relative positions and perceptions of participants in a particular critical conversation. Perhaps it would lead to a situation being seen differently, perhaps to a person seeing his or her faith differently. Another place to start might be with the difficult questions posed by a situation which seemed utterly alien to religious belief and practice. In many ways, the starting point does not matter, the important thing is to find a way into critical conversation which ensures that tradition, contemporary reality and a student's assumptions are all questioned in turn by each other.

An Example

At this point, it might be helpful to exemplify this approach at work. Imagine a student minister going on placement to the Marriage Guidance Council. She goes with a variety of assumptions including the ideas that marriage is inviolable and that ministers should always encourage people to stay together under any circumstances. At the Marriage Guidance Council she may find some aspects which seem to her to affirm some of her presuppositions derived from faith, for example, the importance of trying to help people in practical ways and to mediate love through what counsellors call 'unconditional positive regard'. At the same time, however, she may find things which question her faith and the weight of the Christian tradition, for example, the idea that counsellors should not give direct advice and that clients should be left to make up their own minds on possible courses of action, including divorce. This will make her have to review her own beliefs; should she now leave the Marriage Guidance Council and condemn its ethics because they are not in line with the majority Christian tradition, or should she modify her previous convictions in the light of the fact that telling people what to do and condemning them seems to communicate to them a message of hate and rejection rather than of love and acceptance, things which she might believe to be supreme Christian virtues? Mutual questioning of this kind forms the stuff of theological reflection and even this brief vignette shows how potentially intriguing and challenging it can be. The student mentioned might proceed to analyse the Marriage Guidance Council using some of the questions suggested above. What would she find were the implicit ideas of human nature and purpose, of creation, the fall, redemption, salvation and eschatology which are assumed by this organization? How do these fit in with insights derived from the Christian tradition and from the student's own personal experience and faith?

Limitations

I hope I have now said enough to interest students in the value of theological reflection and to show how it might begin to work using one very simple model. It would be wrong, however, to end without saying something about the limitations of this method. These are manifold. First, it could be argued that asking questions and engaging in critical conversation is not an adequate way of conceiving theological reflection. Surely, it might be said, theology is about providing eternally valid answers and applying these to everyday life today. It is certainly true that the mutually interrogative method I have outlined tends to lead to further questions rather than solid answers an so it is something of a *via negative*, i.e. a way of getting at truth indirectly. I would suggest that this is a good way to proceed because it avoids giving slick and unrealistic answers in complex modern situations, it has the advantage of showing up some of the weaknesses and drawbacks of theological and other assumptions, it is in line with the fundamentally exploratory nature of theology and also with the educational presupposition that students need to find their own answers to situations if those answers are to hold any lasting value. This is not to deny the long-term important constructive task of creating and evaluating systematically theological beliefs and systems, but simply to relegate it to a subordinate position for the time being.

A further criticism concerns the depth of the critical conversation. It is all very well to suggest that a dialogue can be entered into between the student, a contemporary situation and the theological tradition at anything from the most superficial level. But it is, of course, true that deepening conversation might demand extensive research of a fairly academic kind into the social sciences or the sources and tools of Christian theology. I do not want to rebut this point. My hope is that those who practise theological reflection will get drawn into the complexities of analysis using the tools and insights of secular and theological disciplines in order to construct a more nuanced critique and world view.

It would also rightly be pointed out that the use of this method could lead to a great deal of superficial analysis and opinion which was then grandiosely dignified by being called theology. This is indeed a real possibility; it is certainly true that most theological reflections will only be able to deal with some aspects of situations, traditions and assumptions rather than being comprehensive. My only real defence here is the pragmatic one of holding that it is a good thing for people to start theological reflection at their own level and then it might be hoped that their analysis will become more sophisticated. I would, however, want to resist strongly the idea that only when people are highly educated in the classical, literary-based theological tradition should they be encouraged to begin theological reflection. My own experience of working with students suggests that a traditional theological education may indeed inoculate students against being able to analyse experience and to explore creatively the gaps and connections between contemporary reality and the Christian tradition. A particular kind of academic orthodoxy stifles theological imagination in many cases.

It must be acknowledged that the perceptions which emerge from the critical conversation of theological reflection will often have only strictly limited validity and relevance. We need to get used to the idea that theologies can be disposable and contextual; the conclusions of any particular theological reflection do not need to be seen as relevant for all people in all places and they may, indeed, be thoroughly idiosyncratic. Anyone who wants to commend their insights to a wider audience will find themselves entering into a wider conversation which will itself modify their perceptions. This is a valuable and automatic corrective to egotism and the sort of situational fundamentalism which holds that just because something is true in one's own experience, it must be true for all people everywhere.

Finally, and connected with the last point, it must be recognized that any theological reflection undertaken by a particular individual may well reveal more about that person and their particular perspective than it does about a secular situation or the Christian theological tradition. It is important to realize the limitations of one's own perspective and preoccupations in approaching theological reflection and thus to be self-critical. Self-criticism can be fostered and insights generally can be deepened by undertaking the critical conversation of theological reflection in a group rather than on one's own. The group setting creates real rather than imaginary interlocutors in critical conversation and maximizes resources for knowledge and dialogue.

Conclusion

The purpose of this paper has been to engender interest and enthusiasm for theological reflection and to suggest one very particular and inadequate way of starting on this activity. I hope that anyone using it will soon become profoundly dissatisfied with it and will want to find and refine their own method. In this connection, readers may want to consult some of the more sophisticated methods of theological reflection outlined by authors like Don Browning and Michael Taylor.

For my own part, I shall be very happy if I have given people some clue about where to begin and if I have provided for them some manna in the wilderness rather than demanding of them bricks to be made without straw.

SOME POINTS FOR FURTHER CONSIDERATION

- What are the strengths and weaknesses of seeing practical theological activity as a kind of critical conversation?
- Has Pattison identified the right "partners" to take part in what he calls the critical conversation of theological reflection? What others might be engaged or excluded?
- Is Pattison right to see theology as active enquiry rather than historical and doctrinal certainty?
- What practical and theoretical problems might arise in engaging in the critical conversation of theological reflection?
- Should theological reflection be undertaken only by people who are particularly expert in academic theology from their study of the Christian tradition or should it be something everybody can join in?

FOR FURTHER READING AND EXPLORATION

Pattison develops and contextualizes the idea of pastoral theology as critical creative conversation in Pattison with Woodward (1994) and applies this kind of approach more widely in Pattison (1996a). It is best exemplifed in Pattison (1997a and 1997b), where liberation theology is brought into conversation with pastoral care of people with mental health problems. As his thought develops, he becomes more interested in theoretical and practical outcomes of practical theological conversation and the difference that it might make. Pattison's thinking about creating a critical conversation as a basis for theological reflection draws heavily upon Browning (1983), Green (1987), Houlden (1985), Schreiter (1985), Taylor (1983), and Williams (1986). For more recent attempts to devise essentially dialogical, hermeneutic methods for theological reflection see Gerkin (1997), and especially

Patton (1990), which adopts a more contemplative and less intellectual/cognitive approach to theological reflection. Ballard and Pritchard (1996) provide a useful guide to various approaches to theological reflection. Carr (1997) discusses theological reflection further in his chapter 6.

Part Three

Relating Theory and Practice to Perspectives and Issues in Pastoral and Practical Theology

INTRODUCTION TO PART THREE

10 Pastoral Theology and Sociology
    Michael Northcott

11 Liberation Theology and Political Theory
    Peter Sedgwick

12 Ecclesiology and Pastoral Theology
    Nicholas Bradbury

13 Christian Morality and Pastoral Theology
    Nicholas Peter Harvey

14 Spirituality in a Postmodern Era
    Marie McCarthy

15 Sketching the Contours of a Pastoral Theological Perspective: Suffering, Healing, and Reconstructing Experiencing
    Chris Schlauch

16 The Relationship between Pastoral Counseling
    and Pastoral Theology
    Gordon Lynch

17 How Sexuality and Relationships have Revolutionized
    Pastoral Theology
    Bonnie J. Miller-McLemore

18 Culture, Religious Faiths, and Race
    Martin Forward

19 What is the Relevance of Congregational Studies for
    Pastoral Theology?
    Brynolf Lyon

20 Towards Dialogue: An Exploration of the Relations
    between Psychiatry and Religion in Contemporary
    Mental Health
    Mark Sutherland

21 Management and Pastoral Theology
    Stephen Pattison

Introduction to Part Three

Chapters in the first two Parts of this Reader have placed pastoral and practical theology in historical perspective and outlined some of the key methods pertaining to this discipline. Those in this Part consider some of the many perspectives and issues that inform and are of concern within practical theology.

One of the main and most stimulating aspects of contemporary pastoral or practical theology is its use of different disciplinary perspectives and theories, such as those provided by psychology and sociology. This width of interdisciplinary activity is complemented by the broad range of issues and topics that can raise practical and theoretical challenges for pastoral theory and practice. The aim here is to provide a sense of the range of perspectives and issues that presently illuminate and engage pastoral theologians.

This Part can be seen as falling into two sections. The first, consisting of chapters 10 to 15, concerns disciplines, approaches, and perspectives that have shaped and influenced contemporary pastoral theology to varying degrees. The second, from chapters 16 to 21, concerns issues or topics that connect with both theology and care. There will be some overlap in these sections. However, the broad distinction may be a useful one in trying to use this material.

In chapters 10 through to 15 there are a range of pieces which discuss sociology, spirituality, liberation theology and political theory, ecclesiology, pastoral theological method, and ethics. These are all particular disciplines or perspectives which bear upon how pastoral theological theory is shaped, and pastoral care practiced. The papers remind the reader that the context within which theology is done often shapes both theory and practice. All of the writers in this section reflect on the features of the contemporary world that shape pastoral and practical theology. The discipline is explored as a dynamic and changing reality that responds to the contexts and influences that surround it.

Chapters in the second section, from 16 to 21, explore important issues or topics in pastoral and practical theology. These are pastoral counseling, sexuality, race and culture, the worshiping congregation, psychiatry, and management. Each of the chapters explores what its topic has to say to pastoral and practical theology and draws out some key themes and questions. Some of these topics have already been major dialogue partners with pastoral and practical theology (for example, pastoral counseling and psychiatry). Others are likely to shape the discipline in the future (for example, management and Christian dialogue with an expanding Islam).

This Part is not exhaustive. Many other perspectives and topics might appropriately have been included. We have attempted to achieve a balance between British and American writers, though women contributors are in the minority and regrettably all the writers are white. This partly reflects some of the biases and limitations of the discipline. There are topics that we have not been able to include because of space. Those that might usefully have been added are illness, health and disease, the growing interest in and use of narrative and experience in pastoral and practical theology, race, third world perspectives, and the implications of the development of communications and information for pastoral theology. The scope for including such topics demonstrates the width of concern that can be encompassed by practical theology.

10

Pastoral Theology and Sociology

MICHAEL NORTHCOTT

INTRODUCTION

Michael Northcott is an Anglican priest who teaches practical theology and ethics at Edinburgh University. He is best known for his work on environmental ethics (Northcott 1996), but he has a long-standing interest in urban theology and the way in which theology relates to social structures (Northcott 1998).

Along with psychology and some other human sciences, sociology has been one of the most important theoretical perspectives and dialogue partners for contemporary pastoral theology. All pastoral theology and pastoral practice takes place within a social context. It must also relate to social institutions and practices. Sociology, which from its own beginnings has taken a good deal of interest in religion (Weber 1963; Durkheim 1915), provides many methods and insights that can be illuminative within the sphere of practical theology.

This specially commissioned chapter gives the reader an overview of the discipline of sociology and its implications for pastoral care and pastoral theology. Sociology involves analysis of the nature of social structures, systems, classes, and institutions. It can be used as a tool for understanding human behavior. It illuminates how human values and rules are sustained and shared. This enables those participating in pastoral care to analyze dimensions of their work in terms of the social factors that both shape and condition theory and practice.

This chapter explores some of the contemporary features that shape religion including privatization, industrialization, urbanization, and secularization. In particular, Northcott discusses the ways in which secular modes of pastoral care and counseling have been divorced from points of contact with God and any purposive moral framework. He explores the possibility of a relocation of pastoral care and moral guidance within the framework of moral values and narratives which are strongly concerned with the Christian story and a Christian understanding of God.

Northcott also considers the social construction of knowledge and the complex interaction between cultural and social contexts. In the light of these processes, it is not always easy to understand what the concept of God actually means. It is important that pastoral theology takes account of the theological ideas and spiritual practices (especially individualization, psychologization, and professionalization) that shape the pastoral task. Northcott suggests that pastoral theology has been shaped by these influences and should recover its vocation to be challenging to the modern idea of the sovereign individual as entrepreneur or consumer. Northcott concludes that pastoral theology needs to rediscover a concept of personhood as a reflection of the being of God. This would recognize the constitutive significance for personhood of relations between persons and the being of God, and between persons and persons. The concept of God as essentially social and relational provides a direct challenge to many contemporary trends and practices, such as individualization and psychologization.

PASTORAL THEOLOGY AND SOCIOLOGY

The sociological perspective originates from the perception that there is something called 'society' which is conceptually different from the life stories of individuals, and from the history and behaviour of nation states and other political and organizational entities, including churches. This notion of society involves analysis of the nature of social structures, systems, classes and institutions. Such analysis also involves the study of the interaction between these entities or constructs, the individuals which inhabit them, and the ideologies which sustain and legitimate them.

Sociologists recognize that individuals do not act purely according to their own motives and concerns, but are the subject of familial, cultural and social influences. Social interaction between individuals and within and between social groups is therefore the core sociological concept. The study of social interaction takes two forms, one of which involves the study of the macro dimension of social interaction such as relations between church and state, trade unions and corporations, consumers and purveyors of manufactured goods, or between nation states. The other form involves the study of interactions between individuals and interactions in groups and organizational settings, including religious groups and communities.

These two sociological styles can be observed among the originators of the discipline of sociology. Auguste Comte was the first person to coin the term *sociologie* and by it he meant the application of scientific methods to the elucidation and description of the laws which govern human behaviour and social systems, laws which he believed were analogous to the laws of physics or chemistry. The most influential of the early sociologists, including Karl Marx, Emile Durkheim and Max Weber, all deployed historical and contemporary observations of human societies in the delineation of laws or tendencies in their evolution, and of patterns or laws in the development of social processes and institutions, and in the formation and interaction of social groups. The early sociologists placed a great deal of emphasis on the nature of social structure, though they differed in the extent to which they claimed to be able to discern inevitable or determinative laws in their evolution.

Moving away from this early emphasis on structures and laws, later sociologists deployed the study of statistics, and direct observations of the behaviour of individuals in group settings, in the creation of a more empirical sociology focused on the micro features of social practices. Reflecting a reduced confidence in the existence of hidden laws or evolutionary principles in human societies (and not least, following the Holocaust, in the possibility that these principles might involve the necessary progress of human societies from less to more enlightened states), this kind of sociology rose in prominence as a way of studying the complex social problems, including poverty, inequality, deviance and crime, which the emergent welfare states of the postwar era were designed to address. This more empirical style of sociology has also grown in prominence in the social study of religious groups and behaviour. Statistical approaches to the decline of churchgoing have been particularly important in the study and theorization of secularization while qualitative studies of individual and intergroup behaviour have thrown much light on the social character of New Religious Movements, and are increasingly being deployed in congregational studies.

The value of the macro approach to social interaction for the empirical study of the church in relation to society, a central task of practical theology, may be seen in Max Weber's discernment of patterns in the development of religious organizations. In historical and comparative studies of world religions Weber identified a pattern of religious evolution in which each religious innovation is born out of a charismatic experience or prophecy by a particular individual (Abraham, Buddha, Christ, Muhammad, Luther) who shares this idea with members of an existing religious group, challenging existing orthodoxies, rules and practices. As a consequence the group may break away from the existing religion (Christianity from Judaism, Islam from Christianity, Protestantism from Catholicism) and begin a new one. This new religious grouping, which may initially be described as a sect, will often challenge dominant values and practices in society at large as well as in the old religion. However, in time the members of the new religion may acquire property, and attempt to pass on their religion to younger generations. Consequently, they will tend to establish orthodoxies, and prescribe disciplinary and ritual practices of their own so that they can pas on the faith to subsequent generations. They may also begin to be more tolerant of ideas or practices in mainstream society which were earlier rejected. Weber identified this kind of religious life cycle by means of two analytical metaphors, the one being the idea of the *routinization of charisma* where innovation becomes routinized over time. The other is known as the *typology of church and sect*. This typology is used to identify phases in the organizational life cycles of religious groups.

Both concepts have been of considerable importance in practical theology. They provide sociological insight into the history of the church, and in particular into the causes of division between denominations and churches. They help explain different modes of relationship between church and state. They also provide insight into the decline which is taking place in the social influence and membership of established churches in the West, and the correlative rise of new styles of Christianity, and new forms of religiosity.

The macro approach to sociology is also of considerable significance for pastoral studies, as may be illustrated with reference to Emile Durkheim's study of suicide in which he theorized that suicide was a consequence of an individual's lack of integration in society. Durkheim argued that modernizing societies undergoing rapid social change, where established conventions and norms are constantly challenged, are also societies in which anomie (literally lawlessness) and alienation will tend to grow. In such circumstances individuals may experience a loss of meaning and identity, and some may suffer from depression or other forms of mental unease. Consequently certain forms of social deviance such as suicide and criminal behaviour will tend to increase. From a pastoral perspective this approach can help in understanding suicidal tendencies amongst victims of sexual abuse or amongst unemployed young men. Both groups have experienced the effects of anomie or lawlessness as social norms and practices become ineffective in controlling sexual abuse, or in providing secure employment for young adults. In both cases social integration has been distorted or halted altogether and deviant behaviour, including suicide, is a possible consequence. Pastors and counsellors involved with such individuals need to be aware that they are not just dealing with individual pathology but with the effects of more widespread social practices, whose root causes also need to be addressed. This recognition can also be of real pastoral value to individuals caught up in these situations who may tend to blame themselves as individuals and fail to perceive the contribution of larger social and structural changes in their problems.

Durkheim also identified what he called the totemic principle at work in traditional societies around religious symbols and rituals. He argued that the gathering of a tribe or community around a totem or religious ritual played a vital part in the maintenance of social order and the sharing and sustaining of shared values and rules. When human groups gather around totemic symbols and rituals, they are effectively affirming a symbolic representation of the community which in turn gives life and substance to the shared values and welfare of the community as a whole.

This insight seems to indicate that religion primarily has a conserving function in society. But equally Durkheim's perception of the social power of worship has dynamic implications. Worship can be a context in which individuals not only locate themselves in relation to the group, and the group draws individuals into its shared enterprises, but also an environment in which adjustments between the needs of individuals and the social environment can take place.

The totemic principle provides a key insight into the creative and sustaining function of ritual in worshipping communities and in society at large. The growing influence of this insight in practical theology can be discerned in the new emphasis placed by many contemporary practical theologians on the worshipping community as the essential focus for the pastoral and social practice of the church, in contrast to earlier generations of practical theologians who, under the influence of progressive and secular currents of thought, tended to emphasize the witness of the church dispersed in society rather than the church as gathered or sacramental community. The totemic principle affirms the significance of worship, ritual and community gathering as the core practice of the church and of Christians, where the other distinctive Christian practices and virtues, such as neighbourliness, hospitality, care and fidelity are affirmed and sustained.

The totemic principle also points to the possible anomic consequences for moral values and social conscience when religious rituals lose social power as they have done in modern industrialized societies in Northern Europe and North America. Durkheim theorized that the rituals of civil religion around the flag and state and local civic ceremonies in Republican France would effectively supplant the church as the sustainer of the nation's collective conscience and of its members' shared moral values. However, contemporary sociologists have noted an increasing loss of support for common moral projects, such as limits on personal wealth and the minimization of poverty and inequality, in advanced industrial societies. Mobilizing in-depth interview and large-scale survey data they have theorized that this loss of a common moral project may be related to declining participation in worshipping communities.

This sociological insight has advanced talk amongst theologians of the practical significance of Christian worship and belief in the 'public square' and not just in private morals and sprirituality. It also provides an important commentary on the phenomenon of privatization in modern secular societies. As states have taken up many of the communication and community-maintenance functions formerly exercised by the churches, religion has increasingly been confined to the private and domestic spheres of social life, and excluded from the public domain. Practical theologians argue that this has not only reduced the moral and ritual resources of the social collective, but it has also damaged religion, reducing it to a set of personal and therapeutic practices which are better at adjusting individuals to unjust or pathological social structures than at providing resources for critiquing and renewing societies in their service of the common good, and the needs of the majority of their citizens.

Once again this insight has produced in recent years a major new focus in practical and pastoral theology. From the earliest days of Christianity, Christian communities have been associated with practices of care and healing in relation to the sick, the poor, widows, children and the vulnerable. Jesus Christ enjoined his followers to pay special attention to these vulnerable groups who were said to be the particular objects of God's love and concern. The early Christian communities set aside deacons to meet the pastoral needs of the community and monastic communities soon developed a similar pattern of involvement in healing, and later in education of children and the young. The missionary expansion of Christianity manifested a similar pattern with the establishment of hospitals and schools becoming a regular feature of missionary work. Similarly, with the growth of cities in the industrialization of Europe and North America the church was prominent in the establishment of schools and hospitals, and other mechanisms of welfare for the poorest in the slums.

Industrialization and urbanization were accompanied by a new sociological phenomenon, known as secularization, in which churches lost members and influence to other social forces, influences and actors. One cause of this decline in influence was the break-up of the old organic social context of the village and small town in which the church was set as a central institution. In the new cities face-to-face relationships and organic communities were replaced by instrumental relationships, relationships of production and trade which were increasingly characterized by cash and contract, and rationality, rather than personal face-to-face exchanges and moral codes. The church found it difficult to adjust to the new social context and while it retained strongholds in middle-class communities, it lost considerable ground in working-class areas. The demise of the organic community was also characterized by social differentiation whereby whole sectors of social life gradually moved beyond the influence of the church and its functionaries, including criminal law, welfare, education and health care. By the

1960s, in most European countries these functions were now arms of the public services of secular states. The church might remain as a partner in some contexts or in some sectors, but its dominant identity as the provider of social care had fundamentally disappeared.

The consequence of this radical break between forms of therapy and care, and the worshipping communities of the church, was that care itself was secularized and moved apart from the ritual, moral and spiritual frame in which the practices of care had originated, and with which they had been intricately connected for more than fifteen hundred years of Christian influence in Europe. At the same time, and partly in response to secularization, the pastoral care and moral guidance offered by the churches, and particularly the Protestant churches, became privatized and individualized, focusing more on individual conscience and individual need than on the sacramental community of the church and the connections between the spiritual and social reality of church and the ethical norms of society at large. One of the consequences of these dual processes was that practices of care and education became increasingly commodified as they were split from their former moral and community context. Ability to pay became a dominant criterion of access to such services in the Protestant lands of North America, and this is increasingly the case in access to the best public services in some countries in Northern Europe, and not least in the UK. Another consequence was that Protestant churches began to adopt secular modes of pastoral care and counselling which were often divorced from human and transcendental reference points in worshipping communities and spirituality, and from any kind of purposive moral framework.

Traditionally Christians have believed that personal fulfilment is connected with the moral and spiritual direction of a person's life, as manifest in their love for God, and in the quality of relationships with other persons as manifest in such virtues as love, fidelity and hopefulness. Non-directive counselling and psychotherapy, the characteristic modes of secularized pastoral care, express a value-neutrality with respect to both spiritual orientation and the quality of relationships. The principal focus of this kind of care is self-authenticity and the strength and integrity of self-identity which the individual is helped to achieve.

In response to this situation, whose roots can only be fully comprehended with the aid of sociological analysis, a number of practical theologians and ethicists have sought to relocate pastoral care and moral guidance in a framework of moral values and narratives which are strongly connected with the Christian story and the Christian understanding of God as God is revealed in Jesus Christ who is present to Christians in their sacramental gatherings around the preached word and the supper of the Lord. In this approach Christian practices of care are understood to be essentially connected to habits of moral reasoning and behaviour, and to the narrative structure of moral development in the lives of individuals, families and communities. Once relocated in this narrative structure, it becomes possible for pastoral care to achieve a more holistic focus on the network of relationships and social structures within which people live their lives, and the extent to which these structures are sinful or redeeming, and not just on the identity and development of the individual. The dualism which tended to grow in Protestant churches, as a consequence of secularization, between prophetic and pastoral ministries is thus overcome by this approach, as care is reconnected with community and community analysis both in ecclesial and secular contexts.

The Social Construction of God

Durkheim's totemic principle is illustrative of the other core theoretical concept which unites both macro and micro approaches in sociology, which is the idea of the social construction of reality and of knowledge, an idea whose influence is still growing in many other fields of knowledge, including pastoral studies and practical theology. According to this idea, human beings are essentially externalizing creatures, and in groups they construct objects (totems) and ideas from their interior worlds which, over time, acquire a capacity to act back upon the groups which create them. Individuals born into social groups are socialized into shared knowledge constructs and rules, and experience these not as the subjects of human creation but as objective and often powerful features of the social world.

The influence of the idea of the social construction of knowledge is evident in theological studies of the interaction between conceptualizations of God and the modes of power, leadership and social interaction which are adopted in political and ecclesiastical organizations. The idea of God as an absolute, all-powerful, transcendent, lonely (male) monarch was deeply influential in the emergence of the institutions of papacy and monarchy in late medieval Europe. On the other hand, the concept of God as the immanent and dynamic Spirit who inspires and indwells the children of God played an important role in the radical Reformation and in the emergence of democracy and the idea of civil society as a realm in which individuals exercise freedom of thought and association outside the control of popes, priests or monarchs. Studies of the interaction between models of God and modes of human government involve the recognition both of the power of socially shared ideas (externalized knowledge constructs) to influence human behaviour, and the capacity of developments in social structure and behaviour to shape models of God. They are prime example of the increasing influence of sociological analysis on practical theology in recent years.

The social construction of knowledge is an idea whose influence is also clearly at work in pastoral studies and pastoral practice. Counsellors or pastors sometimes encounter individuals who present with a disabling psychological pattern of guilt combined with a weak sense of self-worth and identity, a pattern which may often be associated with experiences of a dominant or inconsistent father in childhood. For such individuals reference to God as father may be positively unhelpful until their own images of fathering, and of selfhood, have been at least partially redeemed and restored. In such circumstances, helping the individual towards freedom from a disabling psychic pattern might involve not only guiding them through a process of uncovering and healing of memories of inadequate or damaging experiences of human parenting, but also enabling them through meditation or other spiritual and intellectual practices to a reformed image of God as lover, mother, friend, nurturer or sustainer, rather than as critical, dominating or demanding father.

Once again we see here the influence of Durkheim's crucial totemic principle. This principle points, as we have seen, to the capacity of groups to create gods and rituals for themselves which externalize features of their social life and collective conscience. It also highlights the possibility that these gods and rituals may reflect patterns of human domination and exploitation and not just of healthy collective governance and a quest for the good of all. Thus certain kinds of ritual procedure or leadership may hide or legitimate exploitative social practices, they may hinder effective engagement by ritual participants, or they may encourage excessive psychic dependence on ritual leaders. Pastoral theologians have often observed the danger that certain styles of religion and of worship leadership can induce a disabling dependence in worship participants. This kind of dependence may hinder or undermine the capacity of worshippers to articulate and mobilize their values and beliefs outside of the worship context, such as in the workplace or the local community. At its worst, unhealthy dependence may manifest in abusive sexual relationships between worship leaders and their congregants, or in other kinds of personal abuse or harassment. Similarly, Marxist and feminist theologians have pointed to the way in which certain conceptualizations of God may have similar social effects. Thus conceptualizations of God as male may legitimate conceptualizations of women as the inferior sex, and conceptualizations of God as monarch may legitimate forms of political or economic elitism and exploitation.

The idea that our models of God and our conceptualizations are socially constructed will not be an uncontroversial one for lay Christians, and even for some theologians. Christians conventionally believe that their ideas of God are primarily mediated by the Bible, the Creeds and the liturgies and rituals of Christian worship. Some theologians identify a hidden, secularizing, agenda in the concept of the social construction of God. It may appear to involve the disavowal of revelation, and the historical authority of Christian orthodoxy, as testimony to the truth and character of God's being. However, the Prophets of the Old Testament were themselves not unfamiliar with the rudiments of social construction. They frequently condemned the worship of idols not just because they were objects of human creation (social construction), but because the people of Israel were led into disastrous social practices as a consequence of their worship of idols who did not exemplify the divine justice and righteousness of Yahweh. Prophets such as Isaiah and Amos condemned social practices which resulted in the oppression of women, children and foreigners, excessive military spending by the Israelite state, or growing inequality between wealthy landowners and the newly landless poor as the direct consequence of the idolatry of Israel and her rulers. Similarly in the New Testament we see the emergence of a much more interactive and immanent concept of God as a consequence of the disciples' encounter with Jesus Christ, and also as a way of speaking about the experience of the Spirit in the lives and communities of the early Christians. God, in other words, may be said to reveal Godself not just in words revealed to chosen spokespersons, but in shared experiences and social contexts which help to shape new perceptions of the human encounter with the being of God.

A strong case can be made for this theological validation of the social construction of reality in terms of the doctrine of creation. The possibility that God may be revealed through social construction and socially constructed knowledge (culture and ideology), and not exclusively to inspired individuals, or to Church Councils, involves the idea that God created human persons essentially as social beings, whose sociality may be said to be a reflection of the sociality of the being of God as Trinity. The idea that divine revelation occurs within cultures, and not outside them, is a *sine qua non* of modern hermeneutic theory. This recognition involves a greater fluidity than is customary in our assumptions about the relationship between church and culture, and between doctrinal understandings of church and of creation.

Despite the claims of Roman Catholicism, Holy Church does not exist in an unbroken line from St Peter until the present day. Besides the historical gaps in the succession of Apostolic ministry which exist in all Christian communions, there are also times when established churches no longer seem to represent the original charism gifted to the early Christians in new or changing cultural contexts. This may be because representatives of established churches come to regard internal cultural practices or procedures, or particular linguistic faith formulae, as unchanging, infallible or divinely inspired even when they no longer effectively communicate the Gospel in new pastoral and social contexts. At such times new leaders and gatherings of Christians may emerge which challenge the established order, as occurred at the Reformation, and as is now occurring in world Christianity as the dominance of European Christianity is being challenged by the increasing numbers of Christians in the South. Such times of change and challenge to established ecclesiastical authority reflect the interaction between faith tradition and its sources, and particularly the Bible, and the new or changing cultural and social contexts of new leaders and new churches. The constant re-fusion between received text and witness, and changing cultural and social conditions reflects a complex interaction between our created and encultured sociality and the historic traditions of faith. The prominence of sociological analysis in many of the newer contextual theologies from both North and South – including feminist theology, liberation theology, political theology and ecotheology – is then a legitimate reflection of the theological reality that we experience God, and God is revealed, in creation and culture as well as in Bible and church.

Recognition of the interaction between cultural and social contexts and concepts of God is common to sociologists and contextual theologians alike. Karl Marx argued that the God of the ruling classes is mobilized in their class interests against the poor and working classes. God functions for the lower classes like an opiate, promising salvation in the next life provided they endure suffering occasioned by exploitation and unjust social structures in this life. For Marx theological constructs are primarily the servants of other social structures, and in particular of production and exchange, relationships under capitalism, and the class struggle these relationships involve. For Weber, on the other hand, religious ideas and concepts have productive power which can be of enormous social significance. Thus Weber proposed that certain elements in Protestant theology and ethics, and in particular the doctrine of double predestination and the Puritan asceticism which this idea encouraged, contributed to a cultural shift in Northern Europe and North America which greatly facilitated the expansion of capitalist modes of trade and enterprise. Another key element in the theological ideas which generated an environment suitable for the development of capitalism was an emphasis on individual destiny and the unmediated relation between the individual and God.

Once again these sociological insights into the social construction and social influence of theological ideas and spiritual practices are of great significance for practical and pastoral theology. As we have seen, Protestant individualism has not only been influential in the development of capitalist entrepreneurialism but also in the development of modes of pastoral ministry in the church which place a strong emphasis on the individual relationships sustained between pastor and members of her congregation. This emphasis has encouraged the mobilization of psychological and counselling skills in many pastoral situations, and the development of a relationship between pastor and people which is sometimes reminiscent of a therapist–client relationship. This development has been criticized for the individualization, psychologization and professionalization of the pastoral task which it seems to represent. From a sociological perspective it may also be said to represent the damaging influence of the modern idea of the sovereign individual as entrepreneur or consumer on the practice of churches and pastors.

Practical theologians have sought to apply a theological as well as a moral critique to the reformation and renewal of pastoral practice and in particular to point up the significance of the social Trinity as a model both for human relationality, and for pastoral relationships in worshipping communities. Once again sociological insight is key to this recent move in practical and pastoral theology. Sociologists understand the formation of the self as a process which is essentially social. The self is formed in relationship. The self is also continually constituted and reconstituted in relationships. Human fulfilment and happiness are said by social psychologists to be closely related to the ability to sustain a reasonable number of in-depth relationships both within and beyond family networks. When we make new friends, our family circumstances change, or we join new churches, there is a sense in which our self-identity is also reconstituted. But this understanding of the self-in-relation does not originate in sociological insight. Rather it involves the recovery of a more ancient and metaphysical conception of personhood, one which sees personhood as a reflection of the being of God, and which recognizes the constitutive significance for personhood of relations between persons and the being of God, and between persons and persons. Once again this recognition is substantiated theologically by the revelation of God as Trinity wherein being itself is understood as essentially social and relational.

SOURCES

Browning, D. S. (1976), *The Moral Context of Pastoral Care*, Philadelphia: Westminster.

Giddens, A. (1993), *Sociology*, Cambridge: Polity Press.

McFadyen, A. (1991), *The Call to Personhood*, Cambridge: Cambridge University Press.

Nichols, D. (1992), *Deity and Domination*, Oxford: Oxford University Press.

SOME ISSUES FOR FURTHER CONSIDERATION

- Explore your understanding of society – specifically what the main influences are upon present-day society.
- What social factors may influence your understanding and knowledge of God?
- What factors may marginalize religion in society?
- What factors shape the ways in which the self is understood in society?
- Is sociology an important resource for pastoral theology and practice? In what ways?

FOR FURTHER READING AND EXPLORATION

For a general introduction to the main readings which present an overview of the relationship between theology and sociology, see Durkheim (1915), Weber (1963), Gill (ed.) (1996). The relationship of sociology to pastoral care is picked up by Furniss (1994). A good general introduction to the sociology of religion is Hamilton (1996). An overview of the contemporary British context is provided in Davie (1994).

___11___

Liberation Theology and Political Theory

PETER SEDGWICK

INTRODUCTION

Peter Sedgwick has had experience of ministry and practical theological education in a wide variety of settings, academic and non-academic. He is presently assistant secretary of the Church of England's Board for Social Responsibility. This reflects a long-standing interest in issues of social concern and justice which is reflected in his writings (Sedgwick 1996).

Like sociology, political theory offers important insights and challenges to pastoral theology. Pastoral theology and practice is "political" in so far as it cannot exist above and beyond debates about power, inequality, and influence in society. One of the main sources of critique in which this challenge from political theory is made specific in the theological sphere is through political theology, especially liberation theology which evolved in Latin America in the 1970s.

In this specially commissioned paper, Sedgwick considers the relevance of political theory and liberation theology to pastoral theology. He offers clear definitions of both liberation theology and politics and draws out some of the main influences of thought in this area both in the United States and the UK.

Sedgwick explores a number of issues that liberation theology and political theory raise for pastoral practice. Liberation theology challenges practice to explore its relationship to the poor. Pastoral theology must, therefore, examine how the realities of power, conflict, and welfare connect with pastoral experience: "pastoral theology and practice are enriched by the study of . . . liberation theology because

[it] enables pastoral care to see how social obligation is carried on, and how poverty and social oppression blight human lives." Sedgwick goes on to highlight the necessity for pastoral practice to develop an awareness of civic loyalty and of how society deals with the socially excluded. He points out that theology is shaped by social anthropology, which enables us to see how groups (for example women) are disadvantaged.

Sedgwick queries the overall aims of pastoral theology, asking if its purpose is "the healing of the damaged [or] an appeal to the strength of persons."

LIBERATION THEOLOGY AND POLITICAL THEORY

What is liberation theology, and why should it matter to students and to those engaged in pastoral care? Equally, why should political theory affect the way pastoral practice is carried out? Liberation theology arose in Latin America around 1960. It faced vigorous opposition from most conservative Roman Catholic priests and Protestant pastors. The type of priest epitomized in Graham Greene's *The Power and the Glory* (1940) is exactly the sort of person who was greatly opposed to liberation theology, and the ambiguous central figure in the novel makes it essential reading for the understanding of where liberation theology came from. So too does the central character in Georges Bernanos's *Diary of a Country Priest* (1936). These are deeply compassionate, caring, apolitical and personally troubled men in a poor, suffering community. They both serve the community and yet are apart from it, for their office symbolizes the divinity of the Church: 'the power of the keys'. Politics is irrelevant: sacrificial priestly ministry is all.

Liberation theology emerged at the same time as the civil rights movement in the United States, which also upset many traditional pastors and yet was equally church-based. Latin American liberation theology spread across the world, and by the late 1970s it was found in Britain. Perhaps the earliest influential British texts are Laurie Green's *Power to the Powerless* (1986), or Ken Leech's writings, such as *The Social God* (1981) and *Struggle in Babylon* (1988). The movement arose in Latin America from the poverty of the great majority of the population, its belief that this poverty was caused by injustice and not by misfortune, and its further belief that this was contrary to the life-kingdom preached by Jesus of Nazareth.

The story of the emergence of liberation theology is intrinsic to its definition. Rebecca Chopp defines it as 'a reflection on God's activity and God's transforming grace among those who are the victims of modern history'. Above all, it is the integrity of a different voice, experience and genre that belongs to the same God, church and Christ. The great meeting of Latin American Catholic Bishops in Puebla in 1979 talked of faces:

the faces of young children, struck down by poverty before they are born
... the faces of the peasants ... they live in exile almost everywhere.
(Chopp, 1997, p. 287)

Liberation theology enables the solidarity of the poor to come into existence, for solidarity does not just happen. Once it exists, it expresses its search for justice. Within this movement, Marxism has been influential as a tool of social analysis. Popular religion has increasingly played its role as well. This religion is made up of indigenous practices, magic, and Afro-American religions. Liberation theology seeks to transform it by making communities self-aware, and to engage it in the changing of communities. Justice is the final goal.

What then is political theory, and why should it matter to pastoral theology and practice? There can be no uncontroversial definition of politics. Raymond Plant, one of the leading political theorists in modern Britain, argues that this is because the term is complex and there are a wide range of criteria which make up this complexity. Not all of them have to be satisfied in order to justify the identification of some event as political. Also, the decision as to which criteria are relevant, and which order they are put in, depends on political preferences. Political theory studies the reasons why someone might call an act or event political. So what might politics be?

It can be about dealing with the conflicts of interests which occur within a state. But what about societies which deny that such conflicts can exist, because they are totalitarian or homogeneous? Despite the long history of this view (in Aristotle, or Bernard Crick today) it excluded women's interests in deeply patriarchal societies in past centuries, or those of the poor in Stalin's Russia, as they were all repressed. Very odd. It can be about the welfare of the community, but could exclude the idea of conflicting interests and interest groups altogether. It could be about a person's relationship to the legally-binding authority of the state in government. But this excludes grassroots groups (as in liberation theology) which might raise levels of awareness but not engage as such with the state. It could be about power and the conflicts which arise from the exercise of power. These can be very wide or very narrow, depending on whether power is seen to be exercised in the way we think and feel about our interests, or whether it is about making decisions and implementing them. Finally it can be held that politics requires formal organizations with clear authority structures. Again, while this rules in trade unions, it rules out the informal meeting on an estate about a social issue.

Nevertheless, political theory must be about the use of these criteria. Why states should be obeyed; what should be done about power; who resolves conflict, or conflicting interests in a state; how the welfare of a community is to be organized – all these are the endemic questions of political theory that have existed for two thousand years, in societies without a place for religion (France during the Revolution), in societies entirely religious (the medieval Holy Roman Empire, or eighteenth-century England), and in societies where religion is a matter of personal preference (see chapter 10 by Michael Northcott).

So liberation theology is a branch of political theory in the light of Christian faith. It deals with power, conflict and the welfare of the community. In the words of Gustav Gutiérrez (1988):

It is an effort to make the word of life present in a world of oppression, injustice and death.

But not all Christian engagement with politics will go in the direction of liberation theology. The debate about political theory is one of the liveliest in the United States and Britain at the end of the twentieth century. Both the British prime minister Tony Blair and the Conservative MP and thinker David Willetts continually engage with political theory, especially as it deals with the welfare of the community. What obligations do we have to the community, and what should we give back to the state? Can we normally draw benefits and not incur an obligation to do something for society? Or is this simply a form of social control, a manipulation of the individual person? Studying political theory enables the pastoral practitioner and theologian to ask how social conflict is being understood, and how it should be regulated, or even reconciled. The primary debate centres around a movement in political theory called communitarianism. It has been hugely influential in the United States through the work of Amitai Etzioni. Religious thinkers have also developed this movement, especially the Chief Rabbi in Britain, Jonathan Sacks in *The Politics of Hope* (1997). Sacks argues that the welfare state inadvertently eroded individual responsibility. We now live in a society strong on preventing the dire poverty found in Latin America in 1960, but

marked by vandalism, violent crime and a loss of civility; by the breakdown of the family and the widespread neglect of children; by an erosion of trust and a general loss of faith in the power of governments to cure some of our most deep-seated problems.

Sacks says that the state has grown too powerful, and smaller forms of association, like the family or the voluntary group, too weak. The relationship between the state and the association needs to be rethought. It should become a covenant, not a contract, which binds people together. Or, in Etzioni's words (1995), we need to become communities again. As he says on criminal policy: 'it takes a village to prevent a crime' (p. 87). Understanding the nature of political obligation is central to communitarianism as a political theory. However, 'political' here means the nature of relationships within a community, and its welfare. Nevertheless, it is a long road from liberation theology (in a society before a welfare state) to some forms of communitarianism (as society despairs of the future of a welfare state now fifty years old). But perhaps this is too simple. Some political thinkers are now trying to unite the insights of liberation theology with communitarianism. While not Christian, Geoff Mulgan and the think tank Demos attempt to tackle social exclusion in urban areas by using local community groups, including the churches, to work with deprived communities and to regain a sense of power. Social exclusion is Mulgan's own phrase, rapidly adopted by government, to mean those who live outside the worlds of work, education or sociability. These make up 8 to 10 percent of the population. Mulgan's political theory is that the role of the state is to offer options which can bring the individual from dependence into independence. Drawing on the work of Julian Le Grand, he sees the task of the state as re-empowering those who might end up dependent on welfare, because all their social contacts have been broken and

> they are stranded in a kind of desert in which they are vulnerable to
> vultures that prey on them. (*New Statesman*, interview with Mulgan,
> 29 August 1997, p. 604)

A book on a similar approach in the United States is called *The New Paternalism: Supervisory Approaches to Poverty*. Published by the Brookings Institution, it is edited by Lawrence Mead of New York University. There is close contact between Demos and the United States intellectual community. Mulgan is also a key advisor to Tony Blair.

So the end of the twentieth century sees a fierce debate (and it is conducted in the hottest language, from academic journals to the tabloid newspapers) on how the poor are to be handled by the state; what obligations each individual should have to society, community and the state; and what role the poor, or the socially excluded, will have in all this. As one commentator from America, Steven Teles of the College of the Holy Cross, puts it, the toughest social problems involve the state providing a blend of help and hassle, commanding and enabling, providing and encouraging.

The revival of the civic order, and the role that civic organizations can play in preserving it, is now central to government action in Britain and the United States. In other words, citizenship in the full and active sense is now central to political theory. Pastoral theology and practice are enriched by the study of political theory and liberation theology because they enable pastoral care to see how social obligation is carried on, and how poverty and social oppression blight human lives. The phrase social, or structural, sin is worth mentioning here. Persons learn their attitudes, values and views of reality from the societal structures in which they are born. These structures pre-exist individual lives, and will continue long after their demise. Such structures are seen as the manner in which actions must be carried out. Social oppression can be overcome, but liberation theologians see ideology as a form of blindness. Consciousness-raising and transforming action together form what is called 'conscientization': ideologies can include violence, racism, sexism and homophobia. Yet at the end of this century of violence and social upheaval it is as well to stress the role of tradition in communities. Paul Clarke in his article on 'Citizenship' in the Routledge *Dictionary of Ethics, Theology and Society* instances the horrific example of Bosnia and East Germany, as well as parts of the former Soviet Union. Social engineering fifty years ago replaced civic tradition, civil society and embedded social values with a totalitarian structure on the grounds of false consciousness and the need for social renewal. When this totalitarian structure itself collapsed in the 1990s the older civic traditions and values had gone (the disappearance is brilliantly documented by the Polish film-maker Andrzej Wajda in *Ashes and Diamonds*, a film made in the late 1950s which is one of the classics of the postwar cinema). The result was the particularizing tendencies of ethnicity, nationality and religious groups, which broke down any sense of common citizenship into genocide and tribal war. The burgeoning civic tradition of a fledgling civil society needs to overcome the particularities of religious faith or ethnic group. A course in political theory ('what does it mean to be a citizen?') is vital for those still at school in such a region, and indeed anywhere in the cosmopolitan, heterogeneous and mobile societies of the late twentieth century. Pastoral practice, without an awareness of such a concept of civic loyalty, could easily become 'ministering to its own'.

Another example which could be given is the current debate (already alluded to) of the New Deal in Britain. Some suggest that civic engagement and the level of volunteer work remain high in Britain, unlike the vision of the United States given by the social scientist Robert Puttnam in a famous essay 'Bowling Alone', which talks of social fragmentation. Nevertheless, 'social capital' or the willingness to be involved in civic engagement varies in Britain. It has increased dramatically among middle-class people, especially women in their thirties. It stagnates in blue-collar workers, the socially excluded and (most importantly) among the young of all classes under the age of twenty. Levels of social trust, another key component of social capital, have declined markedly in the last forty years among young people. As Ian Hargreaves, formerly editor of the *New Statesman*, put it in a radio documentary with Professor Peter Hall of Harvard University (broadcast on Radio 4 on 20 November 1997), this is

a serious warning. If young people are harder to recruit to active citizenship and less trusting of government and each other, it will clearly become harder to build Britain's social capital.

A broad-based organization in East London (called Telco) has worked through local communities, including churches, mosques and temples, to recruit political and community leaders, with considerable success. The ideas of mutuality, reciprocity, rights and obligations are all embodied in such organizations. Similar are mutual organizations which are secular and operate like clubs: employee mutuals for lone mothers, schools or health care. In this example of East London and the New Deal the state works in alliance with mutual organizations. This could lead the state back to its pre-welfare position. Others fear that this alliance of state and voluntary sector could turn voluntary groups into arms of the state. Once again, political theory raises its head. How is accountability addressed, and to whom are mutual bodies accountable since they work alongside democratic local councils but are not elected as the councils are? What regulatory, in the sense of empowering, framework is set up around the mutuals?

These controversial issues are hotly debated in Western political circles, among political practitioners, theorists and journalists. As yet they have only begun to impinge on pastoral theology, but the challenge is for pastoral theology to engage with the issues of state–voluntary partnership, or mutual groups, or civic obligation. The nature of obligation, responsibilities and civic participation should resonate with the Judaeo-Christian tradition in ways that enable the creation of whole and loving communities. Bonhoeffer's theology of responsibility, or deputyship, acting on behalf of others, is a theme that deserves re-attention. So too does the whole tradition of the nature of civic society, and human vocation, in the Lutheran theologies written this century by Emil Brunner and others. Equally, the writing of Reinhold Niebuhr offers a rich vein to explore how political responsibility can be reaffirmed. After years of believing that the 'state can do it all', political philosophy has rediscovered civic order, community and participation. So too must Christian political theology.

What, finally, of liberation theology in Latin America, and in Britain? Two themes above all stand out. One is that poverty is now equated more and more with social exclusion. It is the marginalizing of those who always remain poor, both geographically and in terms of access to positions of influence, that is very important. Social, or structural, sin can make individuals feel that 'it must always be like this: this is natural'. Second, there is a deep awareness among liberation theologians that cultural anthropology must be taken with great seriousness. Women suffer poverty in a particular way as women; so do minority ethnic communities; so do those who are disabled. The work of Stephen Pattison on mental illness and liberation theology is a graphic illustration of this trend.

Pastoral theology will be invigorated as it engages more and more with the disciplines of political theory and liberation theology. The latter is now well advanced, and much pastoral theory and practice is well aware of issues of social power, poverty, exclusion and conscientization. Popular religion and base groups also impinge on pastoral practice. Perhaps the work of Peter Selby and Stephen Pattison would most illustrate this mutual enrichment. The other discipline, of political theory, looms larger in national debate, but Christian theology has yet to catch up in an effective way. It is in the bringing together of these two disciplines, liberation theology and political theory, that the debates of the new century will receive their vigour. There have been some stimulating theological examples, such as the writings of Jonathan Sacks; the interest in political and civic obligation in some of the essays that made up *God in the City*; and the writings of the Relationship Foundation, an evangelical research group. These are straws in the wind, but more is needed for a political-communitarian debate of great intensity to be engaged. The challenge to pastoral theology is to ask what it means to have responsibility to the city. Otherwise pastoral theology becomes the healing of the damaged, but not an appeal to the strength of persons, as Bonhoeffer (himself no mean political activist) saw all too well.

BIBLIOGRAPHY

Chopp, R. S. (1997), 'Latin American Liberation Theology', in D. F. Ford (ed.), *The Modern Theologians*, 2nd edn, Oxford: Blackwell.
Clarke, P. B., and Linzey, A. (ed.) (1996), *Dictionary of Ethics, Theology and Society*, London: Routledge.
Demos Quarterly (1997), 'Keeping the Faiths: the New Covenant between Religious Belief and Secular Power', no. 11, November.
Dwyer, J. (ed.) (1994), *The New Dictionary of Catholic Social Thought*, New York: Michael Glazier, USA.
Etzioni, A. (1995), *New Communitarian Thinking*, Charlottesville, Va: University Press of Virginia.
Green, L. (1986), *Power to the Powerless*, Basingstoke: Pickering.
Gutiérrez, G. (1988), *A Theology of Liberation*, 2nd edn, Maryknoll, N.Y.: Orbis.
Leadbeater, C. (1996), *The Self-Policing Society*, London: Demos.
Leech, K. (1988), *Struggle in Babylon*, London: SCM Press.
Macquarrie, J., and Childress, J. (eds) (1986), *A New Dictionary of Christian Ethics*, London: SCM Press.
Mead, L. (ed.) (1997), *The New Paternalism*, Washington, DC: Brookings Institution.
Mulgan, G. (ed.) (1997), *Life after Politics: New Thinking for the 21st Century*, London: Fontana.
Sacks, J. (1997), *The Politics of Hope*, London: Jonathan Cape.
Sedgwick, P. (ed.) (1996), *God in the City*, London: Mowbray.
Sedgwick, P. (1997), 'Theology and Society', in D. F. Ford (ed.), *The Modern Theologians*, Oxford: Blackwell.
Willetts, D. (1996), *Modern Conservatism*, Harmondsworth: Penguin.

SOME POINTS FOR FURTHER CONSIDERATION

- How are pastoral theology and practice shaped by their political context?
- In the light of this paper, review your articulation of the aims of pastoral care.
- What is the place and meaning of power, poverty, exclusion, and conscientization in pastoral practice?
- What is the meaning of citizenship? Is it a useful or important concept in pastoral theology?
- What is your faith community's response to the socially excluded in your own society?
- What is the relationship between state control and personal freedom from a theological perspective?

FOR FURTHER READING AND EXPLORATION

See Pattison (1997a) for a full account of the outworking of liberation theology and pastoral care and theology. Other texts that explore the place of pastoral theology in political change and the place of power in care are: Hunter and Couture (eds) (1995), Selby (1983), Poling (1991), Gerkin (1991), Green (1988), and Forrester (1997).

12

Ecclesiology and Pastoral Theology

Nicholas Bradbury

Introduction

The ways in which the Christian community understands and reflects upon its nature, roles, and functions change. It responds to a variety of influences, including the particular context within which it exists. Many of those involved in pastoral and practical theology belong to a church and exercise their pastoral care as agents of their churches. The understanding of ecclesiology, the branch of theology that looks at the church's self-understanding, is therefore a significant subject for consideration here.

This specially commissioned chapter has been written by an English Anglican parish priest, Nicholas Bradbury, who has considerable experience of the church and its ministry, as well as of pastoral education, in a variety of settings. It takes and uses his own experience and poses some critical questions.

Bradbury is concerned with the core function of the church. He explores a basic presupposition that participation in church life is limiting, restrictive, and unchallenging. This chapter focuses on the nature of salvation and how the church's understanding of salvation finds expression in its identity and contact with others.

Through the identification of a range of questions that emerge from his own experience, Bradbury concludes the paper by articulating six ways of understanding the church. These models, or understandings, give rise to a number of key ecclesiological issues for pastoral theology. These include: lay ministry; the corporateness in the congregation; and the impact of the human sciences. Bradbury makes a final plea for freedom of thought that can enable the church to be "unblocked, unlocked, open-armed and vulnerable. That way, not the way of infallible pronouncements and institutional certainties, lies the church's road."

ECCLESIOLOGY AND PASTORAL THEOLOGY

Why keep the church going? Is it really worth it?

Pastoral theology asks these questions in the context of a mass of evidence to show that much of the church's effort goes on keeping comfortable people comfortable. Instead of church membership challenging people and nurturing them, it shores up their defences and dispenses a diet of spiritual lollipops. It purveys cosiness, not liberation. It promotes religious thumb-sucking, not justice. Instead of helping people explore the mystery of God, it offers an emotional security blanket.

Ecclesiology is the branch of theology that looks at the church's self-understanding. What do metaphors like 'the Body of Christ' mean in practice? How might a modern outlook differ from a New Testament one? What has been added by recent developments in theology, the ecumenical movement or the human sciences? What is the job of the church? How does the church relate to its ministry? Or the world? Or the Holy Spirit? What is God asking the church to do and be?

In order to get into these questions, let me take you on a personal tour. I was born in 1949 and have lived through a revolution in church affairs. As we travel I'll tell you what mattered to me and what questions I asked. The questions I invite you to ask as we go along are: *what 'salvation' do you think the world needs at the start of this new millennium? What might it look like? Who is it for? How can the church help be part of this salvation? What kind of a church does the bit of it you're involved with need to be?*

Until I was 8, I went to an Anglo-Catholic church in the north of England. Mass was an almost numinous experience with clouds of incense and lots of robed males doing ceremony in the sanctuary. Transcendence ruled OK. I learned something of the holiness and mystery of God and also that through Jesus, His Son, I was invited to be His friend. I had been made in love for love. The stories of Jesus got home. And I knew that the priest also did caring work in the parish. I was impressed by a large parish map in his study. Each street was prayed for by turn at early morning mass where I often served. The liturgy was that of the *English Missal* (1933). I also learned that the priest helped the dying and bereaved and I was aware of church funerals. Finally that church taught me about the Christian Year with its great fasts and feasts. My wanting to be a priest dates from this time and my own prayer was straightforward and easy: I talked to God as a friend. I asked no critical questions and noticed no contradictions. It never occurred to me, for example, that the strange words of the liturgy might be foreign to the working-class language of the community. I accepted that the church was where we should worship God, creator of the world, to whose praise and glory I was supposed to be living my life.

This church of my childhood alerted me to the importance of holiness, silence, ceremony and the transcendence of the mystery of God. When I met 'is Jesus your personal Saviour?' evangelicals for the first time at university, I recoiled, because my upbringing led me to feel that the knowledge of God couldn't be this hearty or wordy. Where the evangelicals wanted me to 'get Jesus', I wanted them to tune in to the ineffable silence of God which for me came with stillness, music, incense and architecture. These prejudices have always remained with me. We tend to retain (or react against) the ecclesiological influence of our early years in the church.

When I was 8, I went off to Christ Church Cathedral School in Oxford to be a chorister, where I sang daily. I loved both the music and the religion. The gaitered ecclesiastical dignitaries still looked straight out of Trollope. But during these years I lost my institutional innocence. I was struck by Christ's poverty and radical demands. I heard about Albert Schweitzer and Trevor Huddleston; surely that was true discipleship, not talking philosophy over vintage claret in Christ Church Hall. How did our expensive Cathedral services promote the Gospel? I began to see my Church of England as a contradiction. If it was supposed to be spreading God's love for the poor why did the Bishop live in a Palace and have an unbelievably posh car with a chauffeur? And why did we need all the pomp and ceremony? I began to think my church was like the religion of the scribes and Pharisees that Jesus preached against. But there was a paradox: the worship and fine-sounding sermons at the Cathedral were deeply reassuring.

Nevertheless, at 13 I lost my faith. A God of love couldn't permit volcanoes and cancer. And Christian faith was clearly nonsense: to what altitude did Jesus ascend? How could it be moral for God to demand the sacrifice of His son? How could someone being crucified deal with the evil of the world? I noticed there were two types of response to my outraged questioning. Those who got frustrated and reiterated orthodoxy. And those who believed that a living God could cope with living questions. It was the era of *Honest to God*, Vatican 2 and Paul Tillich's sermons in paperback. I learned that theology was a lifelong exploration which involved my innermost being.

When I was 18 I spent a year in a Franciscan community in Papua New Guinea. Here at last was the radical joy and simplicity of the Gospel as I understood it. The Franciscans were generous, warm-hearted and dedicated. They showed me what *koinonia* was all about: a community grounded in prayer and expressed in welcome, friendship and practical care, especially for the poor. I was now sure that to be authentic any church would have to be quite like the Franciscans.

Now came five years at Oxford University. This was theological privilege: resources galore, intellectual openness and friends to talk through the issues with. I learned that literature and the arts, psychology and science were important contributors to theology. It was 1968–73: Vatican 2 had brought the Roman Catholic church into the twentieth century and rediscovered the laity as people of God. Group dynamics and hospital placements had been introduced into seminary training. Tillich's *Systematic Theology* in three volumes gave me a modern understanding of Christian faith that made complete sense. A visit to Taizé was greatly inspiring. Off I went to ordination with great theological confidence.

Then came the cataclysm. I was unprepared for the shock. I went to the Elephant and Castle, one of London's poorest and most difficult inner-city neighbourhoods with massive deprivation and widespread human wretchedness. All that through the church was so precious to me seemed suddenly worthless. It simply could not reach where people were. It did not touch their experience. The church as I had known it was impotent. I grasped immediately that the fine theology of Oxford quadrangles was useless, alien. And so was the liturgy.

It was the human sciences rather than theology which helped me understand the situation. Psychology gave me insight into how emotional deprivation works. Sociology helped me to understand the social complexities and injustice I was caught up in. I gained a political perspective. The people of the Elephant and Castle, most of them nothing to do with the church, taught me definitively that if upbuilding and striving to heal a fragmented community of injured people in a brutalized environment is anything to do with the work of God's kingdom, it can be carried on quite apart from the church. The skeletal church did what it could. It identified with initiatives for community development. It supported the secular agencies' activities. Heaven was above the Community Centre rather than the church, and the clergy felt more at home distributing the neighbourhood newspaper or running a children's holiday project than on their knees.

I learned in my three years at the Elephant that wherever the church is, God's love has to be translated into the language and practice of human relationships and community development. Liturgy has to start with people's experience and feelings as they are. The task is to connect these with the resources and inspiration of the Christian tradition. I had to invent liturgies in collaboration with the people around me. Official doctrine had to be recast in the light of people's felt experience as they got to know each other in small groups or in running projects. Talk of salvation, for example, had to be connected to healing.

I then spent three years in New York City with the Jesuits. They were involved in an impressive breadth of ministry, from running a university to subway chaplaincy. They introduced me to the cultural complexity and diversity of Roman Catholicism in the USA: the church in different situations is a very different animal. I found the Roman Catholic church in New York open-minded and experimental. Loyalty to the Pope was in healthy tension with creative imagination and the seeking of new ways of being a church.

In 1979, I returned to another British inner-city parish of 25,000 people in Tottenham, London, including a large West Indian community. Now I was the vicar and had to work out how most appropriately to relate the ministry of the church to the human needs of the parish. So I decided to study at Birmingham University and came across the writings of R. A. Lambourne, which influenced me greatly.

Lambourne's ecclesiology strongly emphasized the corporate calling of the congregation. His work helped me develop the potential of the congregation for corporate care and action. I realized that the church was called to be a worshipping, learning, healing and serving community and that this could only happen by the development of corporateness. Pastoral care, for both theological and practical reasons, is the responsibility of the congregation as a whole.

Lambourne's ideas worked well in the inner city. When I was asked to be priest for six small villages in rural Wiltshire in 1990 I couldn't make them work at all. Culture got in the way. The church had become identified with the annual social and cultural round of the villages. It was there to help run the fete, provide the harvest festival and, above all, to stand for unchanging 'tradition' in a world otherwise surrounded by regrettable change. Any attempt to ask whether this comfortable routine was the best expression of church life for today met with strong resistance. I found myself challenged to the core. How could I gainsay my lifetime of Christian experience? Was this form of the church's existence recognizable as Christianity? I began to wonder if under these circumstances the church was worth keeping going at all.

I was not without allies. A few villagers ardently wanted the church to read the signs of the times and adapt accordingly. So we developed a framework to respond to the question: 'What is God calling the church to be in our parishes in the early part of the next millennium?' We worked on the assumption I have made throughout this chapter, that we can only discern God's will by looking beyond the church and examining how it can address the world's needs. We also assumed that human beings are on the cusp of a new era in their spiritual life. In a climate of uncertainty, the role of the church becomes uncertain. Change is all around us, inevitably being forced upon us. We have to try to understand these changes and find ways to influence our future and that of the church. What does it mean to inherit the Christian tradition of faith? How are we best to use our key resources, the biblical and ecclesial traditions, centred on eucharistic worship and practical caring? What is it to witness to the Gospel in our own context and be free under God to explore its meaning?

We agreed that we needed to examine every aspect of church life to see
if it was suitable for today: worship; how to use our medieval churches;
how or whether we need or use clergy; how we work with young people;
how we spend money, use time, organize life – the syllabus included everything involved in being the church in these villages. We thought the way
forward was prayer, careful listening and sharing ideas. We realized our
questions were far-reaching and that we would probably fail to translate
them into change in our churches. But we felt compelled to ask them.

Surprisingly, a good number of villagers became involved. Meetings were
well attended. Two weekend workshops were held, led by David Jenkins,
former bishop of Durham. Twelve people offered themselves for accredited
lay ministry. A link has been made with an inner-city parish. Church life
began to change and to move forward.

Now I find myself in a suburban parish in the city of Bristol. We have all
the trimmings of a successful middle-class church with its host of organizations and activities. And once again I am confused. Much of what we get
up to seems to be self-serving and complacent, an end-in-itself designed to
make us feel comfortable, pious and secure. But that's not the whole story.
There is a concern for justice, for prayer and for practical service here and
the congregation are, in general, open, welcoming without prejudice and
truly friendly. There is a willingness to explore and adapt. We are working
to establish a collaborative ecclesiology and ministry. I hope that what this
means and implies will gradually emerge.

My story reflects at least six contrasting ways of understanding the church,
presented here in light caricature:

1 The Franciscans: the model of sharing everything in simple, joyful,
   generous friendship and grounding the whole of life in prayer and praise.
2 At the Elephant and Castle a self-effacing church sought allies, however
   secular, and supported, often in hidden ways, their initiatives of reconciliation, justice, peace-making, healing, celebrating, affirming and upbuilding in love which it believed were the Gospel priorities.
3 In New York the Jesuits strove to keep faith with the massive Roman
   Catholic institution but to develop a local expression of it.
4 In Tottenham the church, working corporately, attempted to be a distinctive community embodying and expressing the Christian life in worship, learning, healing and serving. They believed their best contribution
   to the parish was to be a Christian congregation in action: welcoming,
   praying, responding to need and, especially, accepting and befriending
   the socially excluded.
5 In rural Wiltshire the church was more identified with village traditions,
   customs and culture. Sociological factors strongly influenced the rou-
   tines and conventions of church life. Theology was written out of the

script and social needs drove the agenda. A radical reformation seemed needed and was begun.

6   In Horfield, Bristol, the ghost of Constantinian Christendom has not yet accepted its death. Institutional robustness prevails. The bourgeois congregation have plenty to thank God for and are happy to come to church for the purpose. The congregation run a number of worthy associations and activities which tend to be attended by existing church members. They make a hefty financial contribution to the mission and ministry of the church in the inner city and overseas. They are active in the pastoral care of the parish. They strive to be Christian disciples in the workplace, which is often difficult. They are theologically open and questing. Their spirituality is on the move. The liturgy is magnificent.

The key ecclesiological issues for pastoral theology that I have lived through include:

*   a general renewal in the ministry of lay people
*   the recovery of the corporateness in the congregation
*   the impact of the human sciences on pastoral theology. From them ecclesiology has been enriched by a host of ideas including: organizational theory, group dynamics and systemic thinking; the significance of the Unconscious, especially in relation to our defences against anxiety; gender issues and the feminist critique; issues around authority, leadership, power, decision-making and role; appropriate pedagogy and life-long spiritual formation; a sociological perspective (the relation between the congregation and its environment, society and culture); theology as an interdisciplinary venture and the rise of 'theological reflection'

What is needed now is a more trenchant debate about the primary task of the church in the multi-faith, pluralist but increasingly secular world of the new millennium. Authority continues to be a hot issue: as society loses all deference for authority what decision-making structures will work best for the churches of post-Christendom? For the most part the mainstream churches are content to carry on triumphalistically, as if radical reformation was not yet called for by the times we live in.

Ecclesiology continues to be important because it's the discipline where discussion about the church of the future occurs. It helps to connect the past appropriately with the present and to distinguish between gospel and culture. It helps develop a critical eye for what is merely prejudice, jargon and tribal thinking. Most important, it equips us to go forward, in a chosen direction, and to become the best church we can.

We are called first to *be* the church, to be God's people, to be in relationship with God. This is a matter of spirituality. Only from there are we called to *do*, to collaborate with God in plans we hope are worth it for eternity. We need to learn freedom: to be unblocked, unlocked, open-armed and vulnerable. That way, not the way of infallible pronouncements and institutional certainties, lies the church's road.

SOURCES

Sources that I have personally found helpful are:

All the publications of *The Alban Institute*, Bethesda, MD, USA.

Audinet, J. (1995), *Ecrits de théologie pratique*, Ottawa, Canada: Novalis.

Ballard, P., and Pritchard, J. (1996), *Practical Theology in Action: Christian Thinking in the Service of Church and Society*, London: SPCK.

Bradbury, N. (1989), *City of God? Pastoral Care in the Inner City*, New Library of Pastoral Care, London: SPCK.

Cousins, E. H. (1992), *Christ of the 21ˢᵗ Century*, Rockport, MA: Element.

The Documents of Vatican 2. Especially *Lumen Gentium* and *Gaudium et Spes*.

Ecclestone, E. (ed.) (1988), *The Parish Church?*, Oxford: Grubb Institute/ Mowbray.

Furniss, G. (1994 USA/1995 UK), *Sociology for Pastoral Care*, Louisville, KY: Westminster/John Knox Press; London: SPCK.

Gallagher, M. P., SJ (1997), *Clashing Symbols – An Introduction to Faith and Culture*, London: Darton, Longman & Todd.

Jenkins, D. E. (1976), *The Contradiction of Christianity*, London: SCM Press.

Lambourne, R. A. (ed. Wilson, M.) (1985), *Explorations in Health and Salvation*, Birmingham, UK: University of Birmingham, Institute for the Study of Worship and Religious Architecture.

Schillebeeckx, E. (1980), *Ministry: A Case for Change*, London: SCM Press.

Schillebeeckx, E. (1985), *The Church with a Human Face: A New and Expanded Theology of Ministry*, London: SCM Press.

Tillich, P. (1968), *Systematic Theology*, London: James Nisbet.

Viau, M. (1993), *La nouvelle théologie pratique*, Paris: Editions de CERF.

SOME POINTS FOR FURTHER CONSIDERATION

- Describe your own understanding of the nature of the church.
- Describe the model of theological reflection at work in this paper. What are its main theological themes?
- How has your own experience shaped your theological understanding of the nature of the religious community and the world?
- What are the human needs of modern society that the ministry of the church should address? How far should the church community seek to address broad human needs?

• How do the human sciences shape or inform your own understanding of pastoral theology?

FOR FURTHER READING AND EXPLORATION

For a general discussion of different ecclesiological models of the church and some of their implications for practice, see Dulles (1976). For an imaginative, feminist approach to ecclesial existence in practical theology, see Graham (1996). Browning has shown considerable interest in how ecclesial identity and theology are created and expressed (Browning 1991). For more on the ecclesiology of the Church of England and Anglican churches generally, see Sykes (1978); see also Gill (1988, 1989, 1996) and Hardy and Gunton (1989).

___13___

Christian Morality and Pastoral Theology

Nicholas Peter Harvey

Introduction

Christian ethics, pastoral theology, and pastoral practice have always been closely related. Action needs to be guided by principles, while principles may need to be modified or interpreted in the light of experiences and actions. In the Catholic tradition, moral theology or ethics has been the guide for pastoral practice.

In this chapter, reprinted from the *Scottish Journal of Theology*, Peter Harvey, an English Catholic theologian, questions some of the fundamental assumptions upon which traditional moral and pastoral theology have been thought to be founded. He outlines a radical position on the nature of morality, the use of the Bible, and the application of theory to practice.

This subject is a critical one in pastoral theology. The way any theoretical framework conceptualizes the nature of right and wrong shapes practice and the experience of growth and wholeness. Understandings of ethics and morality shape the ways in which boundaries are formed and possibilities for the transformation of human experiences.

Harvey argues against an allegiance to a morality which claims to be comprehensive and distinctively Christian. The chapter argues for an approach to morality that can embrace change, ambiguity, and mystery. It criticizes the position that maintains an approach to the Christian tradition as monolithic and unchanging. Development and adaptation characterize the way Christian history has approached morality. Harvey points out that there is a shadow side to the tradition that has validated feudal and oppressive systems like slavery, serf-dom, and anti-Semitism; further, there is a variety of perspectives on pacifism. No one approach can impose an unchanging pattern to human living and relating. In particular, Harvey argues that the sacralizing of marriage marginalizes other possible forms of relation-ship. This approach has implications for Christian views of remar-riage after divorce and attitudes to same-sex partnerships. Harvey concludes that the key concepts of evolution and development, and the theological virtues of faith, hope, and love need to be worked out afresh "in fear and trembling."

If Harvey's approach to morality were adopted, the Christian tradition of care in the area of sexual relationships, for example, would be transformed with a more inclusive approach to women and gay and lesbian people. This chapter challenges pastoral theolo-gians and practitioners to think more clearly about where moral boundary lines are drawn in theory. It also raises the nature of the relationship between empathy and confrontation in pastoral care. It remains to be seen how pastoral theologians work out the relationship between contemporary experience and the Christian moral tradition.

CHRISTIAN MORALITY AND PASTORAL THEOLOGY

What follows is a set of reflections on the nature of Christian morality. Having been reared on and given allegiance to a morality which claimed to be rigorous, comprehensive and distinctively Christian, I have spent at least the last thirty years unlearning this in the light of experience and observa-tion. The morality of my youth now appears as an ethics of boundaries rather than of transformation.

In the dissolution of this seemingly watertight moral system conversa-tion, thinking, reading and the task of teaching ethics to prospective clergy have all played their part, but the touchstone is observation of what goes on in people's lives. The notion of theology in play, whether or not labelled as pastoral, is essentially that of a reflection on what is happening. From this point of view there is no need to establish connections between theology and ethics, since there can be no separation.

People sometimes ask: 'Where does God come in?' The question is based on a misunderstanding, for what is happening is, if anywhere, the place of God. The past is important only because it has happened, and the future is not yet revealed. The present contains the past and invites the future: all three are inseparable and in a sense indistinguishable. If some sense of the mystery of all things does not burgeon for us in the processes in which we find ourselves involved then attempts to bring God in, or to find God elsewhere, are in vain. The mystical tradition is thus wise to speak of the sacrament of the present moment: that is all we have, that is the gift and the opportunity, that is where possibilities are recognized and embraced – or not.

It is commonly assumed within and outside the church that Christian teaching on moral fundamentals has always been the same. It is also usually supposed that these alleged fundamentals are distinctive, being derived from, or at least in some sense guided by, the moral teachings of the Bible. None of these assumptions can survive critical scrutiny. The Bible is not a book but a library, its components written from cultural and religious standpoints so different from each other as to make synthesis impossible without distortion. It is not possible to draw a morality in our sense either from the Jewish scriptures, tendentiously called by Christians the Old Testament, or from the New Testament.

In the case of the Jewish scriptures it is easy not to notice that some of the most important figures are in our terms morally reprehensible. Abraham, praised by early Christians as our father in faith, heard the Lord's command to kill his son and set out to obey. There is no difference at the level of the application of principles between this state of mind and the response of Peter Sutcliffe, popularly known as the Yorkshire Ripper, to angelic voices telling him to kill prostitutes (cf. Kierkegaard [1985] for Abraham's response as an example of the teleological suspension of ethics in the interests of faith in the living God). Jacob, whose God Christians claim to worship, deceived his blind father in order to cheat his elder brother out of his inheritance. This deceit is a key moment in his rise to a highly honoured role in the tradition. Whatever we are expected to learn from these stories, it is not what is ordinarily called morality.

Then there is Joshua's jihad to exterminate the inhabitants of Palestine, making way for the Israelites. This story, including its racist and religiously intolerant use at times in the past, is dealt with by modern Christians largely by pretending it is not there. This denial is only the most spectacular example of the vain but persistent attempt to homogenize the Bible in the light of currently dominant convictions and concerns. Such attempted homogenization is necessary as long as the traditional claim is made that everything in the Bible is the revealed word of God for all times and places. My contrary contention is that no notion of development, however sophisticated, can make of such disparate materials a coherent whole.

What then of Jesus? Our sources do not corroborate the common picture of him as an outstanding moral teacher and exemplar. The texts present him as involved in a fierce ongoing struggle about the religious identity and future of Israel. This seems to have included an intense dialectic with his theological enemies about the purpose and limitations of the Torah. The Hebrew word *torah*, commonly and misleadingly translated as 'law', has to do with the particular history and self-understanding of the Jewish people. The Torah, including the Ten Commandments, is not a universal code or set of principles or values. There is therefore no reason to suppose Jesus was a moral reformer, still less a personification of the virtues. Indeed, these are sometimes flouted by him in the story as we have it. Two examples, one from his teaching and the other from his life, may help. He insists on hatred of close relatives as a necessary condition of discipleship. True, another source has him referring to the commandment to honour parents, but the commentators' tendency to minimize and distance the 'hard saying' in favour of this generally accepted maxim is to be resisted (Harvey 1991).

The second example: Jesus put himself in line for his own death by setting his face towards Jerusalem, the place of the killing of the prophets. Retrospectively a theology emerged which enabled his followers to acclaim this as a supreme act of love. It is difficult to claim that it was such for his friends at the time: no ordinary human frame of reference could begin to validate any such notion. Whatever is said about the failure of his inner circle to remain in attendance after his arrest, his execution under a curse outside the city wall was a let-down, a desertion of them, a cruel undermining of the hope he had aroused in them. A martyr, or indeed a hero of the revolution, dies for a recognizable cause. Despite modern attempts to say that he died in the cause of justice or freedom, no moral category can accommodate, much less commend, Jesus' approach to his death, which remains unexplained. His approach approximates to that of a suicide. This scandal is the heart of the story (Harvey 1985).

Christians tend to cheat by arguing that it was all in accord with a divine design to which Jesus alone had access. But this is to take away the contingency, and consequent unpredictability, of the events which made up the Passion. Those events, thus accounted for, cease to be the kind of happenings with which we find ourselves engaged. The appeal to a God who always knows in advance what is going to happen removes human responsibility.

Deprived of such a crutch, Jesus' story comes alive. It is not so much a question of finding this story directly useful or helpful, as of finding ourselves in the story. But this does not work at the appropriate depth unless we identify with all the characters. Only moralistic reductionism can produce from this material a tale of goodies and baddies. The gospels are too full of ambiguities and unresolved tensions to generate coherent moral guidance. In so far as these texts remain alive for us, their interest and power lie elsewhere.

In the earliest manifestations known to us Christianity was not characterized by a distinctive approach to morality. For example, the lists of vices in the letters attributed to Paul are largely conventional, products of the milieu in which Christianity came to birth. These letters sometimes go out of their way to stress the moral respectability of Christian behaviour. Notice, for instance, the stress on the importance of obedience to the magistrate, and that of slaves to their masters.

Modern Christians tend to speak as if what is distinctive about their morality is that it is rooted in a love which originates with Jesus. But the gospel material about the life and teaching of Jesus, manifesting as it does a wonderful array of multiple creative ambiguities, does not directly advance understanding of the meaning and practice of love. As for Paul, those remarks in which he reinterprets the Torah in terms of the command to love can offer us no moral guidance, for our struggle is not with the Torah. Furthermore, his often-quoted hymn to love is a description of some of the best in human behaviour: turned into prescriptions, it becomes either unhelpful or dangerous. In any case the claim, whether ancient or modern, that love is what morality is all about is of no help in problematic situations.

What about the Sermon on the Mount? Some Christians have doubtless been deeply influenced in their attitude to morality by particular sentences from this collection, but as a whole it has never formed the basis of any systematic or sustained thinking about morals. Luther thought it represented an unlivable ideal, the function of which was to convince us of our need for divine forgiveness. Some of his medieval predecessors held that the sermon consisted of 'counsels of perfection' for a spiritual elite. The fact that such tortuous interpretations arose within the Christian mainstream indicates the recalcitrance of this material to being treated as a primary text for Christian ethics.

Can the idea of an essence of Christian morality be saved by some concept of development? On the contrary, talk of development prevents a straight look at the history of Christian thinking about morality. Much assimilation from surrounding cultures has occurred, as in the rise of theories of natural law and of virtue and character, now enjoying a revival. Distinctively modern emphases found in western Christianity have also been taken from elsewhere. These include doctrines of human rights and of religious liberty, both once anathema to the church. There are also what might loosely be called existentialist approaches, with a strong stress on authentic individual choice as the constitutive factor in moral living.

Some Christian groupings resist this eclecticism in the name of revealed truth, some appealing to the Bible, others to tradition. They identify Christian faith as such with absolutist answers to particular moral questions. These attempts are not as philosophically innocent as might be supposed, and they depend on a selective use and questionable hermeneutic of traditional texts. These groups could well be asked whether their underlying agenda is the maintenance of a distinctive Christian identity against the perceived inroads of modernity. In other words, is their moral programme pursued not so much for its own sake as in its function of securing a threatened Christian identity? This has certainly happened repeatedly in the past, when moral questions became entangled in attempts to secure boundaries. Ambrose of Milan is a case in point. He gave priority in the Christian moral order to consecrated virginity because he saw consecrated female virgins, with their high symbolic and liturgical visibility, as boundary-stones of the church (Brown 1990).

The phrase 'justice and peace' looms large in some contemporary Christian discourses. In the course of history the church has validated imperial, feudal and egalitarian political systems, including of course slavery, serfdom and anti-Semitism. While it is true that tyrannies of various kinds, from Roman imperialism onwards, have been criticized and even resisted by some Christians, the record of Christian political thinking and practice is from the beginning very mixed. It has been suggested that the New Testament books were written by those in the ascendant in the church who interpreted Jesus in ways which played down his subversive thrust. But it is an illusion to suppose that we can go back behind these diverse and fragmentary texts to establish some certainty about the real, pure Jesus. What we have is a tradition, which allows a variety of interpretations. We lack unmediated access to Jesus (Parker 1997).

Appeals to the Trinity as a model of how humans should relate to one another in the political order are fashionable. It is forgotten that the same doctrine was earlier used with equal sincerity to offer theocratic legitimacy to a hierarchical society. What is happening here is the projection of a preferred notion of the political order on to the doctrine of the Trinity. In any case the forms of justice now so strongly advocated by Christians are characteristic of some of the idealistic political aspirations of our time, and cannot be claimed as a distinctively Christian venture.

As to peace, Christians have held almost every conceivable outlook from outright pacifism (claimed to originate with Jesus) via the just war theory to the crusading spirit. There is also the suggestion that the peace of which Jesus speaks has no direct bearing on the external order or on the particulars of behaviour, but is instead a state of inner harmony with God in all circumstances. Given this range of divergent ways of seeking to follow the tradition, it is not at all clear what Christians mean by peace, still less whether the word has any distinctively Christian resonance (Hauerwas 1983, for an opposing view).

These examples could be multiplied. They are chosen to illustrate the fact that there is not, and never has been, a Christian consensus on moral matters. Whatever resources may be available in the various Christian traditions are not of such a kind as to make it possible to speak of a Christian basis for morality. The current insistence of some Christian leaders and thinkers on a single point of view, especially though not exclusively on aspects of medical and sexual ethics, cannot alter the fact that there are profound disagreements within all the churches on every moral question.

Yet the claim to moral unanimity among Christians, at least on fundamentals, recurs, and prevents healthy debate.

Some recent work argues that the resurrection of Jesus from the dead is the key to Christian morality (e.g. O'Donovan 1986). Part of this thesis is that the resurrection vindicates what is called 'the created order', in which appropriate patterns of relationship are laid down. The moral task then becomes conformity to the original order. We are supposed to find a revealed description of this order in the opening chapters of Genesis. As with a morality of natural law, this tends in practice to be conservative of those patterns of relating familiar at the time, which are all too easily equated with what is thought to be transcultural and transhistorical. In an age when we are being sensitized to the fact that particular forms of human relationship are at least in part social constructions, proponents of 'the created order' insist that there is an unchanging pattern to human living and relating, from which everything else is a falling short.

An obvious case in point is marriage, which has meant and continues to mean different things in different times and places, within the church as much as outside. The attempt to treat it as a univocal term, and as an institution uniquely privileged by God, is an idealization with an oppressive function. It may be argued against this that while the practice is messy and various we must retain allegiance to marriage as an ideal form, for without this there is no basis for criticizing changing patterns of relating. On the contrary, attention to the ideal distracts from properly critical attention to the forms of relationship that are proceeding among us. The insistent sacralizing of marriage marginalizes other possible forms of relationship.

Two examples follow. The usual defence of remarriage after divorce is that it is a second attempt at what marriage is supposed to be (Kelly 1996). This fails to respect the first marriage, since it entails saying either that it was not a real marriage or that the earlier relationship has no enduring significance. The critical question is: In what ways can the first marriage be recognized and valued within the second? This requires accepting that a second marriage is not the same kind of thing as the first, but that both can be equally valid as forms of relationship. A second example is that of same-sex partnerships, the commonest defence of which is that they can approximate to the ideal of marriage. This refuses to take seriously the variety of same-sex relationships that occur, and their possible differences from heterosexual relationships. The question is not whether a gay or lesbian relationship conforms to an ideal transposed from the heterosexual context, but whether it is oppressive or liberating for those involved (Stuart 1995). Concentrating on the ideal of lifelong partnership also overlooks the obvious fact that same-sex friendships with an erotic dimension are sometimes, though by no means always, part of psychosexual development.

The point made in the previous paragraph about oppression and liberation has much wider bearings. Across the whole spectrum of sexual relationships other than marriage the question 'who is getting what out of this?'
opens up a more penetrating line of enquiry than questions of conformity
or otherwise to an ideal. It also has application within marriage, where talk
of fidelity in difficulties may obfuscate the power-play proceeding in the
relationship, usually though not invariably to the detriment of the woman.
In all these ways the invocation of Christian faith to keep the ideal in business militates against clear-sighted analysis and responsible action. Too great
an insistence on an ideal in any aspect of life, not least in a religious context,
can militate against moral development, with destructive consequences.

An odd feature of most theological work on morality is its innocence of
the idea of evolution and of the power of the unconscious mind. There is
something surreal about a conversation purporting to address the fundamentals of behaviour which proceeds as if we lived in a pre-evolutionary
and pre-Freudian world. The churches have in practice long since adopted
the Enlightenment's assumption that what defines us all, except perhaps
those classified as mad, is a core of rationality. This presupposition is also
shared by many theologians who see themselves as attacking the Enlightenment. It has led to simplistic and overly individualistic notions of free will
as the source of human actions. Recognition of the extent to which the
unconscious can dictate individual and corporate behaviour gravely threatens
such moralistic notions; but the churches, in common with one strand in
our culture, have difficulty in hoisting in this very different perception of
what often drives our behaviour. Meanwhile evolution's suggestion that
life spontaneously takes new forms in response to changing circumstances
undermines a morality of static essences and self-conscious virtue.

Nothing said so far need be taken to mean that there are no Christian
resources available which bear on behaviour. It is unfortunate that the
contemporary revival of interest in virtue and character largely presupposes
that the classical notions sit comfortably with the theological virtues. There
is a baneful confusion here, for faith, hope and love are not about virtue
and character in the classical sense at all. They do not demand an understanding of humankind as essentially rational. The character they are liable
to form is unlikely to fit with the norms of prudence, justice, fortitude and
temperance. The classical virtues assume we know what the good life is,
the theological virtues do not (Fuchs 1987, for the suggestion that the
moral task is properly defined as self-realization, provided that reductionist
concepts of the self are avoided). Whereas the classical virtues are acquired
by education, the theological virtues are seen as gifts.

Faith, hope and love are not, of course, confined to Christianity. But they
connect with the story of Jesus, which, as has already been argued, is not a
moral tale. For as long as this story continues to be told, it cannot but

influence our behaviour. It does so by way of interaction between elements in it and what is happening in our lives and in our world (Harvey 1991). Faith, meaning trust in awareness, is the key. The heart of faith is a disciplined wakefulness, a clear-eyed attentiveness to what is going on rather than a prior allegiance to a set of beliefs and practices. If morality in the form of universal principles or imperatives is to hold sway there is no place for faith, for morality has become God. A living faith is liable to insist on quite other and less readily intelligible priorities, which are none the less urgent and taxing for that (cf. Kierkegaard, *Fear and Trembling*).

While a faith-based morality can and will learn from the story of Jesus, there is no question of imitating the particulars. Objection may be made that there is no one version of the story, that from the beginning Christians have used Jesus to justify contradictory things, and that a faith-based morality risks being overly subjective. The truth of these observations can readily be acknowledged. The counter-argument is that while the story of Jesus provides part of the context for our decision-making, we have to take responsibility not only for our actions but for our interpretation of the story (Schüssler-Fiorenza 1995). A living text, it has been said, is always giving birth to meanings.

The critic who says that a faith-based morality provides no viable alternative to a morality of principles or values is missing the point. From the angle of faith the latter kind of morality has no substance other than as an instrument of social control. The insistence on a supplement to faith in the form of principles or values is a demand for a security mechanism. If it is possible to speak at all of a Christian morality it is a morality of gift and call (McDonagh 1979). The theological virtues of faith, hope and love remain to be worked out in fear and trembling.

BIBLIOGRAPHY

Brown, P. (1990), *The Body and Society*, London: Collins.
Fuchs, J. (1987), *Christian Morality: The World Becomes Flesh*, Dublin: Gill and Macmillan; Washington, DC: Georgetown University Press.
Harvey, N. P. (1985), *Death's Gift*, London: Epworth.
Harvey, N. P. (1991), *The Morals of Jesus*, London: Darton, Longman & Todd; American edition: *Morals and the Meaning of Jesus* (1993). Cleveland: Pilgrim Press.
Hauerwas, S. (1983), *The Peaceable Kingdom*, London: SCM Press.
Kelly, K. T. (1996), *Divorce and Second Marriage*, London: Cassell.
Kierkegaard, Søren (1985), *Fear and Trembling*, Harmondsworth: Penguin.
McDonagh, E. (1979), *Gift and Call*, Dublin: Gill and Macmillan.
O'Donovan, Oliver (1986), *Resurrection and Moral Order*, Exeter: IVP.
Parker, D. C. (1997), *The Living Text of the Gospels*, Cambridge: Cambridge University Press.

Schüssler-Fiorenza, E. (1995), *Jesus: Miriam's Child, Sophia's Prophet*, London: SCM Press.
Stuart, E. (1995), *Just Good Friends*, London: Cassell.

SOME POINTS FOR FURTHER CONSIDERATION

- What is your understanding of Christian morality and ethics?
- What is or should be the relationship between ethics and pastoral care?
- What is the role of the Bible in pastoral care and pastoral theology?
- Does the Christian moral tradition change? Explore this issue in relation to an area of moral thinking; for example, peace, sex and sexuality, or marriage.
- How might the theological virtues of faith, hope, and love shape theology as reflecting on the present moment?

FOR FURTHER READING AND EXPLORATION

For a further philosophical consideration of this position, see MacNiven (1993). For a feminist approach to moral development and ethics, see Gilligan (1982) and Frazer, Hornsby, and Lovibond (eds) (1992). For a classic examination of the place of ethics in pastoral care, see Browning (1983); and Underwood (1983). Atkinson and Field integrally connect ethics and care in their dictionary (1995). For background to the traditional Catholic view of moral theology, see Mahoney (1987).

14

Spirituality in
a Postmodern Era

MARIE MCCARTHY

INTRODUCTION

Marie McCarthy is a member of the clinical and training staff of the Center for Religion and Psychotherapy of Chicago. A Catholic, she works as a psychotherapist, spiritual guide, and retreat director. In this specially commissioned chapter, McCarthy draws upon her extensive practical experience to argue that there needs to be a positive dialogue between the disciplines of pastoral theology and of spirituality. Each needs the other.

There has been an explosion of interest in the topic of spirituality throughout the Western world in the last two decades. While there is no agreement about the exact nature of spirituality, it is clear that many people feel the need to explore the meaning and depth of their experience, partly, perhaps, as a reaction to trends such as materialism, commercialism, and anonymity in mass society. Some kinds of spirituality have been engendered and contained within traditional religions such as Christianity. Here retreats and practices such as meditation and spiritual direction have become popular. However, "spirituality" is not the property of any particular religious group. It is common now to hear management experts and health care workers, as well as members of "New Age" religious movement such as paganism, discussing their various spiritual needs and explorations.

McCarthy begins her analysis of the contemporary spiritual quest by examining some of the factors that impinge upon it: postmodern consciousness, technological explosion, space travel, and the Holocaust. These realities have led to a questioning and breakdown of larger frameworks of meaning and long-held values, resulting in the experience of restlessness, spiritual hunger, and wandering. McCarthy describes spirituality as the "deepest desires of the human heart for meaning, purpose, and connection" and as a "deep life lived intentionally in reference to something larger." She invites study of this area in an interdisciplinary way as a discipline which has its roots in a tradition and which is directed towards action. From this perspective, pastoral theologians may discover the dynamic of the discipline through practice.

In conclusion, McCarthy underlines some key aspects of the nature of pastoral and practical theology. First, pastoral theology often starts with human need, experience, and practice. Second, it is orientated towards human wellbeing in the light of the Christian religious tradition. Third, pastoral theology's nature and methods are diversely practiced; it is, therefore, impossible to impose any one framework or pattern upon it.

SPIRITUALITY IN A POSTMODERN ERA

Spirituality as a Topic

The subject of spirituality represents one of the major areas of study and research needing serious attention from the disciplines of practical and pastoral theology. At the same time, the disciplined study of spirituality has a great deal to contribute to the enrichment and renewal of both these disciplines. As we approach the close of the twentieth century, interest in spirituality seems to be exploding on all fronts. Popular magazines and professional journals carry articles on spirituality. Professional associations in both the religious and scientific communities sponsor workshops and devote major portions of their annual conferences to the subject of spirituality. Major television dramas and network news magazines featuring storylines with explicitly spiritual themes and language reach hundreds of thousands of viewers weekly. And a recent check of the local Barnes and Noble bookstore yielded over 1,600 volumes with the word spirituality in the title, as well as over 5,000 volumes addressing some aspect of spirituality.

The Contemporary Climate

To what can we attribute the enormous popularity of spirituality today? Many would locate its roots in the widespread restlessness evident in the lives of individuals, groups, institutions, and businesses. Corporate executives seek opportunities for silent retreats. Major businesses add meditation rooms to the workplace environment. Men and women earning impressive salaries quit their jobs to find a quieter pace, a more peaceful environment, a closer connection with the land, a greater sense of purpose. Much of contemporary society is marked by a restless searching. People from virtually every social, political, cultural, economic, and educational background are searching for depth, meaning, and direction – for a reality and purpose greater than and beyond themselves, which is worthy of their commitment and their life energy.

This restlessness itself is not new. It has been with us, in one form or another, since the dawn of consciousness. It is this restless seeking for meaning, purpose, and enduring values which is the primary maker of the spiritual quest. As Augustine of Hippo reminds us, "Our hearts are restless." We are hungry seekers and that hunger draws us out of ourselves over and over again. It draws us toward connection with people, ideas, and projects worthy of our energies. And whether we experience this hunger as drawing us into relationship with another, with many others, with the whole of creation, or with The Other, we always experience it as being drawn beyond ourselves into connection with something larger than, greater than, beyond our own selves.

While this restlessness has been with us since the dawn of consciousness, it has always taken different shape and form in response to the questions, struggles, accomplishments, preoccupations, and ethos of particular eras. There are four particular factors which I would suggest have had a profound influence on the intensity and character of the spiritual quest at this time in history: postmodern consciousness, the technological explosion, space travel, and the Holocaust.

Our contemporary era has been characterized by many as "postmodern," a designation which is intended to capture a dramatic shift in consciousness which occurred over in the last decades of the twentieth century. This shift in consciousness is marked primarily by the growing awareness of the relativity and particularity of every perspective and position. No longer do we speak of universal principles and laws, valid for all times and places. Instead we look for the particular historical, cultural, social, and familial values that may have contributed to this particular set of principles and laws being useful in this particular set of circumstances. The "postmodern" era is one of intellectual, religious, and political pluralism and diversity – an era of the "conflict of interpretations" (Ricoeur) and of "texts under negotiation" (Brueggemann). It is an era when the "Sacred Canopy" (Berger), if one can be found at all, seems barely to cover the local ball field.

A second factor which has shaped the contemporary ethos and contributed significantly both to the emergence of postmodern consciousness and to the shape of the spiritual quest today is the scientific and technological explosion. People and commodities travel across town, across the country, and around the world in unprecedented numbers, with unprecedented speed and frequency. We meet difference and diversity at every turn. And we need not travel to do so. Communication technology has developed at such an astonishing rate that we can now communicate instantaneously around the world. We can gather unimagined volumes of information, and our computers process that information faster than the human brain can think. As a result we live with a glut of information and, often, with the illusion that information will make us wise. We can communicate what we take to be the facts before we have had a chance to reflect on their meaning. And we can surround ourselves from the moment we wake until we go to sleep with auditory and visual stimuli, which allow little or no time for contemplative attending or focused awareness.

Scientific and technological advances have broken new ground in the prevention and cure of disease while at the same time enabling us to create biological, chemical, and nuclear weapons of mass destruction. And all of this has occurred in an environment where it has been increasingly difficult to articulate a set of guiding values and principles.

Scientific and technological advance also made possible the third factor which has profoundly influenced contemporary consciousness – space travel. When astronauts beamed back the photo of "the big blue marble" they forever changed how we would see this planet earth. This dramatic shift in horizons allowed us for the first time to see the unity and connectedness of the whole of the planet, her great beauty and her extraordinary vulnerability. For the first time we grasped how small she was in the midst of so vast a universe. This shift in vision coupled with the experience of the dark side of technology has led many to abandon the myth of progress and limitless expansion. It has led to a growing awareness of the limits of our resources and the need to preserve and protect those resources.

A final factor which has had a powerful influence on the contemporary spiritual quest is the Holocaust. This historical horror has forced us to see with appalling clarity the extent of the inhumanity of which we are capable. And the continued widespread presence of ethnic cleansing, genocide, and dehumanizing racism lead many to deep soul-searching and to an intense urgency in their spiritual quest.

Given the questioning and breakdown of larger frameworks of meaning and of long-held values and assumptions, it is not surprising to find ourselves hungry and wandering. We seem to find ourselves in an era in which "the mind [has come] to the end of its tether and all its usual patterns of thought have proved fruitless" (Needleman 1982: 3). This breakdown of frameworks of meaning has led some to retreat into entrenched positions and others into directionless wandering. Many search for a larger sense of meaning, for a more adequate grounding, for some alternative to a naive, simplistic piety on the one hand or a religious fanaticism on the other.

In the midst of this reality can the disciplines of practical and pastoral theology offer some insight and direction to our spiritual wandering? And can the retrieval of an authentic spirituality lend renewed vigor, depth, purpose, and vision to the enterprise of practical and pastoral theology? In order to explore these questions I will delineate the arena of the conversation, offer a possible framework for defining spirituality, and explore some of the ways in which spirituality is experienced, perceived, and expressed. I will then suggest some marks or characteristics of an authentic spirituality. And finally I will ask what the study of spirituality might gain from the disciplines of practical and pastoral theology and what practical and pastoral theology might gain from the study and integration of spirituality.

Approaching a Definition

The term spirituality is used in a great variety of ways and with varying degrees of specificity. This is due not only to the character of our contemporary situation but also to the nature of spirituality itself. In some ways defining spirituality is like attempting to delineate a field of study which encompasses the whole of life. Spirituality is a fundamental component of our human beingness, rooted in the natural desires, longings, and hungers of the human heart. It is concerned with the deepest desires of the human heart for meaning, purpose, and connection, with the deep life lived intentionally in reference to something larger than oneself.

There are several distinct, yet interrelated ways in which spirituality can be appropriately understood. Spirituality can refer to the lived experience of depth. It can also refer to a range of expressions of the lived experience of depth, to particular spiritualities which are culture- and context-specific and which have certain requirements that make them effective in a particular culture and context. And spirituality can refer to an academic discipline which studies the first and especially the second of these (cf. Principe 1983: 136–7; Downey 1997: ch. 1).

Spirituality and religion

Given this understanding of spirituality, the distinction between spirituality and religion becomes important. As Diarmuid Ó Murchú points out, spirituality is at least 70,000 years old, while the various formal religious systems are not more than 4,500 years old (1998: vii). Spirituality is broader and more encompassing than any religion. It is an expression of one's deepest values and commitments, one's sense or experience of something larger than and beyond oneself.

While the experience and expression of spirituality is distinct from religion and religious traditions it is not necessarily separate from them. Spirituality is often intimately connected with the rituals, dogmas, rules, and regulations of particular religious traditions and institutions. And these religious traditions hold "flash points with in them" which become vehicles for capturing, focusing, and expressing the spirituality of a people (Harris 1996: 18). Spirituality, then, is always concerned with the quest for meaning.

And when that quest involves an explicit reference to God or the Divine, that spirituality is religious (Downey 1997: 32).

The Study of Spirituality

The defining nature of context

When undertaking the study of spirituality, the nature and breadth of the topic require the use of an interdisciplinary method. It is impossible to understand a person's or a group's spirituality apart from the total context. Psychological, historical, anthropological, sociological, philosophical, linguistic, environmental, and ecological factors give shape and texture to one's spirituality every bit as much as (perhaps even more than) theological and religious attitudes do (cf. Principe 1983: 138). Thus each of these disciplines has a contribution to make to the study of spirituality.

Jacob Needleman suggests the metaphor of many paths to highlight the defining nature of context (cf. 1982: 38, 19). People setting out from quite different and distant regions of the earth to journey to the same destination will encounter vastly different terrain, see different sights and face distinct challenges and joys on their journeys. Those who journey from the arctic regions will have to follow a very different set of rules for survival and carry different provisions than those who journey from the desert regions or the tropical rainforests. It is only as the travelers draw near their common destination that similarities in landscape and in the type of provisions needed begin to emerge. So it is with spirituality. There are many different spiritualities which are expressive of different forms of life, differing world views and experiences, different paths of integration, wholeness, and holiness (Downey 1997: 46). Thus, every study of spirituality has to begin with a consideration of context. We need to know where a spirituality comes from and to what it is related, if we are to understand it in any significant way. To understand a spirituality we must grasp it in the fullness of its concrete particularity.

The place of tradition

Part of the concrete particularity of a spirituality is the tradition in which it is grounded and from which it emerges. Michael Downey makes the point that "any authentic Christian spirituality is expressed in relationship to tradition" (1997: 2). I want to go further and assert that every authentic spirituality, whether religious or not, is rooted in a tradition. Spirituality is not a free-floating amorphous reality that emerges *sui generis*. While spirituality is, indeed, a fundamental aspect of our human beingness, its appearance and expression is always in the form of practices and experiences that are grounded in a tradition.

Tradition, in this sense, involves not just the contents of a teaching, but all of the various external and inner conditions which are necessary for the tradition to be transmitted, experienced, and incorporated into living. To hand on the contents of a tradition apart from the conditions under which it can be heard can only lead to "arid scholasticism or blind fanaticism" (Needleman 1982: 65).

Herein lies part of the dilemma of our contemporary, postmodern era. We are intensely aware of the particularity of the various traditions, of the way in which the parts fit together to make a whole. And we are equally aware that the conditions which fostered, nourished, and enabled the handing on of these traditions are no longer present. Thus, we find ourselves bereft of practices and disciplines that will sustain and nourish us. We find ourselves grasping at bits and pieces of a tradition hoping that the part we latch on to can lead to the same result that once required the whole of the tradition (Needleman 1982: 52).

The New Age myth

Contemporary seekers, with little or no grounding in traditional forms of spirituality and with little historical consciousness, suggest that the current intense interest in spirituality marks the beginning of a new age. Spiritualities which are designated as "New Age" are often characterized as being incarnational, ecological, global, and open to all faith traditions. They are frequently eclectic, non-traditional, and esoteric in nature. While many practitioners of the various forms of New Age spirituality are sincere seekers, there are serious concerns which need to be raised regarding "New Age" approaches to spirituality.

The designation "New Age" itself is problematic. Many of the practices which are referred to as New Age are, in fact, centuries old. What is new is the adoption of these practices apart from the totality of the tradition in which they are grounded. In a culture characterized as "ravenous for soul food" (Gill-Austern 1997: 63), we become indiscriminate eaters. We sample a wide range of appetizers, picking and choosing what suits our taste, without eating a complete and balanced meal. In addition, much of New Age spirituality is marked by privatization and commercialization. As Herbert Anderson has pointed out, spirituality has become "a product to be sold" (1997: 2). It is packaged and marketed to suit the taste of the consumer, promising "relief from the fear of death, peace and enlightenment without a lifetime of discipline" (ibid.).

Finding a postmodern grounding

Part of the task of practical and pastoral theology is to find an effective bridge between the ancient traditions and New Age consciousness. Abandoning the past, picking and choosing discrete elements from the past that suit our interests, retreating to the past or ignoring the wisdom of the current age will not serve us well. Two factors which may assist us in honoring the past and bringing its riches into the present in an active and vital way are a retrieval of the understanding of tradition as a living reality and the identification and exploration of particular charisms.

While our spiritualities are necessarily grounded in tradition, postmodern consciousness has made us keenly aware of the particularities of context and circumstance which have fostered the traditions. We cannot simply import a tradition or a part of a tradition as it existed in another place and time and expect it to be effective in fostering spiritual depth in our current circumstances. We need to understand tradition as a living reality, to uncover the original intentions of a tradition and its practices, and to discover the ways and means by which the original intentions can be served in the current context. Such an exploration, if done well, is a demanding enterprise which requires that we be aware, as fully as possible, not only of the limits and blind spots of the particular traditions, but of the limits of our own perspective and of our tendency to distort the truth to fit our own preconceived notions (cf. Needleman 1982: 63).

The notion of charism can be helpful here. The term refers to the particular or special gift or grace which a spiritual tradition embodies. Seeking out and lifting up the charisms of particular spiritual traditions provides a means of honoring and celebrating the extravagant diversity of God's gifts to us. The retrieval of the original charism of a particular spirituality brings into focus the particular manifestation of truth which is embodied in this particular tradition, while at the same time providing a vehicle for discerning the conditions and practices which will keep that truth a "living truth" in this time and place.

Marks of Authentic Spirituality

While every spirituality, whether eastern or western, traditional or New Age, religious or non-religious, is rooted in particular practices with in a particular context, there are some identifiable characteristics common to all authentic spiritualities. At the broadest level authentic spirituality is an integrative, wholistic response to the command to choose life (Palmer 1990: 143). This response usually includes the dispositions and disciplines of contemplative awareness, effective action in the world, rootedness in community, openness, non-dualistic thinking and action, and discernment.

Contemplative awareness

Authentic spirituality is grounded in the discipline of contemplative awareness. Awareness as a discipline opens us to levels of reality not immediately apparent. It enables us to see ourselves, our circumstances, our world without illusion, to see without prematurely judging both "the terrors of our present situation and the greatness of our possible inner evolution," to grasp the reality both of our divinity and our animality (Needleman 1982: 39, 64). It requires stillness, receptivity, and availability. The discipline of awareness involves deep listening which is marked by waiting, attending, and presence. We must sit in the stillness, wait, and listen deeply. And we must be silent. The discipline of contemplative awareness is nurtured in the practice of silence. We consciously create pools of silence in which to hear. We quiet the many voices around us and within us as we wait to hear a word of revelation.

Effective action in the world

A further mark of an authentic spirituality is that it issues in effective action in the world. Genuine contemplative awareness does not lead to withdrawal from the world, but a deep immersion in the world. One becomes more aware of and attentive to the realities of everyday life, to the joys and sorrows, the sufferings and ecstasies, the struggles and triumphs of very real people in very real circumstances. Authentic spirituality has "consequences for life in society" (Downey 1997: 96); it is concerned with the broken places in our world and is invested in "the repair of the world" (Harris 1996: 14). Authentic spirituality, then, is marked by a dynamic relationship between contemplation and action which works toward the healing of the world and the wellbeing of all creation

Community

Grounding in a community of discourse, belief, and practice is a further feature of authentic spirituality. We do not undertake the spiritual quest alone. We need communities which nurture and hold us, communities which keep the traditions and charisms alive and which hand them on to the next generation. Because we are human beings, we most often come to an encounter with the sacred through the mediation of the traditions, practices, and charisms of particular spiritual traditions. And these traditions and charisms take root, develop, and are handed on only in the context of a community which keeps them alive. Thus an individual, privatized, or purely personal spirituality is an oxymoron. Authentic spirituality can never be an isolated, privatized, individual affair. It is always located in a particular community from which it derives its flavor, character, and efficacy.

A disposition of openness

Authentic spirituality manifests itself in a disposition of openness. It is marked by a letting go of preconceived notions and ideas, an openness to the new and unexpected, an availability for surprise. In authentic expressions of spirituality we experience a sense of hospitality to persons and ideas, a capacity to allow the familiar to become unfamiliar, a willingness to enter into experiences, ideas, relationships, without knowing where they will lead. We learn to sit and wait respectfully before the unfamiliar, making ourselves ready to hear a new word of revelation as well as to hear anew the word of revelation. Thus authentic spirituality is marked by an active opening of oneself to otherness, by careful, active, and respectful listening to positions and perspectives other than one's own, and by a sense of humility before the unfamiliar, the new, the unexpected.

Non-dualistic thinking and acting

Authentic spirituality is marked by an integrative, inclusive, non-dualistic approach to all of life. Polarities are held together and paradox is celebrated. The either/or dichotomies of Cartesian dualism give way to an inclusive, integrative, "both- and" mentality. It is this capacity to integrate, to genuinely hold together opposites and bring them into a larger synthesis which is one of the primary markers of mature spirituality (cf. Dupré 1979: 18–19). In taking a non-dualistic approach to all of life, authentic spirituality will be concerned with both contemplation and action, with both the individual and the social, with both the private and the public, with both the intellectual and the affective, and it will actively seek to overcome the dualism of body and soul so prominent in Western mentality.

Discernment

A final mark of authentic spiritualities is that they generally offer a set of guidelines and practices for discerning the path we are being called to follow. They invite us to put our lives in dialogue with the tradition through prayer, reflection, meditation, individual and group guidance, and other practices. They encourage attentive listening and awareness of how we are being called and where we are being led. In this sense, authentic spiritualities are marked by a sense of obedience to something or someone larger than and beyond oneself. In the process of discernment one looks for certain signs such as a sense of inner and outer freedom, an awareness of the connectedness and interrelation of all creation, a rootedness in tradition coupled with openness to the new, and a sense of deep inner peace.

The Task of Practical and Pastoral Theology

Given these considerations, what do practical and pastoral theology have to contribute to the study of spirituality? Spirituality as a discipline is a practical theological discipline precisely because it aims at effective action in the world. As such, it requires frameworks for understanding, judging, and fostering the various practices which lead to transformation. Given the role of context, particularity, and tradition in the expression of an authentic spirituality it becomes clear that there is no single set of criteria for adequacy and authenticity which can be used to evaluate all the various manifestations and expressions of spirituality. Thus the need for a mutually critical correlation of the various traditions of spirituality with the contemporary context and the wisdom and insights of critical human sciences. It is through such a mutually critical correlation that practical theology can assist us in raising the appropriate questions and developing criteria of adequacy by which to weigh, measure, and critique the various expressions of spirituality.

The tasks of practical and pastoral theology differ somewhat with regard to the study of spirituality. As the broader, more encompassing discipline, practical theology has the task of studying all the various aspects of the contemporary situation, building conversation bridges and common areas of understanding between human experience and the human sciences broadly conceived, and specifically religious and theological understandings of the human situation. Practical theology will need to employ epistemological pluralism to explore, discover, and identify those conditions which would make it possible for the great truths of the various traditions to be living, active, and effective in our contemporary context. It has the task of finding the categories and language which are broad enough and public enough to give voice and expression to the deepest yearnings of the human spirit without becoming bogged down in or wedded to the particularities of any given tradition. In other words, practical theology can assist us in identifying and discerning the signs of spiritual awakening in many varied contexts and traditions. It can likewise assist us in identifying the signs of authentic and inauthentic spiritual awakening and the means of fostering those spiritual practices which lead to personal and social transformation.

Pastoral theology will focus more explicitly and directly on the particular religious, spiritual traditions themselves. In doing so, it can assist us in identifying the roots of various spiritual practices within the different traditions. At the same time it can help us to understand the implications of these practices and to evaluate their efficacy. Finally, pastoral theology will be especially helpful in uncovering the particular gifts or charisms of specific traditions and in discovering ways of renewing those gifts in the current context.

Method

In order to achieve the tasks of practical and pastoral theology we need to engage in a process of retrieval, critique, and reconstruction. This enables us to garner the riches and wisdom of the past without seeking refuge in a thoughtless reproduction of the past. A method of retrieval, critique, and reconstruction encourages and facilitates the reframing and recasting of treasures from the past in ways which are fitting, lively, and meaningful in the contemporary context.

This method honors the role of particularity, recognizing that any authentic spirituality comes organically out of a lived tradition and needs to be expressed in relation to a tradition. It identifies as precisely as possible the traditions which ground particular approaches to spirituality in order to facilitate the process of connecting with and drawing on the riches of the traditions.

A hermeneutics of suspicion

Given our tendency as human beings to distort the truth and to select out of a tradition only those aspects which we like while ignoring other equally important aspects (cf. Needleman 1982: 52–63), we will need to employ a hermeneutics of suspicion in our study of spirituality. Factors which should arouse our suspicion include excessive individualism or any tendency to make personal experience normative. Eclectic, smorgasbord approaches which exploit spiritual practices for monetary gain or which promise spiritual awakening and ecstasy with no suffering or discipline are also suspect. An excessive concern with results and a preoccupation with personal improvement is suggestive of one more example of contemporary narcissistic preoccupation rather an authentic spiritual quest. Authentic spirituality is not goal-oriented. The spiritual life is lived not for the sake of oneself but for the sake of the sacred (Downey 1997: 21). And it involves a process of letting go in a self-surrendering love which leads to personal and social transformation.

Expressions of spirituality which promote an off-handed discarding of the past or which foster a nostalgic return to the past warrant our suspicion. And finally, any spirituality which manifests a lack of connection with ordinary, everyday life in the world, a failure to respond to real human suffering, a lack of openness and respect for differing perspectives, an attitude of knowing the right way, a failure to lead to greater freedom, or a lack of balance between the contemplative dimension of life and effective action in the world must be questioned.

A hermeneutics of restoration

Just as a hermeneutics of suspicion helps us to identify inauthentic expressions of spirituality, a hermeneutics of restoration can help us find effective ways of putting our lives in dialogue with the tradition. It provides a means of retrieving those practices of the various spiritual traditions which have genuine transformative power and doing so in a meaningful way which makes them viable today. In our contemporary, postmodern culture where we have become further and further removed from direct, primary experience, the retrieval of meaningful practices is an especially important and, in some ways, delicate task. Practices such as praying the liturgy of the hours or keeping silence can be quite potent. At the same time these practices are new to many contemporary seekers who have little or no context for understanding their roots or their purpose. Given this, it seems important that such practices be thoroughly explained. Where does the practice come from? What was its purpose? How did it function? Why might we want to retrieve this particular practice and how might it be helpful to us in our current situation? Practical and pastoral theology can make a significant contribution here by exploring the roots of the various practices within the traditions, examining their function and purpose, and building bridges to the present. If practices are retrieved without being situated in this broader context there is a significant danger that they will be adopted in a super-ficial, shallow manner and will be experienced either as a gimmick, one more "New Age" thing to try or as a pious practice without roots.

A hermeneuitcs of restoration can also help us to retrieve the role of community in nurturing a deep spiritual life. It can provide the means for examining and critiquing both ancient and contemporary forms of community living and it can assist us in reconstructing forms of community life which are real and effective in today's society.

The processes of retrieval, critique, and reconstruction, of suspicion and of restoration are the tasks of pastoral and practical theology with regard to the study of spirituality. Taken together they can provide a thorough and effective grounding for the study and pursuit of the spiritual life.

The Gift of Spirituality to Practical and Pastoral Theology

While it is true that the study of spirituality is greatly enhanced by attention from the disciplines of practical and pastoral theology, it is perhaps even more true that practical and pastoral theology are enriched by the study of spirituality. The reason for this is that serious engagement with the study of spirituality will change the practical and pastoral theologian and conse-quently the theology as well. The study of spirituality is never merely an intellectual exercise. It draws one in. It demands an active participation. As we study spirituality we find ourselves drawn into deeper spiritual living. We begin to understand not just with our minds, but with our hearts and our very beings and we begin to reflect in our lives that which we study. Spirituality cannot be studied without being practiced. And this process creates a fundamental shift in the theologian. It transforms the theologian. It leads to the experience of religious conversion which Lonergan describes. It effects a vertical shift in horizons in which our being becomes being-in-love and in which the criteria for all our attending, understanding, judging, and responding become the criteria of love. To the extent that we as theologians reclaim and live out of our spiritual center we become reliable guides for others. To the extent that we allow our study of and engagement with spirituality to touch and transform our own lives, to the extent that we remain faithful to the disciplines of study, teaching, research, and writing as transformative practices, to the extent that we recognize these endeavors as the place where we meet the sacred, to that extent our work will be effective in enabling the personal and social transformation which is the mark of all authentic spirituality. And to that extent we will have received will the gift which the study of spirituality has to offer to practical and pastoral theology.

GENERAL REFERENCES

Dictionary of Pastoral Care and Counseling, ed. Rodney J. Hunter et al., Nashville: Abingdon Press, 1990.
The Journal of Pastoral Care.
The Journal of Pastoral Theology.

SELECTED BIBLIOGRAPHY

Anderson, H. (1997), "Spirituality and Supervision: a Complex but Necessary Connection," *Journal of Supervision and Training in Ministry* 18: 1–6.
Bass, D. C. (ed.) (1997), *Practicing Our Faith: A Way of Life for Searching People*, San Francisco: Jossey-Bass.
Conn, J. W. (ed.) (1996), *Women's Spirituality: Resources for Christian Development*, 2nd edn: New York/Mahwah, NJ: Paulist Press.
Downey, M. (1997), *Understanding Christian Spirituality*, New York/Mahwah, NJ: Paulist Press.
Dupré, L. (1979), *The Other Dimension: A Search for the Meaning of Religious Attitudes*, New York: Seabury Press.
Gill-Austern, B. (1997), "Responding to a Culture Ravenous for Soul Food," *Journal of Pastoral Theology* 7, summer: 63–79.
Harris, M. (1996), *Proclaim Jubilee! A Spirituality for the Twenty-first Century*, Louisville, KY: Westminster/John Knox Press.
Maas, R., and O'Donnell, G. (eds) (1990), *Spiritual Traditions for the Contemporary Church*, Nashville: Abingdon Press.
Needleman, J. (1982), *Consciousness and Tradition*, New York: Crossroads.
Ó Murchú, D. (1998), *Reclaiming Spirituality: A New Spiritual Framework for Today's World*, New York: Crossroad Publishing.
Palmer, P. (1990), *The Active Life: A Spirituality of Work, Creativity, and Caring*, San Francisco: Harper and Row.
Principe, W. (1983), "Toward Defining Spirituality," *Sciences Religieuses/ Studies in Religion* 12/2, printemps/spring: 127–41 (printed in Canada).
Ratliff, B. (1997), "Spirituality and Discernment: a Call to Pastoral Theologians," *Journal of Pastoral Theology* 7, summer: 81–97.
Schneiders, S. (1986), "Theology and Spirituality: Strangers, Rivals, or Partners?," *Horizons* 13, 2: 253–74.
Schneiders, S. (1989), "Spirituality in the Academy," *Theological Studies* 50, 4: 676–97.
Townes, E. (1995), *In a Blaze of Glory: Womanist Spirituality as Social Witness*, Nashville: Abingdon Press.

SOME POINTS FOR FURTHER CONSIDERATION

- How would you define spirituality?
- What is the relationship between spirituality and religion?
- What aspects of culture and society impinge upon or shape the experience of spirituality?
- Is all spirituality acceptable or healthy? What might make spirituality selfish or manipulative?
- Reflect on the role of spirituality in your own (or others') experience of pastoral care. How is it described by others? How does it bear upon pastoral and practical theology?

FOR FURTHER READING AND EXPLORATION

Perhaps the most insightful and critical British writer in this field is Kenneth Leech. Three of his books have been widely read in both Europe and America: see *Soul Friend* (1977), *True Prayer* (1980), and *True God* (1985). For an exploration of spirituality and its relationship to health care, see Cobb and Robshaw (1998). This book points people in the direction of empirical research into spirituality both inside and outside the religious community. For discussion of spirituality and management, see Pattison (1997b). Most of the work of Henri Nouwen, one of the best-known of modern spiritual guides, who was a professor of pastoral theology, is widely available. See, for example, Nouwen (1994). For a good critical essay on the limits and dangers of modern spirituality, see Leech (1997).

15

Sketching the Contours of a Pastoral Theological Perspective: Suffering, Healing, and Reconstructing Experiencing

CHRIS SCHLAUCH

INTRODUCTION

Chris Schlauch is Associate Professor of Pastoral Psychology and Psychology of Religion in the School of Theology, Boston University, USA. He has specialized in examining the relationship between theology and psychology. Experience is often talked about as if everyone understands what it is and what its significance should be in pastoral theological activity. Often, this leads to experience itself as a category in discourse and understanding not being critically considered and examined. In this specially commissioned chapter, Schlauch takes the notion of experience and examines the process whereby pastoral theology handles experiences, exemplifying his argument particularly with relation to the area of suffering and healing.

Effectively, in this demanding chapter, Schlauch offers an alternative way of thinking about the theory and practice of care. From his perspective, pastoral theology is a critical tool, a bridge; "a praxis of experiencing, understanding, and responding to everyday events in a way that expresses the joint heritage of Christian traditions and the human and social sciences." The chapter discusses sources, key topics, methodology, claims, and dimensions constituting a pastoral theological approach. The core thesis is that it is possible to be confident in a confessional approach, that is, an approach based clearly on belief in the central tenets of the Christian tradition. Schlauch believes that the healing which pastoral theology seeks to promote is to do with the formation of faith as understood as a change in nature, specifically as changes in seeing, hearing, and understanding. These changes may be regarded as a fundamental change in "experiencing." This chapter examines experiencing and constructing and reconstructing experiencing.

The process of constructing and reconstructing experiencing, Schlauch concludes, is transformative in two ways. First, *substantively* because the individual may acquire an expanded and meaningful range of categories through a deeper grasp of the dimensions of reality, especially those having to do with love and service of God and neighbor. Second, *methodologically*, it is possible for the individual to acquire a way of being, an attitude which orientates a person to critical attention to their own or another's experiencing and to be engaged with others in pastoral theologizing. The acquisition of these relationships and processes can be transforming of both the theory and practice of care. These points demand further thought and reflection. One of the strengths of the chapter is that it proposes that theology itself may be transformative.

SKETCHING THE CONTOURS OF A PASTORAL THEOLOGICAL PERSPECTIVE: SUFFERING, HEALING, AND RECONSTRUCTING EXPERIENCING

Imagine the following scenario. A man in obvious pain describes how nearly a month ago his entire family died in a horrible accident. Since that moment he has suffered without respite, spending his days sobbing periodically and uncontrollably and his nights, between recurrent nightmares, struggling to rest. He does not want to harm himself; yet the thought of continuing to live without solace or healing is driving him to despair. His formerly vibrant faith has become starkly irrelevant. He yearns for some kind of relief. Is he doomed to a living hell? Where is God in this truly "ungodly" world?

Consider another scenario. A woman tearfully confides that she has recently been raped by a stranger. She remains anxious and fearful, and is acutely troubled by becoming increasingly house-bound, feeling secure only in her home behind locked doors. While tormented by agonizing flashbacks of the rape, she has recently been assaulted by painful memories of having been abused as a child. She is searching for soothing and safety. Is it possible? How might she attain it?

How should one interpret these situations, and intervene accordingly? For some people, the two experiences of suffering are essentially if not exclusively biological (that is, chemical) in nature: "depression" and "anxiety" would respond to what are called psychotropic medications. Others would consider care as having primarily to do with understanding and modifying patterns of thoughts, feelings, and behaviors. Still others would focus on matters of faith and belief. Physical maladies warrant medical intervention, emotional issues merit psychological attention, and spiritual concerns benefit from a religious response. Notice what has happened: illness and healing, cast as "problems" and "solutions," are customarily defined according to specialized theories, practices, and institutions of care which are, for all intents and purposes, mutually exclusive of one another. This fragmentation of the disciplines of care reflects as well as reinforces the fragmentation of the experience of care.

This essay sketches an alternative way of thinking about the theory and practice of care. Concerned with the consequences of such fragmentation, it discusses a "bridge discipline," pastoral theology: a praxis of experiencing, understanding, and responding to everyday events in a way that expresses the joint heritage of Christian traditions and the human and social sciences. The essay opens with a brief discussion of basic issues, namely, sources, key topics, methodology, claims, and dimensions constituting a pastoral theological approach. Proposing that such an approach aims, penultimately, at enhancing meaningful participation in a community of faith and, ultimately, at love and service of God and neighbor, it opens with a consideration of confessional, more specifically scriptural contributions. Within this context, the healing which pastoral theology seeks to promote has to do with formation in faith, understood as a change in nature, more particularly and concretely, as changes in seeing, hearing, and understanding. Changes in seeing, hearing, and understanding are regarded as expressions of something more fundamental: changes in "experiencing." Accordingly, the essay examines the activities of experiencing, and constructing and reconstructing experiencing.

Some Basic Issues: Sources, Key Topics, Methodology

Formulating a pastoral theological perspective is a complex, difficult project. First, a prospective pastoral theologian should become immersed in a spectrum of sources, from her or his confessional tradition, from other religious traditions, and from the human and social sciences. More specifically, she or he needs to examine how religious and secular thinkers discuss a series of *key topics*, especially (a) "human nature", who we are, who we should be and become; (b) brokenness and suffering, as construed through categories such as sin, psychopathology, illness, and disease; (c) wholeness, as interpreted through concepts such as salvation and health; and (d) change, as understood in conjunction with a range of ideas including healing, curing, formation, and sanctification. Second, and more broadly, a prospective pastoral theologian has to specify and carry out a clearly defined *methodology* through which she or he may *interpret* the respective contributions from these areas of inquiry and *coordinate* these areas in a consistent and coherent approach. That is, she or he must be careful to develop accurate and authentic characterizations of the respective contributions and avoid reducting or "collapsing" the ideas and truths of one area into those of another.

Of course, pastoral theologians differ considerably in regard to their choice of confessional and secular sources, key topics, and methodology. In doing so, they express judgments that can be thought about in terms of two different continua: (1) Which *claims* are more fundamental – theological (religious) or psychological (secular)? (2) Which *dimension* is more crucial – elegant theory (i.e. theology) or effective techniques (i.e. ministry)? Understanding some of the options, that is, some of the positions on the respective continua may enable a prospective pastoral theologian to formulate her or his own approach more thoughtfully and clearly.

In regard to the first continuum, pastoral theological positions on one end of the spectrum presume that theological matters are primary and either ignore or selectively employ important but clearly subordinate secular ideas. For example, religious and theological language dominate a particular analysis; psychological terms and ideas are, by contrast, mentioned more or less in passing. Positions on the other end of the spectrum imply the primacy of social scientific discoveries, in terms of which traditional theological ideas are reconstructed. Thus, for example, an analysis pays token homage to the contributions of a confessional tradition but for all intents and purposes strongly resembles secular perspectives. Positions in the middle of the spectrum engage in a complex conversation between confessional and secular contributions and seek to give equal weight to the truths and insights of the different areas.

In regard to the second continuum, pastoral theological positions on one end of the spectrum are singularly concerned with orthodoxy, that is, right belief, and assume that the practice following from good theory is necessarily efficacious. For example, a systematically tight and formally elegant analysis maintains only tangential, tenuous connections with lived experience, and stands "firmly in mid-air." Positions on the other end of the spectrum are preoccupied with orthopraxy, that is, right practice, and take for granted that the theory underlying truly sound practice is necessarily valid. Thus, for example, a discussion focused exclusively on practical skills and techniques neglects to reflect, critically, upon underlying theoretical commitments and assumptions. Positions in the middle of the spectrum assume that neither theory nor practice is primary: each gives rise to and serves to amplify and correct the other, in an ongoing dialectical process. The connections between experience and reflection, between concrete situations and more abstract conceptualizations, are ideally direct and self-evident.

The approach sketched in this essay is located in the middle of each of the two continua. In regard to the first continuum, it follows what is called a "revised correlational theological methodology" (see Tillich 1951; Tracy 1975; Browning 1991), and considers the contributions of confessional and secular traditions as equal partners in the conversation. In particular, it coordinates Biblical ideas of "changing one's nature"; philosophical ideas of "seeing as" (Hanson 1969; Wittgenstein 1958 [1953]), "experiencing" (Gendlin 1962), and "experiencing as" (Hick 1966 [1957]); and, indirectly, psychoanalytic ideas of "transference" (Basch 1980; Gill 1982). In regard to the second continuum, it follows a practice-theory-practice approach (Browning 1991), and assumes the interplay between concrete experience and reflection. Said another way, the proposal about constructing and reconstructing experiencing emerges from practice for the express purpose of making sense of and enhancing future practice. In this spirit, the essay commends the term *theologizing* (in the gerund form) instead of *theology* (in the noun form). The latter term suggests that theology as a set of propositions and/or beliefs is a theory to be "applied" in the practice of ministry, whereas the former avoids this implied theory/practice split as it refers to what we do *through* reflections on past practice.

Sketching the Contours of a Particular Perspective

A revised correlational practice-theory-practice approach evolves in the interplay among: (a) a concrete event, for example, the suffering man or woman discussed at the outset of the essay, (b) religious and theological resources, and (c) human and social science resources. With that in mind, consider some religious resources, namely, contributions of sacred scripture.

Scriptural contributions: healing, formation in faith, changing one's nature
(i.e. seeing, hearing, understanding)

Biblical writers (Revised Standard Version – RSV) characterize the process of healing as having to do with becoming faithful, that is, with a change in "nature." "Put off your old nature which belongs to your former manner of life . . . and be renewed in the spirit of your minds, and put on the new nature, created after the likeness of God in true righteousness and holiness" (Ephesians 4.22–4). Those having been given, by grace, a new nature, no longer live, but Christ lives in them (Galatians 2.20). As "a new creation" (2 Corinthians 5.17) they have "received the Spirit which is from God" and understand "the secret and hidden wisdom of God," "the gifts bestowed on us by God" (1 Corinthians 2). No longer "conformed to this world" (Romans 12.2) they "seek the things that are above" (Colossians 3.1), and in "Whatever [they] do, do all to the glory of God" (1 Corinthians 10.31).

Not infrequently, Biblical accounts portray matters of faith and of one's "nature" in concrete terms having to do with one's senses. "Their idols are silver and gold, the work of men's hands. They have mouths but do not speak; eyes but do not see. They have ears but do not hear; noses but do not smell. They have hands but do not feel; feet, but do not walk; and they do not make a sound in their throat. Those who make them are like them; so are all who trust in them" (Psalm 115.4–8). ". . . seeing they do not see, and hearing they do not hear, nor do they understand" (Matthew 13.13b). Those who are apart from God are not properly oriented: they cannot know who they are, the world in which they live, and the time in which they live. By contrast, in becoming faithful by amazing grace, one who was lost is now found, one who was blind now sees. In becoming a new creation and understanding "the secret and hidden wisdom of God," one sees, hears, smells, feels, and walks in a new way, in a new world.

Thus the contours of a way of thinking about care begin to unfold. The pastoral theologian would approach anyone suffering, such as the man coping with the trauma of the loss of his family and the woman struggling with the trauma of having been raped, in terms of these ideas: *healing* is a matter of *formation in faith, changing one's nature, seeing, hearing, and understanding in a new way.*

Biblical authors often imply that becoming faithful happens instantaneously, following the exemplar of the dramatic Saul-to-Paul conversion: one who has been blind is granted sight; one who has been deaf now hears. More often than not, however, the changes we undergo are as much *partial* as *complete* (we alternate between sight and blindness, hearing and deafness, understanding and incomprehension), as much a matter of *degree* as of *kind* (we see more clearly, but not perfectly, we hear more accurately, but not entirely, we understand more deeply, but not fully). Formation in faith – that is, healing – potentially unfolds according to movement on a trajectory marked by degrees of blindness and sight, deafness and hearing, incomprehension and understanding.

Consider some of the prospective "markers" on that trajectory: (a) Someone seeking healing, formation in faith, a change of nature, may be like *agnostics*, for whom faith life or religious sensibilities are *absent*. She or he may have little if any recognition of "something (that is, faith) lacking or missing"; or they may feel this absence acutely, as if aware of an unactualized potentiality, like being tone deaf. (b) Someone suffering and seeking care may be like on-again, off-again *searchers*, for whom a faith life is more or less present but comparatively *muted and neglected*. Having "the religion of the masses" (Weber), they experience periodic "signals of transcendence" (Berger 1969: 52). (c) Someone seeking care may be like devout *believers*, for whom a faith life is *prominent*, that is, *primary but not exclusive*. Many so-called religious leaders manifest this level of awareness and commitment.

They remain acutely aware of the difference and distance between themselves and the religious genius. (One thinks, for example, of the contrast between the well-known and able Antonio Salieri alongside Mozart.) (d) Finally, someone in need of care may be like what Max Weber called "*religious virtuosi*," "great figures of religious history" (Berger 1992: 132), for whom religious or faith life is *dominant*, more or less *constant and enduring*. Such geniuses have what one might liken to a special gift, as a musician having perfect pitch.

The contours of a way of thinking about care thus unfold further. The pastoral theologian seeks to provide the occasion for healing, for changes in "nature," enabling movement through a trajectory of faith: the suffering man or woman might become increasingly faithful, whether moving from being an agnostic to a searcher, a searcher to a believer, or a believer to a religious virtuoso. Through a relationship and process a person seeking care gains an ability to experience *the new* – features and dimensions of reality that had been unseen, unheard – and, to experience *anew* – dimensions and features of reality that had been seen comparatively dimly, and heard comparatively faintly.

Secular contributions: experiencing, constructing and reconstructing experiencing

Secular contributions constitute the third element in conversation in a revised correlational practice-theory-practice approach, in conjunction with a concrete situation and religious and theological resources. These contributions are, due to limitations of space, restricted to a brief consideration of the concept of "experiencing." This concept is exceptionally well-suited to the discussion, for several reasons. First, experiencing seems to be a general way of talking about how we make contact with and engage the world, encompassing or inclusive of the basic activities of the senses: seeing, hearing, smelling, tasting, and touching. Thus, an analysis of experiencing may serve to "unpack" aspects of the processes of healing and formation in faith, where these processes are understood as concrete "changes in nature." Second, whereas faith is an expressly religious-theological term, experiencing (though found in religious and theological writings) is not. Indeed, it is a technical term in some philosophical as well as clinical (see Gendlin 1981) literature. Third, experience and experiencing are common, everyday words (e.g. "I still don't know how to make sense of that experience"; "have you ever had a religious experience?"). In that regard, they are easily accessible to lay persons as well as to scholars (they are concrete, close to felt experience, "experience-near"). As such, these terms serve as an exemplary point of contact and link among situation, religious resources, and secular resources.

Experiencing, understanding, acting

Human beings relate to themselves, others, and their environment through a series of activities: experiencing (registering information); understanding (reflecting upon that information); and acting (executing meaningful behavior). Although these activities seem to occur *seriatim* – one experiences something, reflects upon that experience, and acts accordingly – they are, more acccurately, concurrent and interactive. Philosophical, theological, and social scientific theories of person variously regard one or another of these activities as primary. Some focus on action and behavior (e.g. behaviorist), others upon thinking and beliefs (e.g. cognitive), and still others on ways of experiencing and engaging the world (e.g. phenomenological). This essay argues that we execute some of our most formative judgments in experiencing, an activity that orients what and how we understand and informs how and why we act; correspondingly, some of the most formative changes we may undergo have to do with becoming aware of, critically reflecting upon, and transforming the categories through which we experience (see James 1958 [1902]).

What is "experiencing"?

Experiencing refers to *registering information*: taking in and recording salient data. Information may be registered in *sensate* form (e.g. a scent draws our attention) or in *verbal* form (e.g. through our window we see "the sun setting"). At times what is initially registered – *apprehended* – in sensate (nonverbal) form is registered anew – *articulated* – in verbal form (e.g. the nameless scent of which I had become aware I now recognize to be roses).

Whether apprehending or articulating, the quality of the engagement between the experiencing subject and the registered information may vary. At times data impress themselves upon and require the attention of a rather *passive* subject (e.g. a loud noise). In some moments information is discovered or uncovered only through *active*, persistent searching (e.g. an astronomer scanning the heavens). In still other moments one senses a peculiar synchrony between knower and known, as if registering presupposed being *receptive* (e.g. a prayer being "answered").

Experiencing is selective, and constructive

Whether comparatively passive, active, or receptive, experiencing is an inherently *selective* procedure. One selects *what* one attends to: some data are sound, other data noise. Furthermore, one selects *how* one attends. To paraphrase British pediatrician-psychoanalyst Donald Woods Winnicott, one creates *as* one finds, one creates *what* one finds (see Winnicott 1971).

Perhaps what most determines selection and "creation" are the categories *through* which one registers information. A person does not experience something-in-general, or something-in-abstraction; she or he experiences something *as* X. Even something unrecognizable or unknown is experienced *as* "unrecognizable" or *as* "unknown." Experiencing is, at basis, "experiencing as" (Hick 1966 [1957]). (Thus, in our respective scenarios, suffering initially is experienced by the man *as* "inconsolable sadness" and "unbearable grief," and by the woman *as* "panic" and "fright.")

Experiencing as involves what cognitive theorists call "perceptual priming": "A perceptual encounter with an object on one occasion primes or facilitates the perception of the same or a similar object on a subsequent occasion, in the sense that the identification of the object requires less stimulus information or occurs more quickly than it does in the absence of priming" (Tulving 1995: 841). A perceptual encounter precipitates retrieving and generating an image from memory, with which an input image is matched. "This sort of image-matching process can also augment the input itself" (Kosslyn and Sussman 1995: 1036).

Experiencing is constructed via *words and languages*

Certainly among the most critical and prominent categories shaping experiencing are linguistic (see Jackendoff 1994). Not unexpectedly, interpretations vary regarding the nature and role of words and languages. Consider two among many well-known approaches. Some persons regard words, if only tacitly, as if "eternal names" which correspond, directly and immediately, to facts of nature. Other persons approach words as tools, and languages as toolboxes. The contrast is particularly instructive.

The former perspective probably has its origins in the mundane process of language acquisition. A child encountering an unfamiliar object is taught what is, for all intents and purposes, that object's "name." "This wooden structure with a flat top and four legs is called a 'table.' " The simple event, practiced repeatedly, suggests that each object in the world has a name; conversely, each word names, or refers to, an object "out there." Progressive understanding seems to unfold in a step-by-step acquisition of word–object connections, implicitly sustaining the assumption of a kind of isomorphism between a word and a reality designated by that word. This view is expressed in various metaphors: words mirror reality (a one-to-one correspondence); words read the book of nature (physical nature can be recast as a book); words carve nature at its joints (the terms we employ cut up reality in preexisting forms). Language as a sort of "book of names" and the independent realities to which names refer and with which they are individually linked exist independently of the learning process (that is, independently of the teacher and the learner). Name, object, and linkage are thus features of the ahistorical, a priori natural order.

This intuitively powerful but utterly simplistic view faces self-evident and fatal challenges. If words correspond to specific realities, how can the same word hook different realities (e.g. "ball" refers to a round object with which one plays, a festive dance, as well as a good time)? How can different words hook the same reality (e.g. "unusual" and "atypical")? How can different languages seem to hook the same, but different realities (e.g. "*Eli, Eli, lama sabach-tha-ni?*" "My God, my God, why hast thou forsaken me?")? How does one account for the fact that the process of making sense of what is unfamiliar is less a process of *uncovering* an unfolding series of a priori matches between names and objects than of *discovering* "unnamed" features of reality and *creating* temporary (often metaphorical) linkages? How does one account for the fact that in the process of understanding reality, the shape and substance of what is sought and found are implicitly formed by the categories of inquiry, that is, that all observation is theory-laden?

These concerns give credence to an alternative point of view. First, we use words as tools in accomplishing various tasks: describing, asking questions, encouraging, praying, remembering, among many other things. Second, particular words only have meaning within their own respective network. Thus, for example, the word sin has no meaning except in conjunction with a host of "theological" terms, including God, covenant, faith, nature, grace, and salvation. Third, the words in particular and the network in general cannot be understood independently of the specific practices for which they are used, within the context of a world they construct. Thus, for example, the word "unconscious" has no meaning except in conjunction with other psychoanalytic terms, including conscious and consciousness, conflict and defense, the pleasure and reality principles, and primary and secondary processes. Further, this network of words has no meaning except as it articulates a particular clinical practice through which psychic processes may be analyzed and therapeutic care may be extended. These words and this language express a world and a way of being in that world. In this regard, experiencing is an activity of selectively registering information through a linguistic network (Wittgenstein's "language game") that articulates a world shaped through a corresponding network of practices (Wittgenstein's "form of life").

If words were names corresponding to reality, we would forever be imprisoned in a linguistic cage, restricted in our experiencing by the necessarily finite nature and number of keys we were granted. If, however, words are tools and languages are toolboxes, our project is considerably more ambitious, and self-consciously creative and constructive. By acquiring proficiency in the use of varied tools and, more significantly, of tools from varied toolboxes, we may participate in building (and living within) several worlds.

How is experiencing constructed?

Through words and actions, patterns of apprehending and articulating are mediated to infants and children (see Ochs and Schieffelin 1984). They learn a language: X-Y-Z. And they learn to experience what they attend to *as* X, *as* Y, or *as* Z. In doing so, they learn to differentiate between what to attend to and what to ignore, and thereby distinguish what is real from what is not. A language thereby determines both *what* can be experienced as well as *how* it is to be experienced: a world is constructed in and through that language. Consider the differences with those who learn a language of A-B-C and attend to the (or "their") world *as* A, *as* B, or *as* C.

For example, some people learn that there are certain kinds of "phenomena" and "events" which can be experienced *as* "God," "Jesus," "the Holy Spirit," "sin," "grace," and "faith." Others learn that there are (other) kinds of phenomena and events which can be experienced *as* "unconscious," "projection," "repression," "conflict and defense." Members of each community are at once learning terms, a language, a spectrum of features and dimensions of reality, and ultimately a world. Most significantly, members of these respective communities live in different worlds, constructed *via* different languages and practices. Furthermore, the others' terms are empty, their language meaningless, events and phenomena invisible (non-existent), and world alien.

Reconstructing experiencing

Reconstructing, like constructing, is a project of acquiring increasingly more complex and accurate tools through which to mediate progressively more satisfactory contact with and adaptation in the world. In the context of pastoral theologizing, it is a project of deepening faith, of fuller love and service of God and neighbor, of augmented sight, hearing, understanding: the agnostic may become a searcher, the searcher a believer, the believer a religious virtuoso. The pastoral theologian mediates, through words and actions, patterns of apprehending and articulating unique to a particular community of faith. For the person seeking care, unused terms and language may become *meaningful*, events and phenomena *visible*, that is, existent, and a world of faith *familiar*.

What does this look like?

The man struggling with his tragic losses has, in his despair, come to experience an unbounded despondency for which his death seems the only exit. None the less, he seeks help, indicating that in the midst of this horror he harbors some lingering hope, some abiding confidence and trust that someone, or Someone, might make a difference. Through pastoral theologizing he may acquire the ability to "pray" to "God" for "hope" and "sustenance," he may know that even as he "walks through the valley of the shadow of death," "Thou art with me," because he can experience certain events and phenomena *through* these now meaning-full words.

The woman managing the crisis of having been raped has experienced evil starkly and immediately, and has lost a basic sense of being safe and protected in a "good" world. By the same token, she reveals an expectation, however tentatively and cautiously, that the person to whom she turns for care is good, safe, and trustworthy, and that a process of candidly discussing her fear, rage, and need will promote healing. Through pastoral theologizing, she may acquire the ability to understand and use words like the following, "Out of my distress I called on the Lord; the Lord answered me and set me free. With the Lord on my side I do not fear" (Psalm 118.5–6a).

Through what means does reconstructing experiencing take place?

Reconstructing experiencing, however welcome and desirable, is neither an easy nor a straightforward project. Telling someone, "It will be all right," "Time heals all wounds," "Don't despair," "Be not anxious," rarely if ever works, and likely does more harm than good. Exhorting someone, "Think about this in another way," "You would feel better if only you looked at this differently," may be said with the best intentions but would probably be useless if not demeaning and demoralizing. So, then, how does one enable others to change the categories through which they experience what is happening?

At basis, the task is twofold: one introduces the person more fully and deeply to her- or himself while (re-)introducing her or him to the faith tradition. On the one hand, the person seeking care typically will not know *that* or *how*, in particular, her or his experiencing is selective and creative – that is, constructive. The reasons for this ignorance are rather self-evident: the patterns of experiencing we acquire are social, that is, more or less common to many persons in our context, and are inevitably regarded as characteristic of the way things are; the seemingly instantaneous activity of experiencing affords little if any perspective; experiencing, occurring as a gestalt, is difficult to parse into patterned and pattern. On the other hand, the person seeking care may not know *that* or *how*, in particular, features of her or his experiencing may be meaningfully articulated through the contributions of the faith tradition. The reasons for this disjunction are rather self-evident: formation in faith is typically initiated – and regrettably concluded – in childhood, and the use of words and ideas from that time is naturally ambivalent, positively connecting one with one's origins, negatively expressing immature, childish thoughts and feelings; formation in faith has, in many Western cultures, been relegated to the private as opposed to the public sphere, and as such, conversations about (and opportunities for prospective maturing in) religious life are restricted.

Pastoral theologizing equips the person seeking care to address this ignorance and this disjunction by maintaining a sustained attentiveness to that person's unique ways of experiencing (see Kohut 1978, 1984; Schlauch

1995): To *what* does this person attend? *How* is it apprehended/articulated? Through what *patterns* is experiencing formed? *What* may be at the edge of awareness? *How* might those dimly perceived phenomena be apprehended/ articulated? What *additional* terms and language would be fitting? What *practices* might one learn? What *world* might one come to know?

Through this process, the person is provided the occasion to apprehend and articulate how she or he apprehends and articulates. And that person is given the occasion to discover a surprising but inevitable fact: she or he *persistently undermines* achieving the consciously desired objectives of feeling, thinking, and acting differently. That is, the person seeking care typically will *resist* becoming aware of and transforming her or his particular patterns of experiencing (see Gill 1982). The motives for this resistance are not unreasonable. The particular shape and texture of the patterns through which one experiences have been forged in one's struggle for survival, for sustaining what Winnicott called "going on being." Disciplined self-examination involves immersion in, that is, re-experiencing of, events having to do with negotiating danger, coping with pain, achieving some modicum of security, and attaining periodic assurance and pleasure.

How, in the face of this resistance, would reconstructing unfold? For example, one would encourage the man coping with tragic loss to talk as plainly and fully as he could about what he is experiencing. When he cried, he would be asked to speak about what he experienced that precipitated his crying, and what he experienced while he was crying. Similarly, he would be asked to talk about his nightmares, and about his fear of never being able to find rest. As the process continued and a healing relationship solidified, he might discover that when alone crying or awakening from a nightmare, the memories of the caregiver's comforting presence are mysteriously with him: he is alone, but not entirely. In talking about these new moments of "being alone but not entirely," he might recall other moments of experiencing the comforting presence other persons – of his deceased family and, from years earlier, of his own parents. Gradually, he may realize he grieves in the company of a "cloud of witnesses" – "no longer alone." His acute unending pain has become a sustained ache. Yet, he gains deepening sustenance in the company of those from and with whom he can receive love and care. His agony is there, but transformed, redeemed.

For another example, one would invite the woman coping with having been raped to confide her fears and panic. She might talk about an abiding sense that evil lurks everywhere, that at any moment she could be again attacked. She might be encouraged to speak with others about her fears, and to ask others to provide needed comfort and support. She may learn to distinguish between those fears that are "reality-based" (e.g. walking in a questionable neighborhood alone at night) and those that have become exaggerated because of her trauma (e.g. working in her garden alone).

Through the process of conversation she might become aware of the fact that her fears are no longer constant and are less intense: "persistent terror" has been transformed into "periodic twinges of fear." What had been "living entirely unprotected in a hostile, evil world" has now become "needing the comforting presence of some truly good souls who help me find my way."

In both instances, each may become aware of an emerging and abiding divine presence, dimly sensed initially in moments in conversation, now more directly known in the company of others whose care makes a palpable difference. As this unfolds, they would be invited to describe these changes, the diminishing of their intense suffering, and the awareness of a process of healing. And they are invited to consider the relevance and meaningfulness of the words of their confessional tradition, in articulating their formation in faith, their reconstructing experiencing.

How Might We Regard the *Telos* of Pastoral Theologizing?

Through pastoral theologizing as reconstructing experiencing, the person seeking care may be transformed in two distinct but related ways. *Substantively*, she or he acquires an expanded and increasingly accurate and meaningful repertoire of categories through which to apprehend and articulate features and dimensions of reality, particularly those having to do with love and service of God and neighbor. *Methodologically*, she or he acquires a way of being, an attitude, disposed to practice disciplined, critical attention to her or his own and another's experiencing, to be engaged and engage others in pastoral theologizing (see Schlauch 1995). Having come to know "in one's bones" how healing unfolds in this kind of relationship and process, that person can "go and do likewise," can witness in action as in word, can love and serve others, by enabling *her or his* reconstructing experiencing.

CORE REFERENCES AND SOURCES

Experiencing and experiencing as

Gendlin, E. T. (1962), *Experiencing and the Creation of Meaning*, Toronto: Free Press of Glencoe.

Gendlin, E. T. (1981), *Focusing*, rev. edn, New York: Bantam Press.

Hanson, N. R. (1969), *Perception and Discovery: An Introduction to Scientific Inquiry*, San Francisco: Freeman, Cooper.

Hick, J. (1966), *Faith and Knowledge*, Ithaca: Cornell University Press (original work published 1957).

Jackendoff, R. (1994), *Patterns in the Mind: Language and Human Nature*, New York: Basic Books.

James, W. (1958), *The Varieties of Religious Experience: A Study in Human Nature*, New York: New American Library/Times Mirror (original work published 1902).

Kosslyn, S. M., and Koenig, O. (1992), *Wet Mind: The New Cognitive Neuroscience*, New York: Free Press.

Kosslyn, S. M., and Sussman, A. L. (1995), "Roles of imagery in perception: Or, there is no such thing as immaculate perception." In M. S. Gazzaniga (ed.), *The Cognitive Neurosciences* (pp. 1035–42), Cambridge: MIT Press.

Tulving, E. (1995), Organization of memory: *Quo vadis?* In M. S. Gazzaniga (ed.), *The Cognitive Neurosciences* (pp. 839–47), Cambridge: MIT Press.

Wittgenstein, L. (1958), *Philosophical Investigations*, 3rd edn, tr. G. E. M. Anscombe, New York: Macmillan (original work published 1953).

Pastoral theologizing

Browning, D. S. (1991), *A Fundamental Practical Theology: Descriptive and Strategic Proposals*, Minneapolis: Fortress Press.

Burck, J. R., and Hunter, R. J. (1990), "Protestant pastoral theology." In R. J. Hunter (general ed.), *Dictionary of Pastoral Care and Counseling* (pp. 867–72), Nashville: Abingdon Press.

Hiltner, S. (1958), *Preface to Pastoral Theology*, New York: Abingdon.

Schlauch, C. (1995), *Faithful Companioning: How Pastoral Counseling Heals*, Minneapolis: Fortress Press.

Tillich, P. (1951), *Systematic Theology*, vol. 1, Chicago: University of Chicago Press.

Tracy, D. (1975), *Blessed Rage for Order: The New Pluralism in Theology*, New York: Seabury Press.

Psychoanalytic ideas

Basch, M. F. (1980), *Doing Psychotherapy*, New York: Basic Books.

Gill, M. (1982), *Analysis of Transference*, vol. 1, New York: International Universities Press.

Kohut, H. (1978), "Introspection, empathy, and psychoanalysis: an examination of the relationship between mode of observation and theory." In P. H. Ornstein (ed.), *The Search for the Self: Selected Writings of Heinz Kohut: 1950–1978* (vol. 1, pp. 205–32), Madison, Conn.: International Universities Press (original work published 1959).

Kohut, H. (1984), *How Does Analysis Cure?*, ed. A. Goldberg, with the collaboration of P. E. Stepansky, Chicago: University of Chicago Press.

Winnicott, D. W. (1971), *Playing and Reality*, London: Tavistock Publications.

Sociological ideas

Berger, P. L. (1969), *A Rumor of Angels*, Garden City, NY: Doubleday.

Berger, P. L. (1992), *A Far Glory: The Quest for Faith in an Age of Credulity*, Garden City, NY: Doubleday.

Ochs, E., and Schieffelin, B. B. (1984), "Language acquisition and socialization: three developmental stories and their implications." In

Shweder, R. A. and LeVine, R. A. (eds.), *Culture Theory: Essays on Mind, Self, and Emotion* (pp. 288–320), Cambridge: Cambridge University Press.

SOME POINTS FOR FURTHER CONSIDERATION

- Draw a diagram of the pastoral theological method outlined in this paper.
- What are the main features of Schlauch's use of the Bible and doctrine in this methodology? Do you approve of this usage?
- In what different ways is experience understood and used in life and practice?
- What kind of responses would you make to the case studies outlined in this paper?
- What theological texts shape your own approaches to pastoral theology?
- In what ways do you think pastoral theology might be transformative?

FOR FURTHER READING AND EXPLORATION

For a comprehensive set of references relating to the methods of practical and pastoral theology see the introductory chapter to this Reader and especially: Pattison with Woodward (1994); Graham (1996); Browning (1991); Farley (1983b); Tracy (1981). For explorations of how experience is used in care see, for example, Rosenwald and Ochberg (1992), and Gersie (1997).

16

The Relationship between Pastoral Counseling and Pastoral Theology

Gordon Lynch

Introduction

This chapter is the first of six that raise issues and challenges for pastoral theology that arise mainly from practical situations rather than from theoretical perspectives or approaches.

Gordon Lynch is an English writer who, while trained in practical theology, is a lay person. A practicing counselor and teacher of counseling, he has written extensively on the relationship between therapy and theology. In this specially commissioned chapter, he considers the present state of relationships between pastoral counseling and pastoral theology.

Counseling and psychotherapy have been important, perhaps the most important, shaping influences upon the theory and practice of modern pastoral theology. They also provide important healing resources for troubled individuals in the contemporary world. Some pastoral workers are trained, skilled, and enthusiastic users of counseling techniques, while many find themselves involved in informal counseling work in the course of their everyday pastoral work. It is therefore important to understand some of the tensions and challenges that may arise from counseling for pastoral theology and practice.

In the first place Lynch establishes the importance of counseling in general, and pastoral counseling in particular. He discusses the influence of both Freud and Rogers and then offers the following definition: "the task of counseling is to give the client an opportunity to explore, discover, and clarify ways of living more satisfyingly and resourcefully." From this starting point the chapter raises the question of the difference between counseling and *pastoral* counseling, concluding that the link with a counselor's belief system and concern for experience and theology become significant pastoral factors. Lynch asks the reader to consider the meaning and implications of pastoral practice being grounded in theological tradition. The chapter ends by addressing the issue of the relationship between experience and tradition. In particular, the main challenge of pastoral theology for pastoral counseling is to consider further how to use "experience" in the critical dynamic between theological traditions and human experience.

THE RELATIONSHIP BETWEEN PASTORAL COUNSELING AND PASTORAL THEOLOGY

In this chapter I will explore the challenge that the discipline of pastoral counselling raises for pastoral theology, as well as the challenge pastoral theology raises for the practice of pastoral counselling. To think about these issues in a purely abstract way would be to miss the point, however. Counselling is not a neat or purely theoretical discipline, but it involves engaging with the real experiences of people who feel confused, anxious, sad or hurt. To get a proper appreciation of the issues that pastoral counselling raises for pastoral theology (and vice versa), it will be most useful for us to begin with a specific story about someone's experience and then to build our reflections on that.

Helen's Story[1]

Helen is a young woman in her early thirties, who for some years now has been a committed member of her local church. The past year has been a very difficult time for Helen. Her husband, Andy, left her just over a year ago to go and live with another woman, and divorce proceedings are now under way between them.

Helen found the aftermath of Andy leaving a terrible time, and her feelings swung between an intense anger towards him for what he'd done, to a desperate longing for him to return to her, to an awful sense of hurt and rejection. As the months passed, these feelings subsided for her into a general sense of loneliness and depression.

In the months after Andy left her, Helen found herself growing closer to James, a work colleague, and starting seeing him socially. One night, when she was feeling particularly lonely, she invited him to stay the night at her flat and they slept together. Over the next few weeks it became increasingly common for him to stay over at her flat after they had been out together and for them to have sex together.

Helen felt terribly torn about sleeping with James. On the one hand, she had really missed Andy as a sexual partner and sleeping with James provided her with some temporary relief from her awful feelings of loneliness. At the same time, though, Helen's church tended to take a very traditional view of sex, seeing any form of sexual activity outside of marriage as sinful. Helen was torn, therefore, between feeling comforted by sleeping with James, and feeling guilty about acting in a way that her church taught was morally wrong.

As time went on, Helen found this tension increasingly unbearable. Eventually, she decided that she needed to talk to someone about her situation. She didn't feel that she could talk to anyone in her church, though, because she expected that they would either simply be shocked at her or that they would listen kindly and then simply tell her that what she was doing was wrong. Helen wanted someone to help her think through what she should do about sleeping with James, rather than just tell her what to do. She was aware of a counsellor, Susan, who was based in another local church. Whilst Helen thought it might be a bit risky consulting her, she was feeling so desperate to talk to someone that she decided to contact Susan and to try her out.

As it turned out, Helen found having counselling with Susan to be very helpful. Initially what she found most useful was simply the chance to tell her story. As Helen did this, Susan simply listened and occasionally made a comment to show that she understood what Helen was saying. What was most important to Helen about this first session was that she was able to express herself honestly to Susan without feeling judged, or that she was a bad person for what she was doing. Over the following sessions, Susan took a more active role to help Helen explore in more detail what she really believed and felt about having sex with James. Through this process, Helen came to realize that although her church would see it as sinful, having sex with James had been a hugely important source of comfort to her at a time when she had felt more miserable than at any other point in her life. Helen decided that her deepest feelings were of gratitude for this comfort, rather than guilt, and that she needed to distinguish between what she thought was right and wrong in her own heart, and what her church told her was right or wrong.

Ultimately, Helen and James decided to stop sleeping together because James did not feel able to make a longer-term commitment to her. They still see each other as friends occasionally, and Helen is still grateful to him for the support that he gave to her during the worst months after Andy had gone. Helen has been changed by this experience. She now has a different view of herself and God, and of sex and sexuality. At the moment she still attends the same church, but she is finding the clear moral and theological teaching within it increasingly hard to accept. Perhaps the future will see her move to another church as she continues to struggle with the issues of what it means to live in a way that is true to herself and true to her faith in God.

What is (Pastoral) Counselling?

This story raises some key issues about the relationship between pastoral counselling and pastoral theology. Before looking at those, however, it will be helpful first to try to get a clearer understanding of what exactly counselling (and pastoral counselling in particular) is.

Although it can easily be argued that therapeutic conversations between individuals in Western culture go right back to pastoral practices within the early Church, the roots of modern, secular counselling and psychotherapy[2] lie in Sigmund Freud's pioneering development of psychoanalysis in the early part of this century (Oden 1989; McLeod 1998). Whilst Freud's theory of psychoanalysis was complex and changed significantly through his career, there were certain basic principles that remained constant in Freud's clinical practice. These were that a 'talking cure' could be brought about in the lives of 'patients' (Freud's preferred term), if they could experience a therapeutic relationship in which they were able honestly to talk about whatever came into their minds and could then be helped to think about the meaning of this experience. The precise ways in which Freud interpreted his patients' experiences to them remain controversial today. Nevertheless, his basic ideas about the importance of a therapeutic relationship in which experience can be honestly talked about and thought about are fundamental to all contemporary forms of counselling and psychotherapy.

Freud's ideas about the value of a therapeutic relationship were developed in a new, and more accessible way by an American psychologist, Carl Rogers, whose humanistic approach to counselling came into increasing prominence from the 1940s onwards (Rogers 1961). Rogers suggested that if a counsellor was able to offer a certain kind of relationship to their client – one characterized by understanding, acceptance and genuineness – then the client would make use of this relationship to get a better insight into their experience and decide how they should live their life. Rogers believed very much that each person had an innate knowledge of how best to live their life and that if people could only be helped to get in touch with how they really experienced things, then they would live in much more constructive and satisfying ways.

Although Rogers's work has itself been criticized as too simplistic and optimistic, and although a wide variety of new theoretical models of counselling have developed since Rogers's work, the basic emphases of Rogers's approach are still fundamental to the practice of counselling today. Thus the majority of counsellors understand their work in terms of providing a therapeutic relationship in which clients are able to think about their experience and to take decisions about their lives. Counselling thus places a strong emphasis on the autonomy of the client – that is, on the client's ability to understand what their authentic experience is and on their right to make their own decisions about their lives. Counsellors do not see themselves as advisers or as 'wise people' able to give guidance to others about how they should live. Rather, counsellors are far more likely to talk about trying to help clients to explore their experience, both through using the kind of personal qualities that Rogers talked about and through other more specific kinds of skill or technique. Indeed, one view of counselling offered by the British Association for Counselling is that 'the task of counselling is to give the client an opportunity to explore, discover, and clarify ways of living more satisfyingly and resourcefully' (McLeod 1998: 3).

If that is counselling, then what is pastoral counselling? A number of definitions have been given for pastoral counselling to date (Clinebell 1984; Lyall 1995). Some people have suggested that pastoral counselling is counselling work that is conducted by people who are ordained clergy. Another suggestion is that pastoral counselling is any kind of counselling that addresses issues of spirituality or of 'ultimate concern'. There are problems with these two definitions, however. The first is too restrictive, in that whilst at one point in the United States pastoral counselling was simply the preserve of ordained ministers, increasing numbers of lay people are now involved in pastoral counselling in Britain and the United States. The second definition is too broad. Many counsellors would today claim an interest in spirituality, but at the same time would not associate themselves with any formal religious doctrine or organization, and would certainly not refer to themselves as pastoral counsellors.

A third, and more helpful approach, is to define a pastoral counsellor as someone whose counselling work arises out of their explicit affiliation to a particular church or religious organization. In other words, the pastoral counsellor is someone who practises counselling either as a paid or voluntary worker with a church or religious organization, or as an individual who wishes to make it clear that their counselling work is shaped by their involvement with a particular religious group. With this third definition, however, it is still possible to identify a wide range of different approaches to pastoral counselling that fall within it. Some pastoral counsellors understand their religious affiliation as meaning that their work should be explicitly influenced by theological (often Biblical) principles. Other pastoral counsellors might never seek to use religious or theological language with their clients, but see their work as implicitly communicating theological truths such as God's loving acceptance of humanity (Lyall 1995). Thus, even if we accept this third definition, then this raises questions about how the pastoral counsellor's religious affiliations influence their counselling work. This leads us into a difficult debate that lies at the heart of contemporary pastoral counselling, and we shall return to this issue shortly.

The Challenge of Pastoral Counselling for Pastoral Theology

Having explored some basic ideas about the nature of counselling, and pastoral counselling, we can now turn our attention to how the disciplines of pastoral counselling and pastoral theology relate to each other. First, I want to suggest that pastoral counselling raises some important issues for pastoral theologians.

If we go back to the story of Helen, we can see a clear tension emerging between her experience of her sexuality and the theological view of sexuality taught by her church. Through the process of her counselling relationship with Susan, Helen was able to clarify how she felt about the experience of sleeping with James and to understand more of what this experience meant for her. Her greater insight into her experience offered Helen a basis for a new understanding of relationships, sexuality and God, and enabled her to make a decision concerning her future with James which was meaningful for her.

It is clear that in this instance the counselling process has privileged Helen's experience of her situation over any abstract theological principle. It is worth noting that this would not always be the case. Not all pastoral counsellors would have been as tolerant or as accepting as Susan, and some might have actively attempted to encourage Helen to become celibate until she married again. Generally, though, pastoral counsellors are primarily interested in their clients' experiences, and seek to help their clients to make decisions that are true to their experience. If Helen's experience of sleeping with James had been different – if, for example, she had come to realize that she deeply believed it was genuinely wrong – then a good pastoral counsellor would have helped her to think about and act upon that insight.

Clearly such a radical emphasis on the specific experience of the individual raises significant questions for theological reflection. Within the broad spectrum of theological disciplines, pastoral theologians are likely to be more sensitive to issues of lived experience when doing theology. The question that pastoral counselling raises for pastoral theology, however, concerns the extent to which the specific experience of individuals should shape or inform theological reflection. If pastoral theology is about facilitating some kind of dialogue between human experience and theological tradition, then what weight is given to the respective voices? Many (though not all) pastoral counsellors would be inclined to give a greater weight to the voice of individual experience than to the voice of theological tradition. Indeed pastoral counsellors, from their experience of working with clients in the Church, are likely to be aware of the pain and suffering that can be caused by abstract doctrinal or moral statements (Lynch, in press). Pastoral counselling generates the insight that (as in the story of Helen) meaningful and authentic existence arises first and foremost out of an honest engagement with one's personal experience. It therefore also highlights the potentially oppressive and abusive nature of theological ideas, when these are imposed on people's experience in ways that distort or deny that experience.

The Challenge of Pastoral Theology for Pastoral Counselling

Earlier in this chapter the question was raised as to the ways in which pastoral counselling might differ from secular counselling. If, as we have just noted, pastoral counsellors may be inclined to accuse pastoral theologians of taking insufficient account of lived human experience, then pastoral theologians might respond that all too often pastoral counsellors have taken too little account of theological tradition (Oden 1989). If we think again about the role of Susan in Helen's story, it seems that Susan has acted in a way that is largely indistinguishable from that of a secular counsellor working to humanistic principles. Susan listened to Helen's experience, accepted it, clarified it, and helped her to make choices on the basis of that experience. A caustic pastoral theologian might observe that Susan's involvement in a church has made no discernible difference to her practice as a counsellor, and that she might just as well have seen Helen in the context of a secular counselling agency. If Susan could defend herself against that charge she might say something like her practice is based on the theological principle that God loves us unconditionally and wishes us to become more fully the people that He created us to be. Whether that is a sufficiently detailed or well thought-through theological rationale for pastoral practice is open to question, however.

Many pastoral theologians, and growing numbers of pastoral counsellors, are now arguing that if pastoral counselling is to be an appropriate form of pastoral practice arising out of the life and faith of the Church, then it needs to be substantially grounded in theological tradition (Lyall 1995; Lynch, in press).[3] This argument is bolstered by the general recognition that secular counselling is itself based on a kind of faith about reality, a faith which perpetuates the Romantic ideal of the individual finding truth within themselves. Increasingly it is being asked whether the assumptions that lie behind secular, humanistic counselling offer an adequate account of the world or of what it means to be a person, and alternative theological frameworks for pastoral counselling are being proposed. Those advocating a more explicitly theological approach are not necessarily wanting to reinforce a strongly conservative theological basis for pastoral counselling (though some do), and it would be a mistake to think that those calling for greater theological integrity for pastoral counselling are unconcerned with the real experiences of individual clients. At the heart of this trend lies the simple argument, which is hard to dispute, that if pastoral counselling does connect authentically with the life and beliefs of the Church then it should be shaped by that life and those beliefs in a distinctive way. Whether this theological approach can actually deliver an approach to pastoral counselling which allows for a sensitive and open exploration of clients' experience remains to be seen, though.

The Swinging Pendulum

It has been suggested that trends in pastoral practice are like the swinging motion of a pendulum. In the 1960s and 1970s, the claim of pastoral counselling that pastoral theology did not give enough emphasis to human experience was in the ascendancy. From the late 1970s until now, however, the pendulum has swung the other way, and the claim of pastoral theologians that pastoral counselling has all too often lost its theological identity is much more strongly heard. In reality, both sides are making points that are crucial to the very heart of the discipline of pastoral and practical theology. Pastoral counselling can warn us of the dangers of theological formulations which hide or distort lived human experience. Pastoral theology can remind us that the pastoral practice of the Church needs its own theological integrity. Both sides force us to think about the respective weight that we give to experience and tradition when doing theology. Reconciling these two emphases of experience and tradition remains a central and difficult task for pastoral theologians and pastoral counsellors as we enter the new milleanium.

NOTES

1 The character of Helen is fictitious, but the tensions in her story concerning sexuality, faith and religious tradition are very real ones for many members of the Church.

2 The difference between 'counselling' and 'psychotherapy' is a major debate in its own right. Some people use the two terms interchangeably to refer generally to therapeutic work with clients. Others argue that it is helpful to distinguish between the two. According to this view, counselling is typically shorter-term work, in which the counsellor seeks to help their client to address a particular problem or to re-establish a sense of coping or self-esteem. Psychotherapy, by contrast, is much longer-term work, generally lasting for months or years, in which the aim is to bring about deeper change within the client's personality. For a discussion of the difference between 'counselling' and the use of 'counselling skills' in pastoral settings, see Lynch (in press).

3   Indeed, some pastoral theologians, such as Bob Lambourne, have suggested that a theological critique of pastoral counselling calls into question the value of a pastoral practice which seems so individualistic in emphasis (Lyall 1995).

BIBLIOGRAPHY

Clinebell, H. (1984), *Basic Types of Pastoral Care and Counselling*, London: SCM Press; Nashville: Abingdon.
Lyall, D. (1995), *Counselling in the Pastoral and Spiritual Context*, Milton Keynes: Open University Press.
Lynch, G. (ed.) (in press), *Clinical Counselling in Pastoral Settings*, London: Routledge.
McLeod, J. (1998), *An Introduction to Counselling*, 2nd edn, Milton Keynes: Open University Press.
Oden, T. (1989), *Pastoral Counsel*, New York: Crossroad.
Rogers, C. (1961), *On Becoming a Person*, London: Constable.

SOME POINTS FOR FURTHER CONSIDERATION

- What is the task of pastoral counseling?
- Reflect on Helen's story (possibly in a small group) and explore the different readings and interpretations of it. Do we understand why we see experiences in particular ways and how might these be connected with theology?
- Are there aspects of the Christian tradition that might pose difficulties for pastors attempting to engage in counseling?
- How might experience shape or inform theological reflection?
- How do religious affiliations shape or influence counseling work?
- What weight is it appropriate to give to human experience and theological tradition respectively?
- How should counseling be related to pastoral care and pastoral theology?

FOR FURTHER READING AND EXPLORATION

For a critique of pastoral counseling dominating pastoral theology and care, see Oden (1983). The work of Patton (1993) and Gerkin (1987) recognizes both the importance and limitations of counseling.

Van Deusen Hunsinger (1995) explores the relationship between pastoral counseling and Barthian theology in a way that tries to respect the autonomy of both but which gives priority to theology. See also McLeod (1997) for a thought-provoking account of how narratives and communities of discourse may shape the therapeutic process. For a critical account of the rise of counseling and the faith assumptions that inform it, see Halmos (1965).

17

How Sexuality and Relationships have Revolutionized Pastoral Theology

BONNIE J. MILLER-MCLEMORE

INTRODUCTION

Bonnie Miller-McLemore is Associate Professor of Pastoral Theology at Vanderbilt Divinity School. Her work in pastoral theology has explored the notion of family in American culture and the roles of women in work and family from a feminist perspective (Miller-McLemore 1994). She has a particular concern for the recent changes in the method and content of pastoral theology in response to feminist theory and theology. These concerns are expressed in this specially commissioned chapter.

The ways within which humans relate to one another are key elements in both the theory and practice of pastoral care. Sexuality may be regarded as basic in understanding human nature. It plays a part, both creative and destructive, in all our human relationships and indeed in imaging the Godhead. It may therefore be regarded as a central subject in this Reader.

Miller-McLemore presents a coherent and challenging case for our valuing the place and voice of women in pastoral theology. By examining the social construction of gender, she highlights how women have been disadvantaged in their relationships with men through an imbalance of power. She then makes a plea for the reconstruction of operative religious ideas which work against an understanding of women and their place in society. This pastoral approach, Miller-McLemore concludes, must always embrace and include a bias against gender injustice. Feminist theory challenges the core functions of pastoral care. She replaces the conventional modes of pastoral care (healing, sustaining, guiding, and reconciling) with four modes: resisting, empowering, nurturing, and liberating. This approach to pastoral theology is orientated to the cry for justice that disrupts and disturbs as much as it comforts and consoles.

The chapter shows the reader that pastoral theology should be a "gendered" process and that the once-hidden voices of women within a male-dominated subject demand to be heard and responded to. It provides a challenge to traditional modes of pastoral care, and a thematic framework is articulated leaving those who participate in care to work out its practical implications.

HOW SEXUALITY AND RELATIONSHIPS HAVE REVOLUTIONIZED PASTORAL THEOLOGY

In the past two decades the study of gender and sexuality has become one of the most exciting areas in pastoral theology in the United States. Up until the middle of this century, men largely defined theology and ministry based on their own experiences and readings of religious traditions within ecclesiastical contexts that prized male knowledge and leadership. Few people even noticed that these experiences were gendered or that these readings were shaped by sexual biases against women. No one thought this influenced what one saw as important in pastoral thought and action. Gender simply did not factor into the equation as a category of analysis. "Mankind" included everyone. Women did not feel left out by the term, so they said, since they assumed their own self-worth, even though few dared to suggest that "womankind" could include men or insisted on having a female senior minister. For the most part, women's public leadership was discouraged and women's experiences and knowledge were largely ignored. No one noticed or cared.

A virtual explosion of literature on gender, sexuality, and relationships has occurred over the past two decades as women gained public voice in both academy and congregation and as feminist theory acquired recognition. This exponential growth of literature represents not just new ideas, experiences, and texts. It indicates an entirely fresh way of perceiving reality. No longer can one study pastoral theology without asking important questions about the role of the social and cultural context. Satisfactory pastoral response to a woman's depression, for example, requires consideration of political components, such as her subordinate position in family, church, and society or her experience of authority or abuse within a patriarchal setting. Beyond the counseling office itself, pastoral care of women and men within the congregation includes considering the ways in which the participation of women in worship or the inclusion of gender-rich metaphors for God influence early development of children and the ongoing spiritual formation of adults. Beyond the confines of the congregation, pastoral theology concerns itself with the ways in which its public voice on gender and religion informs public policies that shape the lives of women, men, and children, such as divorce laws or sexual violence on television.

In this chapter I merely give a taste of some of the discussion of sexuality, gender, and relationships. I introduce some of the representative ideas that have emerged in psychology and pastoral theology and identify implications for pastoral theology in general. While gender is the central subject of this essay, it is important to acknowledge that gender is only one of a variety of fabrications, such as class, race, ethnicity, worldview, and so forth, that feed into the social construction of persons. Roughly speaking, I use the term "sexuality" to refer to the physiological, sensual dimensions of embodiment and "gender" to refer to socially constructed rather than biologically determined sexual identity. Sexuality in relationship always involves gender constructions or strategies of enacting sexuality. As both of these terms indicate, relationships among women and men have come under intense scrutiny. "Relationship" has been a central concept in feminist psychology and theology. This concern extends beyond specific considerations of sex and gender to matters as divergent as sexual harassment, inequitable domestic responsibilities, privileges in the congregation, household violence, and parental duties. Any one of these topics is deserving of a chapter unto itself. This chapter will accent, however, a feminist pastoral commitment that unites all of them – mutuality in relationship or shared responsibility and equality of power and freedom. This commitment represents a fundamental reorientation in gender and sexual relationships.

Psychological Revolutions in Gender, Sexuality, and Relationship

On my office door, I have a cartoon picturing Freud reclining on his couch with a balloon capturing his thoughts, "What does woman want?" Freud belonged to a broader movement of medical and scientific experts intent on solving "*the* women's problem." What was to become of middle-class women in an industrial era in which factory production and the emergence of professions had displaced them from prominent pre-industrial roles in the home and community? Behind him and out of his sight stands Mrs Freud sweeping. The cartoon bubble above her head shows her solution to the problem: she hopes that Mr. Freud will get himself off the couch and pick up the broom. In a word, Freud opened up new vistas of therapeutic intervention, radically altering common perceptions of human sexuality. But his view from the couch had its limits.

Freud contributed several key ideas that have become part of common conversation: (1) the hidden power of the unconscious over conscious thought and action, especially unconscious sexual desires; (2) the importance of early childhood sexual experiences and development; and (3) the powerful role of repressed and misdirected sexual desire in human pathology. These ideas have provoked invaluable reconsideration of human nature. On the other hand, Freud was unavoidably a man of his times and he missed a few things about human sexuality. He capitulated to pressures to deny the reality of early sexual abuse and instead credited fantasies about sexual involvement with one's parents as the primal source of conflict in early development. Equally important, he discounted, misconstrued, and in some cases completely overlooked the particularities of growing up female in a male-dominated culture.

Freud had a mote in his eye: for all his attention to sexuality and the unconscious, he was unable, given the period in which he lived and worked, to see the importance of the cultural construction of womanhood, manhood, and sexuality. He mistook cultural envy of male power for an inevitable biological, psychological, and moral deficiency on the part of the woman. In his opinion, women have only three choices in their desire to compensate for their lack of a penis: (1) neurosis; (2) a masculinity complex, that is, the refusal to accept their castrated state; or (3) optimally "normal femininity." "Normal femininity" entails the passive acceptance of biological fate and even masochistic, narcissistic resignation to a secondary, dependent destiny as a vessel of male activity and a vicarious appendage of male offspring. In short, women can never emotionally, intellectually, or morally attain mature adulthood. In so arguing, Freud gave scientific support to age-old theological and philosophical premises about female inferiority and subordination.

Many recent studies of gender, sexuality, and relationship have contested these and other psychoanalytic "truths." Of particular interest are three prominent theorists: Karen Horney, Nancy Chodorow, and Carol Gilligan. All three make several claims that continue to shape psychological research. Although we still cannot determine the extent to which sexuality and gender are a result of body chemistry or social conditioning, feminist study of sexuality at least suggests that society constructs what it means to be a man or to be a woman to a greater extent than previously imagined. Prior constructions have made male experience the standard and seen female experience as deviant, sick, bad, and immature. Seeing the world from a young girl's and woman's eyes challenges this assumed pattern. The differences between theories of human, or more exactly, *male* development and women's experience no longer signify a problem in women; they indicate an oversight or error in male theory. As pivotal, if sexuality is largely socially constructed, gender roles and identities can evolve and change.

Horney is particularly interesting because she dared to protest Freudian ideas about female sexuality from inside the psychoanalytic movement during its earlier years of institutional consolidation. Partly as a result, until recently she was criticized, ostracized, and overlooked as an important analyst and theorist in her own right. She joined others like Alfred Adler in contending that penis envy, while a valid observation of female sentiment, results not from an ontological or natural female predisposition but from envy of male social domination and authority. Penis envy was in reality envy of male power in a world in which having a penis meant having economic, political, and social rank.

Slightly later, Helen Flanders Dunbar qualifies this further: penis envy is not an inevitable, automatic, or spontaneous reaction. Much more "truly spontaneous" is the remark quoted by Dunbar of a girl who, upon "seeing her baby brother in the nude for the first time," candidly observed, " 'Isn't it lucky that he hasn't got that on his face.' "[1] Horney also named the unnamable male envy of women: "men resent and fear women because they experience them as powerful mothers" – an idea that Chodorow picks up and develops in new directions.[2] Although seldom discussed and explored, the male inability to bear children is experienced as an inborn deficiency on a par with penis envy.[3]

Chodorow and Gilligan choose different entry points into the interior world of human sexuality and gender. An anthropologically-interested sociologist and later trained as a psychoanalyst, Chodorow shifts psychoanalytic attention from the importance of Oedipal struggles between father and child centered around the penis to pre-Oedipal dynamics between mother and child centered around separation and relationship. She proposes that motherhood and, more troubling, misogyny reproduces itself precisely because women mother. When only women participate in primary care of children, daughters have readily available the same-sex parent with whom they identify. While they struggle with enmeshment and self-differentiation in the consuming presence of a parent like them, they learn to value relationships and to fear separation. Boys, on the other hand, do not have the ease of gender identification with the mother and instead must actively disengage and themselves negate the value of connection and ultimately of the mother and women. While sons achieve greater autonomy and individuality, they tend to develop rigid, defensive ego boundaries and repress emotional needs. They struggle with attachment and intimacy. To counteract the devaluation of women and caregiving activities, Chodorow leads psychoanalytic support to a wider social, political premise that men and women should share primary parenting responsibilities.

As a scholar in education, Gilligan broadens the focus from emotional to moral development and significantly undermines the widely accepted stage theory established by Heinz Kohlberg. In his theory, Kohlberg prizes abstract reasoning as the superior moral position and labels derogatorily decisions based on relationships as a lower stage of moral intelligence. Based on interview responses to ethical dilemmas, Gilligan persuasively argues that moral deliberation about relational connections requires comparably sophisticated, if not superior, reasoning of a different sort. Moral theory has unfortunately lost sight of this critical line of development of the capacity for intimacy, relationships, and care for both men and women.

In the short story, "A Jury of Her Peers," a man has died while in his bed sleeping, a rope around his neck. As the mystery of his death unfolds, we witness powerfully alternative ways of seeing key evidence and interpreting the crime. The police inspector laboriously follows the linear lead of the rope, crossing back and forth from bedroom to barn; passing through the kitchen and giving orders he entirely misses and dismisses central evidence as women's "trifles." Meanwhile, while waiting for the men in the kitchen the wife of the inspector and a woman neighbor along to gather the jailed wife's belongings discover key clues by empathy, intuition, and attention to the domestic details of relationship. The wife, the women conclude, murdered her abusive husband in self-defense, self-preservation, even desperation. While they do not condone her action they silently agree not to report the clues they have discovered, suggesting that justice cannot be served under the current circumstances of male-defined law. The crime is not just the killing in itself; the crime is their failure to reach out at an earlier stage; the crime is that domestic work of their own kept them from helping; the crime is that they did not want to visit the somber household.

This story illustrates well central tenets of classic works of women scholars in psychology: if one-half of the population is omitted from research on human wellbeing and sexuality, whether in medicine, psychology, or theology, people cannot see the whole picture. If the measure of the most mature adult rests on male standards based on the study of men, women's reality disappears and women appear deficient. If, however, alternative ways of knowing and deciding are honored, we may see anew. Among other contributions, studies of gender challenge male-defined interpretations of relational thinking as "pathological," identify other key developmental tasks, reclaim the values of dependency, endurance, connection, affectivity, and relationality, question the assigned parental roles of fatherly authority and motherly nurturance, and advance a critique of the dismissal of social and cultural considerations in psychodynamic therapy.

Pastoral Theological Revolutions in Gender, Sexuality, and Relationship

Pastoral theologian Emma Justes wrote one of the first essays on women and pastoral care. She boldly declares, "Pastoral counselors who find that they are unable to travel the route of hearing women's anger, of exploring with women the painful depths of experiences of incest and rape, or enabling women to break free from cultural stereotypes that define their existence, should not be doing pastoral counseling with women."[4] Good skills in pastoral counseling alone are not sufficient. Caregivers must deal with the impact of a variety of sexist attitudes and expectations, from economic matters of unequal pay in the workforce and the unequal second shift of domestic work, to identity issues of low self-confidence and esteem, conflicting roles of paid work and family, and changing lifestyles, to bodily struggles of bulimia, anorexia, rape, incest, and battering, to central religious notions of male headship, female submission, and self-sacrificing love.

Secular and pastoral counseling must connect internal psychic dynamics to "pathological" forces in the culture that uniquely damage women. Goals then encompass several new components: reevaluation of female gender roles; a redefinition and valuing of female sexuality, embodiment, and sensuality; an emphasis on self-worth and on women defining themselves; differentiation between external conditions and internal feelings and reactions; recognition of anger, conflict, pain as a legitimate response; social, political action as an integral part of healing; criticism of women's tendency to put themselves last; and awareness of abuse of power in relationships.

All of these components characterize new perspectives in both secular and pastoral intervention. Pastoral theology and care with men and women adds an important element: careful reconstruction of powerful operative religious ideas. Theologians have reconsidered a rich variety of themes, all of which demonstrate the necessity of dealing with religion when considering questions of sexuality and relationship: the equation of women with Eve as the temptress and source of evil; the double standard that characterizes women's sexual desires as particularly unnatural and motherhood as asexual; doctrines equating love with self-sacrifice, selflessness, suffering; fixed images of God as father and male; the elevation of men as closer to God in institutionalized religious practices and doctrines; scriptural and theological complicity in condoning male domination and female submission; and the related violation and abuse within families and congregations. Fortunately, contrary to the impression given by this laundry list of atrocities, Christianity has not just endorsed male domination and the patriarchal family as a religious norm; it has also acted to liberate people, including women, and has itself created precedent for radically inclusive justice and women's equal worth and participation as created in the image of God.

The power of reconstructing theological doctrines for pastoral purposes can be illustrated by looking at two of these themes – headship and Christian love as sacrifice. Without a doubt, Christianity has taught and continues to teach male headship. In fact, it is impossible to worship in the vast majority of Christian congregations today, even in the more liberal churches, without endorsing it, however subtly or indirectly. Nevertheless, many biblical scholars and feminist theologians now challenge religious sanction of male headship. Since at least the 1980s, feminist theologians have advocated the ideal of mutuality and shared responsibility as grounded in biblical, historical, contemporary, and practical studies in religion and theology.

The creation stories in Genesis to not establish male ascendancy as part of God's plan. Rather recent Biblical theologians demonstrate that Genesis 2–3 portray as normative a shared partnership of women and men in dominion and in fruitful propagation of the species. It is the fall into sin in Genesis 3, not God's intention in creation, that turns dominion into domination of male over female and turns companionship into social enmeshment of the female in human caregiving. The building of Christ's kingdom then calls us toward the renewal of the original creation of balanced alliance of women and men in work and love.

Perhaps the hardest text to contend with, and the texts that have most influenced the ideal of male headship are the household codes of the New Testament. "Household codes" is a term applied to scriptural passages that sought to order family relationships among early Christian converts in two Deutero-Pauline letters (letters attributed to but not authored by Paul) of the New Testament, Colossians and Ephesians. Typically, family members are exhorted to certain behaviors in relation to one another, most specifically, subordinates (e.g. wives, slaves, children) to their superiors (e.g. husbands, masters, fathers). These texts are particularly problematic for feminist interpretations of mutuality. Regardless of their initial intention, from at least the Reformation to the nineteenth century they have given supernatural sanction to patriarchal family roles in which men lead and women follow.

There are sufficient grounds for arguing, however, that the codes were not intended to bolster but to reverse ancient heroic models of male authority in families.[5] In the household codes in Ephesians, for example, the author borrows and yet transmutes the metaphors of the surrounding male culture of strength, dominance, and conflict to suggest new virtues of peace, humility, patience, and gentleness. The husband is called to the self-giving love of Christ and to a kind of mutual subjection not found in similar Aristotelian codes. Over history, it is this accent on male subordination that has been most overlooked. Instead women, more than men, have tended to absorb the message of sacrifice and submission. On occasion, when men have heard the Christian message, they have become less dominant and more giving. None the less, as advocates of women, feminists in religion often deride the codes as a reversal of the more inclusive message within the early Christian community under the social and political pressures of the patriarchal society of that time. The passage ultimately only obtains a modified or benevolent patriarchy. Yet the hierarchical patterns of the Greco-Roman world, if not completely challenged, were at least mitigated in the household codes as well as in some important aspects of the Jesus movement and in some of the practices of the early church.

From early on Christian feminists have contested the idealization of female self-sacrifice and claimed the centrality of radical mutuality in human relationships. In one of the earliest essays in feminist theology, Valerie Saiving suggests that women and men experience the Christian love command in the midst of different struggles. For a variety of anthropological, biosociological, and evolutionary reasons, men tend to face temptations of all-consuming power, prestige, self-assertion, pride, and self-centeredness for those around them. Male theologians have proposed the Christian solution of complete self-giving with no thought for one's own self. Women, Saiving argues, are more often engaged in the minutiae of daily care of others, including young children. As a result, they are more likely to struggle with distractibility, self-loss, dispersion, self-derogation, and fragmentation in the midst of multiple demands – that is, "underdevelopment or negation of the self."[6] Women have been expected to give up needs, desires, opportunities, and space to make way for others. They have been taught to suffer obediently and meekly, as Christ.

However, Christian love modeled after the commandment to love the neighbor as oneself upholds the importance of God's love for each of us and of loving oneself as a source of love of others. A mother, for example, must balance the endless moments of responsive care of the infant with care for herself within a community supportive of the good of children and women. Sacrifice and suffering as ends in and of themselves are not only detrimental to subordinate groups, but neither redemptive sacrifice nor suffering is the primary way to understanding Christ's death on the cross. The cross was an inevitable consequence of Jesus' political pursuit of care for the suffering, and only upholds suffering as a standard of Christian commitment when it serves to liberate the oppressed and free the captives. In short, adequate interpretations of Christian love recognize the dangers in making suffering a central Christian act and emphasize the secondary place of self-sacrifice as a means to the more encompassing end of mutual love.

Implications for the Field of Pastoral Theology

What do changes in understandings of sexuality, gender, and relationship mean for the field of pastoral theology more generally? Feminism is a radical political movement aimed at transforming categories of discrimination, especially but not restricted to categories of gender and sexual stereotype, that rank people as inferior of superior according to particular traits. To think about practical and pastoral theology from this vantage point requires prophetic, transformative challenge to systems of stratification and domination within society and religious life, particularly those that rank men and male activities over women and female activities.

Pastoral theology still focuses on care of persons and finds personality theories, particularly within psychology, primary resources for the enhancement of this practice. However, in the past decade, partly as a result of new studies of gender and sexuality, several feminist pastoral theologians have modified the individualistic leanings of Anton Boisen's metaphor of the living human document as the object of study in pastoral theology by turning to an alternative, related image of the living human web. The metaphor of web affirms the relevant role of other social sciences besides psychology in helping understand sexual roles and social relationships. But it does not mean that the individual or the use of psychology as the primary cognate science for pastoral theology recede in importance. It simply means that the individual is understood in inextricable relationship to the broader context. And in contrast to popular characterizations of psychology as individualistic, psychology is not inherently so, having itself contributed to new understandings of connective selfhood in recent research. Feminist psychology in the different schools of psychoanalytic, self-in-relation, and family systems theory continues to shed light on the ways in which sexuality and gender are culturally determined by distorted patterns of male–female relationship and internalized perceptions of denigration and animosity.

This perspective requires a fundamental reorientation of the core functions of pastoral care. Pastoral care still entails practical religious, spiritual, and congregational care for the suffering, involving the rich resources of religious traditions and communities, contemporary understandings of the human person in the social sciences, and ultimately the movement of God's love and hope in the lives of individuals and communities. However, pastoral care from a liberation perspective is about breaking silences, urging prophetic action, and liberating the oppressed. In place of the conventional modes with which pastoral care has been routinely equated with healing, sustaining, guiding, and reconciling, articulated by Seward Hiltner and amended by William Clebsch and Charles Jaekle, four pastoral practices acquire particular importance: resisting, empowering, nurturing, and liberating.[7] Pastoral theology and care oriented to the cry for gender justice disrupts and disturbs as much as it comforts and consoles.

One day in class, several students responded with mixed feelings to a book on women's struggles in a male-dominated society: an older woman denied gender and sexual oppression as a woman because she has loved mothering;

a younger woman rejected the idea of oppression because changes have occurred and she feels equal rather than personally disadvantaged in her relationships; finally, a younger man disputed his role in oppression of women, having done nothing he could see as exploitative. All three made appropriate claims. They personally do not belong either distinctly inside or outside the role of dominator and oppressed. No one wants to be falsely or rigidly labeled.

None the less, all of these folks stand within a history and society in which social structures prize men more than women; all of us reside in a context in which powerful religious practices, institutions, and doctrines about gender and sexual roles influence our behavior and beliefs about ourselves. Although none of the participants in the discussion above discussed their struggles publicly in the class, I knew from personal conversation with each of them that the older woman suffered in an exploitative, painful marriage; the younger woman came from a home in which her father had sexually abused her; and the young man benefited from unseen economic and educational advantages of his male sex and white skin. Breaking silences about injustice and abuse leads to both relief and fear, shame, even rage. Sometimes it is easier to avoid the kind of pastoral care and theology that surfaces such complex human sentiments. However, the benefits of entering into such conversation are multitudinous. Despite or even as a result of the turmoil created by changes in gender and sexuality, pastoral theology and its approach to human relationships continues to evolve in ever new and exciting ways.

NOTES

1 Helen Flanders Dunbar, *Mind and Body: Psychosomatic Medicine* (New York: Random House, 1947), p. 259, cited by Jeanne Stevenson Moessner, "The psychology of women and pastoral care." In *Women in Travail and Transition: A New Pastoral Care*, ed. Glaz, Maxine, and Jeanne Stevenson Moessner (Minneapolis: Fortress, 1991).

2 Nancy Chodorow, *Feminism and Psychoanalytic Theory* (New Haven: Yale University Press, 1989) p. 6.

3 See E. Jacobson, "Development of the wish for a child in boys," *Psychoanalytic Study of the Child*, 5 (1950): 139–52; John Munder Ross, "Beyond the phallic illusion: notes on man's heterosexuality." In *The Psychology of Men*, ed. Fogel, Saree, and Siebert (New York: Basic Books, 1986), pp. 50–1 (49–70).

4 Emma J. Justes, "Women." In *Clinical Handbook of Pastoral Counseling*, ed. Robert J. Wicks and Richard D. Parsons (New York: Paulist, 1985), p. 298.

5 See chapter 5 in Don S. Browning, Bonnie J. Miller-McLemore, Pamela Couture, Brynhoff Lyon, and Robert Franklin, *From Culture Wars to*

Common Ground: Religion and the American Family Debate (Louisville: John Knox/Westminster, 1997).

6 Valerie Saiving, "The human situation: a feminine view," *Journal of Religion*, 40 (April 1960), p. 109.

7 Partially based on Carroll Weaver's informal remarks during a panel at the American Academy of Religion, November 1996, drawing on her dissertation work on womanist pastoral theology.

SELECTED BIBLIOGRAPHY

Ackermann, D. M., and R. Bons-Storm (eds.) (1988), *Liberating Faith Practices: Feminist Practical Theologies in Context*, Leuven: Peeters.

Bons-Storm, R. (1996), *The Incredible Woman: Listening to Women's Silences in Pastoral Care and Counseling*, Nashville: Abingdon.

Browning, D., B. J. Miller-McLemore, P. Couture, B. Lyon, and R. Franklin (1997), *From Culture Wars to Common Ground: Religion and the American Family Debate*, Louisville: John Knox/Westminster.

Chodorow, N. (1974), "Family structure and feminine personality." In M. Z. Rosaldo and L. Lamphere (eds.), *Women, Culture, and Society*, Stanford, CA: Stanford University Press.

Chodorow, N. (1978), *The Reproduction of Mothering*, Berkeley: University of California Press.

Chodorow, N. (1989), *Feminism and Psychoanalytic Theory*, New Haven: Yale University Press.

Clebsch, W., and C. Jaekle (1983), *Pastoral Care in Historical Perspective*, 2nd edn., New York: Aronson.

Cooper-White, P. (1994), *The Cry of Tamar: Violence against Women and the Church's Response*, Minneapolis: Fortress.

Couture, P. D. (1991), *Blessed are the Poor? Women's Poverty, Family Policy, and Practical Theology*, Nashville: Abingdon.

Culbertson, P. L. (1994), *Counseling Men*, Minneapolis: Fortress.

De Marinis, V. M. (1993), *Critical Caring: A Feminist Model for Pastoral Psychology*, Louisville: Westminster.

Doehring, C. (1992), "Developing models of feminist pastoral counseling," *Journal of Pastoral Care*, 46, 1 (Spring): 23–31.

Dunlap, S. J. (1997), *Counseling Depressed Women*, Louisville: Westminster/John Knox.

Ehrenreich, B., and D. English (1978), *For Her Own Good: 150 Years of the Experts' Advice to Women*, New York: Doubleday.

Fiorenza, E. S. (1984), *In Memory of Her: A Feminist Theological Reconstruction of Christian Origins*, New York: Crossroad.

Freud, S. (1953 [1905]), *Three Essays on the Theory of Sexuality*. In *Standard Edition*, English trans. and ed. J. Strachey, vol. 7, London: Hogarth Press.

Freud, S. (1953 [1931]), *Female Sexuality*. In *Standard Edition*, English trans. and ed. J. Strachey, vol. 21, London: Hogarth Press.

Gilligan, C. (1982), *In a Different Voice: Psychological Theory and Women's Development*, Cambridge: Harvard University Press.

Glaz, M., and J. S. Moessner (eds.) (1991), *Women in Travail and Transition: A New Pastoral Care*, Minneapolis: Fortress.

Graham, E., and M. Halsey (eds.) (1993), *Life Cycles: Women and Pastoral Care*, Cambridge: SPCK.

Greenspan, M. (1983), *A New Approach to Women and Therapy*, New York: McGraw-Hill.

Greider, K. J. (1997), *Reckoning with Aggression: Theology, Violence, and Vitality*, Louisville: Westminster/John Knox.

hooks, bell (1984), *Feminist Theory: From Margin to Center*, Boston: South End.

Horney, K. (1967 [1930]), *Feminine Psychology*, New York: W. W. Norton.

Horney, K. (1973), *Neurosis and Human Growth*, New York: W. W. Norton.

Justes, E. J. (1985), "Women." In *Clinical Handbook of Pastoral Counseling*, pp. 279–99, ed. R. J. Wicks and R. D. Parsons, New York: Paulist.

Lerman, H. (1986), *A Mote in Freud's Eye: From Psychoanalysis to the Psychology of Women*, New York: Springer.

Levant, R., and W. Pollack (eds.) (1995), *A New Psychology of Men*, New York: Basic Books.

Miller-McLemore, B. J. (1994), *Also a Mother: Work and Family as Theological Dilemma*, Nashville: Abingdon.

Miller-McLemore, B. J. (1996), "The living human web: pastoral theology at the turn of the century." In *Through the Eyes of Women: Insights for Pastoral Care*, ed. J. S. Moessner, Philadelphia: Westminster/John Knox, pp. 9–26.

Miller-McLemore, B. J. (1998), "The subject and practice of pastoral theology as a practical theological discipline: pushing past the nagging identity crisis to the poetics of resistance." In *Liberating Faith Practices: Feminist Practical Theologies in Context*, ed. D. M. Ackermann and R. Bons-Storm, Leuven: Peeters, pp. 175–98.

Miller-McLemore, B. J. and H. Anderson (1995), "Pastoral care and gender." In *Pastoral Care and Social Conflict*, ed. P. D. Couture and R. Hunter, Nashville: Abingdon, pp. 99–113.

Miller-McLemore, B. J., and B. Gill-Austern (eds.) (1999), *Feminist and Womanist Pastoral Theology*, Nashville: Abingdon.

Moessner, J. S. (ed.) (1996), *Through the Eyes of Women: Insights for Pastoral Care*, Philadelphia: Westminster/John Knox.

Neuger, C. C. (1992), "Feminist pastoral theology and pastoral counseling: a work in progress," *Journal of Pastoral Theology*, 2 (Summer): 35–57.

Neuger, C. C. (ed.) (1996), *The Arts of Ministry: Feminist-Womanist Approaches*, Louisville: Westminster/John Knox.

Neuger, C. C., and J. N. Poling (eds.) (1997), *The Care of Men*, Nashville: Abingdon.

Plaskow, J. (1980), *Sex, Sin and Grace: Women's Experience and the Theologies of Reinhold Niebuhr and Paul Tillich*, Lanham: University Press of America.

Russell, L. M., and J. Shannon Clarkson (eds.) (1996), *Dictionary of Feminist Theologies*, Louisville: Westminster/John Knox.

Saiving, V. (1960), "The human situation: a feminine view," *Journal of Religion* 40 (April): 100–12. Reprinted in *Womanspirit Rising: A Feminist Reader in Religion*, pp. 25–42, ed. C. Christ and J. Plaskow, New York: Harper and Row, 1970.

Saussy, C. (1991), *God Images and Self-Esteem: Empowering Women in a Patriarchal Society*, Louisville: Westminster John Knox.

Saussy, C. (1995), *The Gift of Anger: A Call to Faithful Action*, Louisville: Westminster/John Knox.

Sturdivant, S. (1984), *Therapy with Women: A Feminist Philosophy of Treatment*, New York: Springer.

Westkott, Marcia (1986), *The Feminist Legacy of Karen Horney*, New Haven: Yale University Press.

SOME POINTS FOR FURTHER CONSIDERATION

- What is your understanding and experience of gender? Compare and contrast it with that of someone of a different sex.
- How does your sense or understanding of gender shape the ways you frame the meanings and practices of pastoral theology?
- If pastoral and practical theology have been dominated by male patterns of thinking, what are the main characteristics of it?
- What injustices of your own particular context need to be addressed by pastoral and practical theology?
- What should be the aims and modes of pastoral care and theology in the light of Miller-McLemore's critique?

FOR FURTHER READING AND EXPLORATION

This chapter has an exhaustive American set of references. For an exploration of the challenge of feminism and gender to practical theology and pastoral care, see Graham (1995), and Graham and Halsey (1993), Glaz and Moessner (1991). For an exploration of men needing to recognize their own genderedness, see Pryce (1996), and Nelson (1992). Two books which examine how the churches have handled debates about sexuality are Stuart (1996), and Stuart and Thatcher (1997).

18

Culture, Religious Faiths, and Race

MARTIN FORWARD

INTRODUCTION

Martin Forward is Lecturer in Pastoral and Systematic Theology at Wesley House, Cambridge, UK. He uses his extensive pastoral experience both in England and abroad to explore the challenges that culture, faith, and race pose to pastoral theology. Forward writes from the perspective of a white, middle-class Methodist minister responding to his experiences in an open and honest manner. Much of the context of pastoral care is multicultural, and the interface between Christianity and other world religions has played a significant part in the theological agenda of the churches, so this subject needs addressing as part of putting pastoral care into a wider social and cultural context.

This specially commissioned chapter offers a clear definition of pastoral theology: "to explore what sort of God, God is, and how God speaks to and cares for creation, particularly human beings." Forward offers a model of dialogue and encounter where there can be interaction between the complex realities of culture, faith, and race. These realities, he argues, can and should take us into a deeper level of reflection and understanding. In particular, Forward asks that pastoral theology consider factors of otherness and power. In other words, he challenges those involved in care to consider what it might feel like to be an immigrant (otherness) and how individuals or groups might be given a sense of power within society (powerlessness). The traditional language of social responsibility, he argues, disempowers because it asks what can be done for or to the other. This disempowering language does not enable individuals and groups to develop a sense of mutual responsibility for those whose experiences are different. Forward challenges all theoretical thinking to engage and connect with the complexity of religion: "religion is far more complex and interesting in real life than many others would warrant." He concludes that pastoral theology must attempt to articulate the incredible diversity of beliefs and world views in the global village and to interpret how God touches it.

CULTURE, RELIGIOUS FAITHS, AND RACE

Some years ago, I spent two weeks in Paurmiana, a small village in the Pakistani province of Punjab. My intention was to improve my knowledge of Urdu which, along with Panjabi, was widely spoken in the village. I lived by myself in a house which was owned by a family in the UK. They usually locked it up except when they came over on holiday. Their family and friends in the village made and brought me meals. Many children and adults from the village wandered over to talk to me.

One abiding conversation was about religion. Everyone there was a Muslim. They all assumed I was a Christian, and most were taken aback when I claimed to know rather a lot about Islam, despite being a Methodist minister. Quite properly, they tested me to make sure I was telling the truth. When my credentials were vouched for, most people's reactions were twofold.

First, they wanted to know why I should wish to remain a Christian after I had read the clear sign of the Qur'an, Islam's holy scripture, which most Muslims believe confirms and fulfils previous revelations. The result is that I had many conversations that, if I were to label them, were about pastoral theology and mission: pastoral theology, because they were about what sort of God, God is, and how he speaks to and cares for his creation, particularly human beings; and mission, for exactly the same reason plus the added factor that there were differences between my understanding of God and their view.

Second, they opened to me their religious treasures. A young man took me to the grave of his mother, and told me how important faith had been in her life and how she had taught it him. He said his prayers whilst we were there, unembarrassed by my presence. Another young man took me to two graves of men who had died many years before. The elder man was a *pir*, a spiritual guide whose teaching is still followed, and intercession with God still sought by many villagers today; also by many people in the surrounding area. His son was also a *pir*. Barren wives come there, tie little 'flags' to the overhanging tree, and pray for children. Others, men, women and children, come and pray for their heart's desires.

There were some indications that religion could be a bad thing. One young woman and her mother took me to a part of the village where Hindus had lived, before the partition of the subcontinent in 1947. Then they were chased out. The mother told me she had friends there, but joined in harrying and expelling them. She said to me: 'Those were difficult times. Why did we do what we did, in the name of God and religion? I don't know.' Further, although only a few villagers had left the area, let alone been outside Pakistan, all were angrily pro-Palestinian and anti-Israeli. The only occasion I felt a prickle of anxiety in the village was when I told a large group that I had visited Israel, and was called upon to explain my outrageous action.

I asked many villagers: why were they willing to share their faith with me? Because you have faith, they told me. Even if it is different faith, it is not secular scepticism or secularized indifference. A few told me, more enigmatically, that I was the sort of person to whom people told things.

Occasionally, it was hard work being in the village. When children came to stare at me, to observe my white skin, hear my accented and feeble Urdu, and teach me some (often rude) expression in Urdu or Punjabi, I alternated between amusement and irritation. One day, irritated, I took myself off to the nearest town, Hasan Abdal. I wandered along the open market, where everything was sold, from a match to a camel. Three young men, silver-beaters, called me over. They gave me a cup of tea and asked me: Are you Japanese? (I assured them I wasn't.) Who are you? What do you do? How much do you earn? It is refreshing to be asked such frank though un-English questions, because you can then ask equally forthright queries. We got on to the subject of marriage and the family. I admitted that I was married, but had no children. Meanwhile, an elderly man had stopped to join in our chat. He took my hand, read my palm, and told me that there would be children; then, he rather spoilt the effect by adding, 'if God wills'. Thereafter, we all giggled and parted amicably.

Another day, I ventured further afield, back to the major city of Rawalpindi. I left it rather late to return to Paurmiana. I caught the last train, and had no great hope of making the necessary connections thereafter to get me 'home'. When I got to the nearest railway station to the village there was one horse and cart there. I took it as far as the man would go. Near where he dropped me, there was a hut. A man came out, and offered to take me to the village on the back of his scooter. I accepted, gratefully. Throughout the journey from Rawalpindi, my Western, Enlightenment convictions about an enclosed universe were in abeyance. I knew that this was the daftest trip I had ever made, with dacoits (robbers) in the area, yet was sure that I was help safe in God's hands.

I returned, not quite the same person. I had lived abroad before, but never like this. I was removed from the phone, from linguistic fluency, from other people like me, from running water: my culture, religious faith, and race were other; I was deskilled and often unnerved. Even so, there were moments of quite extraordinary transcendent luminosity.

What, as a pastoral theologian, has this done for my reflections on culture, religious faiths, and race?

These three areas force one to deal with the fact of 'otherness'. A great deal has been written about 'otherness' in the last twenty or so years. We are often reminded that we are united in a global village, with the World Wide Web linking people to a degree hitherto unimagined. Quite so. Yet in Paurmiana, I discovered how remote one can feel from the known and the taken-for-granted. A few miles away, in Rawalpindi, there were people who shared my language, class identity, reliance on phone and electricity. In Paurmiana, I often felt vulnerable, at the mercy of others' acts of kindness, not so much out of control as unable to control my life.

When I returned to inner-city Leicester, I looked at my black churchgoers, and at Hindu, Muslim and Sikh neighbours rather differently. How did they feel as immigrants? Did they feel differently from their children? When I asked some of them, I had some interesting responses. One Antiguan woman told me that the sense I had of living on a knife-edge and the constant feeling of queasiness in my stomach were exactly her experience of daily living (I had had two weeks only of it!). Her children, however, had far more ambivalent feelings. They were Britons, but often made feel as if they weren't. Yet they had nothing else to be. Antigua was as remote to them as the moon, not the focus of nostalgic childhood reminiscences.

One of the problems I could thereafter identify, but not quite get right, was that of power. In Paurmiana, I had been powerless: deskilled and unnerved. I was fortunate that the villagers were humorous, inclusive and caring. Even so, I felt insecure. How, then, do churches and parsons give to people of different cultures, religions and racial groups a sense of power within society? I found that many of the ways my colleagues espoused did not help. They were so condescending, or could be interpreted as such. Very often, churches and parsons do not ask theological questions of 'otherness', but rather, speak the language of social responsibility: what can be done *for* or even *to* the other. Of course it is good to found community projects, to teach English, to help people fill in necessary forms and so on. People are grateful for such help, and often express gratitude. Yet gratitude is a double-edged sword, often betokening dependence rather than mutuality. I wonder now whether a better theology would not help us get an appropriate sense of mutual responsibility.

Of course theology has responded to the claims of our global village. I want to mention particularly the matter of religious diversity, though another author would emphasize cultural or racial diversity.

Alan Race's book *Christians and Religious Pluralism* (1993), with an important final chapter, 'Ten years later: surveying the scene', has been important in the last decade in describing the parameters of the debate. The subtitle of the first edition drew attention to 'Patterns in the Christian Theology of Religious'. Race sees three: exclusivism, inclusivism, and pluralism. To put these 'patterns' at their simplest: the exclusivist maintains that salvation is only given to those who make an explicit commitment to Jesus Christ; the inclusivist affirms that salvation is bestowed on more than just Christians, because of all that God has done through Jesus Christ; and the pluralist affirms that humans are saved within their own faith traditions, not (except for Christians) because of the person or works of Jesus.

When I was in Paurmiana, I took two theological books with me (distinguished ones, by John Hick and Paul Knitter) than I had to review for academic journals. Both were 'pluralist' in tone and argument. I was angered by both; so furious with one, that I threw it the length of the compound in which I was sitting. So many books in this area, whatever position they espouse, seem excessively theoretical. Further, they actually limit real pluralism. Most pluralists reduce religious difference to questions of salvation, narrowly expressed as to whether others are accepted by God now and will go to heaven later. Muslims in Paurmiana, or anywhere else, who read the Qur'an know that 'salvation' is mentioned only once in that scripture (40.41). It is not of central importance to Muslims. The reasons they adduce for being accepted by God now and entering Paradise hereafter are not Christian soteriological ones, but arise from within the different worldview of Islam.

So I think back to my time in the village, and to convictions I threw away and yet also gained when I was there. I abandoned: the impression that pastoral theology is about *my* care of others; that Western presuppositions about an enclosed universe are self-evidently true and should be taken as read by any intelligent person; that religion can be reduced to boundaried structures, within which people demonstrate appropriate acts of faith and obedience; that pluralism is about everyone being acceptable to God through their own beliefs and practices. I gained the belief that: pastoral theology is about *God's* providential care of all his creation, including me; that life is open to the impress of God's guidance of others and of me; that religious faith and obedience are open-ended; that pluralism is dealing with the bewildering diversity of means and goals.

Let us examine aspects of this change of belief. Some evangelical Christians have questioned whether beliefs of Christians and others, including Muslims, are so divergent that, in practice, they do not point to the same God. I certainly do not hold to the sentimental and unprovable notion that all religions are different paths up the same mountain. They may, in fact, be ascending quite different mountains, some of which are more interesting, dangerous, or attractive than others. This is all of a piece with my conviction that one must be honest about pluralism, and really let the other be other. However, God is God. I believe that he is one, that he is beyond the power of humans to describe, exhaust or explore. Yet we have seen his face in Jesus the Christ. For all the differences between Muslims in Paurmiana and Hasan Abdal, and me, I had a strong sense of the overarching canopy of God's care, of his providential care for others and for me. From my Christian position in this extraordinarily diverse and plural world, I believe that there are not Gods many and Lords many. There is one God, whom Jesus taught was surprised by faith in unexpected places: whether of the Roman Centurion (Luke 7.1–10) or of the Canaanite woman (Matthew 15.21–8). Paul was surely an authentic interpreter of Jesus in drawing out from his message a sense of God's universal grace and of the response of faith as a universal human quality.

If one lives within and tires to think within a different culture, its characteristic ways of locating and responding to transcendence may rub off. My life in Paurmiana was within a culture which expects God *sometimes* to take personal, providential care of individuals, that expects God *from time to time* to work miracles, through intercessors like *pirs* or even directly. This can seem credulous and gullible to outsiders. Sometimes, indeed, it is. But it need not be. It can demonstrate an open-ended, trustful belief in a mysterious God who cares, and whose care is *now and then* demonstrably witnessed by those with the eyes of faith to see. So I do believe that God may be gracious to those who come to *pirs* to implore his mercy, and that he was with me in a quite extraordinary way on my night journey from Paurmiana to Rawalpindi.

I have become sceptical about the phenomenon of postmodernism. It is a curiously Western tool, arising from discontent with some of the assumptions of the European Enlightenment, yet highly indebted to that cultural and historical period. In other parts of the world, grand narratives remain important. Maybe Pastoral Theologians have much to learn from the positive experiences of others, rather than in negative reaction to one's own history?

Grand narratives, however, do not necessarily imply that people enter into every part of the story and make it their own. When I learned Islam, I was taught that people prayed five times a day. In the village, I learned otherwise. The men prayed together on Friday lunchtimes. The few who did not want to were impelled by their mothers or wives to join in. Otherwise, only a few people prayed at the other set times, though quite a few offered occasional, informal, often intercessory prayers. Religion is far more interesting and complex in real life than the way it is systematized in textbooks. As I talked with people about their faith, I came to see that for some it was a comfort, for others an irrelevance (though, because of the nature of the society, never publicly proclaimed by them as such), for a few it was a mystical unity with God, for others a rather superstitious attempt to manipulate spiritual powers to their own advantage. In other words, it had many and varied roles within people's lives, and was of marginal interest to some, though of great importance to others. An obvious difference between Paurmiana and Cambridge is not that everyone in Paurmiana is observant whereas few in Cambridge are. Rather, the social setting in the former place gives religion a centrally important place, which is no longer the fact in many places in the contemporary Western world. In both places, personal faith flourishes or not, according to temperament, means and opportunities, experiences of the world and of the numinous, and so forth.

There are additional, exciting yet complicating factors in the modern West. Paurmiana is a relatively homogeneous society, more so now than before the partition of the subcontinent. Parts of the West are multicultural, multireligious, multiracial. One of the sharp edges in such circumstances is interracial and interfaith marriage.

In the case of mixed-race marriage, it is tempting to quote Paul's words to the Athenians: 'From one ancestor [or, blood], he [God] made all nations to inhabit the whole earth' (Acts 17.26). There is only one human race, created and loved by God. Although Paul goes on to point out that God allotted the boundaries of the places where they would live, in the modern world that has broken down. As a result, interracial marriage is both a natural and a desirable consequence of this. Maybe so. It is certainly a theological truth that all humans are equal before God, loved and graced by him. Yet the meltdown of cultures into a common one has proved contentious. Does not racism prevent many from accepting this end? Anyway, is not variety a good thing? Certainly, many parents worry that their children have abandoned very important matters when they marry out: the Jewish experience illustrates this.

If interracial marriage is readily affirmed by some, what about multiple religious participation? (See the articles by John Berthrong and Julius Lipner, among others, in Forward 1995.) In parts of South-East Asia, particularly China, people have for centuries lived and participated within worlds, not *one* world, of religion: Buddhism, Taoism, Confucianism. They have married within one religion, worshipped in another, they are sent from this world with the prayers of a third. Now some Westerners are claiming to be Christian Buddhists or Jewish Hindus, and so forth. Is this desirable or even possible? What are its effects on understanding a transcendent reality who cares for all?

The contemporary task of pastoral theology in relation to culture, religious faiths and race is to articulate the incredible diversity of beliefs and worldviews in our global village, sometimes illustrated on a single street of a town or city, and to interpret how God's grace in Christ touches and interprets it. There are no easy answers. Much systematic theology and fashionable philosophy is ill-equipped and too parochial to deal with it.

The creation and articulation of appropriate and meaningful models is the next step. Meanwhile, we live in interesting times!

BIBLIOGRAPHY

Butler, T., and Butler, B. (1996), *Just Spirituality in World Faiths*, London and New York: Mowbray. A Church of England bishop and his wife, both deeply involved in racial and interreligious issues, reflect on common themes and images of spirituality. These themes may be more subtly understood than they think, but it is an interesting read.

Forward, M. (ed.) (1995), *Ultimate Visions*, Oxford: Oneworld. Scholars of many faiths who have been existentially engaged in relations with people of other religions reflect upon why they are committed to their own faith.

Griffiths, P. J. (1990), *Christianity through Non-Christian Eyes*, Maryknoll: Orbis. This book contains reflections, some very barbed, by members of other faiths about Christianity. A salutary read.

Haslam, D. (1996), *Race for the Millennium: A Challenge to Church and Society*, London: Church House Publishing. This reflects on the British scene, but incorporates insights from the American situation.

Heim, S. M. (1995), *Salvations: Truth and Difference in Religion*, Maryknoll: Orbis. The model of exclusivism, inclusivism and pluralism as a means of interpreting religious pluralism needs to be changed. Until then, this is its most refined expression.

Heim, S. M. (ed.) (1998), *Grounds for Understanding: Ecumenical Resources for Responses to Religious Pluralism*, Grand Rapids and Cambridge: Eerdmans. North American ecumenical scholars and bureaucrats reflect on their own denomination's resources for responding to religious pluralism. A patchy effort, but well worth attempting.

King, M. L. (1964), *Strength to Love*, London: Hodder and Stoughton. A remarkable set of sermons that say more about racial justice than many more theoretical analyses.

Leech, K. (1988), *Struggle in Babylon*, London: Sheldon Press. This book reflects on racism in the British context, usefully and perceptively but from rather a narrow Anglican perspective.

Mandela, N. (1994), *Long Walk to Freedom*, London: Little, Brown. The extraordinary account of a man's life, committed to overthrowing racial and religious discrimination.

Thangaraj, M. T. (1997), *Relating to People of Other Religions*, Nashville: Abingdon. The best introductory book on this subject, by an Indian Christian with experience of the British and North American situations.

Young, R. (1990), *White Mythologies: Writing History and the West*, London and New York: Routledge. This is a theoretical and Marxist analysis, one-sided but an important contribution to understanding racism in a post-colonial era.

SOME POINTS FOR FURTHER CONSIDERATION

- What problems and opportunities for pastoral practice does racial and/or religious variety in a particular society give rise to?
- Reflect upon your own experiences of faiths, cultures, or races that are different or challenging to your own.
- How would you describe your own faith, culture or race?
- In what ways is Christian faith exclusive, and what are the implications of this for pastoral theology and care?
- In what ways does pastoral theology place limits on God's care?
- How might pastoral theology enable a better sense of mutual responsibility?
- What negative experiences from your own pastoral experience have shaped your understanding of pastoral theology?

FOR FURTHER READING AND EXPLORATION

For an examination of pastoral theology and care from a Black perspective, see Lartey (1997) and Beckford (1998). For a Jewish approach to the area, see Katz (1985). For practical advice about pastoral care, see Augsburger (1986) and Hooker and Lamb (1986).

___19___

What is the Relevance of Congregational Studies for Pastoral Theology?

BRYNOLF LYON

INTRODUCTION

This article is reprinted from the *Journal of Pastoral Theology*. It explores the relationship between congregational studies and pastoral theology. Recent pastoral theology has become interested in groups and communities and not just in individuals. Thus congregational studies has emerged as an area of interest.

Lyon accounts for its core texts and authors: congregational studies is defined as the study of the life of the local congregation. It allows participants to explore a variety of aspects of how a group or congregation works and worships together. The study of congregations is interdisciplinary. The appreciation of their depth and complexity and the recognition of the importance of their significance leads Lyon to argue that pastoral theologians should pay them attention.

The paper outlines four ways in which congregational studies is relevant to the work of pastoral theology. These are: first, deepening a sense of the dynamics of care throughout the whole of congregational life; second, appreciating the "otherness" within congregational life; third, enabling individuals to recognize the complex practices of practical and pastoral theology within congregations themselves; and fourth, facilitating an understanding of congregations' efforts to form and transform their own expressions of care.

WHAT IS THE RELEVANCE OF CONGREGATIONAL STUDIES FOR PASTORAL THEOLOGY?

This essay briefly addresses the relevance of congregational studies to pastoral theology: why it is that those of us who work in the area of pastoral theology might be (and perhaps ought to be) interested in the emerging field of inquiry we now call congregational studies.[1]

What is Congregational Studies?

The use of the term "congregational studies" to refer to a distinct area of research has come into prominence only within the last decade. As with any emerging field, it has a few core texts and authors. Congregational studies is most centrally associated with Denham Grierson's *Transforming a People of God*, James Hopewell's *Congregation: Story and Structure*, the *Handbook for Congregational Studies*, edited by Jackson Carroll, Carl Dudley, and William McKinney, and the earlier volume edited by Dudley, *Building Effective Ministry: Theory and Practice in the Local Church*.[2] While these remain the central texts of congregational studies, new works are being published at a remarkable pace – not only by persons who teach within divinity schools and seminaries, but also by persons whose disciplines are one or another of the human sciences. The academy has rediscovered the congregation.[3]

As Allison Stokes and David Roozen note in their brief history of the field, however, the study of congregations using the tools of the modern social sciences has been going on in this country since at least the turn of the century.[4] The study of congregations in this broad sense, they observe, arose with the urbanization of North American society, the decline of the rural church, and the transformations undergone by inner-city churches. The research of the sociologist H. Paul Douglas was particularly prominent in this early work and much of the work done by the research and survey departments among many mainline denominations during this period was influenced by him.

The historical interpretation offered by Stokes and Roozen implies that the study of the congregation has been guided by a variety of practical interests. In their account these interests have generally followed broader cultural trends. Thus, much of the early work investigated the demographic changes in the social context of establishment churches and was directed toward sponsoring church development in suburban areas and responding to the needs of the new urban immigrants. In the 1960s, they suggest, a more prophetic trend tended to dominate the study of congregations with works such as Gibson Winter's *The Suburban Captivity of the Churches* and Peter Berger's *The Noise of Solemn Assemblies*.[5] James Hopewell argues, however, that this prophetic turn did not alter the basic orientation of the study of the congregation. Such studies tended still to focus on the church's social context as the key to the renewal of congregational life.[6] In many cases, however, it did radically revise the sense of what the congregation was to be about in the world. In the 1970s, mirroring the cultural turn inward, the study of congregations turned from concern with social context to concern with congregational process and questions of what resources for congregational renewal were available from within the church itself. At present, Stokes and Roozen suggest, questions of congregational process have receded somewhat and questions of congregational identity in a fragmented culture preoccupy those studying congregations. In other words, congregational researchers have turned to questions of how the meanings and values that form congregational identity can be relatively cohesive within congregations and be a cohesing force for their members and the culture at large in a way that yet appreciates the richness of diversity and pluralism.

While it is true that questions of congregational identity have gained a certain prominence in congregational studies, it is none the less the case that congregational studies is a quite diverse field of inquiry these days. It is difficult to discern its common features. I want to suggest, however, three very broad characteristics of the field which I think capture something of the tone of its central orientation and hold contemporary forms of congregational studies together as at least a somewhat distinct field of inquiry.

First, as Jim Wind has noted, congregational studies is dominated by an appreciative attitude toward congregational life.[7] While it is generally recognized that there are other important and vital forms of religious association and that congregational dynamics are clearly and painfully subject to systematic distortions of race, class, and gender, congregational studies tends to take the congregation less as a series of problems to be solved – a way of life to be radically altered from without – and more as a rich and persistently significant way of expressing and shaping some of our deepest convictions. The *Handbook for Congregational Studies*, for example, suggests that while congregations are in need of transformation "this is best accomplished when we take seriously and appreciatively, through disciplined understanding, their present *being* – the good and precious qualities that are within them – as means of grace themselves that enable the transformation of congregations into what it is possible for them to *become*."[8]

This appreciative attitude toward congregations marks a significant shift in perspective from the rejection or neglect of congregations and the congregational form of religious association that has tended to dominate the academic study of religion. The emergence of this appreciative attitude no doubt has several sources: the increased awareness of the serious dilemmas facing mainline churches, the more vocal presence and vitality of certain conservative, evangelical, and pentecostal churches in our time, and the emphasis on – and reanalysis of – community that has been nourished within feminist, liberation, post-liberal, and process philosophies and theologies. However these sources have come to form the background for the emergence of the appreciative attitude toward congregations in particular instances within congregational studies, the presence of that attitude is an unmistakable characteristic of this emerging field of inquiry.

A second feature of congregational studies is the recognition of the depth and complexity of congregational life. The use of the notion of congregations as "cultures" in the works of Grierson, Hopewell, and Nancy Ramsay points to this recognition as does the use of the metaphor of congregational life as a "web" in the thought of Brita Gill-Austern and James Fowler's concept of the "ecology of care" within congregations.[9]

It is worth noting in this regard that congregational studies develops a sense of this depth and complexity in the context of the empirical analysis of actual congregations – whether that analysis be quantitative, qualitative, or both. Most theologians tend to think of actual congregations in stereotypic and one-dimensional ways and reserve the idea of a rich complexity of congregational life for the True (and therefore) Invisible Church. While not denying the normative dimension of all congregational studies, congregational studies tends to focus on the understanding of actual congregational life.

What congregational studies is presenting to us, in other words, is increasingly "thick," hermeneutically sensitive understandings of congregational life. The investigation of the thickness of congregational life occurs in at least two formats. On the one hand are the grand methodologies; that is, the development of ways of enriching our grasp of the complexity of the whole of congregational life. The studies of the distinctive idioms within congregations in the works of Hopewell and Robert Schreiter, the analysis of the characteristic patterns of time, space, language, intimacy, consensus, and circumstance in the work of Grierson, the application of a multidimensional model of practical reason to congregational life in the work of Don Browning, and the feminist liberation analysis of class dynamics in congregations by Beverly Harrison are some of the best known examples of this.[10]

On the other hand are the more idiographic studies where the complexity and depth of congregational life is suggested through the study of either distinctive congregational acts or singular congregations. Stephen Warner's provocative analysis of Mendocino Presbyterian Church, Nancy Ammerman's examination of a fundamentalist congregation, Melvin Williams' study of an African-American pentecostal church, and Linda Clark's investigation of congregational hymn-singing are four significant examples of this approach.[11] My point in distinguishing these two formats of congregational studies is to suggest that they do not preclude one another, as Browning's study of Apostolic Church in Chicago makes clear. I simply want to distinguish here two orientations to congregational studies, both of which generate that sense of the thickness of congregational life which characterizes the field as a whole.

The final characteristic of contemporary congregational studies concerns the sheer profusion of disciplinary methodologies which are used nowadays to study congregations. Two things need to be noted about this. First, the recognition of the depth and complexity of congregations has brought with it an avalanche of disciplinary perspectives being brought to bear on congregational life: anthropology, sociology, psychology, semiology, historical studies, aesthetics, literary symbolism, systems theory, and, on somewhat more infrequent occasions, even theology. Even this listing does not do justice to the range of perspectives given the variety of orientations from within each of these disciplines of which congregational studies has made use.

Second, congregational studies are not only multidisciplinary, but increasingly interdisciplinary in character. It is widely recognized today that if one is to mine the immense riches of congregational life one must do so from a variety of different angles of vision. One noteworthy outcome of this is that teams of scholars are often gathered together to carry out the analysis. This was the case with *Building Effective Ministry* and, more recently, with *Tensions Between Citizenship and Discipleship: A Case Study*, edited by Nelle Slater.[12]

The appreciative attitude toward congregations, the recognition of their depth and complexity, and the consequent multi- and interdisciplinary nature of congregational studies merely point in the direction of the most general trends of the field. This characterization is sufficient, however, to gain some purchase on the question of why pastoral theologians ought to pay it heed.

Pastoral Theology and Congregational Studies

I want to address briefly four ways in which I have come to understand congregational studies as relevant to the work of pastoral theology: as deepening our sense of the dynamics of care throughout the whole of congregational life, as assisting our appreciation of the "otherness' within congregational life, as helping us recognize the complex practices of practical and pastoral theology within congregations themselves, and as facilitating our participation in congregations' efforts to form and transform their own expressions of care. This is, obviously, not an exhaustive list of reasons for pastoral theologians to be interested in congregational studies, but I hope that it communicates a sense of why I think this emerging field of inquiry is important to us.

First, congregational studies helps us to see the dynamics of care embedded within the whole of congregational life. As Don Browning has noted, it is startling to realize that pastoral theology has given very little attention to the dynamics of care within congregations.[13] We have focused our attention almost exclusively on the ordained or specially trained lay-person as the

primary agent of care. Our sense of the communal structures which carry
the care of the church, therefore, has often been limited to what can fit in
the pastor's office or what can fit in a parishioner's hospital room. Indeed,
even many of the texts which have been written to facilitate the care of the
laity more generally have tended to take the counseling relationship as the
paradigmatic instance of care and have failed to recognize, in Fowler's
words, the "ecology of care" within congregational life.[14]

Congregational studies opens up the dynamics of care within the whole
of a community's life: its formal and informal rituals, its characteristic
languages, and the overt and hidden ways it orders its life.[15] Congregational
studies, in other words, enables us to see that the care of the church is
constituted not only by the counseling and visitation of the pastor, but also
by the manner and content of its hymn-singing, its preaching, its Bible
study, its prayer, its outreach, its fellowship and the patterns of friendship
that emerge and fail to emerge within it.[16] It is constituted by the ways it
legitimizes and fails to legitimize conflict, the ways it uses its physical space
and the meanings it gives to and discovers in that space, the ways com-
mittees are formed and meetings are run, and the ways it constitutes and
distributes authority and power.

The importance of coming to see the dynamics of care within the whole
of congregational life is not simply a matter of expanding the range of our
vision in pastoral theology, however. It is not just a matter of multiplying
the number of places where we can see care happening. It also alters the
character of our vision by situating the care of the church within those
meaning-laden practices through which the community of faith reproduces
itself.[17] It shows us, in other words, how the question of care is inextricable
from the question of discipline, how it is inextricable from the ways we seek
the persistence of a way of life – even if the fullness of that way of life is
decidedly more "not yet" than "already." When we have taken the paradigmatic instance of the care of the church to be that of the counseling
relationship, we have tended to lose sight of this. Using some of the most
prominent theories and techniques of contemporary psychotherapy, we
often immediately make this very issue problematic: rendering such commitments suspect on one or another intrapsychic or systemic ground.

My point here is not that we ought not to make use of the theories and
techniques of contemporary psychotherapy in pastoral theology. My point,
rather, is that when we take the counseling relationship as the cornerstone
of the care of the church we skew the kinds of questions we ask and the
kinds of answers we will find acceptable in pastoral theology. Congregational studies opens up a way of seeing the care of the church that does
not immediately make problematic its relationship to Christian formation,
but rather sees that care as itself in part constitutive of the variety of ways
congregational life reproduces itself as distinctively Christian community.

This way of understanding the matter does not require us to see the care of the congregation as turned in upon itself. Indeed, if rightly interpreted, it does just the opposite. What it can help us see is the broad range of ways in which the care of the congregation shapes as well as is shaped by the market, the state, and civil society at large: the ways family life is ordered and disordered, the ways gender and ethnicity are constructed, the ways aging persons are understood, and how more generally our communities support and fail to support the flourishing of life. The care of the congregation, seen as embedded within a range of distinctive convictions and practices, is therefore a public resource and public problem in a much broader way than we have often thought in pastoral theology.[18]

By taking congregational studies seriously and by making its own distinctive contributions to congregational studies, pastoral theology can better come to understand how the whole way of life of a community (its distinctive culture[19]) expresses its care – for good and for ill – and the ways that care expresses and fails to express the community's understandings of the requirements of living appropriately in relation to God and neighbor. To use Robert Kegan's phrase, it can better come to understand the "natural therapy" embedded within the belief-full practices of a community's life.[20]

Second, congregational studies can open up to us the "otherness' within congregational life. It is informative in this regard how many of the persons engaged in congregational studies either became or have become intrigued in this field out of the context of the different cultures which the congregations they studied represented or out of the context of their own work in other cultures. James Hopewell's extensive cross-cultural experience, Denham Grierson's first parish experience with a remote mining community in Australia, Don Browning's work with an African-American church in Chicago, and the sociologist Stephen Warner's discovery of the worlds of evangelical and pentecostal Christianity are but a few examples. Each of these persons "left home" as it were and discovered new ways of understanding not only the foreign lands they encountered but also the homes they had left. Each of them reports the sense of discovery, the disorientation from their own assumptive worlds which eventually led them to a more appreciative awareness of the strange and resistant complexity and power – the otherness, if you will – of congregational life.

It might be suggested in this regard that the otherness which has been discovered in congregations is not a product of congregational life itself, but rather a product of the cultures which those congregations represented. That is, it might seem that it is the African-American or the evangelical or the working class cultures which lie behind the congregation that led largely white, male, theologically liberal congregational researchers to an awareness of otherness. In some respects this is true. But the passage through *that* otherness has led many to the recognition of the other within even their own "home" congregations. Hopewell has come close to this in his remark that we have tended to assume that "white Anglo-Saxon churches ... have no cultural particularity and therefore no reason to investigate their own ethos, tradition, and worldview. These features were attributed to 'ethnic' groups; the dominant white Protestant churches considered themselves beyond ethnicity, responsive primarily to universal principles and revelation."[21] What Hopewell did not say, but what I take to be an implication of such a remark, is that this recognition of the ethnicity of a dominant culture suggests more generally not only the awareness of the other that is someone else, but also the other that is already us – albeit marginalized or dissimulated in congregational self-awareness.

Pastoral theology would do well to pay attention to this sense of the "otherness" within the congregation – the recognition that the congregation is not exhausted by our sense of what it is or our wishes for what it might be.[22] It is not simply an object to be manipulated by a technical rationality intent on improving the church nor an antiquated mode of religious association to be ignored or blithely criticized.[23] To recognize that the whole range of communal practices of the church are themselves saturated with the dynamics of care will do us little good without the additional recognition that these practices embody a good deal more than we can control with whatever happens to be the latest therapeutic technique. This is not to endow upon the congregation a new immunity from criticism or to suggest that we cannot facilitate congregational change, but merely to note that we must respect the ways in which congregational life in its concrete lived reality embodies, in fact, an otherness – a something irreducible to a mirror of what we take ourselves or our discipline to be. There is this strange richness within congregations to which pastoral theology has paid little attention over the past several years and that we must come to appreciate more fully, for the care of the congregation can be neither adequately understood nor renewed apart from it.

The third point of relevance of congregational studies for pastoral theology I want to note concerns coming to understand the communal locus of theology. For many of us who teach in seminaries or divinity schools, the doing of theology has been primarily associated with the image of the solitary scholar amid the academic world of "symbols in motion."[24] We have, of course, had some success in perpetuating this image among many pastors and laypersons. Whatever else "real" theology represents to them, it is often something they are confident they do not do and something they most assuredly believe they do not understand. My sense is that telling them the truth, that is, that we do not understand a lot of it either, would not be all that reassuring.

Over the past several decades, a variety of fields of theological inquiry have suggested that theology is best seen less as a matters of the solitary scholar than as a fully communal practice. Congregational studies, when rightly pursued, can make this point also – extending our understanding of the communal locus of theology to the congregation itself. In this sense, practical theology in general and pastoral theology in particular are practices of communities of faith. They are, in the first instance, efforts of particular communities to respond to their situations out of the resources of their interpretations of Christian traditions and their interpretations of the multiple dynamics of their circumstances.

Congregational studies shows us that congregations do, in fact, engage in complex theological work. It may well not be categorized as theological work within the congregation (since theology, the people think, is done by somebody else), but it is theology none the less. Likewise, we are not obligated to think that it is always good theological work by simply recognizing it for what it is.[25] This is significant to pastoral theology for two reasons. First, congregational studies can help us see how actual communities engage in the practices of practical and pastoral theology: how they come to articulate in word and deed the central commitments of their faith within the particularity of their situations, how they go about the business of re-stating or transforming those commitments in situations of crisis or cultural change, and how conflicting practical and pastoral theological methodologies within congregations get mediated or learn to live in isolation from one another. Congregational studies can help us better come to understand, in other words, how practical and pastoral theology are practiced within congregations.

Second, this is also significant to pastoral theology in that it helps us see the congregation as an active partner in the tasks of pastoral theology. Congregations, from this perspective, are not simply to be seen as the last link in the theological food chain – happy consumers of our scholarly wisdom carefully spoon fed to them by those pastors who were once our students. Congregational studies provides certain of the groundwork for those of us in the academy to understand what it would mean to see our work as joined with the theological practice of actual local congregations.

This is not an indictment of so-called academic theology. Theology has a variety of different audiences and purposes. My point is that we do not finally help ourselves by denigrating one locus of theology in order to bolster the esteem of another such locus. For many of us in the academy, however, that is precisely what we have done in relation to the congregation. Congregational studies can help us appreciate the complex theological practice of local congregations and enable us to see the congregation as an active partner in our own work.

Finally, fourth, congregational studies helps us better participate in the work of congregations toward the formation and transformation of their own care. By enriching our understanding of the multiple dynamics of congregational life, something of what the congregation does not want to be seen can be uncovered, something of the gifts it possesses but does not appreciate can be discovered. In short, congregational studies can disclose those "openings for ministry" (to use Grierson's felicitous phrase) within congregational life. As such, congregational studies orients us toward the understanding and renewal of congregations from within the complexity of congregational life itself.

This is not simply a matter of pastoral theologians seeing the congregation as an active partner in their own work, but also of pastoral theologians being active partners in the work of the congregation. However valuable congregational studies are as contributions to the scholarly literature, they are never only that. They are also contributions to the reflective practice of the congregation itself. To recognize this fact and find ways fruitfully to participate *as* pastoral theologians in congregational life on its own terms represents an important challenge which comes to us from the congregational studies literature.

Indeed, congregational studies as a field has grown somewhat more sensitive to the role of the results of its inquiries in the lives of those congregations it studies. It is increasingly common for congregational researchers to wonder aloud about how such studies ought to feed back into the self-understanding of the congregation. It is also significant to note in this respect that an increasing number of congregational studies are being initiated from *within* congregations as part of their own efforts to renew their lives.

It is important to note one particularly vexing problem related to this issue, however. Congregational studies has not been particularly adept thus far at situating its work within clear and compelling theological methodologies. As has been noted by several commentators on the current state of the field, congregational studies has generally proceeded without sufficient attention to the roles of the kinds of analyses it offers in distinctively theological inquiry. The work of Don Browning is, I think, a sustained and significant exception to this.[26] None the less, for pastoral theology to make the kind of contribution to the renewal of congregational life that is required of it, it must pay greater attention to how the kinds of judgments that arise from congregational studies fit within an overarching practical or pastoral theological methodology.

To put it bluntly, what I mean is this. What congregations need from pastoral theologians is not simply keen psychological insight, but also ways to situate those kinds of insights within the reflective practice of the church as it seeks to order its life as expression of the gospel of Jesus Christ. For it is here (in the realization of this *theological* task) that – even within the partiality of its self-understanding – the congregation's own otherness can disclose both the depths of its sin and the redemptive history of God in which it participates and which it proclaims. It is here that the care that is actually expressed within the whole of congregational life can be situated within the congregation's distinctive identity. It is here that we must finally make sense of the congregation's own efforts to transform its life.

Final Comments

Congregational studies enjoys a growing popularity today. The results of its early work are significant enough to justify pastoral theologians reading this literature and contributing to it. It provides one tool for broadening our understanding of the dynamics of care within the church, for gaining a sense of the otherness within the congregation, for coming better to understand the theological practices of the local congregation, and for participating in the reformation of congregational life – all worthy purposes for pastoral theology in our time. Whether congregations will turn out to make as interesting case studies as clients to our field, however, remains to be seen.

NOTES

1 This is not the same as discussing why pastoral theology ought to be interested in the *congregation*. While this is a not too subtle distinction, it seems important to underscore that this essay is concerned principally with the body of literature called congregational studies.

2 Denham Grierson, *Transforming a People of God* (Melbourne, Australia: Joint Board of Christian Education of Australia and New Zealand, 1984); James Hopewell, *Congregation: Story and Structure* (Philadelphia, PA: Fortress Press, 1987); Jackson Carroll, Carl Dudley, and William McKinney (eds.), *Handbook for Congregational Studies* (Nashville, TN: Abingdon Press, 1986); Carl Dudley (ed.), *Building Effective Ministry: Theory and Practice in the Local Church* (San Francisco, CA: Harper and Row, 1983).

3 See the remarks of William McKinney, "Sociological perspectives on congregational care in discipline in contemporary American culture," in *Congregational Care and Discipline: Sustaining Christian Life in Our Time*, ed. K. Brynolf Lyon and Charles Blaisdell (manuscript in preparation).

4 Allison Stokes and David A. Roozen, "The unfolding story of congregational studies," in *Carriers of Faith: Lessons from Congregational Studies*, ed. Carl Dudley, Jackson Carroll, and James Wind (Louisville, KY: Westminster/John Knox, 1991).

5 Peter Berger, *The Noise of Solemn Assemblies* (Garden City, NY: Doubleday, 1961); Gibson Winter, *The Suburban Captivity of the Churches* (Garden City, NY: Doubleday, 1961).

6 One exception to this that is particularly important to our field was James Dittes's remarkable study *The Church in the Way* (New York, NY: Scribner's, 1967).

7　Oral communication.

8　*Handbook for Congregational Studies*, p. 7.

9　In addition to the works of Grierson and Hopewell noted above, see Nancy Ramsay, "The congregation as culture," *Encounter* (forthcoming); Brita Gill-Austern, "Rediscovering hidden treasures for pastoral care," in *Congregational Care and Discipline*; and James Fowler, *Faith Development and Pastoral Care* (Philadelphia, PA: Fortress, 1987).

10　Hopewell, *op. cit.*; Robert Schreiter, *Constructing Local Theologies* (Maryknoll, NY: Orbis, 1985); Grierson, *op. cit.*; Don Browning, *A Fundamental Practical Theology* (Philadelphia, PA: Fortress, 1991); Beverly Harrison, "Toward a Christian feminist liberation hermeneutic for demystifying class reality in local congregations," in *Beyond Clericalism: The Congregation as a Focus for Theological Education* (Atlanta, GA: Scholars Press, 1988).

11　Stephen Warner, *New Wine in Old Wineskins* (Berkeley, CA: University of California Press, 1988); Nancy Ammerman, *Bible Believers: Fundamentalists in the Modern World* (New Brunswick, NJ: Rutgers University Press, 1987); Melvin Williams, *Community in a Black Pentecostal Church* (Pittsburgh, PA: University of Pittsburgh Press, 1974); Linda Clark, Hymn singing: the congregation making faith, in *Carriers of Faith*.

12　Nelle Slater, ed., *Tensions Between Citizenship and Discipleship: A Case Study* (New York, NY: Pilgrim Press, 1989).

13　Don Browning, "Pastoral care and the study of the congregation," in *Beyond Clericalism*.

14　See Fowler, *op. cit.*

15　While not developed in relation to the field of congregational studies, a variety of works on ritual and pastoral care are now appearing that are very helpful in understanding some of these issues. Elaine Ramsbaw's marvelous *Ritual and Pastoral Care* (Philadelphia, PA: Fortress Press, 1987) is richly suggestive in this regard. See also Kenneth Mitchell, "Ritual in pastoral care," *Journal of Pastoral Care* (Spring 1989): 68–77; and Robert Kinast, *Sacramental Pastoral Care* (New York, NY: Pueblo Publishing Company, 1988).

16　African-American scholars in pastoral theology have been making this point for some time. See, for example, the work of Edward Wimberly, especially *Pastoral Care in the Black Church* (Nashville, TN: Abingdon, 1979) and his "The contributions of Black Christians to the discipline of pastoral care," *Reflections* (January 1983): 4–8. See also the recent remarks of Robert Franklin, "Defiant spirituality: care traditions in Black Churches," in *Congregational Care and Discipline: Sustaining Christian Life in Our Time*.

17　This way of phrasing the matter was suggested to me by Anthony Giddens's notion of the "recursive" character of social practices. See his *The Constitution of Society* (Cambridge: Polity, 1985).

18 It is interesting to read the congregational studies in David Roozen, William KcKinney, and Jackson Carroll, *Varieties of Religious Presence* (New York, NY: Pilgrim Press, 1984) from this broad pastoral theological perspective.

19 One must be cautious here. The "culture" of a congregation (as well as its care) is received or appropriated – or, if one must, internalized – in a host of different ways within that congregation. Here, indeed, is one of the places that pastoral theology might well ply its trade to the benefit of congregational studies: how is the care that is expressed through the beliefs and practices of congregational culture differentially appropriated within the congregation? What does this then mean for the care and ordering of congregational life? On the issue of the differential use of culture, see Peter Stromberg's interesting *Symbols of Community: The Cultural System of a Swedish Church* (Tucson, AZ: University of Arizona Press, 1986).

20 Robert Kegan, *The Evolving Self: Problem and Process in Human Development* (Cambridge, MA: Harvard University Press, 1982).

21 Hopewell, *Congregation*, p. 11.

22 The discontinuity with itself that is suggested by the notion of the "otherness" within the congregation is not something that is overcome by new knowledge on our part. This is the point of saying that it is a genuine "otherness." Thus, congregational studies does not eradicate the discontinuity, but rather discloses (even as it hides) it – allowing us to respond more appreciatively to its "manifestation" and its "proclamation." The "other" at issue in this discussion is most helpfully seen, I think, from a variety of perspectives: critical theory, psychoanalysis, and theology being the most prominent. One way to get at some of this – as is suggested above through the notions of manifestation and proclamation – would be to reflect on the otherness within the congregation in terms of its "prophetic" and "mystical" dimensions. On these distinctions see David Tracy, *Dialogue with the Other: The Inter-Religious Dialogue* (Louvain, Belgium: Peeters Press/Grand Rapids, MI: Eerdmans, 1990), pp. 9–26.

23 Indeed, one of the strongest impressions I come away with from this literature is that talk of *the* congregation is dubious at best. The sheer variety of congregational life, its irreducible particularity in significant respects is an important lesson of congregational studies.

24 I have adapted the phrase "symbols in motion" from Peter Berger's description of modern bureaucracy as "files in motion." See Peter Berger, Brigitte Berger, and Hansfried Kellner, *The Homeless Mind* (New York, NY: Random House, 1973). It may well seem that this is not true for pastoral theologians who, above all in the academy, have sought to develop theological reflection out of the very stuff of the fragility of life. There is some truth to this, but in itself this strikes me

as a bit too self-congratulatory on our part. Our difficulty in bringing the distinctively theological task to fruition in our work in a way that does not make it sound like an afterthought, an obligatory preface, or a naive methodological "applicationalism" has all too often served to reinforce the sense among our colleagues (and among ourselves?) that what we are really about is keeping the church up-to-date on psychological ideas and theories.

25 I have argued elsewhere that much of the conversation of the congregation takes place in the languages of popular psychology and business management and that this impedes congregations from taking fuller theological responsibility for their lives (see "The discipline of congregational life: prospects and resources for renewal," *Mid-Stream* 26: 399–407). I still believe this to be true, but being too cynical about this obscures the theological work that actually takes place in this truncated discourse.

26 Browning, *A Fundamental Practical Theology* (1991). There are, of course, a variety of other persons in pastoral theology who have developed theological perspectives that could be transformatively appropriated in this regard. Browning's work is the only one of which I am aware, however, that does this directly in relation to the literature on congregational studies. None the less, the work of Charles Gerkin on narrative practical theology might be particularly helpful here (*Widening the Horizons*, Nashville, TN: Abingdon, 1986), as would John Patton's recent work on clinical theological method (*From Ministry to Theology*, Nashville, TN: Abingdon, 1990) and the work of James Poling and Donald Miller, *Foundations for a Practical Theology of Ministry* (Nashville, TN: Abingdon, 1985).

Some Points for Further Consideration

• In what ways might the context within which you live or work form a source for learning about pastoral theology?
• Can "congregational analysis" be relevantly applied outside congregations?
• What factors shape the life of a congregation?
• How would you define a healthy congregation?

For Further Reading and Exploration

Hopewell (1987) provides a useful introduction to the area of congregational studies. See the work of the British pastoral theologian

Elaine Graham (1995, 1996) for an imaginative feminist approach to ecclesial existence; Browning (1991) explores how ecclesial identity is created and formed. See also Dulles (1976). The work of Gill (1996) and Gerkin (1997) looks at dimensions of the congregation's identity and ministry.

20

Towards Dialogue:
An Exploration of the Relations between Psychiatry and Religion in Contemporary Mental Health

MARK SUTHERLAND

INTRODUCTION

The world is full of mental distress. This chapter is included here because psychiatry and theology have been major dialogue partners for pastoral theology. It is worth noting that Anton Boisen evolved Clinical Pastoral Education out of his own experience of mental distress. In pastoral practice it is probable that there will be encounters with significant numbers of individuals who suffer from poor mental health.

Mark Sutherland, an Anglican mental health chaplain, working at the Maudsley Hospital in London, opens up this vast and complex area in this specially commissioned chapter. He takes an overview of the relations between religion and psychiatry from a mainly theoretical perspective, raising a range of challenges and questions that have significant practical implications.

Sutherland offers a framework within which the resources of the Christian tradition might be made available to those who suffer from mental health problems. He argues for a dialogue between psychiatry and the religious tradition by explaining how and why these traditions have arrived at aspects of their respective positions and understandings. Sutherland reminds the reader of the marginalization of people who experience mental distress and of the links between this and factors such as race, poverty, and exclusion. In the main substance of the chapter he addresses mental health as an area of competing and mutually exclusive ideologies. These, he argues, fall into three major discourses: the psychological-social discourse; the psychiatric discourse; and the spiritual-theological discourse. The factors inhibiting dialogue are discussed. A way forward is proposed based on an understanding of the diverse elements within the web of human experience of mental health. He concludes: "Perhaps the real task of practical theology is to recall the wider religious tradition to the central task of facilitating human cooperation with a God who maintains an intention and purpose for the whole of the creation."

While asserting that the Christian tradition offers a holistic view of the person, it is important (from a pastoral perspective) to bear in mind that Christianity offers a variety of perspectives including the radical dualism of demon possession. Turner (1995) argues that the mystical tradition was a rational one which had little sympathy for affect and emotion. Further, in this theoretical discussion, it is important to consider how one should respond pastorally to a person whose distress appears to be driven and informed by religious concepts and images.

TOWARDS DIALOGUE: AN EXPLORATION OF THE RELATIONS BETWEEN PSYCHIATRY AND RELIGION IN CONTEMPORARY MENTAL HEALTH

> Pastoral or practical theology can be defined as the place where contemporary experience and the resources of the religious tradition meet in a critical dialogue that is mutually and practically informing.
>
> (See the editors'
> Preface, pp. xiii–xviii)

Reflections on the Status Quo

It is a matter of some importance that students of practical theology concern themselves with mental health. There is an urgent need for the resources of the religious tradition to be both better understood, and made more widely available, to those who suffer with poor mental health. Generally speaking, there has been little critical dialogue within the contemporary experience of mental health between psychiatry and the religious tradition. This situation is somewhat paradoxical, to say the least. This state of affairs invokes the use of the word *critical* in both senses of its meaning, indicating the idea of significance, as well as that of judgement.

If practical theology is to adequately address contemporary mental health issues, attention will need to be focused upon two principal questions. Given the social significance attaching to the causes of much mental health disturbance in our society, how are we to account for the comparative uninterest in mental health within the dominant elements of the religious tradition? Second, on what basis can a renewed dialogue be developed with biological psychiatry which avoids the getting bogged down in the usual failure of science and theology to understand one another?

Mental health is central to any critical theological analysis of contemporary social experience. It is the one area where the lines of multiple social and individual deprivation intersect. It is not a new idea to suggest a link between disturbances in the mental health of individuals and the larger social and political factors of race, poverty and exclusion. In any first-world context the numbers of mentally disturbed, homeless people is a key indicator of a society's ease with itself. Outside of the criminal justice system, poor mental health is the major symbol of exclusion in our society. Mental health legislation throughout the first world gives to the psychiatric establishment powers of detention and exclusion unparalleled in any other area of society. Pattison (1997a) has identified mental health sufferers as the *biblical poor* of the modern age. To the biblical notion of the poor we could also add the other archetypal biblical image of exclusion, that of the leper.

The challenges mental health issues pose for the religious tradition concern the essential importance of levels of non-rational mental functioning to any understanding of the human condition. In having capitulated to the claims of medical science in the area of mental health, the religious tradition has, together with other elements within society, colluded in the medicalization of yet another significant area of human experience. This collusion has masked at the social level, the way the concept of 'mental illness' operates as a social construction designed to avoid having to ask deeper and more disturbing questions about the nature and dynamics of our first world societies. It is not only that the religious tradition had failed to openly confront this state of affairs, but that this failure results in a situation where the Church has placed itself under the critical judgement of elements within its own spiritual and pastoral tradition.

Over centuries the Christian spiritual tradition has drawn its own maps for the exploration of the deeper regions of the human experience. It has some knowledge of the emotional vicissitudes resulting from the desires and frustrations experienced by human beings in their heartfelt pursuit of living in creative relationship with God. This is a holistic and human-oriented understanding which locates the manifestations of disturbance in mental health within this larger spiritual quest.

Anton Boisen stands out as a theologian-pastor who clearly understood the importance of the spiritual components in mental health disturbance. In the early battle for the heart and mind of the Clinical Pastoral Theology movement, the importance of the psychiatric hospital was emphasized as the laboratory for the development of the pastoral practitioner. He believed that here the pastoral practitioner would be brought face to face with the painful search for meaning in the lives of others, and consequently be brought to a more honest confrontation with searching and disturbing questions within his or her own life. This idea is captured well by Patricia Dunker in *Hallucinating Foucault*. In a passage the young woman psychiatrist responds to the protagonist's question about why she is a psychiatrist:

> Pain. Madness is a greater form of suffering than any other kind of disease. . . . It is the saddest world I know. . . . It is the most terrible thing that can ever happen to you. It destroys every aspect of your life. . . . Society has a terrible fear of letting those they call mad live among them. . . . But [by working with madness] you do learn to see things differently. . . . You see things more coherently. You accept things. You are more open. More tolerant. If I have a more generous open mind than I had when I was a medical student it is largely due to *this work*. (Dunker 1996: 92–3)

Competing Ideologies

For the student of practical theology the first encounter with the area of mental health is often a confusing experience. Mental health is an area of competing and mutually exclusive ideologies. I have grouped these ideologies into three major discourses. Since Foucault, we have come to more fully recognize that the function of a discourse is not simply to describe what is out there, so to speak. Rather, it is to create a closed system presenting a particular perspective on the world as normative.

The *psychological-social discourse* groups together a number of different psychological models, each differing in the degree of importance given to a balance between the internal 'intrapsychic' world of the individual and the external interaction between individuals and the social. Although largely displaced by psychiatry in the treatment of major mental disturbance, this discourse retains a highly complex and sophisticated hold in the popular imagination. The psychosocial discourse is concerned with the creation of a *ideology of the mind*. Psychoanalytic (Freud), humanistic (Maslow), and analytical (Jung) psychology represent a core of 'depth psychologies', so called because of their emphasis upon the dynamic interaction between the unconscious and conscious elements in human mental functioning. These psychologies emphasize personal life history and the relationship between the unconscious consequences of life events and psychological development. Treatment of mental health disturbance is through the therapeutic reconstruction and reworking of an individual's emotional biography within the here-and-now experience of a relationship between patient and therapist. This is a dynamic relationship which is concerned with the nature and quality of interaction between patient and therapist.

The *psychiatric discourse* is currently the most influential discourse in mental health. Psychiatry, a branch of medicine, and clinical psychology, a science of mental measurement and observation concern themselves with the *ideology of the brain*. Psychiatry employs the biological concept of brain illness to characterize severe mental disturbance. Treatment involves the application of the medical model of diagnosis. Diagnosis is the reduction of an individual's experience to a group of symptoms which locate the individual's disturbance within larger categories of reference. There are several major diagnostic categories, but in the main, psychiatry recognizes two principal groups of conditions. These are disturbances of mood, as in the case of depression and manic conditions, and disturbances of thought, as in the case of the schizophrenias.

Psychiatric research posits the causes of mental illness in dysfunctional brain activity. In its clinical practice it displays little interest in the origin of mental disturbances in individual psychosocial histories. It has no interest in the possibility of illness resulting from factors in an individual's existential-spiritual history. Its main concern continues to be pharmacological and behavioural treatments aimed at the amelioration of symptoms. It has become increasingly successful in its clinical aims with new generations of drugs able to offer amelioration of symptoms with less disruptive side effects.

Psychiatry is the most powerful of ideologies and during the last fifty years has more or less seen off any real challenge from the theories of the mind represented by depth psychologies. This situation is the result not of its overwhelming success, for whatever success it claims, those who suffer from mental health problems maintain that this comes at too high a price for them. Psychiatry owes its prominence to society's tacit and unquestioning acceptance of the mythical power of doctors, and its fear of those who suffer from mental illness.

Clinical psychology is concerned with the identification of dysfunctional psychological patterns through scientific methods of measurement. It is also concerned with treatment using cognitive and behavioural therapies. These therapies do not attempt to understand the origin of mental disturbance. Neither do they require a relationship between the therapist and patient. In this sense they are mechanistic rather than dynamic in approach. Their aim is to modify actual behaviours and thought patterns rather in the way psychiatry focuses on the treatment of symptoms.

The *spiritual-theological discourse* is the oldest of the ideologies applicable to the area of mental health. It is in essence a *holistic ideology of personhood.* This discourse is comprised of the long-established tradition of mystical theology, and the more recent one of clinical pastoral theology. The mystical theological tradition emphasizes the human journey towards deeper integration with God. This journey is perceived within the clinical pastoral tradition in terms of a natural quest for health. Both traditions recognize that deeper integration with God and the pursuit of health involve a negotiation with the deeper parts of emotional life not normally accessible to rational consciousness.

The spiritual-theological discourse engages with mental health disturbance through the process of discernment of an individual's life journey. Boisen developed the concept of the living human document to express this. The process of discernment seeks to understand the function of mental disturbance by attempting to read a purpose in an individual's journey into deeper, non-rational levels of emotional experience.

Except in cases of organic damage to the brain, manifestations of mental disturbances often accompany a wide range of life experiences. For example: a response to a radical call of conversion to faith, the negotiation of stressful life events such as bereavement and loss, an attempt to reorganize one response to existential questions about the meaning of one's life, or a falling into psychological disorganization as a defence against emotional and psychological pain. The process of discernment relies on the development of a trusting and containing relationship between an individual and their priest/pastor, pastoral counsellor or trained spiritual director.

Factors Inhibiting Dialogue

Increased biological influences have introduced into psychiatry the prejudices of a mechanistic Newtonian science. Galileo's dictum 'whatever can not be measured and quantified is not scientific' has long ago come to mean, what ever cannot be quantified is not real. Increasingly, psychiatry has come to reject the notion of human experience in favour of human behaviour. Both the spiritual-theological and psychological-social discourses stress the importance of the interrelationship of elements within a person's experience. Psychiatry stresses the divisibility of such elements and is capable of viewing only those elements compatible with its methods of investigation. Consequently, much human experience falls outside psychiatry's study. The view of the human being which emerges from this study is consequently an impoverished one. The human person ceases to exist, becoming simply a collection of symptoms and behaviours which have to be modified and brought under control. Over time, the lines between the three discourses have become more firmly drawn than ever.

I have already referred to the absence of critical dialogue in contemporary mental health between psychiatry and religion as paradoxical. As psychiatry has increasingly adopted a biological orientation, it has become preoccupied with demonstrating its scientific credentials to the rest of medical science, which remains sceptical of these claims. The difficulties for a creative dialogue in mental health between science and religion is only partly due to the dismissal of religious insights by psychiatry. As I have noted earlier, there has been a collusion on the part of rational religion with the reductionist attitudes of the very scientific viewpoint it most abhors in other areas of thought.

Rational religion has always felt uneasy about mystical theology. If this is somewhat to be expected, its marginalizing of clinical pastoral theology in mental health is less easy to understand. Until, at least, it is recognized that a psychoanalytically informed pastoral theology, travelling by a different route, nevertheless arrives at the same spiritual insights as mystical theology. They both view mental disturbance as having a purpose for the individual. There is something about these shared insights which disturbs the uncritical espousing of Newtonian rationalism in both science and religion. It needs to be remembered that Newton did not conceive of his work in opposition to religion. His ideas emerged within the context of an already developing rationalist religious deism. If mechanistic rationalism, and its mechanistic view of the universe, has led medical science to reject large parts of human experience as subjective and anecdotal, the same rationalism has led mainstream religion to turn its back on the most important insights from its own authentic spiritual-theological tradition.

Put most succinctly, what is frightening is the idea that the root of religious experience lies in a region of the human emotions (the psychological unconscious) which we recognize in the phenomenology of psychotic disturbance. Mystical theology has always recognized the pursuit of God as a non-rational process which can involve periods of acute disturbance in an individual's capacity to function rationally. The 'Boisen' tradition in pastoral theology has likewise recognized that conversion and other powerful religious experiences share a common phenomenology with manifestations of psychosis. As R. D. Laing most eloquently put it:

> Mystics and schizophrenics find themselves in the same ocean, but the mystics swim whereas the schizophrenics drown.   (Capra 1989: 135)

Does this mean then, as psychiatry contends, that religion is a kind of madness? On the contrary, religious traditions provide, throughout all human societies, mechanisms for the safe containment and social management of the experience described in the Psalms as 'deep calling unto deep'. The rationalist tradition has turned religion into a bulwark against the non-rational instead of remaining a mechanism for its management. Failure to manage what Reed has termed the oscillation between rational and non-rational levels of experience has only further increased the sense of alienation in Western society, increasing the likelihood for individual mental breakdown. It is significant that as rationalism in religion has reached its apotheosis over the last fifty years, as if to provide a necessary counterpoint, there has been a considerable revival of charismatic and pentecostalist religious expression. Much of this remains out of balance and unhealthy only because it is forced by the dominance of rationalism to remain split off from the theological-ecclesiological mainstream.

A Possible Way Forward

Pastoral theology's espousal of depth-psychological models has not proved a useful basis for establishing a dialogue with psychiatry about mental health. To follow this route has entangled pastoral theology in the contentions between theories of mind and theories of brain. A new basis for dialogue has to be found.

Recent thinking in physics and theology attests to a shift in the boundaries between the major paradigms of physical science and religion. New paradigm thinking describes the application of the insights from the quantum theory in physics to analyses of contemporary paradigms from physics, through medicine, biology, economics, to theology and spirituality. The significant impact of new paradigm thinking is that it recasts what have hitherto been conflicts between science and religion, opening up an exciting new panorama of converging understandings.

Quantum mechanics currently perceives networks of communicative processes where Newtonian mechanics saw only discrete material objects. The quantum theory arose in order to account for the fact that subatomic particles were discovered to be both particles and information waves. According to the quantum theory, what we see when we look at the subatomic world is the result of a complex interaction between the intention of the observer, i.e. what s he is looking for, and the position from which s/he looks. The physicist sees either particles or waves, but never both. This introduces a concept of relativity to the observer who influences what s/he observes. It comes as little surprise to pastoral and psychological practitioners that to observe is to enter into a relationship which has dynamic consequences for the observed.

Biological psychiatry is still rooted in the Newtonian mechanical mindset. It shares the current mood of biological scientific omnipotence, which needs to be seen as an understandable legacy of the startling scientific advances in biological understanding of DNA and the genetic map. However, to view thoughts as the result of the firing or misfiring of electrical impulses is to see only the hardware of the brain. The mind is the software. Thoughts are more properly the property of the activity of the mind. Mind is a higher conceptualization and results when the processes of interconnection and interrelation, the wave instead of the particle, is observed. The relation of brain to mind is analogous to the relation between words and story. One of the leading quantum physicists, David Bohm, has put it this way:

> A centrally relevant change in descriptive order required in the quantum theory is thus the dropping of the notion of analysis of the world into relatively autonomous parts, separately existent but in interaction. Rather, the primary emphasis is now on undivided *wholeness*, in which the observing instrument is not separate from the observed. (Davies, 1990: 112)

The human brain is not simply a collection of separate elements which interact. It is a network of relations which display a quality of purposeful self-organization which theology identifies by the term personhood. Animals have brains and consciousness, but human beings have self-consciousness. Self-consciousness is a higher level of conceptualization than consciousness. At this level of complexity it becomes meaningful to speak of concepts of mind and soul. The brain is a highly complex biological entity, but it belongs to a lower level of conceptualization with which the concepts of mind should have little correspondence. To offer a crude example: an electronic sign is a series of electrical impulses which switch lights on and off in organized sequences. To talk of it only this way is to miss the point that it is also a device for communicating a message and that this message is related to a product which is designed for a specific purpose. If the electrical impulses are equivalent to the brain, the message is the equivalent of the mind. The relationship between message and purpose could be likened to the area concerned with the soul. Brain, mind and soul are concepts which, if not confused, can be seen to be complementary. 'Each reveals an aspect which is there to be reckoned with, but is unmentioned by the other' (Davies 1990: 84).

Under the influence of new paradigm thinking, biological science has the possibility of finding new meaning in a concept of holism. This offers us a more fruitful starting point for the exploration of the dialogue in the area of mental health between science and the religious tradition. Suddenly, concepts such as experience, perception and intentionality emerge as thoroughly scientific concepts. The theories of biology, psychology and spirituality become complementary articulations, from different vantage points, of the same set of phenomena, i.e. the human being.

For practical theologians working in the area of mental health, a working knowledge of the discourses outlined in this chapter is an essential prerequisite. However, I believe the issues outlined above have implications which go beyond any particular interest individual practical theologians may have in mental health. Theology has traditionally claimed to be the 'queen of the sciences'. It is time for this somewhat lofty and archaic claim to be substantiated in practice.

Practical theology is theology's link with the way life is lived. Practical theology is no less affected than biological science by new paradigm thinking. When practical theology and biology meet on the conceptual field of new paradigm thought, itself a consequence of the quantum revolution in physics, religion and science find they have enough of a shared conceptual framework to reconstruct dialogue.

Practical theology is concerned with the interrelationship of widely differing elements within the web of human experience which build upon the consciousness that there is within us the echo of a sense of higher purpose in our creation beyond that explainable by the concept of random accident. Mental health is the area where connections are made between society and some of its deepest fears. For each of us, our mental health is the area where the struggle for wholeness and holiness can seem most imperilled and precarious. Perhaps the real task of practical theology is to recall the wider religious tradition to the central task of facilitating human cooperation with a God who maintains an intention and purpose for the whole of the creation.

BIBLIOGRAPHY

Reflections on the status quo

Asguith, Glen Jr (1992), *Vision from a Little-known Country: A Boisen Reader*, Decatur: Journal of Pastoral Care Publications.

Dunker, P. (1966), *Hallucinating Foucault*, London: Picador.

Foucault, M. (1967), *Madness and Civilisation*, London: Tavistock.

Laing, R. D. (1968), *The Politics of Experience*, New York: Ballantine.

Pattison, Stephen (1997a), *Pastoral Care and Liberation Theology*, London: SPCK.

Competing ideologies

Laing, R. D. (1982), *The Voice of Experience*, New York: Pantheon; Harmondsworth: Penguin.

Sutherland, Mark (1996), 'Mental Illness or Life Crisis', in D. Bhugra, *Psychiatry and Religion*, London: Routledge.

Sutherland, Mark (1997), 'Pastoral Care and Mental Health', *Contact: Journal of Interdisciplinary Pastoral Care*, no. 123, pp. 12–19.

Symington Neville (1986), *The Analytic Experience*, London: Free Association Press.

Factors inhibiting dialogue

Capra, Fritjof (1983), *The Turning Point*, London: HarperCollins.

Capra, Fritjof (1989), *Uncommon Wisdom*, London: Flamingo.

Laing, R. D. (1982), *The Voice of Experience*, New York: Pantheon; Harmondsworth: Penguin.

Reed, Bruce (1978), *The Dynamics of Religion*, London: Darton, Longman & Todd.

A possible way forward
Capra, Fritjof (1982), *The Tao of Physics*, London: Flamingo.
Capra, Fritjof (1983), *The Turning Point*, London: HarperCollins.
Capra, Fritjof (1989), *Uncommon Wisdom*, London: Flamingo.
Davies, Paul (1990), *God and the New Physics*, Harmondsworth: Penguin.
Ward, Keith (1998), *God, Faith and the New Millennium*, London: One World:
Wilber, Ken (1996), *A Brief History of Everything*, Dublin: Gill & Macmillan.
Wilber, Ken (1998), *The Marriage of Sense and Soul: Integrating Science and Religion*, Dublin: Gill & Macmillan.

SOME POINTS FOR FURTHER CONSIDERATION

- What shapes your understanding of, and response to, individuals or groups who are suffering from mental distress?
- What is the relationship between the "objective" and "subjective" within your view of religion?
- Is theology a master-language that embraces a comprehensive understanding of human experience?
- What are the pastoral and practical implications and significance of Sutherland's framework?
- What have you learned that is of personal or theological significance from any experiences of mental distress of people with whom you are acquainted?

FOR FURTHER READING AND EXPLORATION

This area is discussed in detail in Foskett (1984). For an exploration of supervision in pastoral care, see Foskett and Lyall (1988). For background information about Clinical Pastoral Education, see the entry on Anton Boisen in Hunter (1990). For a fuller discussion of the relationships between religion, mental health, and pastoral theology and care, see Pattison (1989, 1997a), Bhugra (1996), and Malony and Spilka (1991).

21

Management and Pastoral Theology

Stephen Pattison

Introduction

Management and organizational leadership have become key practices in the modern world. Most organizations of whatever kind now feel the need for some kind of formal management arrangements. Church communities and their ministers are beginning to see the importance of management. In the UK, for example, there is now quite a significant demand for business administration courses that equip clergy with management skills. And the Church of England has adopted new structures of governance that are widely perceived as management-orientated. The skills and techniques of counseling and groupwork that were eagerly sought in the past are now being supplemented by those of management and leadership. The theory and practice of management carries with it distinctive views of the world and people. It therefore presents an important subject for reflection to practical theology in so far as it attempts critically to evaluate contemporary practices that affect people's worldviews and wellbeing.

In this specially commissioned paper, Stephen Pattison, an English pastoral theologian who has studied and researched extensively into management, outlines the challenge that management poses to pastoral theology in theory and in practice. Pattison describes the nature of management before going on to discuss its importance and value. He argues that management is probably a necessary, useful, and inevitable part of the life of any contemporary organization, including that of the church. However, he then goes on to suggest that churches need to be cautious and critical in their adoption and adaptation of management ideas and techniques. The reason for this is that management has its own implicit faith assumptions about the world that are embodied in its practices. These assumptions may not always be compatible with those of the Christian community.

If management is a kind of faith system accompanied by its own distinctive symbols, rituals, narratives, and practices, then these need to be theologically evaluated before they begin to change the nature of ecclesiastical life and thought. To this end, Pattison sets out some preliminary critical comments on three aspects of management theory and practice: the worldview and assumptions underlying management, the language of management, and a particular managerial practice, namely individual perfomance appraisal.

If Pattison is right in arguing that management and other "secular" practices such as counseling have their own implicit faith systems and world views, an interesting implication of his argument for practical theology generally is that the analysis of faith and religion might extend far beyond the confines of the Christian community. This means that managers and others might profitably become critical practical theologians of their own belief systems and practices. Thus the scope and usefulness of practical theology is widened to include theological activity and analysis outside the church.

MANAGEMENT AND PASTORAL THEOLOGY

Ever since the pharaohs plotted the construction of the pyramids, there has been a need for coordination, leadership and administration to ensure that things get done. In other words, there has been the need for, and the practice of, some kind of management. Management as it is presently understood is, however, mostly a product of the nineteenth-century industrial revolution. Much modern management theory and practice has its origins within industry and commerce in the USA (Locke 1996). From there, it has spread around the world and throughout society to public and voluntary organizations as well as those in the private sector.

There is increasing interest in management and leadership techniques in churches and religious groups. This is partly due to the influence and fashionable nature of management in society as a whole. It is also the result of the need to use scarce human and financial resources effectively and properly at a time when many denominations are declining in membership. It therefore makes sense to examine management critically here with a view to assaying its nature, strengths, weaknesses, dangers and challenges.

I want to suggest that, while management theories and practices may often be useful and to a large degree inevitable in any organization such as a church, they should not be uncritically accepted as an uncontroversial, universal panacea that has no negative effects. To the extent that management may be regarded as a faith and belief system that manifests itself in practice, it can be problematic from a religious or theological perspective. I will start, however, by saying a bit more about the nature of management.

What is Management?

According to Peter Drucker, one of the founders of modern management theory, management aims to improve organizational performance. Within this overall aim, managers exist to (a) set objectives; (b) organize; (c) motivate and communicate; (d) measure and evaluate performance; and (e) develop people (Drucker 1974: 20–1). While theories of management multiply and vary according to fashion and context, it is difficult to conceive of any meaningful kind of management that does not in some way embody these five basic notions.

It has been said that 'Managers manage messes.' It could be added that managers manage messes in a muddled way. In reality, practical management is often a much more complex and confused activity than Drucker's theoretical formulation of five basic tasks suggests.

A moment's thought about Drucker's formulation of general functions of management reveals that they are by no means confined to managers. It is certainly true that, for example, people who run households and look after children do many, if not all, of these things without describing themselves as 'household managers'! This points up the fact that (a) many so-called distinctive management skills and functions are widespread throughout society; (b) many of us perform management functions within roles that we might not regard as primarily managerial; and (c) there may be a sense in which who regards what task as one of management is relative – management is in the eye of the beholder (Grint 1995).

It is perhaps not surprising then that, although management qualifications like MBAs do exist, it is not always necessary to have such a qualification to practise as a manager (Pattison 1997: 14). Most are trained in other disciplines and functions before they become managers and they often have little training for a specifically managerial role. People often become formally designated as managers by being good at something completely different like engineering, or educating people. Many very senior managers have no formal management qualifications of any kind. They rely on life experience, personal leadership abilities or native wit to accomplish their managerial tasks. Curiously, despite the emphasis on measurement and evaluation in management, it is often quite difficult for managers to actually state what they achieve by their activity. This is because organizational success often depends on the combined efforts of many individuals, not just managers.

Within the general management function with its generic tasks outlined by Drucker above there are specialized management functions for which particular skills may be needed. These include:

* financial management
* human resource management
* marketing management
* planning and strategic management

In a large organization, these functions may be discharged by individual specialists or departments of specialists working under the direction of some kind of overall general manager. In a small organization, they may all be undertaken by a single general manager whose job is to ensure that all these aspects are taken into account and efficiently discharged. The aim of all managers, whether general or specialist within an organization, is to help ensure that the organization attains its goals and purposes (e.g. to make a profit for shareholders). 'Good' management ensures that the necessary organization for this to happen occurs. Thus, inputs of capital and resources (e.g. raw materials, human labour) are used to produce the desired outputs (e.g. health care, cars) in a way that follows the three virtuous 'e's of effectiveness, efficiency and economy.

All manner of theoretical domains and practical skills contribute to understanding and performing management functions. Organization theory, sociology, psychology, politics, human relations, systems theory, communication theory and accountancy are just some of the organizing perspectives that may be introduced to illuminate particular aspects of management practice. Some theorists like to describe management as a science and to emphasize its empirical and quantitative basis in statistics and hard information. Others prefer to see it as a practice, a creative art, or a science of understanding that includes subjectivity and personal judgement as well as objectivity (Mintzberg 1989).

The Importance and Value of Management

Management is idolized by some as a creative universal panacea for any organizational or social problem. Others resent its perceived narrowness and instrumental approach. However, management is unlikely to disappear. It is important for Christian pastoral workers and others to appreciate its significance and value.

First, in practical terms, it is hard to imagine how organizations of any size, including church communities, could function or survive in the contemporary world without some version of the kind of management functions described above, albeit people might prefer not to label these functions as management or to see themselves as managers. 'Leadership' seems to be a more acceptable term in the church, having resonances with NT writings (Gill and Burke 1996; Higginson 1996; Banks and Powell, in press). I am not sure whether this usage does not create as much confusion as it solves since leadership both inside and outside the church is an ambivalent concept capable of many interpretations and (mis-)understandings. No responsible organization can wholly ignore the importance of defining purpose, organizing, motivating, evaluating and developing its members even if a different vocabulary is used to describe these functions. The alternative is chaos, confusion and a lack of clarity that means that people do not know what they should be doing and resources are wasted purposelessly – a recipe for frustration and decline.

Second, management of some kind is not only necessary in churches, it is already there and has been for a long time. Historically, religious communities have always had some form of management. Benedictine communities of monks are cited as early examples of highly organized groups that may be seen as ancestors of modern managed organizations (Grint 1995). It has been claimed that the Catholic Church was the first, and for a long time the only, centrally managed organization upon earth! Religious communities have pioneered and influenced the development of organization and management in the past (compare sociologist Max Weber's famous exploration of the influence of Calvinist religious ideas upon the spirit and growth of capitalism). It would be unfortunate if this heritage were to be disavowed now. In fact, many churches have introduced managerial techniques and ideas at national and local levels to help them to meet challenges such as shortages of resources, decline in membership and scarcity of workers. Management is therefore already in the church and likely to become more dominant as time goes on. It seems sensible to understand and use it appropriately rather than to pretend that its insights and techniques do not exist, or to re-invent the wheel by thinking up new ideas and practices. It would be no more sensible to avoid management in thinking about ecclesiastical organization than it would be to ignore counselling techniques and ideas that might be adopted when trying to help individuals in need.

Third, from the point of view of the Christian pastoral and theological tradition that emphasizes the importance of groups and the corporate aspect of religious existence exemplified in notions of the Kingdom of God, the church as a Christ's body etc., it seems important to take very seriously the ways of organizing and structuring groups and their work suggested by management. To fail to make use of modern ideas and practices about organizations would be to adopt the posture of the ostrich, head in the sand. Taking some management ideas and practices seriously does not, however, imply that religious communities should be uncritically comprehensive in adopting them.

Fourth, management is becoming a world phenomenon. It provides a set of beliefs and world views embodied in practices and disciplines that are highly influential in shaping the behaviour and views of many people. Sometimes this happens in ways that people do not consciously recognize. It would be ludicrous for Christians who claim to have a concern for the contemporary world not to be interested in learning from, dialoguing with, and critically evaluating, one of the main social practices that informs organization and living today.

On Having a Critical Faith

Management theories and practices owe something to the religious tradition (Pattison 1997: 45ff). They are already present in the churches and are likely to become more prevalent. They will provide some of the means necessary for meeting the challenges facing any organization in the modern world. For any organization with a strong interest in corporate and social wellbeing, like the church, management ideas and techniques cannot be ignored. In so far as management is an increasingly important global practice and intellectual force, it is, or should be, of interest to Christians seeking to work out God's purposes today.

None of which means that management is totally unproblematic, has wholly beneficial effects, or is merely a set of techniques that have no religious or theological implications. The use of words with religious associations in management like mission and vision should be enough to alert us to the fact that management may have a more than passing resemblance to Christianity. When it is remembered that some of the roots of management theory and practice lie in ecclesiastical control practices in medieval Catholicism and nineteenth-century entrepreneurial Protestantism in the USA, it should come as no surprise that management can credibly be seen as in some ways a religious activity embodying a certain kind of faith. This has led me to suggest elsewhere that management can be regarded as a Christian heresy and that it is therefore possible to analyse the 'faith' of the managers (Pattison 1997).

In this final part of the chapter I want to suggest that management theory and practice has in itself some of the features of a religion or faith system, some of its theories and practices may be ambiguous or harmful, and so it needs to be adopted critically within churches (and, indeed, within other organizations) if it is to be beneficial rather than baneful. I will cast a critical eye over just three aspects of management that may cause questions to arise about the nature and effects of management. These are the world view and assumptions underlying management in general, the language of management and a particular practice common in managed organizations, appraisal.

The worldview of management

Pick up almost any popular book on management technique and you will find in it a set of techniques and concepts that, if followed, claim to be able to transform organizations and to guarantee success. This is particularly true of the books produced by so-called 'gurus' like Tom Peters and Charles Handy, which are characterized by a sense of forward-looking optimism about the possibilities of management in a changing world. While many theorists are very sober, not to say boring, it can be argued that much of the theory that gains currency in the popular managerial imagination is of this kind. (The only book to be found in the office of a very senior health care manager I once knew was Tom Peters's *Thriving on Chaos* – this was not reassuring to his visitors!) In many ways, management theorists and consultants are selling faith, hope and meaning as much as any kind of specific knowledge or technique. The sort of faith or action-informing world view that they are propounding often embodies some or all of the following assumptions:

- Human beings can control the world and colonize the future effectively so long as they have the right techniques.
- Individuals should be subservient to organizational goals and to their superiors.
- Relationships are fundamentally hierarchical and require clear lines of upward accountability and downward responsibility.
- The nature of organizational work should be such as to extract the maximum from the employee.
- Everything that is significant can and should be measured objectively.
- Clear goals and objectives can be set for the future and they can and will be attained.
- The prosperity and flourishing of the organization is the greatest good and the priority for all organization members.
- Productivity and profitability determine the value of individual and organizational endeavour.

Management practices and beliefs are often very uncritical of society in general, of the capitalist system of economic production and exploitation. They are mostly developed by those who depend on managers for making their living. Christians, however, should perhaps be wary of uncritically adopting a set of practices that embody a world view that could be characterized as wildly overoptimistic, narrow in its view of human nature and relationships, Pelagian (i.e. ignorant of the fallen, sinful and harmful nature of human being and endeavour), utopian, exploitative, and trivializing of the chaotic and unpredictable nature of the world.

The language of management

Much of the theory of management that has seized the popular imagination in the last decade or so has overtly appealed to ideals and values with notions such as the 'value-driven' organization etc. (Huczynski 1996). It is not surprising, then, that many concepts with overtly religious resonances have entered the managerial vocabulary.

Two of the most prominent of these are the concepts of 'mission' and 'vision'. Vision is what is supposed to motivate an organization and given it a sense of ultimate direction. The mission of the organization, often embodied in a short 'mission statement', is a description of what the organization intends to do in order to realize its vision. It is worth being alert to the presence of religious words and concepts, whether explicit or implicit, that are used to obtain commitment and legitimacy in managerial practice. It is also a good idea to subject these concepts to some kind of theological analysis.

Metaphors like mission and vision may have important, unintended secondary meanings, and the historical experience of the Christian tradition can alert us to some of the limits of using these concepts. Thus, in the case of mission, this concept has positive connotations of clarity of purpose, urgency, outward-directedness, and the need for change. However, it has the more negative connotations evidenced in Christian history such as unquestioning response to a command 'from above', dualism, seeing the world as a hostile place that needs changing and regarding those outside the organization as alien or demonic 'objects' needing conversion or elimination. Christian mission has often been aggressive, violent, exploitative and colonial – hence the utility of the concept of mission within the military. Those who use this concept in management need to be aware of its capacity for harm as well as good.

Similar comments could be made about vision. On the one hand it has connotations of changing things for the better, not accepting an unsatisfactory present, and thinking about the future. However, it can also be associated with arbitrariness, fending off challenge (who dares to challenge a vision?), top-down planning, and obedience and passivity in the face of authority that cannot be questioned.

Here again, it must be emphasized that there is a real need for Christians to be critical of management words and practices, not necessarily with a view to dismissing or discarding them, but with a view to using them judiciously and with full awareness of their implications.

Appraisal: governing the soul

It is not just management theories and language that may have theological or problematic aspects to them. Managerial techniques themselves are ideology- and theory-laden. Like all human practices, they contain and incarnate particular fundamental world views and assumptions. Browning notes that

> All our practices, even our religious practices, have theories behind and within them. We may not notice the theories in our practices. We are so embedded in our practices, take them so much for granted, and view them

as so natural and self-evident that we never take time to abstract the theory from the practice and look at it as something in itself.   (Browning 1991: 6)

One example of a common management technique that may pose interesting problems is that of appraisal or Individual Performance Review (Jacobs 1989). It is common in many organizations, including churches, for individuals to have a regular appraisal with their line manager or immediate superior with a view to evaluating their past performance and setting measurable goals and objectives that promote the mission and purpose of the organization for the future. While this process has many enthusiasts and some people find it very useful, appraisal presents many practical problems. For example, the goals and scope of an effective appraisal scheme should be very clear, it should not be used for multiple purposes (e.g. career development *and* determining performance-related pay); organizational objectives and measures need to be clear if the scheme is to be fairly applied; the workforce should understand and actively assent to its introduction and operation; staff should be effectively supported in working towards agreed goals; time is needed for useful appraisal; and trust and a non-punitive attitude are required if people are to be honest about their performance. In many organizations these criteria are not met, so that, for example, time is not made available for preparing for appraisal and resources are not available to follow through the goals identified. If appraisal is conducted infrequently, goals become superseded – the OOPS phenomenon, whereby objectives are ousted by other priorities (Pattison 1997: 109). It is this sort of slippage, which will be familiar to anyone who has been employed in an organization which uses appraisal, that has led one critic to conclude that 'Rarely in the history of business can such a system have promised so much and delivered so little' (Grint 1995: 75).

Appraisal is just one example of a practice that has become canonical and enshrined in many organizations without much question being raised as to whether it actually accomplishes what it claims. If appraisal does not necessarily improve individual and organizational performance, it can be asked what purpose it does serve. Perhaps it is a way of ensuring top-down control and surveillance of the workforce so that they perceive themselves to be seen by their superiors and are encouraged to conform to organizational norms. In this sense, far from being a tool of personal development and liberation, appraisal can be regarded as a tool of social control, rather like the rite of confession to a priest in the medieval Catholic church. In this connection it is interesting to note that appraisal tends to be much lauded by senior managers for the benefit of their juniors while mostly they do not subject themselves to appraisal from below.

Appraisal can be seen as a tool for reinforcing hierarchical obedience and control. It is just one example of a managerial practice that is perhaps less innocent and unequivocally helpful than its advocates would like to suggest. It incarnates and moulds a particular view of human beings and social relationships and is not just a simple, useful tool.

Conclusion

In the New Testament, Jesus advises his followers to be as cunning as serpents and as innocent as doves. The same advice might usefully be applied to approaching management theories and practices in society and church. Management is becoming an increasingly universal phenomenon that not only helps to run organizations but is also helping to shape fundamental world views and metaphors of reality in the lives of many individuals and groups.

One response to the rise and prevalence of management would be to ignore or dismiss it. This is probably neither realistic or responsible in a world of complex organizations. However, it behoves Christians and others to think carefully and critically about the implicit ideologies and effects that management ideas and techniques may carry with them if they are to make management a tool rather than becoming unwitting tools of management. If part of the mission of religious groups is to be critical of assumptions and practices that may be dubious, dehumanizing or destructive, it is necessary that the nostrums of popular management theory should not be adopted wholesale by churches and pastoral workers.

BIBLIOGRAPHY

Banks, R., and Powell, K. (eds) (in press), *The Role and Practice of Faith in Leadership*, San Francisco: Jossey-Bass.
Browning, D. (1991), *A Fundamental Practical Theology*, Minneapolis: Fortress Press.
Drucker, P. (1974), *Management: Tasks, Responsibilities, Practices*, Oxford: Butterworth Heinemann.
Gill, R., and Burke, D. (1996), *Strategic Church Leadership*, London: SPCK.
Grint, K. (1995), *Management: A Sociological Introduction*, Cambridge: Polity Press.
Higginson, R. (1996), *Transforming Leadership*, London: SPCK.
Huczynski, A. (1996), *Management Gurus*, London: International Thompson Business Press.
Jacobs, M. (1989), *Holding in Trust: The Appraisal of Ministry*. London: SPCK.
Locke, R. (1996), *The Collapse of the American Management Mystique*, Oxford: Oxford University Press.
Mintzberg, H. (1989), *Mintzberg on Management*, New York: Free Press.
Nelson, J. (ed.) (1996), *Management and Ministry*, Norwich: Canterbury Press.

Pattison, S. (1997), *The Faith of the Managers*, London: Cassell.
Peters, T. (1989), *Thriving on Chaos*, London: Pan Books.

SOME POINTS FOR FURTHER CONSIDERATION

- What attitude should church leaders and communities take to techniques and theories of management?
- Think of a contemporary "secular" practice such as counseling, teaching, or management. What basic assumptions does it make about the nature of the world and people? How far are these assumptions compatible with Christian traditions and practices?
- Is it useful to see management as a kind of faith system that performs some of the same functions as religion?
- What are the main differences between the Christian religious faith system and the managerial "faith" system?
- Which "secular" techniques and practices in the contemporary world would benefit from some kind of practical theological analysis, and why?

FOR FURTHER READING AND EXPLORATION

For a general, authoritative introduction to the nature of management, Drucker (1974) is still very helpful. The history of management is well captured in Huczynski (1996) and Locke (1996). For management in the churches, see Gill and Burke (1996), Higginson (1996), and Nelson (1996). For critical assessment of management and leadership in religious communities and some theological assessment see, e.g., Percy and Evans (in press) and Banks and Powell (in press). For an extended version of Pattison's analysis of management as a faith system, see Pattison (1997b). The notion of management as a kind of irrational ideology is well explored in Alvesson and Willmott (1996). For more on various types of appraisal and their alternatives within the church setting, see Jacobs (1989).

__ Part Four __

Evaluating Pastoral and Practical Theology

INTRODUCTION TO PART FOUR

22 An Introduction to Evaluation in Pastoral Theology and
    Pastoral Care
    Stephen Pattison and James Woodward

23 Pastoral Care as Performance
    David Lyall

Introduction to Part Four

Pastoral and practical theology relate to practice, to action, to doing things. They might therefore be supposed to make a difference to people, to transform or change their lives in some way. The question is, in what way or ways might pastoral theology make a difference? Furthermore, is the difference that pastoral or practical theology makes a useful or desirable one? These questions underlie this part of the Reader, which is concerned with evaluation in pastoral and practical theology.

Evaluation has become a significant aspect of many activities in the contemporary world. It is an important part of being critical and ensuring that activities both make a difference, and make a difference that is wanted. If people do not evaluate what they are doing in terms of its processes and outcomes, they cannot know whether or not their efforts are being well applied or accomplishing anything useful. It is therefore highly appropriate to take stock of what any kind of study, thought or action actually accomplishes. Only thus can it become clear whether anything useful or desirable is being accomplished at all.

For the most part, pastoral and practical theologians have assumed that their analysis, teaching, thinking, and acting have made a difference to pastoral carers. They have also assumed that their effect on practice and thought has been beneficial and positive. Like many other professional groups, they have largely failed to be critical and evaluative of their own work and its effects, preferring rhetoric and assumption to analysis. This raises the question of whether pastoral, or any other kind of education, actually has useful, desired, and intended effects, or whether its main value is to socialize people into a particular group and world view (this in itself might be evaluated as being a useful, positive thing).

In future, it is likely that pastoral theologians and pastoral carers will have to be able to demonstrate the value and significance of their activity. They will need to account for themselves to justify the support and confidence of peers in the academic and care worlds. Critical evaluation and the capacity to give an account of what is being done and why is therefore becoming important in the interests of accountability. It is also important in terms of using time, energy, and money appropriately.

Evaluation can take many forms. It may use many different techniques and kinds of evidence, and cover many spheres of thought and activity. It need not necessarily be lengthy, complicated, or focused upon objectively measurable results. So, for example, it could be argued that studying pastoral theology is intrinsically interesting and pleasurable, stimulating the imagination and making people more consciously aware of their circumstances without necessarily making those who study it better pastoral carers. In this case, evaluation might consist in asking whether pastoral theology does achieve these ends. Is it intrinsically enjoyable, stimulating, consciousness-raising, etc?

The point is that evaluation requires people to look at their claims, their purposes, their values, and their actions to find out whether what they think they are doing is what they and/or others think they really want to do.

Often, evaluation is a very subjective, informal activity – have I done what I set out to do in line with what I think should be done? Whatever level and means are selected, asking basic questions about the worth and value of what one is doing or thinking is an important part of developing critical reflection in pastoral theology and practice.

Appropriate evaluation in pastoral theology and practice is still at an early stage in its development. In this part of the Reader, we include two papers that begin to explore the nature and significance of this activity.

In "An Introduction to Evaluation" Pattison and Woodward set out some of the basic concepts and issues that arise in thinking about appropriate evaluation in pastoral theology as intellectual activity and formation, and in pastoral practice. They argue that evaluation is an important and useful function because it is the process of establishing the worth or value of an activity. They conclude the paper with a series of questions that may help readers to define the kind of evaluation appropriate to their own context.

This is followed by David Lyall's article, "Pastoral care as performance." Lyall is a theological educator of many years' standing. He evaluates his long experience of the nature of pastoral theological education and the actual effects that it might have upon those who then go on to engagement in pastoral ministry and care. Having conducted empirical research on the effects of theoretical and pastoral education on students, Lyall points up the limits of the quantitative approach in evaluation. He argues that something more is required that is appropriate to the fundamental nature of pastoral care as an art form rather than a science. Lyall usefully complicates and broadens the understanding of evaluation in pastoral theology and pastoral care, showing that this must be sensitive to the nature of the activity being evaluated. Although evaluation may have to be complex, subtle, and multifaceted in the case of pastoral care and pastoral theology, this does not mean that it should be uncritically dismissed or discarded. Lyall sees an important future for this activity within practical theology.

22

An Introduction to Evaluation in Pastoral Theology and Pastoral Care

STEPHEN PATTISON AND JAMES WOODWARD

INTRODUCTION

Evaluation has become an important part of the lives of many individuals and organizations. Strangely, pastoral theology and pastoral care have not given it much priority, though there is some evidence that it is becoming more important.

In this specially commissioned paper, Pattison and Woodward argue that appropriate types of evaluation can perform a very important and useful function within academic and practical pastoral activity. Evaluation is the process of establishing the worth or value of an activity. There is inevitably a subjective, contextual aspect to evaluation, so it is never entirely objective. This means that evaluation must necessarily be flexible and varied in structure and method if it is to be useful.

Useful, appropriate evaluation can help people to map their activities and progress as well as allowing them to articulate their values and purposes and account for what they are engaged in. There are pitfalls in evaluation, for example people evaluating the wrong things or becoming concerned with measurement of tangible things instead of with the issue of worth. Evidence and methods must be fit for the purpose of evaluation. However, in principle it is still possible to design and execute appropriate evaluations. These can and should take into account theological and religious values and practices in the context of pastoral theology and pastoral care.

Pattison and Woodward conclude with a series of questions that may help readers in defining the kind of evaluation that may be appropriate for their own activity and context. Evaluation, they argue, is ultimately what people want it to be, and they should feel free to make it relevant to their needs within their own particular contexts. Pattison brings to this paper his experience as a writer of distance-learning materials in the School of Health and Social Welfare at the Open University, where materials are constantly under review and evaluation. Woodward has worked in the British National Health Service where chaplaincy faced the challenges of monitoring and evaluation. He is working at the moment on methods of evaluating care with older people.

AN INTRODUCTION TO EVALUATION IN PASTORAL THEOLOGY AND PASTORAL CARE

The Origin of Evaluation

In the beginning God created the heaven and the earth . . .

And God saw everything He made. 'Behold,' God said, 'it is very good.'

And the evening and the morning were the sixth day.

And on the seventh day God rested from all his work; His archangel came then unto Him asking:

'God, how do you know what you have created is "very good"? What are your criteria? On what data do you base your judgement? Aren't you a little close to the situation to make a fair and unbiased evaluation?'

God thought about these questions all that day and His rest was greatly disturbed.

On the eighth day God said, 'Lucifer, go to hell.'

Thus was evaluation born in a blaze of glory.

(Halcom's *The Real Story of Paradise Lost*, quoted in Katz and Peberdy 1997: 269)

Introduction

Pastoral theology, pastoral care and pastoral education have paid a good deal of attention to the need for theological reflection upon practice and experience. However, they seem to have been less willing to think about critical assessment of their own worth, effects and results. The implicit assumption often seems to be that these activities, buoyed up by habit, tradition and good intentions, must in and of themselves be helpful and beneficial to those who are affected by them. This assumption may be correct. However, the issue of evaluation in various kinds of pastoral activity is not one that can be entirely avoided.

The aim of this essay is to consider some of the issues pertaining to evaluation. It does not provide any definite recommendations or techniques for evaluation in pastoral theology. However, it explores some aspects of the nature of evaluation and factors that need to be borne in mind when contemplating undertaking it in any particular form or context. Contrary to the little story above about the origins of evaluation, if prudently undertaken, evaluation need not be a dreaded, intimidating, elaborate, expensive, formal, or judgemental activity. It can, in fact, usefully add to practice of many kinds, whether it be in the academy or the parish.

The Nature of Evaluation

Evaluation is nothing more and nothing less than the matter of judging the worth of an activity or an entity (Katz and Peberdy 1997: 269ff). It will immediately be apparent that this is something that most human beings do in an informal way a great deal of the time. People are constantly asking themselves how things are going, how could things be better, is that appropriate or useful? *Informal evaluation* on a personal basis is just part of life.

Formal evaluation is a somewhat different matter. In formal evaluation, activities or entities are (or should be) judged against carefully thought-through and articulated criteria such as aims and objectives (Pattison 1996; in press). Here, groups of people may set out to establish whether an activity or object attains the standards that are set in such a way that it can be deemed formally acceptable. Have the purposes that were originally intended been fulfilled, in what ways, and to what extent?

By contrast with informal evaluation, formal evaluation is likely to be a more lengthy, elaborate and time-consuming process. This does not necessarily mean that informal evaluation is less useful or appropriate. The kind of evaluation that is undertaken should be determined by what is appropriate in a particular context. Formal evaluation of occasional, trivial, short-lived or one-off activities would be wasteful and inappropriate. It might, however, be appropriate in the case of activities that are habitual, long-term, costly, and of great significance in the lives of individuals, groups or societies.

Values are created by human beings. They are various, and they can change considerably from culture to culture, even from individual to individual (Pattison 1998; Tschudin 1992). There are many different things and activities in the world that are valued differently. So, for example, some people value the money that they are paid for working; this is the valued outcome or product of their labours. Others might value as an outcome the difference that their labours make. A teacher, for instance, might value the fact that a student has made real progress in mastering academic skills because of her efforts. Yet others may value the process of working. A teacher might enjoy teaching for the pleasure it brings in and of itself, rather than because of seeing a set of excellent grades acquired by students because of the teaching they have experienced. And some people in their work might principally value the chance to get out of their homes and mix with friends from different backgrounds, seeing the actual tasks for which they are paid as part of the price of having an interesting life. Of course, there is nothing to stop any of the people in the examples discussed from equally valuing all the elements that go into their work, or valuing some of them differentially.

A number of important points relating to evaluation arise out of these examples. First, in many situations, there are any number of things that might be valued and so evaluated positively or negatively to a greater or lesser extent.

Second, it all depends on whose point of view or interests are prioritized as to what is evaluated and what is thought to be valuable. Would students studying in a college value different things from their teachers who come to the college to earn their living? It seems likely they often would and they would not be very interested, or interested in the same way, in what the teachers valued about their work.

Third, there are significantly different kinds of things that are valued – valuing working is not necessarily the same thing as valuing the results of work such as a pay packet, though these two kinds of valuing may be very compatible.

Fourth, it should be noted that not everything that is valued can be easily measured. If people primarily value money as an outcome or reward for their labours then presumably the more they earn the more satisfied they feel. Thus, their earnings represent a good, relatively objective measure of what they value which can easily be compared with other people's earnings. However, it may be much more difficult to measure the amount of job satisfaction that a teacher has in working with students on a day-to-day basis. Just because something cannot be weighed, measured or counted does not mean that is should not matter in terms of evaluation. It just means that it may be more difficult to take it into account. In evaluation, one danger is that things that can be easily measured, e.g. exam results, sums of money, numbers of commodities are assumed to be more valuable or significant that those that cannot – 'If you can't count it, it doesn't count' (Handy 1996: 137). This obsession with measurement can be very off-putting. It disguises the basic nature of evaluation, which is simply to assay the worth of something against the standards and values of the assayer or assayers, however intangible or unmeasurable those values or standards may be.

Finally, an important distinction can be made here between process and outcome. It is different to value or evaluate the process of a particular activity from evaluating the product of that activity. So, for example, a college might produce very good exam results and be evaluated as excellent on the basis of these (an evaluation based on product or outcome). However, if it were found that all the staff and students hated the work they had to do and felt they got little out of being there, an evaluation of process that gave weight to how people felt about their educational experience might find that the college was rather poor.

All of these points go to show that evaluation must be a subtle, clearly thought-through activity if it is really to be appropriate and of some use. If people are not clear about what they are evaluating and what kind of worth they are trying to determine, evaluation may well be a misleading, unhelpful waste of time and resources. So given the difficulties of undertaking evaluation, why is it important to evaluate activities and entities?

The Need to Evaluate

Evaluation has become an integral part of many activities in modern society. In what is called postmodern society there is an emphasis on reflexivity, looking at the self or the organization all the time to see what is going on (Giddens 1991). This seems to be related to a need to plan, organize and avoid risks which goes along with the process of rationalization or 'McDonaldization' with its principles of efficiency, calculability, predictability and control (Ritzer 1996). It is not surprising, then, that the need constantly to evaluate is also entering the arenas of pastoral theology and pastoral care. Some religious practitioners, particularly those who work in secular organizations and institutions, are being forced formally to evaluate and plan their work by managerial and professional pressures. In the UK, hospital chaplains, for example, have to create business plans, adhere to standards, and then evaluate their performance in the light of these (Williamson 1992; College of Health Care Chaplains 1993; Woodward 1995, 1999).

The pressure to engage in evaluation is not necessarily an unhelpful thing. As we have already seen, many people undertake all kinds of informal everyday evaluation anyway. Thinking more carefully about this activity might make it more useful and focused. And there are several very positive benefits that appropriate evaluation might bestow.

First, evaluation might encourage pastoral theologians and pastoral workers to articulate what it is that they do, why, and why this is valuable. Even if the aspects of pastoral theology and care that are valued are more to do with process, imagination and creativity than they are to do with achieving more definite outcomes or results such as saving a certain number of souls per year, there is really no excuse for people working in these areas not to be able to explain to themselves and others what exactly it is that is valuable about their activity. It is, of course, perfectly possible to articulate a complex, multidimensional view of the value of these activities. This is different from refusing to articulate any kind of view at all.

Once it has been established what it is that is valued about pastoral care or pastoral theology and what is accomplished through these activities, it will be possible for people engaged in these activities to sharpen their focus and perhaps do more of what it is that is valued and less of those things that are not valued. This may lend helpful clarity and purpose to these activities. It will also help in creating a direction and purpose for future action.

One of the advantages of evaluating one's activities is that it is then possible to be much more clearly accountable for them to other people. Most people have some kind of responsibility to others in their work. In so far as they consume resources and may have an impact on other people's lives for good or ill, it seems important that they should be able to render an account of what they do and why it is valuable to those to whom they are responsible. In commercial and public service organizations, individuals and groups are often measured against the values of effectiveness, economy and efficiency. These are not necessarily the right criteria for evaluating pastoral work and pastoral theology. However, it seems reasonable that these activities should be able to justify their existence and their value in their own terms through appropriate evaluation.

A further advantage of appropriate evaluation of activity is that it helps people to have a sense of the value of their own work, to have a sense of direction, and also to gain a sense of achievement. This may help to avoid purposeless meandering and a sense of being lost or useless. These feelings can sometimes bring people to a point of depression or burn-out as they perceive their efforts to be of little use or worth. Evaluation may therefore be an important part of staying alive, interested, stimulated and well in the context of one's activity, particularly if that evaluation is shared with sympathetic others.

Some Pitfalls in Evaluation

Despite the positive benefits of evaluation that have been outlined, many people remain resistant to the notion of evaluation in pastoral care and pastoral theology. For some, this resistance stems from a feeling that they would not know how to begin to evaluate their activity. Others might argue that pastoral work and pastoral theology have a proper mystical, intangible quality to them which eludes evaluation. How can one begin to evaluate the worth of visiting an old person for a cup of tea, or writing an article about mental health and religion (Pattison 1996; in press)? Some people may fear that evaluation means having to formulate or adhere to some agreed values or aims that then preclude flexibility and individual discretion.

They want to be free to follow where the spirit leads them, and evaluation threatens to get in the way. Others might fear that any kind of evaluation means that they may be judged by others and found to be wanting in their academic or practical performances.

Then there are anxieties that evaluation might mean that things they value that are intangible or difficult to measure will be displaced by attention to things that can be counted. Worth may be displaced by measurement. So, for example, a person's pastoral work might be evaluated against the number of people who attend religious worship in a particular church on a Sunday morning. Finally, there are those who would argue that they need the time that could be spent in evaluating their activity to actually perform it. Evaluation is seen as a self-indulgent waste of time and energy that distracts people from actually doing their work.

These fears and fantasies are not entirely ill-founded. Evaluation has often been experienced as a crude, clumsy, externally-imposed, time-consuming, judgemental process that fails to do justice to the subtleties of a particular situation or kind of work. However, this is not an argument against evaluation as such. It is an argument against crude and inappropriate evaluation that is not adequate for the kind of activity or situation upon which it is being imposed. The solution is to ensure that evaluation is suitable and acceptable for the purpose for which it is intended.

A good deal of thought and preparation may need to go into thinking through the methods, aims, purposes and intended outcomes of the evaluative process. It is silly to use a very large sledgehammer to crack a very small nut. Would-be evaluators of self, other individuals, organizations or situations need to take control of the evaluation process to ensure that it serves the needs of the people it is intended to serve, not some idealized notion of evaluation as such.

Evidence and methods

The clear implication of the discussion above is that there is no one correct way of undertaking evaluation. It needs to be sensitive and appropriate to the purpose for which it is undertaken and it needs to be useful to those who are evaluating a particular situation or practice.

An enormous variety of evidence and methods may be used according to the ends and values of the evaluators. There is certainly no imperative to adopt complex, time-consuming empirical research methods such as questionnaires, outcome studies, or in-depth interviews in evaluation unless this directly serves the nature and purpose of the evaluation that is being undertaken.

In the case of informal evaluation undertaken for the sake of everyday self-monitoring, for example, it may be enough to simply try and gain some immediate verbal feedback on one's performance from people who witness it in some capacity, e.g. colleagues, students, parishioners. Beyond this, mechanisms such as supervision can also help in evaluating what is going on (Lyall and Foskett 1988). At a slightly more formal level, individual appraisal can also be relevant here, especially if appraisers collect evidence from other people about one's activities and performances (Jacobs 1989; Pattison 1997b). It may also be possible to evaluate how far one has succeeded in one's work by more objective measures such as articles published, number of people visited, amount of pastoral work done.

None of these informal means of evaluating individual performance on its own necessarily forms a full evaluation. Furthermore, the significance of the evidence must itself be weighed and evaluated. Writing a lot of articles or visiting a lot of people may not reveal much about the quality or significance of this work. Here again, the importance of perspective and the subjective element comes into play.

Formal evaluation may take place on a larger scale and over a longer timescale, particularly if the whole of a particular kind of activity is being evaluated. The full panoply of empirical research techniques may be deployed to find out what effects a particular activity or approach may have. However elaborate and complex the methods and evidence are that are used, the main principle of evaluation is still relevant: Is this evidence relevant and appropriate to the kind of activity that is being evaluated? It is not possible to escape from the matter of judging and discerning what is in fact relevant and appropriate. Human valuation is essential to appropriate evaluation at whatever level it occurs.

Evaluation in Theological Perspective

In the case of evaluation within pastoral theology and pastoral care, it might be thought appropriate that religious and theological perceptions drawn from the Christian religious tradition should inform the nature and process of appropriate evaluation, as well as the standards or values that these activities are evaluated against.

It is perfectly appropriate that an activity that serves religious ends and values should be evaluated against theological or religiously defined criteria. So, for example, a group of Christian pastoral workers might conclude that their work should be evaluated not by ecclesiastical managers or external consultants but by the poor and oppressed people who are excluded by society. It could be argued that this would reflect Jesus' bias to putting the interests and perspectives of the excluded and marginal first in the Kingdom of God, as revealed in teachings such as the parables of the Good Shepherd or the Prodigal Son and in his actions such as eating with tax-gatherers and sinners.

Similarly, the success of pastoral endeavour or pastoral theology might be evaluated against Biblical values such as promoting love, justice and peace. So, for example, ministerial activity could be wholly or partially evaluated in terms of Micah 6.8 (Authorized Version): 'and what doth the LORD require of thee, but to do justly, and to love mercy, and to walk humbly with thy God.' In this case, pastoral workers might ask to what extent their work has helped to promote social justice, loyalty and humility. Of course, they might have to think carefully about what these categories mean in modern society.

The point that is being made here is that the process and criteria that inform evaluation can be derived from theological interests and categories. Evaluation does not have to be a matter of the wholesale adoption of 'secular' values, methods and structures.

Some Helpful Questions in Approaching Evaluation

Evaluation can be as flexible and varied as the people who wish to be evaluators want it to be. It can be exactly what people want it to be and do whatever they want it to do. If, for example, pastoral care is regarded as more like an art than a science, it needs to evaluate itself against artistic or aesthetic criteria using methods that allow it to do this, rather than adopting the quantitative methods that might be appropriate to evaluating more discrete 'scientific' endeavours. There is no need to narrow or exclude important things that are valued in pastoral theology or pastoral care to conform to some kind of externally imposed template of evaluation. Evaluators have the freedom to create their own type and process of evaluation according to their own values and interests.

To create appropriate, sensitive and relevant structures of evaluation, it is important to become clear about what sort of evaluation is required and what criteria should be used within it. From this flow issues like what methods should be used, what kind of evidence should be collected and regarded as significant, etc.

Here are some questions, adapted from Katz and Peberdy (1997: 284ff) that may be helpful in trying to clarify what sort of evaluation may be appropriate to any particular activity or situation:

- Why do we want to evaluate?
- What is the purpose of the evaluation?
- Why evaluate now?
- What will be done with the products of any evaluation?
- Who should evaluate whatever is being evaluated?
- Who will be involved in the evaluation, and how?
- Whose values should inform the evaluation and what values should they be?
- From whose perspective, and in whose interests, is evaluation to occur?
- When should evaluation take place?
- Against which criteria should evaluation be undertaken?

- What information is required for evaluation? How can it be acquired?
- What methods are appropriate to use in evaluation (quantitative, qualitative, interviews, surveys, etc.)?
- What should count as evidence?
- What weight is to be given to different types of evidence?
- What place should theological themes, ideas, principles etc. occupy in evaluation?
- How is theological evaluation to take place?
- In what way will the findings of the evaluation be presented?
- To whom will the findings be presented, and for what purpose?

Conclusion

To parody Socrates, while the over-evaluated life may never be lived, the under-evaluated life may be lived in the wrong direction, or, indeed, in no particular direction at all. In this essay, we have tried to show that the evaluation of activities and practices can form an important, useful, even necessary, part of pastoral theology and pastoral practice, that does not require practitioners to engage in elaborate, complex, extraneous or distorting activity. The key to useful evaluation is to ensure that it is appropriate to its function and purpose. If this dictum is borne in mind then evaluation can become a useful tool of critical practice that helps to leaven and enliven the theory, practice and teaching of pastoral theology.

REFERENCES

Bryman, A., and Burgess, R. (eds) (1994), *Analyzing Qualitative Data*, London: Routledge.

College of Health Care Chaplains (1993), *Health Care Chaplaincy Standards*, London: Hospital Chaplaincies Council.

Giddens, A. (1991), *Modernity and Self-Identity*, Cambridge: Polity Press.

Graham, L. K. (1992), *Care of Persons, Care of Worlds*, Nashville: Abingdon Press.

Handy, C. (1996), *Beyond Certainty*, London: Arrow.

Jacobs, M. (1989), *Holding in Trust: The Appraisal of Ministry*, London: SPCK.

Lyall, D., and Foskett, J. (1988), *Helping the Helpers: Supervision and Pastoral Care*, London: SPCK.

Pattison, S. (1996b), 'Should pastoral care have aims and objectives?', *Contact* 120: 26–34.

Pattison, S. (1997a), *Pastoral Care and Liberation Theology*, London: SPCK.

Pattison, S. (1997b), *The Faith of the Managers*, London: Cassell.

Pattison, S. (1998), 'Questioning values', *Health Care Analysis* 6: 352–9.

Pattison, S. (in press), 'Objections to aims and objectives'. In M. Percy and G. Evans (eds), *Managing the Church*, Sheffield: Sheffield Academic Press.

Ritzer, G. (1996), *The McDonaldization of Society*, rev. edn, Thousand Oaks, CA: Pine Forge Press.

Tschudin, V. (1992), *Values*, London: Bailliére Tindall.

Williamson, C. (1992), *Whose Standards? Consumer and Professional Standards in Health Care*, Milton Keynes: Open University Press.

Woodward, J. (1995), *Encountering Illness: Voices in Pastoral and Theological Perspective*, London: SCM Press.

Woodward, J. (1999), 'A Study of the Role of the Health Care Chaplain in England', unpublished PhD thesis, Open University.

SOME POINTS FOR FURTHER CONSIDERATION

- What is your experience of evaluation?
- What value does evaluation have in pastoral theology and pastoral care?
- What sort of evaluation might be appropriate in trying to assess the worth of pastoral theology?
- What sort of evaluation might be appropriate in trying to assess the value of pastoral care?
- In the case of both pastoral theology and pastoral care, whose interests and values should be taken into account, and how?
- What theological ideas and principles might form a basis for the structure and content of evaluation in pastoral care and pastoral theology?
- How would you go about evaluating your course in pastoral theology?

FOR FURTHER READING AND EXPLORATION

Various techniques of evaluation together with a checklist are to be found in Katz and Peberdy (1997). Their approach depends on first having established aims and objectives against which things can be evaluated. This book is useful in giving a succinct account of evaluation techniques in health and social care. They expand on notions like the reasons for undertaking evaluation, as well as giving a list of techniques. However, we suggest that it is read in the light of the concerns and questions highlighted above.

For an up-to-date exploration of research methods from a theological perspective, see Van de Creek, Bender and Jordan (1994).

23

Pastoral Care as Performance

David Lyall

Introduction

David Lyall is a Scottish Presbyterian minister who has taught practical theology at the University of Edinburgh for many years. Prior to becoming a full-time teacher, Lyall was a hospital chaplain who supervised pastoral placements, having experienced the methods of Clinical Pastoral Education in the USA. He is one of the few people in Britain to have attempted an empirical evaluation of the effect of pastoral theological education upon students. David Lyall has written widely and influentially upon pastoral theological education, pastoral counseling, and supervision.

In the specially commissioned article included here, David Lyall argues for a broad framework of evaluation for pastoral theology that reflects the nature of pastoral care as a creative art, rather than exact science. Drawing upon his own research and experience, he reflects upon the extent to which pastoral education and pastoral theology affect the practice of ministry. In quantitative research conducted some years ago, he found that the attitudes and skills of students were affected – in unexpected ways – by pastoral theological education. Subsequently, Lyall has come to think that more qualitative research methods of evaluation might be more useful in helping to understand what happens to particular individuals as they experience this kind of education.

Lyall goes on to suggest that students and teachers have important, but different expectations of what pastoral education should achieve. Students often want to acquire relevant knowledge and skills for ministry. Educators may want them to acquire the ability to use supervision, to learn how to tolerate ambiguity and ambivalence and how to practice pastoral care as an art form that awakens the imagination and evokes an awareness of new possibilities. This combination of expectations, together with leaving open the possibility for unexpected discoveries, makes it very difficult fully and appropriately to evaluate pastoral theology and pastoral theological education.

That is not to say that such evaluation should not be undertaken, however. If, in fact, pastoral theology does not meet anyone's needs or expectations, there must be an argument that it should cease or radically change its nature and methods. Lyall leaves open an important question with which he began and which lies at the center of practical theology: Does pastoral or practical theology actually in any way help to transform or improve ministry and pastoral practice?

PASTORAL CARE AS PERFORMANCE

The past thirty years have seen an enormous growth in the discipline of pastoral studies, of which this volume is one tangible expression. When I was a divinity student at Edinburgh University in the early 1960s, 'Practical Theology' was not examinable as part of the BD degree. Rather, a wise and experienced professor told those of us who would be ministers what he considered we needed to know in order to perform acceptably as servants of those congregations which would be entrusted to our care. Since then a 'new' discipline of practical theology has been born, generated from the intercourse of theology and the social sciences, the story of which is told in earlier chapters of this volume. The outcome has been a more rigorous approach to the training of women and men for pastoral ministry. It is difficult to train for ministry now without encountering the major insights of psychology and sociology, supervised placements both in-role and out-of-role are *de rigueur* and everybody knows that theological reflection is important (even if they are not quite sure how to do it).

The unexamined assumption behind all this activity is of course that we now have a more effective way of doing things, that we now produce a better class of minister (ordained or lay), more knowledgeable, more sensitive, more perceptive, more skilled in the pastoral arts. But can we be sure about this? It was this question which I thought I was being asked to explore when one of the Editors wrote and asked whether I might appreciate the opportunity to reflect critically about the extent to which doing pastoral theology courses in the UK shapes the practice of ministry. My first reaction was that this seemed a vast project, more appropriate for a doctoral thesis than a 3,000-word paper. I began to think about what might be involved in such a project – contacting a cross-section of those who had trained under the new dispensation in practical and pastoral theology, designing a questionnaire or conducting interviews to see what they thought now of their training. Maybe it would be possible to interview members of their congregations – now *that* would be revealing! Was there a control group (I wondered) who had trained under the old regime? What if the method of training made not a blind bit of difference or, even worse – is there such a thing as value-free research? – what if the old-fashioned ministers were regarded as 'better' pastors? It was obvious, of course, that such a huge project was not what was wanted, though it must be recognized that these questions are still unanswered in what is still the adolescence, if not the infancy, of pastoral studies and that there are some interesting research projects awaiting the next generation of practical theologians.

My own doctoral research, now twenty years old, attempted to investigate the effect of training on Divinity students, though now with hindsight I am much more critical of the methods I then used. I investigated the impact of the courses being offered in Edinburgh upon the attitudes and skills of students participating in them.[1] Alastair Campbell was teaching the academic component and three of us, hospital chaplains associated with the university department, were offering various kinds of hospital experience. The impact of two kinds of courses was explored. First, for years there had been a week-long Easter vacation conference for the first-year students. Reactions to this often seemed a bit 'over the top'. 'This has been the greatest week of my life'. (What had they been doing with the rest of their lives?) So a questionnaire was devised to measure attitude-change on four dimensions. These were attitudes to (a) hospitals, (b) ethical issues, (c) ministry, and (d) psychiatry. The analysis was statistical and the results at first disappointing. Taking the group as a whole there was not one single statistically significant change on any of the 40 items in the questionnaire. So what was all the fuss about? I had also, however, used with the students an attitude inventory which categorized them according to their conscious motivation for entering ministry. Was it predominantly pastoral, or predominantly evangelistic? As it happened, the class split along these lines into two groups of twelve – a researcher's dream. When the results of the attitude change were measured for these two groups separately, the results were dramatic. Both groups changed in statistically significant ways, but in totally different directions. The 'pastoral' students became (even) more liberal and the 'evangelistic' students became (even) more conservative.

The second part of my research consisted in measuring the counselling profiles of the students at the beginning and end of an academic year in which they attended an academic class on Pastoral Care and Counselling and undertook a supervised hospital placement. The bottom (statistically significant) line was that we taught the students to say 'Mmmh' instead of incessantly asking questions – a not inconsiderable contribution to pastoral ministry.[2] While these results were of some interest, I have more questions to ask of them now than twenty years ago. As early as 1973, James Dittes of Yale Divinity School had questioned the value of this kind of research in pastoral care.[3] He argued that in pastoral research, still in its adolescence, there was an inherent tension between reliability and relevance.

> ... (the) identity of reliable servanthood is not easily obtained by any adolescent. Research is no exception. ... When its pitiful pretensions run most rampant, research gives us a lot of reliable information – usually with elaborate icon-like tables of data and sophisticated statistical analysis – that is not recognizably useful to any important pastoral concerns, or relevant to any other significant questions.

In view of the fact that I had studied under Dittes and respected his judgement, I am surprised now that I did not then take on board what he was saying. But that was the culture of hospital-based research at the time, and in a previous incarnation I had been a scientist, so the seduction of statistically significant numbers is perhaps at least understandable. In recent years, there has been a significant development in qualitative research methods in pastoral research as opposed to the quantitative approach described above. This is to be welcomed. While there is certainly a value in measuring changes within groups of people, to be able to track what is happening in the lives of individuals is surely more congruent with the nature of pastoral care itself as well as providing us with the kind of information we need to improve our pastoral training. It is interesting to note that students of an evangelistic disposition became more conservative as a result of exposure to the hospital, that the conservative students were even more opposed at the end of the course than at the beginning to the idea that 'Alcoholism is more of an illness than a sin'. That is not, however, the end of this story. Two years later the research was repeated with another cohort of students. On that occasion, a leading and much respected evangelical minister took part in the course and spoke warmly of the work of the Alcohol Problems Unit. That year the students *as a whole* moved towards regarding alcoholism as an illness! Such information, valuable as it is, does not, however, tell us what is happening in the case of any particular student. It is only the more qualitative methods of research which will help us to access this information. It is when individuals are allowed to tell their stories that deep truth is expressed; it is often in the particularity of a personal story that we find an expression of a reality which resonates most authentically and generally.

What stories do we imagine would be told by those who have undertaken courses in pastoral theology? It is always worthwhile, perhaps even necessary, to explore the expectations of those who set out on a course in pastoral studies. Sometimes these expectations can be affirmed and sometimes they must be gently challenged. Those who teach pastoral studies may also have expectations of the course which it will be difficult to share with those set out on the pilgrimage of learning for there are some things which cannot be described in advance but only identified in their discovery.

Common Expectations

Among the common expectations which students bring to a course in pastoral studies are the acquisition of (a) knowledge and (b) skills.

Acquiring knowledge

It must be recognized that it is not unreasonable that one will know more at the end of any course than at the beginning. The problem is that the knowledge base for pastoral ministry is large and expanding. Human growth and development, the psychology of religion, the sociology of religion, models for relating theology and pastoral practice, studies in Christian spirituality – all of these (and more) can stake a claim for their inclusion in the knowledge base necessary for good pastoral practice. Few courses can include everything, and individual teachers will decide what is appropriate for their own courses. But knowledge base there must be. While 'learning from experience' is an important feature of pastoral education there must also be a conceptual framework within which experience can be located and reflected upon. The danger is of course that 'knowledge' becomes not a framework for reflection but a straitjacket within which experience must be contained. If, however, students are introduced at an early stage to an 'action-reflection' model of learning this danger can be minimized. As we shall see later, students in this field (as in many others) must also come to live with the reality of 'not knowing'.

Learning skills

Students also bring to courses in pastoral studies the expectation that they will learn new skills, sometimes in the area of counselling. The acquisition of new skills is not an unreasonable expectation but we must be quite clear about what is on offer. The significant expansion of pastoral studies over the past thirty years has paralleled, and sometimes been linked with, the phenomenal expansion of the counselling movement. Indeed both national and international organizations have been set up for the promotion of 'pastoral care and counselling'. It must be recognized, however, that most institutions in the business of teaching pastoral studies do not teach 'counselling' as such, and certainly not to the extent of offering a qualification in counselling. Perhaps the time has come for pastoral care to redefine its relationship with counselling. I offer this suggestion for a number of reasons. First, the expansion of counselling has been accompanied by courses of widely different standards. We cannot compete with the best of them (not least because that is not our main aim); we should not seek to be identified with the worst of them. More fundamentally, however, we need to affirm the value of pastoral care in its own right, a helping relationship rooted within the historic diaconal ministry of the church.

This does not mean that there is nothing that pastoral care can learn from the modern counselling movement, quite the contrary. Counselling *skills* must be an integral part of training for pastoral care. Learning how to listen is fundamental; a basic awareness of the reality of transference and countertransference will greatly enhance pastoral ministry (and prevent some disasters); and good supervision should be integral to all pastoral education. There are, however, some significant differences between counselling and pastoral care. First, pastoral care is usually far less structured with contracts implicit rather than explicit. Second, boundaries are far less secure, a fact which can cause anxiety for some counsellors but is a reality which ministers must simply learn to manage. Finally, it must be recognized that pastoral care takes place within a context of beliefs and values, individual and communal, held in differing degrees by carer and cared for, a recognition of which state of affairs seems to be anathema to many counsellors. It is no part of pastoral care for the carers to impose their own beliefs and values upon those whom they seek to help; it is of the very stuff of pastoral care to recognize and explore beliefs and values, for therein may lie both the source of pain and the resource for healing.

Unexpected Discoveries

A student undertaking a course in pastoral studies will have some of his expectation fulfilled at least in part. It may also be, however, that there will be other benefits and unexpected insights which because they can only be appreciated retrospectively are difficult to describe in advance. Among these might be: (a) the ability to use supervision; (b) the ability to live with ambivalence and ambiguity; and (c) the ability to practise pastoral care as an art form.

Learning to use supervision

Most students do not look forward to their first experience of supervision. The word carries so many negative connotations. It smacks of someone looking over your shoulder, of having your inadequacies exposed, of being found out. It is worse than the thought of failing a written examination. There can be reasons for failing an exam, not that you are personally inadequate, but that the 'wrong' questions came up, or that you did not have time to do all the required work. Supervision is different, or at least imagined to be different. It is not your lack of knowledge which is being exposed but your personal inadequacies – and precisely at that point where you have the heaviest personal investment, namely, in learning to be a minister or a pastor. Such anxieties must be taken seriously at the beginning of the supervisory relationship, for the gift of the initial experience of supervision is the appreciation of its value for continuing ministry. This means that learners should come to experience supervision as essentially affirmative of their skills and their personhood. Feedback, both positive and negative, there will assuredly be but negative criticism will only be heard in the context of a safe relationship. Coming to an awareness of 'mistakes' must not be seen as a threat to the very personhood of the learner, but as an opportunity for learning. The rewards of good supervision are rich. They include growing self-awareness and self-confidence, the freedom genuinely to 'learn from experience' and, in theological terms, having experienced grace in the supervisory relationship to be able to mediate that grace in the pastoral relationship. All of these gains, rooted in a good supervisory experience, are fundamental to the two points which follow.

Tolerating ambiguity and ambivalence

We have already noted the legitimate expectation that those who set out on a course in pastoral studies will be provided with an adequate knowledge base. This is not the same as satisfying an illegitimate expectation that they will be provided with an answer for every human dilemma. Sometimes in general conversation people say that they could never become counsellors or pastors because they 'wouldn't know what to say'. This is an anxiety, sometimes unexpressed but nevertheless real, which learners may bring to the study of pastoral theology. The reasons why there are 'no answers' are of course varied. Sometimes situations are of such ethical complexity that there is no obvious right thing to do; sometimes life is so tragic that there is nothing to be said which will 'make things better'; usually (and this much pastoral care can learn from counselling) there are good reasons why pastors should not seek to provide answers. To learn to live with ambiguity and ambivalence, to be able to experience the apparent absence of God in the face of the tragedies of life, to have no answers *and not to be overwhelmed with anxiety about this state of affairs*, is one of the positive outcomes of a course in pastoral studies. For it is often when men are struck dumb that God speaks the enlightening word, the way forward becomes clear, grace breaks through. While supervision cannot be programmed to provide this kind of experience for the learner, it is as the supervisory process is able to model this experience amidst the mutual 'not-knowing' of supervisor and learner that the toleration of ignorance becomes an enabling grace.

Practising pastoral care as an art form

If the ability to tolerate not having answers is one positive outcome of a course in pastoral studies, a complementary one is to know how to be proactive in the care of others. There is a right and proper professionalism that needs to be developed in pastoral care, independent of whether or not the carer is either paid or ordained. It consists of a willingness to take calculated risks on behalf of those for whom one has some pastoral responsibility. This is not a lack of care stemming from ignorance but care based on a realistic appraisal of what one knows and does not know. It is not a care independent of either knowledge base or acquired skills but a care which builds upon knowledge and skill – and then goes beyond them. It is a way of doing pastoral care which makes creative use of the imagination, thinking oneself into the situation of those cared for and envisaging new possibilities for the future. It is pastoral care as performance, pastoral care as creative art form. It is a care rooted in the personal and pastoral identity of the carer: an identity which is shaped by supervision. Brian Thorne, a leading exponent of person-centred counselling who has also written of the spiritual dimension of counselling speaks of the need to be 'sensitive to those moments in therapy when prose gives way to poetry'.[4] The same is true of pastoral care at its best. Like good poetry it awakens the imagination and evokes an awareness of new possibilities, of seeing things differently. Fortunate is the prospective student who sets out on a course of pastoral studies and reaches the next stage on the journey filled with new knowledge and having acquired new skills. Even more blessed are those who can live with what they do not know and yet are enabled to reach out in imaginative pastoral care to others.

NOTES

1 Lyall, D., 'Theological education in a clinical setting'. Unpublished PhD thesis, Edinburgh University, 1979.
2 For a more detailed description of this research, see Lyall, D., 'Theological education in a clinical setting', *Contact* 65, 4: 11–17.
3 Dittes, J. E., 'A symposium on pastoral research', *Journal of Pastoral Care* 27, 4: 253–8.
4 Thorne, B., *Beyond the Core Conditions: Person-Centred Counselling – Therapeutic and Spiritual Dimensions*, London: Whurr: 83 (1991).

SOME POINTS FOR FURTHER CONSIDERATION

- What are the advantages and disadvantages of thinking of pastoral care as an "art form"?
- Does constituting pastoral care as an "art form" place it beyond effective evaluation of any kind?
- What questions, methods, and assumptions should inform an evaluation of pastoral theology as an educational experience?

- What might be the questions, methods, and assumptions that could be used in evaluating the activity of pastoral care?
- Does practical theological study and education make any real desired difference to people's lives, thinking, practice, and action? Should it make any difference?

FOR FURTHER EXPLORATION AND READING

Surprisingly little has been written by way of specifically evaluating the worth and effects of pastoral theology, pastoral theological education, and pastoral care. No major textbook on pastoral care or pastoral theology even indexes "evaluation," though clearly works on theological reflection, supervision, and appraisal do imply quite a strong element of evaluation. See, e.g., Patton (1990), Jacobs (1989). For more on Lyall's own research, see Lyall (1979a) and (1979b). Lyall's writing on supervision is to be found in Foskett and Lyall (1988), while his work in pastoral counseling can be consulted in Lyall (1995).

Bibliography

Ackermann, D. M. and Bons-Storm, R. (eds) (1998), *Liberating Faith Practices: Feminist Practical Theologies in Context*, Leuven: Peeters.

Aden, Le Roy and Ellens, Harold J. (eds) (1990), *Turning Points in Pastoral Care*, Grand Rapids, Mich.: Baker Books House.

Alvesson, M. and Willmott, H. (1996), *Making Sense of Management*, London: Sage.

Anderson, H. (1997), "Spirituality and Supervision: a Complex but Necessary Connection," *Journal of Supervision and Training in Ministry*, 18, 1–6.

Asguith, Glen Jr. (1992), *Vision from a Little-Known Country: A Boisen Reader*, Decatur, Ga.: Journal of Pastoral Care Publications.

Atkinson, D. and Field, D. (eds) (1995), *A New Dictionary of Christian Ethics and Pastoral Theology*, Leicester: Inter-Varsity Press.

Audinet, J. (1995), *Ecrits de théologie pratigue*, Ottawa, Canada: Novalis.

Augsburger, D. (1986), *Pastoral Counselling across Cultures*, Philadelphia, Pa.: Westminster Press.

Ballard, P. (ed.) (1986), *The Foundations of Pastoral Studies and Practical Theology*, Cardiff: HOLI.

Ballard, P. and Pritchard, J. (1996), *Practical Theology in Action: Christian Thinking in the Service of Church and Society*, London: SPCK.

Banks, R. and Powell, K. (eds) (in press), *The Role and Practice of Faith in Leadership*, San Francisco, Cal.: Jossey-Bass.

Barnett, R. (1994), *The Limits of Competence*, Buckingham: Open University Press.

Basch, M. F. (1980), *Doing Psychotherapy*, New York: Basic Books.

Bass, D. C. (ed.) (1997), *Practicing our Faith: A Way of Life for Searching People*, San Francisco, Cal.: Jossey-Bass.

Bauman, Z. (1989), *Modernity and the Holocaust*, Cambridge: Polity.

Beckford, R. (1998), *Jesus is Dread*, London: Darton, Longman & Todd.

Benhabib, S. (1992), *Situating the Self: Gender, Community and Postmodernism in Contemporary Ethics*, Cambridge: Polity.

Berger, P. L. (1969), *A Rumor of Angels*, Garden City, N.Y.: Doubleday.

Berger, P. L. (1992), *A Far Glory: The Quest for Faith in an Age of Credulity*, Garden City, N.Y.: Doubleday.

Bernstein, R. J. (1985), *Habermas and Modernity*, Cambridge: Cambridge University Press.

Bhaskar, R. (1989), *Reclaiming Reality: A Critical Introduction to Contemporary Philosophy*, London: Verso.

Bhugra, Dinesh (ed.) (1996), *Psychiatry and Religion*, London: Routledge.

Biggar, N. (1998), "Should Pastoral Theology Become Postmodernist?," *Contact*, 126: 22–7.

Boisen, A. (1990), in Hunter (1990).

Bons-Storm, R. (1996), *The Incredible Woman: Listening to Women's Silences in Pastoral Care and Counseling*, Nashville, Tenn.: Abingdon.

Bourdieu, P. (1992), *The Logic of Practice*, Cambridge: Polity Press.

Bradbury, N. (1989), *City of God? Pastoral Care in the Inner City*, London: SPCK.

Brown, P. (1990), *The Body and Society*, London: Collins.

Browning, D. S. (1966), *Atonement and Psychotherapy*, Philadelphia, Penn.: Westminster.

Browning, D. S. (1976), *The Moral Context of Pastoral Care*, Philadelphia, Penn.: Westminster.

Browning, D. S. (1983), *Religious Ethics and Pastoral Care*, Philadelphia, Penn.: Fortress Press.

Browning, D. S. (ed.) (1983), *Practical Theology*, San Francisco, Cal.: Harper & Row.

Browning, D. S. (1991), *A Fundamental Practical Theology: Descriptive and Strategic Proposals*, Minneapolis, Minn.: Fortress Press.

Browning, D. S., Miller-McLemore, Bonnie J., Couture, P., Lyon, B. and Franklin, R. (1997), *From Culture Wars to Common Ground: Religion and the American Family Debate*, Louisville, Ky.: Westminster/John Knox Press.

Bryman, A. and Burgess, R. (eds) (1994), *Analyzing Qualitative Data*, London: Routledge.

Burkhart, J. E. (1983), "Schleiermacher's Vision for Theology", in D. S. Browning (ed.), *Practical Theology: The Emerging Field in Theology, Church, and World*, San Francisco, Cal.: Harper & Row.

Butler, J. (1990), *Gender Trouble: Feminism and the Subversion of Identity*, London: Routledge.

Butler, T. and Butler, B. (1996), *Just Spirituality in a World Faiths*, London: Mowbray.

Callahan, D. (1970), *Abortion: Law, Choice and Morality*, New York: Macmillan.

Campbell, A. (1985), *Paid to Care?*, London: SPCK.

Campbell, A. (1986), *Rediscovering Pastoral Care*, London: Darton, Longman & Todd; 2nd edn 1987.

Campbell, A. (ed.) (1987), *A Dictionary of Pastoral Care*, London: SPCK.
Capps, D. (1984), *Pastoral Care and Hermeneutics*, Philadephia, Penn.: Fortress Press.
Capps, D. (1990), *Reframing*, Minneapolis, Minn.: Fortress Press.
Capps, D. (1993), *The Poet's Gift*, Louisville, Ky.: Westminster/John Knox Press.
Capra, F. (1982), *The Tao of Physics*, London: Flamingo.
Capra, F. (1983), *The Turning Point*, London: HarperCollins.
Capra, F. (1989), *Uncommon Wisdom*, London: Flamingo.
Carr, W. (1997), *Handbook of Pastoral Studies*, London: SPCK.
Chodorow, N. (1974), "Family Structure and Feminine Personality," in R. Zimbalist and L. Lamphere (eds), *Women Culture and Society*, Stanford, Cal.: Stanford University Press.
Chodorow, N. (1978), *The Reproduction of Mothering*, Berkeley, Cal.: University of California Press.
Chodorow, N. (1989), *Feminism and Psychoanalytic Theory*, New Haven, Conn.: Yale University Press.
Chopp, R. S. (1997), "Latin American Liberation Theology," in D. Ford (ed.), *The Modern Theologians*, Oxford: Blackwell.
Christ, C. P. (1988), "Embodied Thinking: Reflections on Feminist Theological Method," *Journal of Feminist Studies in Religion*, 5(1): 7–15.
Clare, A. (1980), *Psychiatry in Dissent*, London: Tavistock.
Clarke, P. B. and Linzey, A. (eds) (1996), *Dictionary of Ethics, Theology and Society*, London: Routledge.
Clebsch, W. and Jaekle, C. (1983), *Pastoral Care in Historical Perspective*, 2nd edn, New York: Aronson.
Clinebell, H. (1984), *Basic Types of Pastoral Care and Counselling*, London: SCM Press; Nashville, Tenn.: Abingdon Press.
Cobb, M. and Robshaw, V. (eds) (1998), *The Spiritual Challenge of Health Care*, Edinburgh: Churchill Livingstone.
College of Health Care Chaplains (1993), *Health Care Chaplaincy Standards*, London: Hospital Chaplaincies Council.
Conn, J. W. (ed.) (1996), *Women's Spirituality: Resources for Christian Development*, 2nd edn, New York/Mahwah, N.J.: Paulist Press.
Connell, R. W. (1987), *Gender and Power*, Cambridge: Polity.
Cooper-White, P. (1994), *The Cry of Tamar: Violence against Women and the Church's Response*, Minneapolis, Minn.: Fortress Press.
Cousins, E. H. (1992), *Christ of the 21st Century*, Rockport, Mass.: Element.
Couture, P. D. (1991), *Blessed are the Poor? Women's Poverty, Family Policy and Practical Theology*, Nashville, Tenn.: Abingdon Press.
Couture, P. D. and Hunter, R. (eds) (1995), *Pastoral Care and Social Conflict*, Nashville, Tenn.: Abingdon Press.
Culbertson, P. L. (1994), *Counseling Men*, Minneapolis, Minn.: Fortress.

Cupitt, D. (1994), *After All: Religion without Alienation*, London: SCM Press.

Davie, G. (1994), *Religion in Britain since 1945: Believing without Belonging*, Oxford: Blackwell.

Davies, J. G. (1973), *Every Day God*, London: SCM Press.

Davies, P. (1990), *God and the New Physics*, Harmondsworth: Penguin.

Davis, C. (1994), *Religion and the Making of Society*, Cambridge: Cambridge University Press.

Day Williams, D. (1961), *The Minister and the Cure of Souls*, New York: Harper & Brothers.

De Marinis, V. M. (1993), *Critical Caring: A Feminist Model for Pastoral Psychology*, Lousville, Tenn.: Westminster.

Deeks, D. (1987), *Pastoral Theology: An Enquiry*, London: Epworth.

Demos Quarterly (1997), "Keeping the Faiths: the New Covenant between Religious Belief and Secular Power," no. 11 (November).

Dittes, J. E. (1973), "A Symposium on Pastoral Research," *Journal of Pastoral Care*, XXVII: 4, 253–8.

Doehring, C. (1992), "Developing Models of Feminist Pastoral Counselling," *Journal of Pastoral Care*, 46(1) (Spring) 23–31.

Downey, M. (1997), *Understanding Christian Spirituality*, New York/Mahway, N.J.: Paulist Press.

Drucker, P. (1974), *Management: Tasks, Responsibilities, Practices*, Oxford: Butterworth Heinemann.

Duffy, R. (1983), *A Roman Catholic Theology of Pastoral Care*, Philadelphia, Penn.: Fortress Press.

Dulles, A. (1976), *Models of the Church*, New York: Doubleday.

Dunbar, H. F. (1947), *Mind and Body: Psychosomatic Medicine*, New York: Random House.

Dunker, P. (1996), *Hallucinating Foucault*, London: Picador.

Dunlap, S. J. (1997), *Counseling Depressed Women*, Louisville, Ky.: Westminster/John Knox Press.

Dupré, L. (1979), *The Other Dimension: A Search for the Meaning of Religious Attitudes*, New York: Seabury Press.

Durkheim, E. (1915), *The Elementary Forms of the Religious Life*, London: Allen & Unwin.

Dwyer, J. (ed.) (1994), *The New Dictionary of Catholic Social Thought*, New York, N.Y.: Michael Glazier.

Dyson, A. (1977), "Pastoral Theology – Towards a New Discipline," *Contact*, 78, 2–8.

Ecclestone, E. (ed.) (1988), *The Parish Church?*, Oxford: Grubb Institute/Mowbray.

Ehrenreich, B. and English, D. (1978), *For Her Own Good: 150 Years of the Experts' Advice to Women*, New York: Doubleday.

Etzioni, A. (1995), *New Communitarian Thinking*, Charlottesville, Va.: University Press of Virginia.

Farley, E. (1983a), "Practical Theology: the Emerging Field in Theology, Church and World," in D. S. Browning (ed.), *Theology and Practice outside the Clerical Paradigm*, New York: Harper and Row, pp. 21–41.

Farley, E. (1983b), *Theologia: Fragmentation and Unity in Theological Education*, Philadelphia, Penn.: Fortress Press.

Farley, E. (1996), *Deep Symbols: Their Postmodern Effacement*, Minneapolis, Minn.: Fortress Press.

Fiorenza, E. Schüssler (1995), *In Memory of Her: A Feminist Theological Reconstruction of Christian Origins*, New York: Crossroad.

Flax, J. (1990), *Thinking Fragments: Psychoanalysis, Feminism, and Postmodernism in the Contemporary West*, Berkeley, Cal.: University of California Press.

Flax, J. (1993), *Disputed Subjects: Essays on Psychoanalysis, Politics and Philosophy*, London: Routledge.

Forrester, D. (ed.) (1990), *Theology and Practice*, London: Epworth.

Forrester, D. (1997), *Christian Justice and Public Policy*, Cambridge: Cambridge University Press.

Forward, M. (ed.) (1995), *Ultimate Visions*, Oxford: Oneworld.

Foskett, J. (1984), *Meaning in Madness*, London: SPCK.

Foskett, J. and Lyall, D. (1988), *Helping the Helpers: Supervision and Pastoral Care*, London: SPCK.

Foucault, M. (1967), *Madness and Civilisation*, London: Tavistock.

Fowler, J. (1996), *Faithful Change: The Personal and Public Challenges of Postmodern Life*, Nashville, Tenn.: Abingdon Press.

Frazer, E., Hornsby, J. and Lovibond, S. (eds) (1992), *Ethics: A Feminist Reader*, Oxford: Blackwell.

Freud, S. (1953 [1905]), *Three Essays on the Theory of Sexuality*, in *The Standard Edition*, English trans. and ed. James Strachey, vol. 7, London: Hogarth Press.

Freud, S. (1953 [1931]), *Female Sexuality*, in *The Standard Edition*, English trans. and ed. James Strachey, vol. 21, London: Hogarth Press.

Fuchs, J. (1987), *Christian Morality: The World Becomes Flesh*, Dublin: Gill & Macmillan.

Furniss, G. (1994), *Sociology for Pastoral Care*, London: SPCK.

Gallagher, M. P., SJ (1997), *Clashing Symbols – An Introduction to Faith and Culture*, London: Darton, Longman & Todd.

Gay, P. (1973), *The Enlightenment: An Interpretation*, vol. 1: *The Rise of Modern Paganism*, London: Wildwood House.

Gendlin, E. T. (1962), *Experiencing and the Creation of Meaning*, Toronto: Free Press of Glencoe.

Gendlin, E. T. (1981), *Focusing*, rev. edn, New York: Bantam Press.

Gerkin, C. (1987), *The Living Human Document*, Nashville, Tenn.: Abingdon Press.

Gerkin, C. (1991), *Prophetic Pastoral Practice*, Nashville, Tenn.: Abingdon Press.

Gerkin, C. (1997), *An Introduction to Pastoral Care*, Nashville, Tenn.: Abingdon Press.

Gersie, A. (1997), *Reflections on Therapeutic Storymaking*, London: Jessica Kingsley.

Giddens, A. (1991), *Modernity and Self-Identity*, Cambridge: Polity Press.

Giddens, A. (1993), *Sociology*, Cambridge: Polity Press.

Gill, M. (1982), *Analysis of Transference*, vol. 1, New York: International Universities Press.

Gill, R. (1985), *A Textbook of Christian Ethics*, Edinburgh: T. & T. Clark.

Gill, R. (1988), *Beyond Decline*, London: SCM Press.

Gill, R. (1989), *The Myth of the Empty Church*, London: SPCK.

Gill, R. (1993), *Competing Convictions*, London: SCM Press.

Gill, R. (ed.) (1996), *Theology and Sociology: A Reader*, London: Cassell.

Gill, R. and Burke, D. (1996), *Strategic Church Leadership*, London: SPCK.

Gill-Austern, B. (1997), "Responding to a Culture Ravenous for Soul Food," *The Journal of Pastoral Theology*, 7 (Summer) 63–79.

Gilligan, C. (1982), *In a Different Voice: Psychological Theory and Women's Development*, Cambridge, Mass.: Harvard University Press.

Glaz, M. and Moessner, J. S. (eds) (1991), *Women in Travail and Transition: A New Pastoral Care*, Minneapolis, Minn.: Fortress Press.

Goodliff, P. (1998), *Care in a Confused Climate: Pastoral Care and Postmodernist Culture*, London: Darton, Longman & Todd.

Graham, E. (1995), *Making the Difference: Gender, Personhood and Theology*, London: Mowbray.

Graham, E. (1996), *Transforming Practice*, London: Mowbray.

Graham, E. and Halsey, M. (eds) (1993), *Life Cycles: Women and Pastoral Care*, London: SPCK.

Graham, L. K. (1992), *Care of Persons, Care of Worlds*, Nashville, Tenn.: Abingdon.

Green, L. (1987), *Let's do Theology*, London: Mowbray.

Green, L. (1988), *Power to the Powerless*, Basingstoke: Marshall, Morgan and Scott.

Greenspan, M. (1983), *A New Approach to Women and Therapy*, New York: McGraw-Hill.

Greider, K. J. (1997), *Reckoning with Aggression: Theology, Violence and Vitality*, Louisville, Ky.: Westminster/John Knox Press.

Griffiths, P. J. (1990), *Christianity through Non-Christian Eyes*, Maryknoll, N.Y.: Orbis.

Grint, K. (1995), *Management: A Sociological Introduction*, Cambridge: Polity Press.

Grisez, G. (1970), *Abortion: The Myths, the Realities and the Arguments*, New York: Corpus Books.

Gutiérrez, G. (1974), "Liberation, Theology and Proclamation," *Concilium*, 6, 57–77.

Gutiérrez, G. (1988), *A Theology of Liberation*, 2nd edn, Maryknoll, N.Y.: Orbis.

Habermas, J. (1971), *Knowledge and Human Interests*, Boston, Mass.: Beacon Press.

Habermas, J. (1984), *The Theory of Communicative Action*, vol. 1: *Rationality and Rationalization*, trans. T. McCarthy, Boston, Mass.: Beacon Press.

Habermas, J. (1989), *The Theory of Communicative Action*, vol. 2: *Lifeworld and System: The Critique of Functionalist Reason*, trans. T. McCarthy, Boston, Mass.: Beacon Press.

Hall, S. and Gieben, B. (eds) (1992), *Formations of Modernity*, Cambridge: Polity.

Hall, S., Held, D. and McGraw, T. (eds) (1992), *Modernity and its Futures*, Cambridge: Polity.

Halmos, P. (1965), *The Faith of Counsellors*, London: Constable.

Hamilton, M. (1996), *The Sociology of Religion: Theoretical and Comparative Perspectives*, London: Routledge.

Handy, C. (1996), *Beyond Certainty*, London: Arrow Books.

Hanson, N. R. (1969), *Perception and Discovery: An Introduction to Scientific Inquiry*, San Francisco, Cal.: Freeman, Cooper.

Haraway, D. (1991), *Cyborgs, Simians and Women: The Reinvention of Nature*, Cambridge: Polity.

Harding, S. (1986), *The Science Question in Feminism*, Milton Keynes: Open University Press.

Hardy, D. and Gunton, C. (eds) (1989), *On Being the Church*, Edinburgh: T. & T. Clark.

Harris, M. (1996), *Proclaim Jubilee! A Spirituality for the Twenty-First Century*, Louisville, Ky.: Westminster/John Knox Press.

Harvey, D. (1989), *The Condition of Postmodernity*, Oxford: Blackwell.

Harvey, N. P. (1985), *Death's Gift*, London: Epworth.

Harvey, N. P. (1991), *The Morals of Jesus*, London: Darton, Longman & Todd.

Haslam, D. (1996), *Race for the Millennium: A Challenge to Church and Society*, London: Church House Publishing.

Hauerwas, S. (1983), *The Peaceable Kingdom*, London: SCM Press.

Heim, S. M. (1995), *Salvations, Truth and Difference in Religion*, Maryknoll, N.Y.: Orbis.

Heim, S. M. (ed.) (1998), *Grounds for Understanding: Ecumenical Resources for Responses to Religious Pluralism*, Grand Rapids, Mich.: Eerdmans.

Hick, J. (1966), *Faith and Knowledge*, Ithaca, N.Y.: Cornell University Press.

Higginson, R. (1996), *Transforming Leadership*, London: SPCK.

Hiltner, S. (1958), *Preface to Pastoral Theology*, Nashville, Tenn.: Abingdon Press.

Hodgson, P. C. (1994), *Winds of the Spirit: A Constructive Christian Theology*, London: SCM Press.

Holifield, B. (1983), *The History of Pastoral Care in America*, Nashville, Tenn.: Abingdon Press.

Hooker, R. and Lamb, C. (1986), *Love the Stranger: Christian Ministry in Multi-Faith Areas*, London: SPCK.

hooks, bell (1984), *Feminist Theory: From Margin to Center*, Boston, Mass.: South End.

Hopewell, J. (1987), *Congregation: Story and Structure*, London: SCM Press.

Horney, K. (1967), *Feminine Psychology*, New York, N.Y.: W. W. Norton.

Horney, K. (1973), *Neurosis and Human Growth*, New York, N.Y.: W. W. Norton.

Houlden, L. (1985), *Connections*, London: SCM Press.

Huczynski, A. (1996), *Management Gurus*, London: International Thompson Business Press.

Hunter, R. (1990), "Wisdom and Practical Knowledge in Pastoral Care," in R. Hunter (ed.), *Dictionary of Pastoral Care and Counseling*, Nashville, Tenn.: Abingdon Press.

Hunter, R. (ed.) (1990), *Dictionary of Pastoral Care and Counselling*, Nashville, Tenn.: Abingdon Press.

Hunter, R. and Couture, P. (eds) (1995), *Pastoral Care and Social Conflict*, Nashville, Tenn.: Abingdon Press.

Jackendoff, R. (1994), *Patterns in the Mind: Language and Human Nature*, New York, N.Y.: Basic Books.

Jacobs, M. (1989), *Holding in Trust: The Appraisal of Ministry*, London: SPCK.

James, W. (1982), *The Varieties of Religious Experience: A Study in Human Nature*, New York, N.Y.: Penguin Books.

Jameson, F. (1991), *Postmodernism: Or the Cultural Logic of Late Capitalism*, London: Verso.

Jenkins, D. E. (1976), *The Contradiction of Christianity*, London: SCM Press.

Justes, E. J. (1985), "Women," in *Clinical Handbook of Pastoral Counselling*, ed. Robert J. Wicks and Richard D. Parsons, New York, N.Y.: Paulist.

Katz, R. (1985), *Pastoral Care and the Jewish Tradition*, Philadelphia, Penn.: Fortress Press.

Katz, J. and Peberdy, A. (eds) (1997), *Promoting Health: Knowledge and Practice*, London: Macmillan.

Kearney, R. (1994), *Modern Movements in European Philosophy: Phenomenology, Critical Theory, Structuralism*, 2nd edn, Manchester: Manchester University Press.

Kelly, K. T. (1996), *Divorce and Second Marriage*, London: Cassell.

Kierkegaard, Søren (1985), *Fear and Trembling*, Harmondsworth: Penguin.

King, M. L. (1964), *Strength to Love*, London: Hodder & Stoughton.

Kohlberg, L. (1971), "From Is to Ought," in T. Mischel (ed.), *Cognitive Development and Epistemology*, New York: Academic Press.

Kohut, H. (1971), *The Analysis of the Self*, New York: International Universities Press.

Kohut, H. (1984), *How Does Analysis Cure?*, ed. A. Goldberg, with collaboration of P. E. Stepansky, Chicago, Ill.: University of Chicago Press.

Kosslyn, S. M. and Koenig, O. (1992), *Wet Mind: The New Cognitive Neuroscience*, New York, N.Y.: Free Press.

Laing, R. D. (1968), *The Politics of Experience*, New York: Ballantine.

Laing, R. D. (1982), *The Voice of Experience*, New York, N.Y.: Pantheon; Harmondsworth: Penguin.

Lakeland, P. (1997), *Postmodernity: Christian Identity in a Fragmented Age*, Minneapolis, Minn.: Fortress.

Lambourne, R. A. (1963), *Community, Church and Healing*, London: Darton, Longman & Todd.

Lambourne, R. A. (1985), *Explorations in Health and Salvation*, ed. M. Wilson, Birmingham, UK: University of Birmingham, Institute for the Study of Worship and Religious Architecture.

Lapsley, J. N. (1972), *Salvation and Health: The Interlocking Processes of Life*, Philadelphia, Penn.: Westminster Press.

Lartey, E. (1987), *Pastoral Counselling in Inter-Cultural Perspective*, Berne: Peter Lang.

Lartey, E. (1997), *In Living Colour: An Intercultural Approach to Pastoral Care and Counselling*, London: Cassell.

Leadbeater, C. (1996), *The Self-Policing Society*, London: Demos.

Leech, K. (1977), *Soul Friend*, London: Darton, Longman & Todd.

Leech, K. (1980), *True Prayer*, London: Darton, Longman & Todd.

Leech, K. (1981), *The Social God*, London: Darton, Longman & Todd.

Leech, K. (1985), *True God*, London: Darton, Longman & Todd.

Leech, K. (1988), *Struggle in Babylon*, London: Sheldon Press.

Leech, K. (1997), *The Sky is Red*, London: Darton, Longman & Todd.

Lerman, H. (1986), *A Mote in Freud's Eye: From Psychoanalysis to the Psychology of Women*, New York: Springer.

Levant, R. and Pollack, W. (eds) (1995), *A New Psychology of Men*, New York: Basic Books.

Locke, R. (1996), *The Collapse of the American Management Mystique*, Oxford: Oxford University Press.

Lonergan, M. (1972), *Method in Theology*, New York: Herder and Herder.

Lyall, D. (1979a), "Theological Education in a Clinical Setting," *Contact*, 65(6), 11–17.

Lyall, D. (1979b), "Theological Education in a Clinical Setting," unpublished PhD thesis, University of Edinburgh.

Lyall, D. (1995), *Counselling in the Pastoral and Spiritual Context*, Milton Keynes: Open University Press.

Lyall, D. and Foskett, J. (1988), *Helping the Helpers: Supervision and Pastoral Care*, London: SPCK.

Lynch, G. (ed.) (in press), *Clinical Counselling in Pastoral Settings*, London: Routledge.

Lyotard, J. F. (1984), *The Postmodern Condition: A Report on Knowledge*, trans. G. Bennington and B. Massumi, Manchester: Manchester University Press.

O'Donovan, Oliver (1986), *Resurrection and Moral Order*, Exeter: Inter-Varsity Press.

MacIntyre, A. (1987), *After Virtue: A Study in Moral Theory*, 2nd edn, London: Duckworth.

MacNiven, D. (1993), *Creative Morality*, London: Routledge.

Macquarrie, J. and Childress, J. (eds) (1986), *A New Dictionary of Christian Ethics*, London: SCM Press.

McFadyen, A. (1991), *The Call to Personhood*, Cambridge: Cambridge University Press.

McLeod, J. (1997), *Narrative and Psychotherapy*, London: Sage.

McLeod, J. (1998), *An Introduction to Counselling*, 2nd edn, Milton Keynes: Open University Press.

McNeill, J. (1977), *A History of the Cure of Souls*, New York, N.Y.: Harper & Row.

Maas, R. and O'Donnell, G. (eds) (1990), *Spiritual Traditions for the Contemporary Church*, Nashville, Tenn.: Abingdon Press.

Maddox, R. L. (1990), "The Recovery of Theology as a Practical Discipline," *Theological Studies*, 51(4), pp. 650–72.

Mahoney, J. (1987), *The Making of Moral Theology*, Oxford: Oxford University Press.

Malony, H. N. and Spilka, B. (eds) (1991), *Religion in Psychodynamic Perspective*, New York, N.Y.: Oxford University Press.

Mandela, N. (1994), *Long Walk to Freedom*, London: Little, Brown.

Mead, L. (ed.) (1997), *The New Paternalism*, Washington, D.C.: Brookings Institution.

Milhaven, A. L. (ed.) (1991), *Sermons Seldom Heard: Women Proclaim their Lives*, New York, N.Y.: Crossroad.

Miller-McLemore, B. J. (1994), *Also a Mother: Work and Family as Theological Dilemma*, Nashville, Tenn.: Abingdon.

Miller-McLemore, B. J. and Anderson, B. (1995), "Pastoral Care and Gender." In *Pastoral Care and Social Conflict*, ed. P. D. Couture and R. Hunter, Nashville, Tenn.: Abingdon Press, pp. 99–113.

Miller-McLemore, B. J. (1998), "The Subject and Practice of Pastoral Theology as a Practical Theological Discipline: Pushing Past the Nagging Identity Crisis to the Poetics of Resistance," in Denise Ackermann and Riet Bons-Storm (eds), in *Liberating Faith Practices: Feminist Practical Theologies in Context*, Leuven: Peeters, pp. 175–98.

Miller-McLemore, B. J. and Gill-Austern, Brita (eds) (1999), *Feminist and Womanist Pastoral Theology*, Nashville, Tenn.: Abingdon Press.

Mintzberg, H. (1989), *Mintzberg on Management*, New York: Free Press.

Moessner, J. S. (ed.) (1996), *Through the Eyes of Women: Insights for Pastoral Care*, Philadelphia, Penn.: Westminster/John Knox Press.

Moltmann, J. (1974), *The Crucified God*, London: SCM Press.

Mulgan, G. (ed.) (1997), *Life after Politics: New Thinking for the 21st Century*, London: Fontana.

Murphy, N. and McClendon, J. W. (1989), "Distinguishing Modern and Postmodern Theologies," *Modern Theology*, 5(3), 191–214.

Needleman, J. (1982), *Consciousness and Tradition*, New York, N.Y.: Crossroads.

Nelson, J. (1992), *The Intimate Connection: Male Sexuality, Male Spirituality*, London: SPCK.

Nelson, J. (ed.) (1996), *Management and Ministry*, Norwich: Canterbury Press.

Neuger, C. C. (1992), "Feminist Pastoral Theology and Pastoral Counselling: a Work in Progress," *Journal of Pastoral Theology*, 2 (Summer), 35–157.

Neuger, C. C. (ed.) (1996), *The Arts of Ministry: Feminist–Womanist Approaches*, Louisville, Ky.: Westminster/John Knox Press.

Neuger, C. C. and Poling, J. (eds) (1997), *The Care of Men*, Nashville, Tenn.: Abingdon.

Nichols, D. (1989), *Deity and Domination*, London: Routledge.

Northcott, M. (1996), *The Environment and Christian Ethics*, Cambridge: Cambridge University Press.

Northcott, M. (1998), *Urban Theology: A Reader*, London: Cassell.

Nouwen, H. (1994), *The Wounded Healer*, London: Darton, Longman & Todd.

Oden, T. (1966), *Kerygma and Counselling*, Philadelphia, Penn.: Westminster Press.

Oden, T. (1983), *Pastoral Theology: Essentials of Ministry*, New York, N.Y.: HarperCollins.

Oden, T. (1984), *Care of Souls in the Classic Tradition*, Philadelphia, Penn.: Fortress Press.

Oden, T. (1989), *Pastoral Counsel*, New York, N.Y.: Crossroad.

Ogden, S. (1963), *The Reality of God*, New York, N.Y.: Harper & Row.

Oliver, G. (1991), *Counselling, Anarchy and the Kingdom of God*, Lingdale Papers no. 16, Oxford: Clinical Theology Association.

Ó Murchú, D. (1998), *Reclaiming Spirituality: A New Spiritual Framework for Today's World*, New York, N.Y.: Crossroad.

Pagels, E. (1982), *The Gnostic Gospels*, London: Penguin Books; New York, N.Y.: Random House (1979).

Palmer, P. (1990), *The Active Life: A Spirituality of Work, Creativity, and Caring*, San Francisco, Cal.: Harper & Row.

Parker, D. C. (1997), *The Living Text of the Gospels*, Cambridge: Cambridge University Press.

Pattison, S. (1983), "Pastoral Studies: Dustbin or Discipline?," *Contact*, 80, 22–6.

Pattison, S. (1986), "The Use of the Behavioural Sciences in Pastoral Studies," in P. Ballard (ed.), *The Foundations of Pastoral Studies and Practical Theology*, Cardiff: HOLI, pp. 85–97.

Pattison, S. (1989), *Alive and Kicking: Towards a Practical Theology of Illness and Healing*, London: SCM Press.

Pattison, S. (1993), *A Critique of Pastoral Care*, 2nd edn, London: SCM Press.

Pattison, S. (1996a), "Can We Speak of God in the Secular Academy?," in F. Young (ed.), *Dare We Speak of God in Public?*, London: Mowbray.

Pattison, S. (1996b), "Should Pastoral Care have Aims and Objectives?," *Contact*, 120, 26–34.

Pattison, S. (1997a), *Pastoral Care and Liberation Theology*, London: SPCK.

Pattison, S. (1997b), *The Faith of the Managers*, London: Cassell.

Pattison, S. (1998), "Questioning Values," *Health Care Analysis*, 6, 352–9.

Pattison, S. (in press), "Objections to Aims and Objectives," in Martyn Percy and Gillian Evans (eds), *Managing the Church*, Sheffield: Sheffield Academic Press.

Pattison, S. with Woodward, J. (1994), *A Vision of Pastoral Theology*, Edinburgh: Contact Pastoral.

Patton, J. (1985), *Is Human Forgiveness Possible?*, Nashville, Tenn.: Abingdon Press.

Patton, J. (1990), *From Ministry to Theology*, Nashville, Tenn.: Abingdon Press.

Patton, J. (1993), *Pastoral Care in Context*, Louisville, Ky.: Westminster/ John Knox Press.

Percy, M. and Evans, G. (eds) (in press), *Managing the Church*, Sheffield: Sheffield Academic Press.

Peters, T. (1989), *Thriving on Chaos*, London: Pan Books.

Plaskow, J. (1980), *Sex, Sin and Grace: Women's Experience and the Theologies of Reinhold Niebuhr and Paul Tillich*, Lanham, Md.: University Press of America.

Poling, J. (1991), *The Abuse of Power*, Nashville, Tenn.: Abingdon Press.

Principe, W. (1983), "Towards Defining Spirituality," *Sciences Religieuses/ Studies in Religion*, 12(2), 127–41.

Pryce, M. (1996), *Finding a Voice: Men, Women and the Community of the Church*, London: SCM Press.

Rahner, K. (1968), *Theology of Pastoral Action*, New York: Herder & Herder.

Ramsey, P. (1970), "Reference Points in Deciding about Abortion," in J. T. Noonan (ed.), *The Morality of Abortion*, Cambridge, Mass.: Harvard University Press, pp. 60–100.

Ratliff, B. (1997), "Spirituality and Discernment: A Call to Pastoral Theologians," *The Journal of Pastoral Theology*, 7 (Summer), 81–97.

Reader, J. (1997), *Beyond all Reason: The Limits of Post-Modern Theology*, Cardiff: Aureus.

Reed, B. (1978), *The Dynamics of Religion*, London: Darton, Longman and Todd.

Richardson, A. and Bowden, J. (eds) (1983), *A New Dictionary of Theology*, London: SCM Press.

Ritzer, G. (1996), *The McDonaldization of Society*, rev. edn, Thousand Oaks, Cal.: Pine Forge Press.

Robinson, J. A. T. (1963), *Honest to God*, London: SCM Press.

Rogers, C. (1951), *Client-Centred Therapy*, London: Constable.

Rogers, C. (1961), *On Becoming a Person*, London: Constable.

Rogers, C. (1980), *A Way of Being*, Boston, Mass.: Houghton Mifflin.

Rosenwald, G. and Ochberg, R. (eds) (1992), *Storied Lives*, New Haven, Conn.: Yale University Press.

Russell, A. (1980), *The Clerical Profession*, London: SPCK.

Russell, L. M. and Shannon Clarkson, J. (eds) (1996), *Dictionary of Feminist Theologies*, Lousville, Ky.: Westminster/John Knox Press.

Sacks, J. (1997), *The Politics of Hope*, London: Jonathan Cape.

Saiving, V. (1960), "The Human Situation: a Feminine View", *Journal of Religion*, 40 (April) 100–12; reprint. in *Womanspirit Rising: A Feminist Reader in Religion*, ed. Carol Christ and Judith Plaskow, New York: Harper & Row, 1970.

Saussy, C. (1991), *God Images and Self-Esteem: Empowering Women in a Patriarchal Society*, Louisville, Ky.: Westminster/John Knox Press.

Saussy, C. (1995), *The Gift of Anger: A Call to Faithful Action*, Louisville, Ky.: Westminster/John Knox Press.

Schillebeeckx, E. (1980), *Ministry: A Case for Change*, London: SCM Press.

Schillebeeckx, E. (1985), *The Church with a Human Face: A New and Expanded Theology of Ministry*, London: SCM Press.

Schlauch, C. (1995), *Faithful Companioning: How Pastoral Counselling Heals*, Minneapolis, Minn.: Fortress Press.

Schleiermacher, E. F. (1966), *Brief Outline on the Study of Theology*, trans. T. N. Tice, Richmond, Vir.: John Knox Press.

Schleiermacher, F. (1988), *Christian Caring: Selections from Practical Theology*, Philadelphia, Penn.: Fortress Press.

Schneiders, S. (1989), "Spirituality in the Academy," *Theological Studies*, 50(4), 676–97.

Schneiders, S. (1993), "Theology and Spirituality: Strangers, Rivals, or Partners?," *Horizons*, 13(2), 253–74.

Schreiter, R. (1985), *Constructing Local Theologies*, London: SCM Press.

Schüssler-Fiorenza, E. (1995), *Jesus: Miriam's Child, Sophia's Prophet*, London: SCM Press.

Sedgwick, P. (1996), "Theology and Society," in D. F. Ford (ed.), *The Modern Theologians*, 2nd edn, Oxford: Blackwell.

Sedgwick, P. (ed.) (1996), *God in the City*, London: Mowbray.

Segundo, J. L. (1982), *The Liberation of Theology*, Maryknoll, N.Y.: Orbis.

Selby, P. (1983), *Liberating God*, London: SPCK.

Selby, P. (1996), *Grace and Mortgage*, London: Darton, Longman & Todd.

Shweder, R. A. and LeVine, R. A. (eds), *Culture Theory: Essays on Mind, Self and Emotion*, Cambridge: Cambridge University Press, pp. 288–320.

Smith, A. (1997), *Navigating the Deep River: Spirituality in African American Families*, Cleveland, Oh.: United Church Press.

Stokes, A. (1985), *Ministry after Freud*, New York, N.Y.: Pilgrim Press.

Stuart, E. (1996), *Just Good Friends*, London: Cassell.

Stuart, E. and Thatcher, A. (eds) (1997), *People of Passion: What the Churches Teach about Sex*, London: Mowbray.

Sturdivant, S. (1984), *Therapy with Women: A Feminist Philosophy of Treatment*, New York, N.Y.: Springer.

Sutherland, Mark (1997), "Pastoral Care and Mental Health," *Contact*, 123, 12–19.

Sykes, S. (1978), *The Integrity of Anglicanism*, Oxford: Mowbray.

Symington, N. (1986), *The Analytic Experience*, London: Free Association Press.

Taylor, M. (1983), *Learning to Care*, London: SPCK.

Thangaraj, M. T. (1997), *Relating to People of Other Religions*, Nashville, Tenn.: Abingdon.

Thorne, B. (1991), *Beyond the Core Conditions: Person-Centred Counselling – Therapeutic and Spiritual Dimensions*, London: Whurr.

Thornton, M. (1961), *Pastoral Theology: A Reorientation*, London: SPCK.

Tillich, P. (1951–63), *Systematic Theology*, vols 1–3, London: Nisbet.

Tillich, P. (1952), *The Courage to Be*, London: Nisbet.

Toulmin, S. (1970), *An Examination of the Place of Reason in Ethics*, Cambridge: Cambridge University Press.

Townes, E. (1995), *In a Blaze of Glory: Womanist Spirituality as Social Witness*, Nashville, Tenn.: Abingdon Press.

Tracy, D. (1975), *Blessed Rage for Order: The New Pluralism in Theology*, New York: Seabury Press.

Tracy, D. (1981), *The Analogical Imagination: Christian Theology and the Culture of Pluralism*, London: SCM Press.

Tschudin, V. (1992), *Values*, London: Ballière Tindall.

Turner, D. (1995), *The Darkness of God*, Cambridge: Cambridge University Press.

Underwood, R. (1983), *Empathy and Confrontation in Pastoral Care*, Philadelphia, Penn.: Fortress Press.

Van de Creek, L., Bender, H. and Jordan, M. (eds) (1994), "Research in Pastoral Care and Counselling: Quantitative and Qualitative Approaches," *Journal of Pastoral Care Publications*.

Van Deusen Hunsinger, D. (1995), *Theology and Pastoral Counselling*, Grand Rapids, Mich.: Eerdmans.

Viau, M. (1993), *La nouvelle théologie pratigue*, Paris: Editions de CERF.

Ward, G. (1997), *The Postmodern God*, Oxford: Blackwell.

Ward, K. (1998), *God, Faith and the New Millennium*, London: One World.

Weber, M. (1963), *The Sociology of Religion*, Boston, Mass.: Beacon Press.

Welch, S. D. (1985), *Communities of Resistance and Solidarity: A Feminist Theology of Liberation*, Maryknoll, N.Y.: Orbis.

Westkott, M. (1986), *The Feminist Legacy of Karen Horney*, New Haven, Conn.: Yale University Press.

Wheeler, B. G. and Farley, E. (eds) (1991), *Shifting Boundaries: Contextual Approaches to the Structure of Theological Education*, Louisville, Ky.: Westminster/John Knox Press.

Wilber, Ken (1996), *A Brief History of Everything*, Dublin: Gill & Macmillan.

Willetts, D. (1996), *Modern Conservatism*, Harmondsworth: Penguin.

Williams, M. (1986), "The Dichotomy between Faith and Action," in P. Ballard (ed.), *The Foundations of Pastoral Studies and Practical Theology*, Cardiff: HOLI.

Williamson, C. (1992), *Whose Standards? Consumer and Professional Standards in Health Care*, Milton Keynes: Open University Press.

Wilson, M. (ed.) (1983), *Explorations in Health and Salvation*, Birmingham: University of Birmingham, Department of Theology.

Wilson, M. (1988), *A Coat of Many Colours*, London: Epworth Press.

Winnicott, D. W. (1971), *Playing and Reality*, London: Tavistock Publications.

Wittgenstein, L. (1958), *Philosophical Investigations*, trans. G. E. M. Anscombe, 3rd edn, New York, N.Y.: Macmillan.

Woodward, J. (ed.) (1990), *Embracing the Chaos: Theological Responses to AIDS*, London: SPCK.

Woodward, J. (1995), *Encountering Illness: Voices in Pastoral and Theological Perspective*, London: SCM Press.

Woodward, J. (1999), "A Study of the Role of the Health Care Chaplain in England," unpublished PhD thesis, Open University.

Young, F. (ed.) (1995), *Dare We Speak of God in Public?*, London: Cassells.

Young, R. (1990), *White Mythologies: Writing History and the West*, London and New York: Routledge.

Index

administration, 5, 284
American Association of Pastoral
    Counselors (AAPC), 53
applied theology, 3, 31, 34, 62, 79,
    109, 211
Association for Clinical Pastoral
    Education (ACPE), 53
Association for Pastoral Care and
    Counselling (APCC), 67
Augustine, St, 23, 137, 194

Bible, 8, 14, 28–9, 32, 37, 39, 44,
    62, 81, 105, 138–9, 182, 184,
    186, 191, 211, 222, 227, 240,
    262, 307
Black churches, 60–1
Black theology, 128, 131, 138,
    256
Boisen, Anton, 27, 49, 50–3,
    57, 242, 272, 275, 277–8,
    282
British Association for Counselling
    (BAC), 227
British and Irish Association for
    Practical Theology (BIAPT),
    4, 67, 104, 128

class, 49, 151–2, 156, 169, 235,
    251, 259–60
cleric *see* pastor

Clinical Pastoral Education (CPE),
    27, 47, 50–3, 57, 66, 272,
    275, 282, 311–19
Clinical Theology Association
    (CTA), 64, 67
community work, 64
congregation, 150, 173, 177,
    178–9, 235, 240, 257–71
*Contact: The Interdisciplinary
    Journal of Pastoral Studies*, 69
context, 55, 143, 149, 152, 173,
    197, 201, 202, 216, 234, 259,
    285, 302
counselling, 7, 8, 64, 66, 141, 150,
    154, 157, 223–32, 262, 283,
    287, 293, 313, 315–17
culture, 30, 33, 43, 44–5, 50,
    55–6, 105, 110, 133, 152,
    160, 170, 176–9, 234, 248,
    250, 253, 259–60, 263–4

disability, 111–12, 170, 212

ecclesiology, 173–81
education, 5, 52, 122–5, 129, 156,
    190, 301, 311–19
ethics, 28–9, 49, 53–5, 57, 73,
    89–90, 92, 93, 96, 97–100, 105,
    129, 131, 138, 151–2, 157,
    182–91, 226, 229, 238, 317

evaluation, 285, 297–319
experience, xiii, 12, 15–16, 23, 25,
  27, 49, 50–4, 56, 64–5, 73–4,
  76, 109, 118–19, 132, 138,
  150, 196, 201, 203, 207–22,
  224, 228, 230, 234, 249, 263,
  274, 277–8, 315, 317

faith, xiv, 12–13, 29–31, 41–2, 45,
  50, 54, 74, 95, 104–5, 108–9,
  112, 118–19, 122, 129,
  131–2, 137–8, 141, 175, 178,
  190, 211, 212–13, 217–18,
  226, 229, 248, 250, 252,
  253–4, 265, 284–5, 288–9,
  293
family, 7–8, 56, 152, 233, 240,
  242, 250, 263
feminism, 55, 74, 104, 106, 107,
  111, 131, 161, 233–47,
  259–60, 271
feminist perspectives *see* feminism

gay people, 15, 183, 188
gender, 49–50, 55, 57, 106–7,
  109, 179, 233–47, 259, 263
God, 5, 8, 12, 14, 23, 29, 39,
  43–4, 54, 65, 76, 80, 83–4,
  86, 95, 97, 105–6, 108,
  112–13, 132, 137, 152,
  157–60, 174–5, 177, 179,
  183–4, 187, 197, 208–9, 212,
  216–17, 225–9, 233, 235,
  239, 248–50, 252–4, 263,
  266, 273–4, 277, 281, 287–8,
  307, 317

healing, 12, 51, 56, 112, 150, 156,
  176, 200, 207–22, 234, 239,
  242, 276
hermeneutics, 49, 53–5, 74,
  105–6, 109, 111, 113,
  118–27, 144, 203–5, 254

Hiltner, Seward, 24–53, 66, 79,
  80–3, 93, 119, 242
homiletics *see* preaching

illness *see* healing
imagination, 85, 134, 143, 298,
  304, 318
Industrial Mission Association
  (IMA), 63, 67
Institute of Religion and Medicine
  (IRM), 64
interdisciplinarity, 15, 64, 76, 132,
  149, 257, 261
International Academy of Practical
  Theology (IAPT), 89
interpretation *see* hermeneutics
Islam, 249, 252, 253

Jesus, 10, 23, 32, 42–3, 83, 95,
  132, 141, 157, 174–5, 184–7,
  190, 217, 241, 252–3, 266,
  291, 307
Journal of Pastoral Theology, 257

lay people, 12, 34, 57, 60, 66,
  159, 173, 176, 179, 213, 261,
  312
liberation theology, 14, 65, 84,
  109, 111, 112, 131, 138, 144,
  149, 161, 164–72, 259
liturgy, 5, 8, 24, 61, 79, 105, 123,
  155, 156, 158, 174–8, 203,
  235, 262, 284

management, 130, 283–93
men, 234–47, 249
mental health/distress, 9, 11–12,
  49, 51, 144, 170, 209–10,
  224, 235, 272–82, 305
method in pastoral and practical
  theology
  conversation, 13, 16, 75, 110,
  135, 196, 220, 243

correlation, 27, 44–5, 73–4, 89–90, 93, 95, 130, 202, 211–22
critical attention to experience, 207–22
deduction, 10, 77, 81, 84
experiential, 56, 74
hermeneutic, 144
induction, 10, 77, 81, 84, 104
retrieval/critique/reconstruction, 202–4
minister *see* pastor
ministry, 6–7, 52, 54, 62–3, 79, 84, 93, 122–4, 129, 158, 173, 178–9, 210–11, 266, 299, 308, 312–13, 315
morality *see* ethics
multi-faith issues, 179, 248–56

narrative, 111, 150, 152, 157–8, 184–5, 225, 284, 314
New Age religious movements, 198–9

pastor, 1, 7, 11, 31–3, 51, 54, 61–2, 84, 108, 125, 154, 227, 261–2, 283, 312–13, 316
pastoral care, 5, 23, 50, 53–5, 79–80, 91, 96, 98, 106, 123, 149, 152, 157, 173, 177, 183, 235, 239, 242–3, 248, 297, 299–301, 305, 307, 311–19
pastoral counselling, 5, 50, 52, 54, 91, 108, 129, 223–32, 239
pastoral psychology, 31, 34
pastoral studies, 3–4, 59, 64, 68, 135–6, 158, 312, 314–15
pastoral theology
background, 2
definition, xii, 4–7, 28–32
history, 1–2, 23–69
methods, 42–4, 46
nature, 7–8

Paul, St, 23, 35–6, 185–6, 212, 240, 253–4
philosophy, 93–5, 105
pluralism, 49, 62, 66, 75, 91, 94–6, 100, 107, 129, 179, 202, 252–3, 259
politics, 14–15, 77, 84, 120–1, 161, 164–72, 176, 235, 237, 239, 241–2, 274, 286
political awareness *see* politics
postmodern, 104–8, 192, 194, 198–9, 253, 304
postmodernism *see* postmodern
poverty, 7, 9–10, 12, 67, 86, 153, 160, 165–6, 170, 176, 273–4
power, 49, 55, 57, 120, 158, 164, 166, 170, 179, 235, 237, 248, 251, 263
practical knowledge (phronesis), 104, 110, 113
practical theology
definition, xii, 4–7, 24
history, 23–69
methods, 9–10, 73–145
models for reflection, 128–34, 136–45
nature, 7–8, 77–88
purpose, 75
scope, 8–9
as theological discipline, 24–48, 73, 77–88
praxis, 11, 65, 124, 130, 207, 210
preaching, 5, 24, 61, 79–80, 106, 123, 262
prophet, 133, 158–9, 185, 242, 258
prophecy *see* prophet
profession, 63–4, 152, 161
professionalisation *see* profession
psychiatry, 33–5, 40–1, 51, 60, 272–82

psychoanalysis, 25, 64, 92–3, 96, 111, 157, 189, 216, 223, 226, 235–8, 262, 275, 278–9
psychoanalytic psychology *see* psychoanalysis
psychology, 9, 24, 27–8, 31, 34, 40–1, 50–1, 56, 82, 108, 149, 176, 207, 210, 235, 242, 261, 266, 275–6, 280, 286, 312, 315
psychotherapy *see* psychoanalysis

race/racism, 49, 55, 57, 60, 120, 150, 195, 235, 248, 259, 273–4
ritual *see* liturgy

salvation/atonement, 8, 29, 43, 83–4, 121, 124, 140, 173–6, 216, 252
Schleiermacher, Friedrich, 24, 61, 78–9, 83, 108–9, 129
secularisation, 63, 66, 85, 151, 153, 156–7, 178
sexuality, 150, 225–6, 228, 236, 243
shepherd/shepherding, 1–2, 27–8, 32–4, 36, 40, 44, 61, 80–1
situation, 10–12, 14, 16, 73, 83, 85, 118–27, 132, 135–6, 139, 143
social construction, 158–61, 188, 233, 235, 237, 274

social work, 64
sociology, 31, 41, 82, 149, 151–63, 176, 178–9, 261, 286, 312, 315
spirituality, 64, 106, 131, 149, 152, 157, 161, 179, 192–206, 227, 235, 254, 274–7, 279, 280, 315
story *see* narrative
suffering, 14, 207–22, 229, 241

theological reflection, 15, 64, 75, 85, 123–4, 128, 135–45, 211, 228, 301, 315
Tillich, Paul, 27, 36, 44–5, 65–6, 82, 89, 130, 175–6
tradition
    Catholic, 3, 61, 97, 176–7, 182, 191
    Protestant, xii, 2, 4, 24, 34, 49, 61
transformation, xii, 10, 13, 104–17, 204, 208, 242, 259, 265, 267, 297

Westminster Pastoral Foundation (WPF), 64
white people, 150, 243, 263–4
women, 15, 60, 74, 108, 121, 150, 170, 233–47, 249
worship *see* liturgy